Labor in the South

Labor in the South

F. Ray Marshall

HARVARD UNIVERSITY PRESS
CAMBRIDGE, MASSACHUSETTS
1967

Foreword

Labor in the South is a significant volume because it fills a major gap in providing an authoritative history of organized labor in our southern states. But it is much more than a narrative. It analyzes the interactions between industrialization and union development, and it makes a contribution to the theory of union growth in this country. The study also provides much needed historical perspective on the diversity and changing policies and attitudes of unions toward Negro workers. This discussion helps us to understand the reform potentials and limitations of our labor organizations at local and national levels.

Professor Marshall's contribution should be required reading for all those who speculate on the future size and growth of the labor movement. Union membership in the south has increased at a more rapid rate than in the nonsouth since 1939. Professor Marshall finds that union growth and the spread of collective bargaining is related to the industrial composition of a region, the size of establishments, the presence of branch plants of national companies, the occupational mix, and the location of enterprises in urban rather than rural areas. There is an inverse relationship "between the proportion of the industry located in the south and the extent of collective bargaining coverage."

One of the most interesting of Professor Marshall's conclusions relates to the role of legislation on union growth. He states that "the writer's observations in the south and the analysis of NLRB election results fail to produce evidence that the right-to-work laws have had a significant effect on union growth. The laws are probably most important as symbols registering union political strength, which does have important implications for union operations" (chap. XX). The analysis of the influence of community and legislative factors, as well

v

as employer policies, on union growth should be of interest to all concerned with the strategy of organizing and collective bargaining.

The long-term fortunes of labor organizations in the south have been directly related to the course of industrialization. The relative decline in agriculture, the break-up of the company-dominated town, the diversification of industry, and the introduction of new, advanced industry; the influence of branch plants under national personnel and collective bargaining policies; the growing national homogenization of the country through transport and communications; and the presence of the federal government in developmental projects and social legislation are all aspects of industrialization which have influenced labor organization in the south. At the same time, the detailed narrative helps us to keep in mind the theme of diversity within the southern states. The south has never been monolithic. The contrasts within the region are a major theme of this story. As time goes on, industrialization appears to be diminishing the differences within the economy and the industrial relations of the south, compared to the rest of the country.

Some of the most effective and militant state federations of labor at the present time are in southern states. This volume helps us to understand some of the reasons: the political party and legislative power in these states, the low standards of social legislation of concern to union members, the absence of organized contending forces, and perhaps the difficulty which southern labor leaders may have in achieving national leadership, thereby attracting able leadership to the state federations. Professor Marshall might well have brought together more explicitly his rich knowledge of the operation of these state federations.

Professor Marshall brings to this volume an unrivaled knowledge of southern labor-management relations acquired both from documents and from a rich experience in the field. He is eminently qualified to place these southern developments in the national perspective. He has also researched and written widely on the problems of the Negro worker. This volume will long remain a standard work.

July 1967   John T. Dunlop

Author's Preface

THIS VOLUME SEEKS primarily to analyze the factors influencing the growth of organized labor in the south. The material covered is therefore selective in the sense that attention has been focused primarily on influences which have affected the growth of unions and not on their collective bargaining, political, or other activities. Obviously, however, a discussion of the growth of unions requires us to understand the distinguishing features of the south's basic political, economic and social institutions. Part I therefore concerns itself with an analysis of the main factors which make the institutions unique. The other parts attempt to show how these institutions have influenced the growth of organized labor. The material in Part I demonstrates, for example, that the south can be identified quantitatively as a unique region in terms of economic and demographic factors, as well as in terms of geography and politics. The south was the only region of the United States, for example, with anything resembling a "traditional" society in terms of economic development. Its basic political, social and economic institutions originated in slavery, the plantation system, the Civil War, Reconstruction, and an agricultural system based on share-cropping and cotton culture. The economic backwardness of the south after the Civil War was caused by an agricultural system that depleted the soil and offered limited possibilities for many farmers and tenants to improve themselves, a shortage of capital, high birth rates, relatively slow rates of increase in capital per head, low wages, low value-added in industry, and inadequate education facilities.

The south's economic dilemma was not helped by the undemocratic, backward-looking political system that prevented attention to important problems by exaggerating the race issue for political purposes. Although it looked for a time during the 1870's and 1880's as if the south might establish a diverse political system based on economic differences, racial segregation and the one-party system had become firmly established by 1900.

Even though there were many obstacles to economic development, there were some steady improvements even during the 1870's, and industrialization was accelerated during the 1880's and 1890's. Economic development was spurred mainly by autonomous economic forces, but there also were conscious efforts by southerners to attract and build industry. Indeed, despite some opposition from those who favored the agrarian way of life, the idea that industrialization could cure the region's economic ills became a pervasive philosophy of the leaders of the new south. It also became part of the southern ideology that economic development was being promoted as a public service to help the region in general and poor whites in particular. It is not surprising therefore that industrialists should have been considered public benefactors, even when they made higher profits, paid lower wages, and maintained poorer working conditions than their nonsouthern competitors.

The southern white worker's attitude toward employers also was influenced by the racial and ethnic homogeneity of southern white workers and managers, who had been unified by the Civil War and Reconstruction. This unity was strengthened by the fact that southern industries, unlike their northern competitors, did not employ many immigrants, but drew their workers mainly from the reservoir of poor whites who had been neglected by slavery and the plantation system.

While the south thus had many unique political, social, and economic characteristics, its institutions were gradually modified by changes associated with industrialization, technological development, wars, depressions, population shifts, and external political developments. These changes have tended to draw the south increasingly into the mainstream of American life and to cause its institutions to converge gradually with those of the rest of the United States.

Parts II, III, and IV deal with the development of organized labor within the institutional environment discussed in Part I. It will be seen that the south's environment had important effects on the growth of unions. The unity of white managers and workers, the race problem, the surplus of labor in a low-income agriculture, the nature and composition of southern industry, the undemocratic political tradition, the idea that industrialists were benefactors, all created relatively unfavorable conditions for the growth of unions. At the same time, however, union growth was spurred by other factors. Many southern workers, like those everywhere, turned to unions as a means of maintaining and improving the conditions of their working lives and to gain some voice in politics. Southern union growth also was stimulated because many national labor organizations were motivated to try to organize the industrializing south in order to protect union conditions elsewhere.

In spite of the hostile environment, therefore, some unions became relatively strong. Sometimes this was because they were willing to conform, but other factors were at work. It is the purpose of Part V to analyze the reasons for the differential rates of union growth in many industries. Wherever available, statistical data is analyzed to show the differences between union strength within the south and between the south and the nonsouth; this is done in Chapter XIX. Chapters XX and XXI relate union growth to the south's basic political, social, and economic institutions, and Chapter XXIII discusses the prospects for the future growth of unions in the south.

Although the south's labor organizations have been conditioned by unique forces, other circumstances have unified southern and national unions. After all, most unions in the south have been affiliated with the nation's main labor organizations and therefore share the structure and philosophy of the American labor movement. Moreover, we shall see that all industrial relations systems have certain common or basic aspects and that the singular features of union growth in the south can be discussed within a conceptual framework that is useful in understanding the development of unions anywhere.

While the people who helped me in various ways with this study are far too numerous to list here, some of my debts are too great to go unacknowledged. I am particularly grateful to the various participants in the Southern Union Staff Training Institutes held at the University of North Carolina in 1963, the University of Texas in 1965 and the University of Georgia in 1966. The international union representatives who participated in these institutes permitted me to use them as sounding boards for ideas and supplied many valuable insights and much useful material on unions in the south. Similarly, officials of the southern state AFL-CIO federations and the Southern Labor School have been very helpful; I am especially indebted to H. S. "Hank" Brown, Roy Evans, and Lymon Jones of the Texas AFL-CIO; Victor Bussie and E. J. Bourg of the Louisiana State Labor Council; Claude Ramsey and Ray Smithhart of the Mississippi Labor Council; Stanton E. Smith, Matthew Lynch and Charles M. Houck of the Tennessee State Labor Council; E. H. "Lige" Williams, AFL-CIO Region VII and Carey Haigler, AFL-CIO Region V.

In addition, numerous national AFL-CIO officers have been extremely helpful, especially Lawrence Rogin, George Guernsey, and Otto Pragan of the Department of Education; Donald Slaiman and

E. T. Kherer of the Civil Rights Department; Nat Goldfinger of the Department of Research; Nicholas Zonarich of the Industrial Union Department; and Franz Daniel of the Organizing Department. The late George Googe, AFL Southern Director from 1928 to 1948, provided me with much useful information from his files and from his experiences. Similarly, H. L. Mitchell former president of the National Agricultural Workers' Union (which succeeded the Southern Tenant Farmers' Union) permitted me to use his records and discussed at great length the organization of agricultural workers in the south. James Carey and George L-P Weaver permitted me to use the records of the Congress of Industrial organizations. William Mitch, Director of United Mine Workers' District 50, who has directed the UMW's activities in Alabama since 1933, turned over to me his very valuable personal records and newspaper files. My colleague Professor Ruth Allen gave me the benefit of her vast knowledge of organized labor in Texas and permitted me to use some of her unpublished materials. I am likewise grateful to Professor Leo Troy of Rutgers University for unpublished statistical material on union membership by states for 1939 and 1953. Professor Mark Perlman of the University of Pittsburgh provided some valuable material on the early history of the machinists. Daniel A. Powell of the AFL-CIO Committee on Political Education gave me the benefit of his vast knowledge of labor politics in the south and let me use some of his personal records. Father Jerome A. Drolet, active in labor affairs around New Orleans since the 1930's lent me some of his private papers and discussed his experiences with me. Several librarians have assisted me with materials, especially from the Industrial Relations Library at Harvard University, the Library of Congress, New York Public Library, the AFL-CIO Library, and the libraries at the following universities: California, Louisiana State, Mississippi, Texas, and Tulane.

I am grateful to a number of publishers for permission to use some of my previously published materials. The Institute of Race Relations in London allowed me to use my "Industrialization and Race Relations in the Southern United States," in *Industrialization and Race Relations,* Guy Hunter, ed., 1965. The editors of *Labor History* and my coauthor Lamar B. Jones gave me permission to use "Agricultural Unions in Louisiana," *Labor History,* Fall 1962. The Industrial Relations Research Association permitted me to use "Some Factors Influencing the Growth of Unions in the South," *Thirteenth Annual Proceedings* of the Industrial Relations Research Association, 1960; the editors of *Industrial Relations* gave me permission to use "Union Racial Problems in the South," *Industrial Relations,* May 1962.

Other published sources found to be particularly helpful include:

Ruth A. Allen, *Chapters in the History of Organized Labor in Texas* (University of Texas Press, 1941); W. J. Cash, *The Mind of the South* (Alfred A. Knopf, 1941); James McBride Dabbs, *The Southern Heritage* (Alfred A. Knopf, 1958); Walter Galenson, *The CIO Challenge to the AFL* (Harvard University Press, 1960); William H. Nicholls, *Southern Tradition and Regional Progress* (University of North Carolina Press, 1960); Sterling D. Spero and Abram L. Harris, *The Black Worker* (Columbia University Press, 1931); Tom Tippett, *When Southern Labor Stirs* (Jonathan Cape and Harrison Smith, 1931); and C. Vann Woodward, *Origins of the New South* (Louisiana State University Press, 1951).

The person most responsible for this volume is John T. Dunlop who was an indispensable source of encouragement and assistance. Professor Dunlop not only gave me much valuable advice but, along with other members of the Wertheim Committee at Harvard University, gave me financial support to permit freedom from teaching duties and to allow the extensive travel which this study required. I am also indebted to the Ford Foundation and the University Research Institute at the University of Texas for financial help. Special thanks also are due to Walter Galenson, Paul S. Taylor, Kenneth Stampp, H. M. Douty, and Lawrence Rogin for reading and making valuable comments on various drafts of this manuscript.

F. RAY MARSHALL

Austin, Texas
September 1966

Contents

PART I

Institutional Setting and General Development

CHAPTER   PAGE

   I   The Institutional Setting 3
  II   General Developments and Problems of Unions before 1928   20

PART II

Development of Unions by Trade and Industry before 1932

  III   Printing and Building Trades 41
   IV   Railroad Workers and Longshoremen 50
    V   Coal Miners and Textile Workers 71
   VI   Agricultural and Lumber Workers 86
  VII   Revolt of the Textile Workers 101
 VIII   The 1930 AFL Organizing Campaign 121

PART III

The Depression and the New Deal

   IX   Coal Mining 137
    X   Communists, Socialists, and Sharecroppers 154
   XI   Textile and Clothing Workers 166
  XII   Growth of CIO Unions 182
 XIII   Growth of AFL Unions 202

PART IV

War and Postwar Development

 XIV   World War II 225
  XV   Operation Dixie 246

xiii

XVI   Organizing Experiences after Operation Dixie 270
XVII Paper, Coal, and Agricultural Workers 283

PART V

Union Growth in the South:
Status, Causes, and Prospects

XVIII Quantitative Aspects of Union Membership in the South..... 297
  XIX Factors Influencing Union Growth in the South 309
   XX Industrial Development and the Law 319
  XXI The Unions and the Workers 332
 XXII The Future of Unions in the South 344
Notes 353
Index 395

Tables

1. Strikes in the south and the United States by industry, 1887–1905.   30
2. Membership of railway operating unions in Georgia, 1890–1928.   59
3. Membership in railroad unions affiliated with the Louisiana Federation
   of Labor, 1912, 1920, 1928.   57
4. Southern membership in some selected national unions, 1939 and 1953.   267
5. Union membership and per cent of nonagricultural employment organized, southern states and United States, 1939–1964.   299
6. Change in nonagricultural employment by industries, 1940–1962.   301
7. Southern membership of selected international unions, 1964.   303
8. Collective bargaining coverage, proportion of industry in the south, and
   concentration ratios by industry group.   317
9. Production workers and manufacturing employment in metropolitan
   areas, 1954, 1958, and 1962.   318
10. Production workers in manufacturing in the south and in the nonsouth
    by major industry group, 1939, 1947, and 1962.   346
11. Distribution of civilian employment by major industry group, south and
    nonsouth, 1940–1962.   348
12. Distribution of employment by occupations, south and nonsouth, 1940–
    1964.   349

PART I

Institutional Setting and General Development

CHAPTER I

The Institutional Setting

Considerable attention in recent years has been devoted to the study of labor movements in different countries. These studies have given us insight into the basic factors shaping the origin, growth, objectives, and effects of labor movements. Although much less has been done in regional comparisons, studies of this kind are equally valuable. Students of labor movements, as well as economists generally, have discovered that analyses based on national aggregates frequently cannot be applied to particular regions because, as John T. Dunlop has demonstrated, "the features that are ordinarily regarded as distinctive to a national system do not enter equally into each industrial relations system within its borders."[1]

It may well be questioned, however, if the labor movement of the American south is sufficiently unique to provide a significant comparison with the nonsouth. It is the purpose of this chapter to demonstrate that it is indeed unique.

Unless otherwise indicated, we shall define the south as the states of the Confederacy plus Kentucky and Oklahoma.[2] Sometimes, however, it will be necessary to use the census definition, either because it is difficult to separate out the states that we exclude from the census' south Atlantic (Delaware, West Virginia, Maryland and the District of Columbia) classification, or because an economic or geographic area extends logically into a "border" state. In discussing organizations of coal miners, for example, we include West Virginia because of common usage in the industry.

3

Although we shall note that the south's individual characteristics are being dissolved by industrialization, causing its economic, political, and social institutions increasingly to be patterned after those of the nation, there can be little question that from an historical viewpoint the south is unique by almost any definition. George T. Renner defines regions as "genuine entities, each of which expresses both natural and cultural delineation from its neighbors,"[3] and V. B. Stanberry defines a region as an "area of which the inhabitants instinctively feel themselves a part."[4] Economic historian W. W. Rostow asserts that the south was an exception to the American experience of being "born free" or not having a traditional society which had to be overcome before rapid industrialization could begin. He argues that "The United States . . . created for itself a kind of traditional society in the South, as an appendage to Lancashire, and then New England's cotton mills; and the long, slow disengagement of the South from its peculiar version of a traditional society belongs clearly to the general [European] and not to the special [American] case."[5]

In 1931, Broadus Mitchell noted a number of "important differences between industry in the south and industry in the north."[6]

The introduction of manufacturing was later and more abrupt than elsewhere. "Cotton mills were set down suddenly in the cotton fields," and there was a "definite revolt against agriculture—a feeling that single devotion to agriculture had failed the south and needed to be supplemented by industry."

Southern industrialists have a peculiar pride in their achievement. They began their work following a period, during Reconstruction, of political humiliation, and their tools were only such as were offered by determination in the midst of poverty. These things gave to the whole movement a social sanction, I might almost say social sanctification, which was largely lacking elsewhere. An added element to this end was the fact that industry, particularly the cotton factories, furnished bread and meat to the hordes of poor whites who waited to be reclaimed after the destitution which slavery entailed upon them.

The presence of the Negro depresses wages, reduces skill, curtails purchasing power, diverts "white workers' attention from the economic to the race issue," and furnishes "an enormous potential supply of industrial workers." In addition the race question has tended to obscure the role of economic issues in southern politics.

"And one of the most important [differences] is that the South's industry is little diversified, and is relatively localized geographically."

The south's character as a distinctive and homogeneous region is confirmed by the statistics on its economic and demographic characteristics. First of all, it has been relatively unindustrialized. The per cent of nonagricultural labor force to total labor force in southern areas as a percentage of the national averages were: 49 per cent in the south Atlantic in 1840 moving up to 93 per cent in 1950; in the east south central, 38 per cent in 1840 and 83 per cent in 1950; west south central, 67 per cent in 1840 and 92 per cent in 1950.[7]

Thus, while the degree of industrialization is converging to the national average, at no time since 1840 has any southern region equaled any nonsouthern region. It also has consistently had lower per capita incomes than other areas of the country. And after 1840, the service incomes per worker were consistently lower than in other regions (except for 1950 when agricultural income in the west south central was higher than in New England).

Statistics show that the per capita income of southerners started declining relative to the United States around 1840 and began to converge toward the national average around 1900. The reasons for this are not clear, but it is perhaps significant that similar north-south patterns exist in many other countries.[8]

Although relative per capita incomes two decades after the Civil War were little higher than they had been in 1840, the Civil War and Reconstruction obviously were not the only causes. The divergence after 1840 was probably associated with the impact of slavery and the Civil War on the south. The convergence is probably due to the extension of industry into the area after the rates of return on investment began to decline in the nonsouth. There was a sharp increase in its relative per capita income around 1900. Indeed, the average rates of per capita income growth in the south Atlantic and west south central states led the nation between 1900 and 1920. However, the southern regions exhibit some tendency to be dependent, growing faster than the national average during periods of rapid national growth and declining relative to the national average during downswings. During the 1930's, therefore, the south suffered a serious setback in relative income growth but by 1940 had more than regained its 1920 position. In 1950 the relative level of all the southern areas exceeded the levels of 1900, but by that date only the south Atlantic exceeded its 1840 standing.[9]

The south's large Negro population has undoubtedly been its most distinctive characteristic, and many of its unique features have developed from this. The defense of slavery united southern whites and made the region much more homogeneous than its internal geographic, economic and social differences would have warranted.

In 1840, slaves constituted 15 per cent of the population of the United States, but the following proportions in the southern states:

Virginia, 36 per cent; North Carolina, 33 per cent; South Carolina, 55 per cent; Georgia, 41 per cent; Florida, 47 per cent; Kentucky, 23 per cent; Tennessee, 22 per cent; Alabama, 43 per cent; Mississippi, 52 per cent; Arkansas, 20 per cent; and Louisiana, 48 per cent. Outside the south, no state had sufficient slave populations to be recorded by the 1840 census except Delaware (3 per cent), Maryland (19 per cent) and Missouri (15 per cent).

Since emancipation, however, emigration has caused the south to converge with the nonsouth with respect to Negro population, and the influence of this factor on the region has diminished through time. The proportions of all nonwhites in the United States in the south for various census dates were as follows: 92 per cent in 1890, 74 per cent in 1930, and 57 per cent in 1960. The 1960 figure of 57 per cent really overstates the proportion of nonwhites in the south because it is based on the census definition, which includes Maryland, the District of Columbia, and Delaware, with 1,098,146 nonwhites. If we subtract this total, the states of the southeast and southwest contained only 10.4 million of the 20.5 million nonwhites in the United States. The "south" as defined in this more restricted sense had the following proportions of the nonwhite population: 1940, 73 per cent; 1950, 60 per cent; and 1960, 51 per cent.

The presence of Negroes and the region's rural character explain the lower proportion of foreign-born people. In 1930, for example, the only state outside the south with less than 2.5 per cent foreign-born was New Mexico, and the only southern state with more than 2.5 per cent was Florida. At the same time, Negroes did not constitute as much as 10 per cent of the population of any nonsouthern state, while Kentucky and Oklahoma were the only southern states where Negroes constituted fewer than 10 per cent of the population. The percentage of foreign-born in the south in 1960 was only 1.8 per cent, as compared with 4.4 per cent in the north central, 6.9 per cent in the west and 10.2 per cent in the northeast. The percentages of natives with foreign or mixed parentage were: northeast, 23.3 per cent north central, 14.1 per cent; south, 4.2 per cent and west, 15.5 per cent.

Generally, the south has had higher fertility rates (children born per 1000 women fifteen to forty-four years old) than other regions; a relatively larger percentage of its population under twenty years of age than any other region;[10] lower levels of education and higher illiteracy rates, shorter average school terms and lower proportions of school enrollment; higher proportions of Protestants; and smaller average acres per farm and lower amounts of horsepower per agricultural worker.

Although we have emphasized the factors unifying the south and have noted the economic changes which have drawn the region increasingly into the American pattern, it is homogeneous only when compared with the nonsouth. Once we take a closer look, we discover much diversity and many souths. As might be expected, its subdivision depends upon one's purposes, and there are numerous geographic, historical, physical, economic, social, agricultural, industrial and other classifications that might be employed. Rupert B. Vance has identified a minimum of fifteen homogeneous human-use regions.[11] More generally, the south is sometimes divided into five subregions: (1) the mountains, (2) the Piedmont, (3) the plantations, (4) the coastal flatwoods or piney woods, and (5) the southwest. These geographic subdivisions have greatly influenced economic activity and population characteristics. The Negro population, for example, has been concentrated in the plantation belt and its surrounding major cities. Poor whites were pushed out of these areas into the highlands and piney woods. Many of them migrated to the new lands of the southwest and into textile mill villages following the Civil War. The industrialization which followed the Civil War was generally outside the plantation areas, and most manufacturing activity was based on white labor.

SLAVERY, CIVIL WAR, AND RECONSTRUCTION

In adapting the slave to his needs, the planter sought to turn him into a machine and to keep him in that status by a system of firmly established controls and customs.[12] As James McBride Dabbs says: "Into that machine he tried to build certain gadgets. The slave was to be docile, submissive, unreflecting. In general, he was to be inferior, and therefore by various methods he was made inferior."[13] While the planter was never really able to reduce the slave to this ideal, the mark of inferiority became firmly stamped upon him in the minds of whites, and the Negro was in some degree forced to conform with this image in order to survive.

The effects of slavery extended far beyond the Negro, however; it produced an economy which made progress extremely difficult at a time when other areas were advancing rapidly. Slavery did very little to improve the productive powers of whites. The slave owner did not have the stimulus to reduce costs that the wage system gave the northern employer. While slaves acquired some skills in order to produce the goods and services required by the plantation economy, the abilities were usually very rudimentary and too crude to permit the freed Negro to compete with more highly skilled white artisans (except for traditional occupations like the trowel trades). Since the plantation was largely a self-contained economic unit, few towns grew up to promote nonagricultural pursuits and diversify the economy. Moreover, since foreigners generally avoided the south, the region lost the advantages of the intellectual and social stimulation given to other areas by immigrants. The south was also largely ignored by American capitalists, because the agricultural creed that buttressed slavery and the plantation system was hostile to commercial and industrial undertakings; indeed, men like John C. Calhoun evolved fairly elaborate philosophies to defend slavery and the agricultural system as a means of avoiding the class conflicts which they saw as the inevitable consequences of industrialization. Calhoun told the United States Senate that slavery exempted the south from the "conflict between labor and capital" which always came in "an advanced stage of wealth and civilization." Calhoun also advocated slavery as a means of avoiding the "class struggle."[14]

The diverging pattern of the south's economy from that of the north produced growing ideological differences. While the economy of the north was industrializing, that of the south was comparatively static; as the political and social institutions of the north were responding to this changing economic base, the institutions of the south continued to reflect the system upon which they were founded.

Slavery also had profound intellectual effects on southern whites. Although slave owners were a minority of the south's total white population in 1860, their values and interests dominated the political life. White supremacy arguments caused common whites increasingly to identify themselves with planters. There were many reasons for this white unity in spite of the economic and social barriers. One was undoubtedly the region's relatively homogeneous white population. And, as W. J. Cash emphasized, the free and easy life of the common white caused him to be unreflective or unanalytical and therefore blinded him to his real interests. In addition, "If he had no worth-while interest at stake in slavery, if his real interest ran the other way about, he did nevertheless have that, to him, dear treasure of his superiority as a white man, which had been conferred on him by slavery; and so was as determined to keep the black man in chains, saw in the offensive of the Yankee as great a danger to himself, as the angriest planter."[15] We must add to this the sectional pride and patriotism of any group under outside attack. Moreover, the common white's patriotism and identification with the planter was strengthened by his lack of class feeling and the contrast which his leaders painted between the southern gentlemen (with whom he identified) and the crass, uncouth Yankee:

> For continually, from every stump, platform, and editorial sanctum, they gave him on the one hand the Yankee—as cowardly, avaricious,

boorish, half Pantaloon and half Shylock—and on the other the South-erner—as polished, brave, generous, magnificent, wholly the stately aris-tocrat, fit to cow a dozen Yankees with the power of his eye and a cane —gave him these with the delicate implication that this Southerner was somehow any Southerner at random.

Poor whites, forced to compete sometimes directly and always in-directly with slaves, were largely pushed out of the pre-Civil War economy into poor lands not suited for the plantation system.[16] Mitchell points out that native whites were also frequently overlooked by em-ployers who imported skilled craftsmen.

The half century following the Civil War was of tremendous im-portance in economic and social relations for the south and for the United States, because during this period the southern economy re-adjusted itself to the abolition of the slave economy, and southern whites institutionalized their relations with Negroes. The fundamental problem was to reestablish relations in an economy a large part of whose capital had been freed by emancipation and depleted by the war. The freedmen in some instances were so exhilarated by their new freedom that they refused to work, but their dream that the Yankees would provide them with forty acres and a mule soon faded, and they were forced to turn to their old masters and to sharecropping for sub-sistence. Under this system there was little incentive for the worker to improve either his condition or that of the land he worked. Moreover, the exigencies of cotton growing were such that little food was raised, the diet was poor, the fertility of the soil was rapidly depleted. Farming techniques were unchanged and required little other than brute strength from the sharecropper. Negroes also had great difficulty im-proving their conditions by moving into urban areas because the rate of growth of nonagricultural industry in the south was very low until after 1880, and even then the Negro generally found only disagreeable or low-status jobs. His inferior education and low degree of skill was also a barrier. Moreover, the planters and their political allies took measures to restrict the Negro's movements from agriculture in order to assure a continuous supply of agricultural labor; the so-called "Black Codes" were ostensibly vagrancy laws but had as one of their primary objectives the assurance of labor supplies for plantations. Finally, sharecroppers were frequently in debt to the planters and thus not allowed to leave the plantation until this debt was cleared. As we shall see, their disfranchisement after 1890 made it virtually impossible for Negroes to improve their conditions through political action.

It would be very misleading, however, to leave the impression that the system established after the Civil War was entirely the fault of the planter. The planters were also impoverished by the war, which had practically destroyed the region's credit structure. Credit was therefore available only on very harsh terms from bankers or supply merchants, who sprang up throughout the region during these years. (As we shall see in the following chapter, agrarian protest movements between Reconstruction and World War I frequently were directed against these merchants.)

War and Reconstruction also strengthened the unity of southern whites. The fact that the south was defeated only served to make southern whites more conscious of their regional indentification. As C. Vann Woodward and others have emphasized,[17] the Negroes' part in the Reconstruction governments probably did not suffer too much by comparison with governments in other areas; but this is irrelevant for the formation of attitudes. Even though few Negroes were elected to public office, southern whites remember this as the period of "nigger domination" and for years defended their actions as preventing the Negro from "taking over" again. Southern whites were therefore unified behind their traditional leaders, because the Civil War conditioned the common whites to follow and the officers to lead, preventing the formation of any significant class movement except for the abortive efforts of the Knights of Labor and the Populists. Of course, the whites of the region were also unified by their poverty. This influenced their racial attitudes, too, since they feared that their economic condition and forced competition with Negroes would dislodge them from their position on next-to-the-last rung of the status ladder. Also, the Negro was a galling symbol of the recent defeat. Finally, we must not discount the fact that in their conflict with the north, southerners were probably as interested in the contest as in the issues involved.

This helps to explain the solid political front in the south for so many years, but political solidarity was not established immediately. For some time after the withdrawal of federal troops, the Negro vote was coveted by conservatives and liberals alike. According to Woodward, during the 1880's southern Democrats and Republicans competed vigorously for the Negro vote. "The Negro voters were therefore courted, 'mistered,' and honored by Southern white politicians as never before."[18] Not only was the Negro disfranchised by the turn of the century, but the Democratic Party became the party of the south, and Republicanism was equated with "Treason to race, country, God and Southern womanhood," and the race question was elevated to paramount importance in southern politics.

Just as disfranchisement of Negroes did not occur immediately after the withdrawal of federal troops, it took some time for a rigid form of legal racial segregation to become the pattern. Whether out of fear of the return of Yankee troops or fear of the Negro vote, it was about a decade after the end of military occupation before the first segregation laws were passed. In Mississippi, Vernon L. Wharton found that saloons in Jackson served Negroes and whites at separate tables,[19] and the governors of Louisiana and South Carolina went on record in favor of protecting the Negroes' right to vote.[20]

Complete legal segregation became the accepted way by 1900, however, because of a number of circumstances, one of the most important being a general feeling that a majority of northern whites favored segregation and second-class citizenship for the Negro and therefore would not send the troops back south. This conviction was supported by: the segregation of the Negro in the federal army and the refusal of many northern states to enfranchise the Negro, even after they insisted that the south do so; the prevalence of *de facto* segregation in the north; the acquiescence of northerners in the political compromise of 1877, which resulted in the withdrawal of federal troops; and, finally, a series of U.S. Supreme Court decisions between 1873 and 1898 establishing the legality of "separate but equal facilities" and denying the Negro federal protection for acts committed against him by private individuals.[21]

By 1900, therefore, the southern Negro had become almost completely segregated by law or custom. He rode in separate compartments or in the back of public conveyances, went to segregated public schools, could not marry whites, ate in separate restaurants, and was buried in segregated cemeteries. Employment was also segregated, and Negroes generally were frozen out of occupations they had formerly held and relegated to "Negro" jobs in urban occupations. The jobs set aside for them were usually ones that whites would not take.

INDUSTRIALIZATION

While we have stressed the predominantly agricultural nature of the antebellum south, the region actually had achieved a significantly high level of industrialization before cotton culture became its predominant economic characteristic. In 1810, for example, the south produced 20 per cent of the value of manfactures in the United States—a proportion it has not since equaled. After 1810, however, agriculture absorbed the region's economic resources, a constellation of political, social, and economic forces arose which greatly impeded the growth of manufacturing until after the Civil War.[22]

Although students of the south differ as to whether or not the region experienced an "industrial revolution," there can be little doubt that a rapid increase in industrial activity took place during the decade of the

1880's. William H. Nicholls[23] and C. Vann Woodward[24] do not consider this growth to be impressive, while Broadus and George Mitchell[25] argue that for the south during this period there "arrived nearly overnight an Industrial Revolution as swift and vigorous as that in England." Woodward apparently bases his conclusion on its relative lack of urbanization, its small share of the nation's capital, and the small number of manufacturing establishments in 1904 as compared with 1860.[26] This, however, is hardly a convincing comparison because of the debilitating effects of the Civil War and Reconstruction and because much of the south's industry was not located in urban areas. Moreover, the number of manufacturing establishments and the share of capital are hardly important measures of economic development. Woodward's conclusion that "It does not appear that the South as a whole advanced in manufactures faster than the nation as a whole," is true for 1890 as compared with 1860, but is not true for the 1890 compared with 1880. In the 1870-1880 decade, manufacturing wage earners increased by only 19.6 per cent and the value of manufacturers by only 24.6 per cent, while the comparable figures for the 1890 to 1899 were 108.7 per cent and 111.4 per cent. The south's proportion of the nation's manufacturing wage earners increased from 7.7 per cent to 12.6 per cent between 1880 and 1899, and its proportion of the value of manufacturing rose from 5.9 per cent to 8.3 per cent in the same period.

Although the south failed to regain the relative position that it had held in 1860 with respect to its proportion of the value of the nation's manufactures (10.2 per cent), the percentage increases in the number of manufacturing wage earners and the value of manufactures were very rapid in the 1880-1890 decade. Moreover, when we consider the rapid growth of manufactures in the United States after 1860 and the fact that the geographic territory of the United States was expanding while that of the southern states remained unchanged, phenomenal progress was necessary for the south to regain its position by 1900.

An examination of the factors converging around 1880 to accelerate economic development reinforces the statistical evidence on the rapidity of industrial growth. One of the most significant was the change in the attitudes of leading southerners toward industrial change. Indeed, in spite of some who lamented the passing of the "agrarian way of life,"[27] the desire to attract industry assumed almost crusading proportions, particularly in the Piedmont areas where campaigns of industrialization were launched by Henry Watterson of the Louisville *Courier-Journal*, Francis W. Dawson of the Charleston (S. C.) *News and Courier* and Henry W. Grady of the *Atlanta Constitution*. As Woodward put it, these champions of industrialism also "were preaching laissez-faire capitalism, freed of all traditional restraints, together with a new philosophy and way of life and a new scale of values."[28] Although the lure of profits, which averaged 20 per cent in 1882 and more later, probably was not overlooked by those who sought to bring the cotton textile mills to the cotton, Mitchell assures us that "To give employment to the necessitous masses of poor whites [who had been neglected parts of the antebellum labor force], for the sake of the people themselves, was an object animating the minds of many mill builders."[29] The new economic order seems to have been based largely on white labor and to have grown up outside the plantation belt.

[It was considered] a fact of tremendous significance in the history of Alabama that the agricultural and industrial forces conspired to transfer economic supremacy from the Black Belt to the white northern counties. The new Alabama was growing out of what had been the waste lands before the war. These developments were based largely on the labor of whites. The political slogan of the white counties—"This is a white man's country"—was in a large sense as true of the economic life of the state as it was the political. The Negro was playing relatively an insignificant role in the upbuilding of the state.[30]

Ten years after the start of the cotton mill movement of the 1880's, however, the chief motive for building factories seems to have been the exploitation of cheap labor. Indeed, although the availability of raw materials was very important, most students of the south seem to agree that cheap labor and the absence of protective labor legislation were predominant factors in the region's growth during these years.[31] Although there is some disagreement as to the importance of the desire to help poor whites in the early cotton textile movement in the 1880's,[32] the assumption that it was a moral consideration is important for our purposes.

Whatever the reasons, there is little doubt that the growth of the cotton textile industry was greatly accelerated during the 1880-1900 period. Indeed, the industry was concentrated outside the plantation belt and appears to have been less blighted by Reconstruction than other areas. Between 1880 and 1890 the number of cotton mills increased by 48.4 per cent as compared with 19.7 per cent for New England. The south's proportion of the cotton textile spindles in the United States increased from 22 per cent in 1890 to 57 per cent in 1929.[33]

While cotton textile manufacturing led the south's industrial advance, many other industries were stimulated by the convergence of events around 1880. The region's potential and its progress were advertised widely by a series of expositions during the 1880's. The withdrawal of federal troops not only had favorable psychological affects on the south, but also made the region more attractive to outside investors. Moreover, the increase in the south's political power led to a rise in federal expenditures for railroads and other public improvements.

Since the south's progress seems to depend heavily on developments in the national economy, the end of the 1873-1879 depression was an important business stimulant. The cigarette machine was patented by a Virginia teenager in 1880, leading to the formation of James B. Duke's American Tobacco Company in 1890.

There were, at the same time, a number of developments which attracted outside capital. For one thing, the north had experienced considerable expansion in the immediate post-Civil War period. Therefore, not only were costs lower in the south, but railroads and raw materials offered investment opportunities in industries which were already developed in the north. In 1876 the federal government adopted a land policy which stimulated railroad building and led to rapid exploitation of the south's timber resources by lumber companies and land speculators.[34] The rapid depletion of much of the south's timber resources stimulated activity for a while as lumber companies denuded a wide area of the region. A government forestry expert referred to this as "probably the most rapid and reckless destruction of forests known to history."[35] By 1899 the southern states became the leading timber-producing region of the United States, a position they held until 1930 when they were superseded by the Pacific states.[36]

There were also important developments in the south's coal, iron and mineral resources around 1880.[37] The iron industry had existed in the south long before 1880, but a number of events at that time stimulated and changed its character. Especially important was the discovery of large deposits of coking coal in Tennessee and Alabama, and the technological changes which made it possible to substitute coke for charcoal and to use Alabama red ores. The first area to experience extensive development in the iron industry was Tennessee, where pig iron had been made using coke as a fuel in 1867. Chattanooga became an important iron-making town in 1877 when the Chattanooga Iron Company was established. By 1885, several hundred coke ovens were in operation in Tennessee, and nine furnaces and seventeen foundries and machine shops were in operation around Chattanooga.[38]

The development of the iron, coal, and railroad industries were all mutually stimulating and led to an important industrial triangle of Birmingham, Atlanta, and Chattanooga by the turn of the century. Around 1874 an important seam of good coking coal was discovered in the Warrior Field near Birmingham, which had been founded three years earlier.[39] In 1878 the first important Birmingham coal company—Pratt Coal and Coke—was formed to exploit this seam. The first of the "Big Four" in the Alabama iron and steel industry, the Woodward Iron Company, was formed in 1881 and started its first furnace in 1883.[40] The Sloss Furnace Company, which later became U.S. Pipe and Foundry, was formed in 1881. The Pioneer Mining Manufacturing Company, organized by the Thomas Brothers of Pennsylvania, founded Thomas, Alabama, and built two blast furnaces in 1888-1889. Pioneer sold out to Republic Iron and Steel in 1899. The biggest of the "Big Four" was the Tennessee Coal Iron and Railroad Company, organized in 1860, which began commercial production of basic open hearth steel in 1899 and was taken over by United States Steel in 1907.[41]

Thus, while the stage for the expansion of the south's iron industry had been set before 1880, the business revival of 1879 stimulated the rapid expansion of the industry.

> In 1879 an English syndicate with millions at its command opened its first furnace in Tennessee, and the same year Northern and English capitalists made large investments in the mines and furnaces of Virginia . . . Expansion was rapid in several Southern states, but none so fast as in Alabama. Her production of 1889 was over ten times her tonnage of 1889, more than twice the combined production of her nearest rivals, Tennessee and Virginia, and more than all the other Southern states together.[42]

The cast iron pipe industry developed rapidly after 1877, when the first pipe shop in the south was built in Chattanooga. The cast iron pipe industry was greatly stimulated by the growth of water works and sewerage installations as the nation urbanized during the 1880's and 1890's.[43] Southern pipe was produced at a much lower cost than elsewhere[44] and, unlike the basic iron and steel industry, benefited from being classified with pig iron for freight purposes.[45]

Although we shall see that there is some question as to how important the freight rate differentials were in impeding the economic development of the south during these years,[46] there can be little doubt that the favorable rates on raw materials and unfavorable rates on manufactured products shipped out of the south tended to hamper the growth of manufacturing. Indeed, the lower rates on raw materials benefited the nonsouthern manufacturer primarily. Because of lower wages and the close proximity of coal, iron ore, and limestone, Birmingham produced steel at a cost 26 per cent lower than Pittsburgh. But Birmingham could not capitalize on its advantage because of unfavorable freight rates and the so-called "Birmingham differential," imposed by the United States Steel Company on the output of Alabama mills.[47] Under this pricing arrangement, the consumer of Alabama steel had to pay the price at Pittsburgh and a differential of $3.00 a ton plus freight from Birmingham. This policy gave northern steel fabricators an advantage over their southern competitors even in southern markets.

Thus a Birmingham rival company found that the differential amounted to 9 per cent of the price of its product and that it was excluded from competition in Kentucky, Virginia, Missouri, and Arkansas because of this. A bridge company in Chattanooga discovered that the Birmingham Differential placed it under a disadvantage of 7 per cent in competition with Pittsburgh for construction in Winston-Salem and prohibited it from competing with the same city for business in Memphis.

Thus, while intervention of northern investors in southern markets perhaps introduced an element of security and stability, it also held the industry back and was at least partly responsible for the fact that between 1903 and 1913 production of pig iron in the south remained relatively stationary, while output in the United States was increasing by 70 per cent; the south's share of national production declined from 22 per cent in 1893 to 11 per cent in 1913.[48] Although the southern steel industry fared better than iron, "under the Pennsylvania rules of 'Pittsburgh Plus' and 'Birmingham Differential,' the captive industry came far from living up to possibilities obviously unexploited."[49]

A study by George Stocking supported the position that Birmingham, though enjoying the nation's lowest costs on some basic steel products, was prevented from developing because the United States Steel Company adopted practices which "subordinated the management of its southern properties to the combined interests of its national operations."[50]

These and other problems caused Howard Odum and others to observe that the south's economy occupied a "colonial" status. Odum declared in 1936, "Until recently, the South was a furnisher of raw materials to manufacturing regions, essentially colonial in its economy."[51] Odum felt that this colonial status perpetuated the south's "uneven technology," resulting in part from the region's limited access to capital, which caused higher interest rates and required southern enterprises to earn a higher return in order to get capital. "Accordingly most sorts of manufacture involving elaborate technologies have avoided the South because, as a rule, the elaborate technology is expressed in expensive and elaborate plants."

The notion that the south's economy was colonial was perpetuated by the 1938 report of President Franklin D. Roosevelt's Conference on

Economic Conditions in the South.[52] This report pointed to the detrimental effects of absentee ownership of industries and resources, adverse freight rate differentials, and high tariffs (which caused it to pay higher manufacturing prices and reduced the ability of other countries to purchase the south's agricultural products). "The South, in fact, has been caught in a vise that has kept it from moving along with the main stream of American economic life; on the one hand, the freight rates have hampered its industry; on the other hand, our high tariff has subsidized industry in other sections of the country at the expense of the South." The ideas expressed in the CECS report were not new, of course, because they had been expressed for years by southern politicians and scholars.[53]

Some scholars have, however, denied that the south's economy suffered for these reasons. Although there was scarcely a question that freight-rate inequities existed, Hoover and Rachford concluded that "high freight rates are not now, and never were, a major barrier to the economic development of the South."[54] Some economists also denied that northern monopolies had produced an adverse effect on the south,[55] while others pointed out that it was necessary for southerners to go outside the region to get capital and that the loss of control and the drainage of income from the south into other areas was the price that had to be paid for the advantages derived.[56] Clarence Danhof concludes with respect to this controversy, "The colonial-imperialistic thesis of conspiracy must be considered an unfortunate episode—a resurgence of a crude sectionalism—that diverted attention of some of the South's ablest men from constructive approaches to the region's problems . . . That the thesis dealt with significant matters is obvious, but they were national problems and their relationship to the South's economic retardation highly doubtful."[57]

The development of railroads was closely related to the growth of other industries and had an important influence on the total economic development of the region. The Civil War virtually destroyed the south's railroads, and, despite many bond issues and much political chicanery, relatively few miles of rails were laid during the 1870's. Rail mileage in the southern states east of the Mississippi increased by 24.9 per cent during the 1870's and 108.6 per cent during the 1880's. In the whole south, it increased by 135.5 per cent during the 1880's as compared with the national increase of 86.5 per cent. A construction and consolidation boom in southern railroads started in 1879 with the investment of large amounts of northern and foreign capital. In spite of the formation of 180 new railroad companies between 1881 and 1890, by then more than half the region's railroad mileage was in the hands of a dozen large companies and their affiliates, directed largely from New York.

Increased economic activity and federal subsidies between 1880 and the First World War greatly increased the region's seaports, especially in the Gulf states. Exports increased by 95.5 per cent as compared with 64.9 per cent for the nonsouth between 1880 and 1901. The ports at New Orleans and Galveston experienced such rapid growth that they were for a time second and third to New York in the value of exports. In 1888 the furniture manufacturing industry was established in High Point, North Carolina. Fertilizer manufacturing also became important after 1880 as did the cottonseed-oil industry. The south became the nation's leading oil-producing region after the discovery of the famous Spindletop well, near Beaumont, Texas, in 1901. Sulphur was developed after 1903 because 95 per cent of the nation's deposits are in the Texas and Louisiana Gulf Coast. Four southern states—Arkansas, Georgia, Alabama, and Tennessee—produced the entire domestic supply of bauxite.

While we have emphasized the relative rapidity of industrial change around 1880, the region continued to lag far behind the rest of the United States in manufacturing activity. A number of factors account for this. In some cases, like timber resources, the rapid growth during the 1880's was based on exploitation which soon was exhausted. Moreover, industrial development was impeded by the south's "colonial" status during these years.

But not all economic disadvantages can be blamed on northern monopolists. While industrialization did indeed erode some of the south's traditional values, the values themselves were impediments to economic development. And the leaders seem rarely to have been aware either of the changes implicit in industrialization or of the incompatibility of the old values with economic development. William H. Nicholls argues that whether or not the south should have the economic progress to which a majority of its leaders seem committed is a value judgment, but that the region could not have economic progress *and* its traditional social values. Joseph J. Spengler has summarized a number of impediments to the expansion of income and output associated with the south's economic and cultural history: the age composition of the region's population has been such that its labor force participation rates have been relatively small; its high population growth and low rate of capital expansion has resulted in a comparatively slow growth of capital per head which has retarded the growth of wages and output per worker and restricted southern industry's capacity to absorb its excess farm labor; the south's labor force has been concentrated in relatively low income employments; and the south's capacity to increase its low average income has been "depressed more by lack of training in the population than by any other condition, especially in the rural white population and in the non-white population rural and urban."[58]

CHAPTER II

General Developments and Problems of Unions Before 1928

The earliest labor organizations in the south were "mechanics' societies" (which were mainly fraternal), and temporary or spontaneous associations formed during the eighteenth century. Before the Civil War there were, for example, many sporadic, organized uprisings of white workers. One of the most famous was the unsuccessful strike by 200 whites in 1847 to prevent the Tredegar Steel Company at Richmond from expanding its force of 600 slaves.[1]

However, many bona fide unions were formed in the major cities before the Civil War. Probably the earliest southern union was organized in 1810 by printers in New Orleans. Although the important printers' unions in the region did not appear before 1835, typographical unions were formed in most of the south's leading cities before the Civil War. Besides the printers, local unions of longshoremen, machinists, blacksmiths, cigar makers, molders, carpenters, and brickmasons existed before 1860. The Civil War thus interrupted an expanding southern labor movement.

THE NATIONAL LABOR UNION

The National Labor Union (NLU), organized in 1866, was active until 1872. Southern delegates were at the NLU's founding convention,

20

and William Sylvis, the NLU's president, journeyed through the south in 1868 in an effort to align white and black workers against a "non-producing aristocracy."[2] Richard Trevellick, a British immigrant who had lived in New Orleans between 1855 and 1860,[3] returned to the south as an NLU organizer in 1869. Trevellick worked at establishing "uplift" associations. In the spring of 1869, for example, he spoke in Atlanta on the "Right of Labor and Producer,"[4] and established Workingman's Union No. 1 in April of that year. This organization proposed to establish a library and reading room in Atlanta and to promote better feeling between workers and employers. However, it became involved in municipal elections of November 1869 and disappeared later that year.

The National Labor Union also attempted to solve the race problem. And when two leading southern delegates to the 1869 convention voted for the admission of Negroes, it looked as though it might succeed.[5] But, although the NLU called for the organization of all workers without "distinction of race or nationality,"[6] the initial convention announced that it could reach no conclusion concerning the race question because it found "the diversity of opinion among our members" too great. The NLU felt that working-class problems could best be solved by "greenbackism," cooperation, and homesteads; southern whites supported the Democratic Party, while most Negro leaders were Republicans. The Negroes therefore formed a National Negro Labor Congress (NNLC), and, although the NNLC and NLU were willing to exchange delegates, the differences between Negro and white workers doomed these efforts to failure. The NNLC met in New Orleans in 1872, "repudiated the National Labor Union, declared unflagging loyalty to the Republican Party and passed into oblivion."[7] The NLU also ceased to function after Judge David Davis of Illinois declined its nomination for President of the United States.

THE KNIGHTS OF LABOR

The most significant general labor organization formed before the 1880's was the Noble Order of the Knights of Labor (KL), organized in 1869. The main reasons for the Knight's rapid growth in the south were its membership policies and its structure. The order organized all who worked for a living, and local assemblies admitted workers in particular trades or industries or in mixed assemblies. In 1878, as business began to improve following the recession of 1874, the Knights sent 15 organizers into the south, thus launching the first concerted southern organizing drive. Seven of them worked in Alabama, five in Kentucky, and one each in North Carolina, Florida, and Georgia. The

Knights' southern activities seem to have been concentrated in Alabama and Kentucky until 1883, when a great general increase in southern membership occurred.[8] Four local assemblies, with 336 members, were reported in Alabama in 1879; Kentucky had two assemblies with 139 members that year, but reported 18 assemblies with 1484 members in 1880. Three of the four lodges in Alabama were in Mobile, the earliest center of union organization in that state, and the other was at Birmingham.[9] The only other southern states to report membership in the Knights before 1883 were Tennessee, where a local with 20 members was formed in 1881; Virginia, where a 15-member local was organized in 1882; and Texas, where the first local assembly appeared in 1882.[10] The first year of general activity throughout the south was 1883; locals were reported that year in every state except North Carolina and Florida—where the first locals were formed in 1885. There were at least 17 southern locals in 1883 with 858 members; by 1888 there were a least 487 locals with 21,208 members. In the southwestern states, not included in these figures, there were over 200 locals and 15,000 members in 1886.[11]

Thus, the 12 southern states for which estimates are reported—which comprise our definition of the "south" except Oklahoma, for which estimates are not available—had approximately 45,700 members in the Knights at a time when the order's national membership reached a peak of some 730,000 members. The Knights' southern membership later probably became a larger proportion of the total because it increased after 1886, while national membership was declining.

Although their main activity was concentrated around such centers as Birmingham, Knoxville, Galveston, Louisville, and New Orleans, the Knights also were active in many rural areas.[12] In North Carolina, a few professionals and some small merchants joined the Knights, but wage earners and farmers constituted the bulk of the membership.[13] The Knights were not very active among workers in the growing textile industry except for a long and costly strike in Augusta, Georgia, in 1886,[14] but they had affiliates of coal miners in Tennessee, Kentucky, and Alabama; lumber workers in Alabama; longshoremen in the Gulf and south Atlantic ports; sugar cane workers in Louisiana; and railroad workers throughout the region; as well as numerous mixed assemblies.[15]

Negroes, barred from membership in many craft organizations, took advantage of the Knights' policy of organizing "to uphold the dignity of labor and to affirm the nobility of all who earn their bread by the sweat of their brow."[16] The 1885 KL convention proposed the appointment of a colored organizer for each of the old slave states, and the

1886 convention was told that Negroes were flocking to join the Knights in the south, apparently mainly in all-Negro assemblies. In Richmond, Virginia, there were seven Negro assemblies by 1885, and one in Manchester to the south of Richmond. There was a Negro district assembly in Richmond with 13 locals.[17] There were eight Negro assemblies in Alabama[18] and four in Atlanta.[19] In North Carolina, Negroes apparently were also organized in segregated locals, and an assistant state organizer, presumably colored, was engaged to work among Negroes.[20] White workers in North Carolina sometimes prevented Negroes from getting jobs. In Texas, it was found that "no ideological slogans could wipe out the reality of the racial barriers, and the Negroes from a Harrisburg [Texas] assembly petitioned the General Assembly to instruct the white members to treat them as brothers."[21]

Then Knights' official racial position was widely publicized at the 1886 national convention in Richmond. When a New York Negro delegate was denied service in hotels, restaurants, theaters and other public places, the delegation moved to another hotel, and Master Workman Terence V. Powderly (who headed the Knights from 1879-1893) chose the colored delegate to introduce him before he introduced Governor Lee of Virginia.[22]

When Powderly, who had at least once advocated exclusive Negro assemblies, was widely criticized in the southern press, he replied that he had no intention of interfering with social relations in the south, but wanted to promote the education of the Negro and the elevation of labor irrespective of race and color. The Knights adopted a statement at this convention which recognized "the civil and political equality of all men and, in the broad field of labor recognizes no distinction on account of color, but it has no purpose to interfere with or disrupt the social relations which may exist between different races in any part of the country."[23]

One of the most significant acts of the Knights of Labor, in the south or elsewhere, was the "Great Southwest strike" against Jay Gould's railroads in 1886. The events leading to this walkout suggest a plot to undermine the rapidly growing and undisciplined Knights.[24] Gould's victory, which ultimately involved approximately 9000 men on 5000 miles of railway, contributed greatly to the Knights' decline.

The Knights also were active politically, electing a congressman and 11 of 15 members of the city council at Lynchburg, Virginia; a majority of the city and county officials and several state legislators in Macon, Georgia; and several officers in Mobile, Alabama, in 1887. The Knights also claimed to have elected mayors at Jacksonville, Florida, Vicks-

burg, Mississippi, and Anniston, Alabama, in 1888, and a Mayor at
Selma, Alabama, the following year.[25] As we shall see in Chapter VI
the Knights also formed a political alliance with the Populists during
the 1890's.

The widespread and much publicized activities of the Knights of
Labor brought unionism to the attention of workers and citizens in
every southern state. The Knights' peak membership in the south
came after 1886—the top year for their national strength—probably
because the order's southern membership comprised a higher percentage of farmers in mixed assemblies. The farmer members were
more interested in political activity than in collective bargaining, and
their membership therefore was less influenced by business conditions.

The great strength of the Knights of Labor—from an organizing
viewpoint—was their philosophy and structure; these, paradoxically,
were also the organization's greatest weaknesses. The broad social
philosophy, ideally suited for political action and cooperative schemes,
was ill suited for the establishment of a strong trade union movement
in the environment of nineteenth-century America. Its activities and
policies were more akin to the agricultural protest organization origi-
nating in the south during these years than they were to those of the
American Federation of Labor.

THE AMERICAN FEDERATION OF LABOR, 1881-1928

Although the Knights of Labor publicized the idea of unionism in
the south, it was the American Federation of Labor (AFL) which consolidated the local unions (which remained aloof from the Knights) into
what might be called a labor movement. This was not accomplished
immediately, however, because many southern locals remained unaffiliated with both the Knights and the AFL's predecessor—The Federation of Organized Trades and Labor Unions (FOTLU), organized
in 1881.[26] One of the reasons for not joining the AFL during these early
years was the desire by many of the region's union leaders to form a
political coalition with farmers and other groups not affiliated with
the federation. The real beginning of the AFL's activities came during
the late 1880's, after a decade of rapid industrial expansion in the
south.[27] Union activity was especially great in Birmingham, where
there were some 7000 union members in 1894 and where a trades
council was organized in 1890;[28] New Orleans, where there were 95
local unions, 49 of which, with a membership of "over 20,000 laborers,"[29] were affiliated with the AFL; and Louisville, Paducah, and
Dallas, where trades and labor asesmblies were organized before 1895.
Although only three southern delegates attended AFL conventions

during the 1880's, 93 delegates attended AFL conventions during the 1890's; the 1894 convention was the only one during this decade without southern delegates. The first southern convention of the AFL was held at Birmingham in 1891, and the delegates were warmly received by Governor Jones of Alabama.[30]

The AFL's president, Samuel Gompers, who had long been interested in strengthening the AFL in that region, toured the south in 1895.[31] In 1893 a resolution was introduced recommending that two general organizers be appointed in the south "to assist in more thorough organizations of all the allied crafts and the extensive and general formation of local federal labor unions."[32] A southern delegate to the same convention introduced a resolution calling for the appointment of a Negro organizer.

This activity apparently produced rapid increases in southern union membership in the following years. The AFL issued 26 new local union charters between 1890 and 1891, and 50 the following year. A total of 99 new southern local charters were issued between 1890 and 1894, and central labor unions were established in most of the major cities by 1900, when five state federations of labor (Alabama, Georgia, Kentucky, Texas, and Virginia) were chartered; by 1919, when the Mississippi state body was chartered, every southern state had a federation of labor. By 1919 there also were AFL organizers in 173 different cities in every southern state. Only two of these organizers were salaried, however. There were 11 Negro organizers in the south in 1919; six in Texas, three in Virginia, one in Louisiana, and one in Tennessee.

The general pattern of union growth during the period between 1890 and 1928 resembled that of unions in the rest of the country. Although we do not have membership figures for every state, the available statistics reveal that unions in the region started first among the printers, building tradesmen, railway operating employees, and longshoremen, and then spread to lesser-skilled workers in these same occupations. Within the building trades the older crafts like carpenters and brick masons were organized first, but plumbers and electricians were organized on commercial construction work in every major city by the early years of the twentieth century.

Union membership was stimulated in the south as in the rest of the country by the economic expansion and the favorable attitude of the Federal Government toward unions during the First World War. In 1914, when the war started in Europe, the United States was passing through a period of depression. By 1916, the European allies' demand for goods had produced prosperity conditions in the United States.

The war also improved the conditions of workers by halting the flow of immigrants from Europe. Although few immigrants had come south, many southerners, particularly Negroes, migrated to meet the demands for unskilled labor in the north. In order to counteract the influence of the Industrial Workers of the World and other pacifist groups and to gain labor support for the war, AFL unions formed the American Alliance for Labor and Democracy in 1917. Gompers and other leaders also served on numerous special boards and committees created during the war. The boards were particularly important in encouraging the growth of unions in the shipbuilding, longshoring, railroad, coal-mining, and various defense industries. Particularly important was the National War Labor Board (NWLB) which sought, by mediation, conciliation, and arbitration, to prevent disputes in essential industries. The board recommended that there be no strikes or lockouts during the war and that employers recognize the workers' right to organize. Employers were not to discharge workers or otherwise interfere with their right to engage in union activities. Union security provisions were to remain unchanged, and all employers in an area were to pay prevailing wages. Although exact membership figures are not availble for the south, the pattern in that region was similar to that of the country as a whole, where membership increased from 3.0 to 5.1 million between 1917 and 1920 and declined thereafter until the upsurge of the 1930's. In the south, as in the United States, the main membership gains were among skilled workers.

The wartime gains among skilled workers and the postwar efforts to extend unionism to industrial workers, who remained virtually unorganized, were vigorously resisted by employers and their allies during the so-called open-shop movement of the 1920's. Some employers in the south's manufacturing industries resisted unions by paying attention to the workers' needs and motives and adopting employee representation plans to give workers some voice in management. Although some of these schemes failed when economic recession forced employers to disregard the workers' opinions and cut wages, they were nevertheless successful in keeping unions out during the 1920's.

But nonunion employers in the south appear to have continued to resist unions by such traditional tactics as yellow-dog contracts, injunctions, labor spies, blacklisting, discharging workers for union activity, and supporting anti-union local officials. Southern employers also adopted the so-called "American Plan of Employment," which is sometimes mistakenly referred to as an "open-shop" movement. Under the open shop, employers are willing to hire workers regardless of whether they are union members; under the "American Plan," union members were not to be hired. In addition, the National Open Shop Association was supported by local organizations and chambers of commerce in virtually every southern city. As a result of these activities, unions were able to survive during the 1920's only among the south's most strongly organized workers. As in the rest of the nation, only the strongest unions were able to survive the open-shop period of the 1920's.

The antiunion campaign was particularly vigorous in Texas. In San Antonio, for example, the chamber of commerce ran a free employment agency which placed over 2000 nonunion workers in 1920, by which time it had become almost impossible for union carpenters to get jobs. Mexican workers were brought in by the thousands, and special schools were set up to train nonunion workers. In San Antonio, this program defeated union electricians, carpenters, planning mill operators, butchers, printers and others.[33] Beaumont, which had been a strong union town, became almost "open shop" after the antiunion attacks led by a member of the National Metal Trades Association. The antiunion forces in Dallas imported 1500 strikebreakers, and even the printers were forced to accept nonunion conditions. The Southwest Open Shop Association opened a trade school at Dallas to supply workers and persuaded the governor to send militia to Galveston to break the 1920 longshoremen's strike.

The open-shop movement was not completely successful, however, because the unions at Fort Worth and Houston were able to survive— and at Houston they were even strong enough to get rid of the antiunion secretary of the chamber of commerce.

In Mississippi, unions apparently were not powerful enough to arouse open-shop opposition, but organized resistance was active in Georgia, North Carolina, and eastern Tennessee.[34] Not only was the open-shop movement a response to the general increase in union membership during and after the First World War, but it also seems to have been most vigorous in those states and areas where unions had grown the most.

Except for the information on unions presented in the following chapters, the main evidence of the nature of worker protest in the south during the 1887-1905 period comes from statistics on strikes compiled by the United States Commissioner of Labor. A careful analysis of these statistics reveals that strikes in the south and the nonsouth apparently became more formal and less spontaneous as industrialization proceeded, but that strikes in the south were much less likely to be successful. In the 1887-1904 period, for example, 61.3

per cent of the southern strikes failed, compared with 43.8 per cent for the nonsouth; the related figures for other periods were: 1895-1900, 53.7 per cent and 23.3 per cent; 1900-1905, 52.7 per cent and 36.9 per cent. Until 1900, the proportion of strikes led by formal labor organizations was about the same in the south as elsewhere; however, in the 1900-1905 period, 78.0 per cent of nonsouthern and 75.8 per cent of southern strikes were led by formal labor organizations. Between 1887 and 1900, about a third of all strikes in the south and the non-south were spontaneous walkouts.

Table 1 reveals that southern strike activity was concentrated in fewer industries during 1887-1905 than was true of the United States. Over half the strikers were in the coal and coke and building trades industries. As might be expected, the location of strike activity follows the pattern of economic activity.

It is significant that relatively few strikes occurred in the south's leading manufacturing industry, cotton textiles. During the entire period between 1887 and 1905, there were only 32 cotton textile strikes involving 9274 workers. Indeed, of the south's rapidly expanding industries the only ones to have a significant number of strikes during the 1887-1894 period were transportation and tobacco. However, the tobacco strikes did not occur in the newer cigarette plants but in the older Florida cigar industry, which accounted for 66 of the strikes between 1887-1894. There was not a single tobacco strike in North Carolina during this period, and only five involving 56 workers in Kentucky; of 22,447 tobacco strikers during this period, 21,127 were in Florida. About one third of the south's strikes came in the coal and coke industry which was expanding rapidly during these years. During the earliest period, 1887-1894, the south's proportion of the nation's total strikes (5.39 per cent) was much less than its proportion of strikers (8.08 per cent), although during the 1901-1905 period the proportion of strikes (9.07 per cent) was greater than the proportion of strikers (7.72 per cent). This suggests that some of the earliest strikes in the south were relatively large but then diminished in comparison with the rest of the country.

These statistics also give some indication of the relationship between strikes and business conditions. The number of strikes in the south and the nation more than doubled in the 1895-1900 depression as compared with the period of prosperity, 1887-1894, and declined again in the gainful years between 1901 and 1905. During 1895-1900—when business conditions were more depressed than in either the 1887-1894 or the 1901-1905 periods—a smaller proportion of the strikes were called by unions in the United States, though the proportion of unsuccessful strikes increased greatly in the south. This indicates that southern unions were less successful in resisting wage cuts during recession periods than their northern counterparts. Kentucky, the state with the oldest, most established labor movement, had about the same proportion of unsuccessful strikes (24.7 per cent) as the United States (24.4 per cent); Texas also had a relatively low proportion of unsuccessful strikes during this period (27.3 per cent).

AFL racial practices and policies. The AFL, like the Knights of Labor and the National Labor Union, found it necessary to deal with the race problem. Since Negroes were concentrated in many of the occupations which AFL affiliates were trying to organize, and since the AFL entered the region at a time when racial segregation had become firmly institutionalized, it faced more serious difficulties than earlier labor organizations. The AFL's problem also was complicated by the fact that its affiliates, unlike those of the Knights of Labor or the National Labor Union, were mainly strong collective-bargaining organizations whose locals often restricted membership in order to enhance their control of jobs.

The AFL's affiliates also were social and fraternal organizations formed at a time when it was not considered proper to have social relations with Negroes. Of course, the policies of many of the AFL's skilled trades affiliates were motivated by a desire to monopolize their jobs. Moreover, the problem of racial discrimination existed more among the locals than it did in the AFL and national unions. Local unions are more vulnerable to social environment and are more restrictive. Indeed, national officers are rarely, if ever, interested in limiting membership, because they acquire power by expanding it. National officers also are in a better position to see the detrimental influence of racial restriction on the whole labor movement. It was for this reason that the leaders of such unions as the cement masons, longshoremen, carpenters, painters, bricklayers, firemen and oilers, electrical workers, and teachers attempted at a very early date to overcome discrimination. As early as 1868, for instance the constitution and bylaws of the Bricklayers, Masons and Plasterers' Union imposed a $100 fine on any member found guilty of discrimination. The leaders were not, however, always successful, since the locals often enjoyed considerable autonomy. And national union leaders rarely enforced their views when they thought these views jeopardized their political positions or the survival and growth of the union.

The official policy of the AFL from its inception was to admit no union which refused membership to Negroes. The federation declared in 1890, for instance, that it "looked with disfavor upon trade unions

Table 1. Strikes in the south and the United States by industry, 1887–1905.

Industry	Number of strikes	Per cent south of U.S.	Number of strikers	Per cent south of U.S.
	1887–1894			
United States				
Building trades	2,490	2.33	273,121	11.87
Clothing	1,015	4.93	68,102	1.38
Coal and coke	709	11.99	675,128	7.09
Cotton goods	234	2.14	35,616	1.31
Printing and publishing	299	8.03	11,425	4.88
Mining, ore	—		—	—
R.R. Car building	38	13.16	8,272	12.46
R.R., canal, road building	—		—	—
Stone quarrying and cuttings	587	8.18	45,922	5.68
Transportation	626	14.54	173,418	12.39
Tobacco	645	12.87	82,221	27.30
Woolen and worsted	155	1.29	16,200	4.31
Other	3,689	3.09	444,668	3.97
Total	10,487	5.39	1,834,093	8.08
		Per cent of total		Per cent of total
South				
Building trades	58	10.27	32,420	21.87
Clothing	50	8.85	938	0.63
Coal and coke	85	15.04	47,896	32.31
Cotton goods	5	0.89	468	0.32
Printing and publishing	24	4.25	558	0.38
Mining, ore	—		—	—

Table 1. (Continued)

Industry	Number of strikes	Per cent south of U.S.	Number of strikers	Per cent south of U.S.
Railroad car building	5	0.89	1,031	0.70
R.R., canal, road building	—	—	—	—
Stone quarrying and cuttings	48	8.50	2,609	1.76
Transportation	91	16.11	21,494	14.50
Tobacco	83	14.69	22,447	15.14
Woolen and worsted	2	0.35	699	0.47
Other	114	20.18	17,674	11.92
Total	565	100.00	148,234	100.00

1895–1900

Industry	Number of strikes	Per cent south of U.S.	Number of strikers	Per cent south of U.S.
United States				
Building trades	4,440	3.72	559,230	7.66
Clothing	1,638	3.97	461,416	0.26[a]
Coal and coke	2,515	11.93	1,584,084	6.79
Cotton goods	512	4.30	113,994	5.98
Printing and publishing	765	9.15	30,267	4.92
Mining, ore	—	—	—	—
R.R. Car building	94	5.32	20,580	5.01
R.R., canal, road building	—	—	—	—
Stone quarrying and cuttings	856	8.41	93,724	4.67
Transportation	1,265	15.73	366,737	15.54[b]
Tobacco	1,509	15.51	200,734	24.82
Woolen and worsted	484	1.65	45,254	4.34
Other	8,715	3.98	1,218,829	3.47
Total	22,793	6.52	4,694,849	6.74

Table 1. (Continued)

Industry	Number of strikes	Per cent south of U.S. / Per cent of total	Number of strikers	Per cent south of U.S. / Per cent of total
South				
Building trades	165	11.10	42,827	13.54
Clothing	65	4.37	1,220	0.39a
Coal and coke	300	20.17	107,523	33.99
Cotton goods	22	1.48	6,819	2.16
Printing and publishing	70	4.71	1,490	0.47
Mining, ore	—	—	—	—
Railroad car building	5	0.34	1,031	0.33
R.R., canal, road building	—	—	—	—
Stone quarrying and cuttings	72	4.84	4,376	1.38
Transportation	199	13.38	56,998	18.02b
Tobacco	234	15.74	49,815	15.75
Woolen and worsted	8	0.54	1,964	0.62
Other	347	23.34	42,236	13.35
Total	1,487	100.00	316,299	100.00
		1901–1905		
United States				
Building trades	5,076	7.74	356,237	6.25
Clothing	281	12.46	131,009	0.90
Coal and coke	8,823	16.28	422,739	11.77
Cotton goods	165	3.03	52,153	3.81
Printing and publishing	278	13.31	18,911	6.10
Mining, ore	85	5.88	22,574	2.25

Table 1. (Continued)

		Per cent of total		Per cent of total
R.R. Car building	—	—	—	—
R.R., canal, road building	130	6.92	38,208	1.64
Stone quarrying and cuttings	216	5.56	28,638	1.67
Transportation	442	12.22	99,585	19.80
Tobacco	312	21.15	43,953	63.39
Woolen and worsted	131	2.29	31,552	1.32
Other	6,025	8.51	787,637	3.95
Total	13,964	9.07	2,033,196	7.72
South		Per cent of total		Per cent of total
Building trades	393	31.04	22,269	14.18
Clothing[a]	35	2.76	1,184	0.75
Coal and coke	134	10.58	49,737	31.67
Cotton goods	5	0.39	1,987	1.27
Printing and publishing	37	2.92	1,154	0.73
Mining, ore	5	0.39	508	0.32
Railroad car building	—	—	—	—
R.R., canal, road building	9	0.71	628	0.40
Stone quarrying and cuttings	12	0.95	479	0.31
Transportation[b]	54	4.27	19,718	12.56
Tobacco	66	5.21	27,863	17.74
Woolen and worsted	3	0.24	415	0.26
Other	513	40.52	31,098	19.80
Total	1,266	100.00	157,040	100.00

a Men's clothing.
b Railroad freight.
Source: U.S. Commissioner of Labor, *Annual Reports*, 1894, 1901, 1906.

33

having provisions in their constitutions excluding from membership persons because of race and color and requested they be expunged."[35] In spite of this, the AFL later admitted discriminating unions and chartered segregated locals and central bodies. The first significant tests of the nondiscrmination policy came between 1890 and 1895 when Gompers sought unsuccessfully to prevent the Machinists' Union from being affiliated because of a race bar in its constitution. The machinists were admitted in 1895, however (the only year between 1886 and 1924 that Gompers was not president), by transferring the race bar from the constitution to the ritual.[36] After the machinists were admitted, the AFL accepted several other discriminating unions and permitted others already affiliated to erect formal racial barriers. In 1900, the federation adopted the policy of organizing Negroes into directly affiliated federal locals and central labor unions where, "in the judgment of the Executive Council, it appears advisable and in the best interest of the trade union movement to do so."[37] The affairs of the federal locals, affiliated directly with the AFL, were handled by the executive council, which proved very unsympathetic to the Negro workers. The federal locals not only lacked effective bargaining power to protect their jobs, but under the AFL Constitution they had no appeal from decisions of the executive council, which often surrendered the Negroes' interests to those of the international unions when these interests clashed. In fact, several leaders of the most discriminatory national unions were always on the executive council.

The race problem greatly weakened unions in the south for a number of reasons. In the first place, partly because of discrimination by unions and white workers, Negro leaders like Booker T. Washington actively allied themselves with employers and encouraged Negroes to act as strikebreakers. Of course, union discrimination is not a complete explanation for the use of Negro strikebreakers and the alliance between Negro leaders and employers, because Negroes also broke strikes of nondiscriminatory unions like the United Mine Workers. The Negro was encouraged to ally himself with employers because, in Booker T. Washington's words, "When he gets a job . . . he is inclined to consider the source from which it comes."[38] Will Winn, a Columbus, Georgia AFL organizer, reported in 1898: "Unfortunately there are but few unions in the South which have the negro as an active competitor that can truly lay claim to stability; and inasmuch as he is an active competitor in 90 per cent of Southern industry it would appear that time and money spent in a general organization of white workingmen is, at best, experimental—notwithstanding that there are industries which public sentiment will not permit the negro to engage in that are not organized."³⁹ Winn said that he had "participated in the organization of several unions that were, in time, forced to disband because their members could not procure work at a union wage in the face of negro competition." Ironically, however, Winn did not advocate an active campaign to organize Negroes. He felt that with few exceptions Negroes lacked "those peculiarities of temperament such as patriotism, sympathy, sacrifice, etc., which are peculiar to most of the Caucasian race and which alone make an organization of the character and complicity of the modern trade union possible."

Although the need to organize the rapidly industrializing south undoubtedly influenced the AFL's racial policies, we do not know how much the attitudes of southern AFL organizers like Winn influenced Gompers and the federation's national leaders. Although Gompers visited Columbus, Georgia, in 1895, he probably felt that equalitarian racial policies were less important than the growth of the AFL. Gompers said, "In making the declaration for the complete organization of all workers [the AFL] does not necessarily proclaim that the social barriers which exist between the whites and blacks could or should be obliterated."⁴⁰ Citing the advice of some Negro leaders that colored workers should be controlled by their employers, Gompers added: "The antipathy that we know some union workers have against the colored man is not because of his color, but because of the fact that generally he is a 'cheap man.'"

Gompers' most mature thinking on the race question was probably his statement to a group of Negro leaders who urged the executive council in 1918 at a time when unions were expanding to organize Negro workers on a more equitable basis and have "these assurances pledged by not with words only, but by deeds—pledged by an increasing number of examples of groups of Negro workmen given a square deal."⁴¹ The Negro leaders added: "With these accomplished we pledge ourselves to urge Negro workingmen to seek the advantages of sympathetic cooperation and understanding between men who work."

Gompers replied by reviewing the AFL's racial policies and added that he did not think the AFL was completely at fault.

> The fact of the matter is, and I am going to speak as plain to you as a man ought to men . . . in many instances the conduct of colored workmen, and those who have spoken for them, has not been in asking or demanding that equal rights be accorded to them as to white workmen, but somewhat conveying the idea that they are to be petted or coddled and given special consideration and special privilege. Of course that can't be done . . . The colored workers have been the victims of many of

the colored misleaders who have sought advantage to themselves at the sacrifice of the interests of the rank and file of colored workmen, to ride into power, to ride into position, to ride into emolument or advantage . . .

You must have in mind the fact, gentlemen, that this is a Federation of organized workers, and is a voluntary body, that is, its existence depends upon the good will, the desire, the cooperation of the workers organized in their unions. We have all sorts of people to deal with . . . We must maintain our Federation and we cannot always do that which we would like to do and yet maintain our Federation, which as you have said has grown into power and influence. It is because we have tried to keep abreast and perhaps a little ahead of the great mass of workers. We can't rush too far ahead and then find ourselves high and dry without a Federation, without a following, without anything of the support for the existence of which we can only continue.

Regardless of the causes, there can be little question that hostility between Negroes and unions weakened labor organizations before the 1930's. Not only were Negroes used as strikebreakers, but the unions' refusal to organize Negroes made it impossible for them effectively to organize their jurisdictions. Of course, the incompatibility of discrimination and strong unions became increasingly obvious as more Negroes moved into nonagricultural jobs. We shall see, however, that the way in which different unions handled this problem depended mainly on the number of Negroes in the trades and occupations and their location. And, although we shall argue that racial differences became less important impediments to union growth after the 1930's, the problem has been constant for southern unions, as it has been for the larger southern society.

POLITICAL ACTION

In the early days of the twentieth century, many union leaders in the south attempted to form political alliances with other groups, particularly the farmers. Indeed, the AFL's insistence that unions avoid such connections with nonlabor groups caused some southern unions to remain unaffiliated for many years. The Texas State Federation of Labor, for example, was chartered initially in 1900, but gave up its charter in an effort to form political alliances with other bodies, especially the railway brotherhoods and the farmers. Farmers' Union members also were affiliated with several other southern federations of labor.[42]

In 1900, the railway brotherhoods and the Texas State Federation of Labor (TSFL) established the Joint Labor Legislative Board of Texas. This board formed an alliance with the Farmers' Union, organized in 1902.[43] The Texas Joint Board was instrumental in securing the passage of favorable labor legislation during the 1900-1915 period, particularly: a 1901 measure outlawing the issuance of company checks, tickets or symbols of any sort redeemable only in merchandise at company stores; a child labor law first adopted in 1903 and improved in 1911; a 1907 law giving railroad telegraphers an eight-hour day; an eight-hour law for state employees and persons working on government contracts in 1911; a 1913 law establishing a nine-hour day and a 54-hour week for women in manufacturing; antiblacklisting and mine safty codes in 1907; apprenticeship requirements for loco-motive engineers and conductors, a full crew law for passenger trains and a requirement that railroads repair their equipment in Texas shops, and workmen's compensation legislation for railroad workers in 1909; workmen's compensation was extended to industrial workers in 1911; a bureau of labor statistics in 1909 to enforce protective labor legislation; and the abolition of the convict lease system in 1910.

Much of this favorable legislation was adopted because of the TSFL's alliance with the railroad brotherhoods and the farmers, but cooperation with the latter group began to weaken in 1911 when the Farmers' Union secured the passage of a bill—over labor's objections —to establish a textile mill in the Rusk penitentiary and in 1913 when the farmers lobbied against the railway brotherhoods' full crew bill. The Farmers' Union had been infiltrated by the antiunion Commercial Secretaries Association.

The joint board was also weakened by a split between the TSFL and the railroad brotherhoods. The brotherhoods had five of the six seats on the joint board and only about one sixth of the TSFL's member-ship. This struggle led to the withdrawal of the engineers, firemen, conductors and trainmen in 1914.[44]

The common political, social and economic problems confronting the region's workers also produced attempts to get southwide coopera-tion among farmers, railroad organizations, unions affiliated with the AFL, and other prolabor groups. In 1912, for example, southern unions and farmers' organizations launched the Southern Labor Congress (SLC) to "unite the farmer, railroad and working man to bring about certain reforms so sadly needed in the south."[45] The 1912 meeting, held in Atlanta and attended by "influential men, mapped out the pos-sibility of a strictly sectional, largely advisory adjunct of the AFL. The congress formed an alliance with the Farmers' Union and railway brotherhoods to secure the passage of "remedial and constructive legis-lation." The first session was attended by 188 delegates from 12 south-ern states and the American Federation of Labor. The second session, held at Nashville, Tennessee, in 1914, was attended by 115 delegates from 12 states; the third session, at Birmingham in 1914 was attended by 91 delegates from 11 states, and the 1915 session at Chattanooga attracted 106 delegates from ten states. These delegates came from all trades and the railway brotherhoods, and many were "from locals where no central bodies exist, and in some instances sections of the country where labor organizations are practically unknown."

Colonel Jerome Jones represented the Southern Labor Congress at the 1915 AFL convention at which George Berry of Tennessee, president of the Printing Pressmen's Union, introduced a resolution urging all organizations and the AFL Executive Council to help the SLC. Jones told the 1915 convention that the labor movement in the south needed missionaries—"something more than organizers who often only gather together certain units and leave them before they cohere." "Without the cooperative help of the farmers and railroad men," Jones added, "We cannot hope to solve the problem in the lifetime of most of us in the South—certainly not in mine. With the cooperation of the AFL, and these elements in the Southern Labor Congress, we can get results in the immediate future."

However, the Resolutions Committee took a dim view of the Southern Labor Congress and adopted the following report.

> This Congress may and no doubt is doing much good in its own way. From information received we learn it consists of trade unions affiliated and unaffiliated with the American Federation of Labor, farmers' organizations, women's clubs, welfare associations and the like. It takes unto itself the right to direct state federations of labor in the South as to the course they should pursue in education and legislative matters. This we consider the business of the American Federation of Labor and not the Congress. We therefore cannot see our way clear to recognize it as a component part of the American Federation of Labor; nor do we believe it should be represented in the conventions of the American Federation of Labor by a fraternal delegate.

PART II

Development of Unions by Trade Industry Before 1932

CHAPTER III

Printing and Building Trades

PRINTERS

The earliest bona fide union in the south was the New Orleans Typographical Society of 1810.[1] The oldest local in the International Typographical Union (ITU) is Local 101 in Washington, D.C., but short-lived locals were organized in New York as early as 1786.[2] There were also printers' organizations elsewhere in the south before 1836. The New Orleans Typographical Society disappeared sometime after 1810, but another organization was formed in 1830. This group struck for higher wages in 1832, collapsed sometime after 1833, and was reorganized in 1835. It struck successfully for higher wages in 1836 and 1839, in spite of the importation of 42 strikebreakers from New York, but died out in 1845.[3] Another New Orleans Typographical Society was organized in 1852, at the time of the first convention of the National Typographical Union (NTU), and was chartered in 1853 as Local 17. The NTU changed its name to the International Typographical Union (ITU) in 1869 and is the oldest national labor union in the United States. ITU Local 17 is still in existence, and New Orleans printers have played an important role in the history of the international organization. Gerald Stith of New Orleans was president of the National Typographical Union from 1853 to 1854, and Lewis Graham and William J. Hammond of that city were presidents during 1854-1855 and 1870-1873 respectively.[4] The New Orleans organization was disrupted by the Civil War but emerged in 1868 as one of NTU's strongest unions.

41

The NTU also had solid affiliates at Nashville and Louisville at an early date. Local 10 in Louisville has been active since 1852. Typographical societies were also functioning in Richmond, Charleston, and Louisville in 1834, and Mobile and Natchez the following year. Probably the first union organized in Texas was the Texas Typographical Society formed at Houston in 1838.[5] Printers' unions were in operation in Vicksburg, Frankfort and Tallahassee in 1839 and Jackson, Mississippi in 1840, and one was formed at Savannah in 1850.

Almost all the strikes before the Civil War involved either wages or apprenticeship standards. The New Orleans society amended its constitution in September 1839 to prohibit any member from working "on any English daily morning paper, on which any apprentices may be employed."[6]

Impact of the Civil War. The Civil War disrupted relations between most of the southern locals and the NTU, although delegates from Louisville and Memphis remained active and served on the executive committee in 1864 and were joined by delegates from New Orleans and Nashville the following year. Although they did not participate in the NTU's affairs, locals existed in New Orleans, Mobile, Atlanta, and Raleigh during the war.

The Civil War apparently did not cause bitterness within the union. The NTU's president announced in 1866 that those southern unions which had absolved themselves from "allegiance to our constitution and seceded from our national organization," were welcome back with no conditions. A resolution was adopted remitting the per capita due from any of these organizations between 1861 and 1865 if they so requested. At the time of the 1866 convention there were 4013 members of the NTU in some 90 local unions, including 17 from the south; 15 of the 56 members of the executive committee in 1866 were from the south.

The first typographical unions were concentrated in the older colonial cities, and were followed by other towns usually situated along the heads of navigable rivers which flowed from the Appalachian region to the Atlantic or Gulf. Later, with the growth of the railroads and industry, unions were formed in the newer towns which served inland areas.

The race problem. Because there were relatively few Negroes in the industry, the typographers had little difficulty with racial problems. The first time the question came up was at the 1869 convention when the Washington local proposed that all qualified workers be admitted to the union, but refused to accept L. H. Douglas, a Negro. The local later accepted him, however, and a committee at the following convention expressed its "severe regret that negro question was ever introduced." Although the 1870 convention was willing to leave the question of admitting Negroes to the locals, this did not solve the problem of Negro members in good standing transferring from one local to another. This was brought up at the 1879 convention, and it was decided that no subordinate union could refuse to accept a properly accredited traveling card.

Growth after the Civil War. Some southern typographical unions were among the strongest in the nation after the Civil War. The power of the Memphis local apparently was due to militant tactics. In 1868, for example, there were unsuccessful strikes in Nashville, Galveston, Selma (Alabama), and various nonsouthern locations (although one in Memphis did succeed). The NTU's president used this as an argument for a national strike fund.

The ITU's membership, like membership generally, fluctuated with business conditions during this time. Immediately after the war most of the prewar unions were revived, but expansion was limited by depressed conditions until around 1870. Membership declined again after 1873 because of the recession which began that year. There were unsuccessful strikes in New Orleans, Montgomery and Little Rock in 1874. Membership declined from over 10,000 in 1875 to 8688 in 1876 and reached a low point of 4260 in 1878. Business conditions in the south were also aggravated by the yellow fever epidemic of the late 1870's.

In spite of setbacks, the ITU survived in practically every southern state and grew when economic conditions started improving in 1881. In 1882, when the ITU began appointing state delegates where it had locals, every southern state was represented except Georgia and Florida (and delegates were appointed from there the following year).

The ITU orginally contained all printing trades within its ranks, but as technological developments and the growth of large newspaper establishments differentiated the trade into more distinct groups, the pressmen in 1899, followed by the stereotypers and electrotypers and the photoengravers, seceded and formed their own international unions.

The earliest reference to a printing union in Alabama was the Mobile Typographical Society formed in 1836; Mobile ITU Local 127 was organized in 1853, and the International Pressmen and Assistants organized a Mobile local in 1899. The Montgomery Typographical Society was formed in 1858. Birmingham ITU Local 104 was organized in 1886, and the Printing Pressmen-Stereotypers No. 6 was formed in that city by 1896.

The printing trades, especially the typographers, were successful in surviving the postwar recession and the antiunion movement of the twenties. Union strength was concentrated in the newspapers. Mercer G. Evans, who made a careful study of Georgia unions, estimated that the industry in Georgia "was 37 per cent organized in 1920, and 31 per cent organized in 1925; and there has been very little change, probably, since the latter date."[7]

In Georgia, workers on newspapers accounted for 64 per cent of the total membership of printing trades unions in 1919, and 50 per cent in 1925. By 1928 all the newspapers in the major cities were fully organized.

Employers have sometimes wanted to deal with unions in order to "stabilize" their industries. Such was the case with a citywide agreement in the Atlanta printing industry in 1901, the first time every shop in the city had been unionized. This agreement was for five years between the Atlanta Employing Printers' Club and locals of pressmen, compositors, stereotypers, electrotypers, bookbinders, and any other willing printing union. The contract provided that only members of the unions would be hired by the Printers' Club, and union members would work only for employers in the club. A nine-hour day was established with time and a half for overtime; employers were given complete freedom in hiring and firing, and small employers were permitted to assign both typesetting and presswork. Men who chose not to join the union were given six months to find other jobs. Disputes were to be settled through arbitration.[8] The agreement apparently was accompanied by one among the employers not to bid against each other.

The agreement broke down in 1903 when the ITU ordered several union workers to return to work for a printing firm which had violated the employers' agreement. The firm had violated the compact by cutting prices but refused to pay a $300 fine levied by the club. The employing printers then called upon the unions to strike the price-cutting firm. However, President Lynch of the ITU ruled that the firm had not violated his contract with the unions, and that the ITU would not help the Employing Printers' Club "assault some other man's legitimate business."[9] This conflict then became involved in the growing national dispute between the ITU and the pressmen. The pressmen's President Higgens sided with the Employing Printers' Club, and when the dispute could not be settled, the employers declared open-shop conditions. The compositors then struck all members of the club except the price-cutter, and the pressmen struck him; he "worked with union compositors and nonunion pressmen, while club firms employed union pressmen, feeders, and bookbinders, and nonunion compositors."[10]

The Atlanta employers' open-shop campaign was temporarily suspended during the First World War but started anew in 1921 after Atlanta participated in a general strike to obtain the forty-four hour week. The Atlanta unions lost their strike which had been called after employers repudiated a national agreement. The employing printers were joined by Atlanta building contractors, the chamber of commerce, and the manufacturers' association in a vigorous and successful open-shop campaign throughout the 1920's. Of the 65 printing firms in Atlanta in 1928, only 12 were organized, and only one of these employed 50 or more workers. Four of Macon's six shops were nonunion, including the largest.[11]

THE BUILDING TRADES

Although they were not organized on a continuous basis as early as the printers, the building trades were among the first to form unions in the south and have been numerically the most important in the region. Indeed, one of the earliest examples of labor activity was a strike for a wage increase by Savannah carpenters in 1746.[12] The oldest building trades organizations in the region were the carpenters, bricklayers, painters and stone workers. A carpenters' organization was formed at Houston in 1839, but there is no information on its activities.[13] Although it ceased to exist after World War II, in 1941 the oldest building trades union probably was Carpenters' Local 7 in Galveston which had not been reorganized since 1860. Like many other Texas "mechanics' societies" of the nineteenth century,[14] this union was established by Germans and many of its records were kept in German.[15]

Carpenters' unions were organized earlier and extensively not only because the carpentry is an old craft, but also because carpenters have always been numerous. Organizations of plumbers, electricians, and elevator constructors appeared much later in the region. The International Brotherhood of Electrical Workers, for example, was not organized until 1891, and the oldest surviving southern locals were established at San Antonio in 1896 and 1899, New Orleans in 1900, Louisville in 1903 and Fort Worth and Birmingham in 1912. The electrical workers became well entrenched in the south by 1928.

Growth. Building trades unions were organized in the principal towns of Alabama very early. At Mobile, carpenters formed locals in

1867, 1885, and 1886; the 1886 local was for Negroes. Painters and decorators organized a Mobile local in 1887, bricklayers and plasterers in 1891, plumbers in 1899, and the International Brotherhood of Electrical Workers and the Journeymen Stonecutters' Association of America in 1900. Two carpenters' locals (one for Negroes) and locals of the bricklayers' and masons', painters', and plumbers' unions were organized in Montgomery in 1900. Many locals of the building trades unions had been organized in Birmingham by 1900. In March 1901, the Mobile City Trades council, organized in August 1889, had fourteen affiliated unions; of these the building trades had carpenters', electrical workers', plumbers' and painters' unions.[16]

Building trades unions also started organizing effectively in Georgia in the 1880's. There were many sporadic strikes from 1879 through the 1880's, and Augusta had a building trades council in 1887, which included carpenters, bricklayers and painters.[17]

The national carpenters' union established its first branch at Savannah in 1884, at Macon in 1887, and at Atlanta in 1889; the painters' union was the only other national organization to establish unions in Georgia between 1889 and 1893, when it conducted an organizing campaign in the south. Painters' locals affiliated with the national union were established in Augusta in 1889, and in Atlanta in 1892. Building trades unions benefited from the building boom (1886-1889), which was particularly pronounced in the west and south.[18] In many cases, however, these locals lasted only a few years. Building trades union membership also grew rapidly during the prosperous period of 1897 and 1904.

In 1928, the locals had most of their membership in the larger towns and cities in Georgia. Indeed, approximately 71 per cent of Georgia building trades unionists were in the five leading cities. In addition union membership declined much less in the larger cities during the 1920's than in the smaller towns.[19]

Building trades unions also began in Louisiana very early. The bricklayers were organized in New Orleans in 1865.[20] These unions were strong in New Orleans by 1892, but a general strike of 24,000 workers that year greatly reduced their power.[21] There was a revival of union membership around 1900, and in 1901 an organizer reported: "Taking it all in all, New Orleans is fast going back to what she was in '92, that is one of the best organized cities in the South."[22] New Orleans carpenters, plumbers, and electrical workers had successful strikes in 1901, and at that time the Negro carpenters were organized.

By the time the Louisiana Federation (LFL) became effectively organized in 1912, many building trades had already become well established. Of 20 locals in the LFL that year, seven were in the building trades and five were in unions affiliated with the railroads. Total membership of all affiliated unions was 1016, of which the building trades had 508 and the railroad unions 245. The peak membership in LFL unions before 1930 was 9468, reached in 1920, of which 4161 were in the building trades.

Florida unions developed a hard core of strength in the late 1920's, despite losses from the wartime high; for example, the Florida State Federation of Labor, formed in 1901, had over 200 delegates at its 1926 convention, with approximately 35,000 members represented.

Although there were independent carpenters' locals in the south at the time, no southern locals were represented at the founding convention of the United Brotherhood of Carpenters and Joiners (UBCJ) in 1881. After the convention, however, a New Orleans local applied for a charter and became the first southern local (Local 16) on January 30, 1882.[23]

Only 15 of the first 100 UBCJ locals remained in continuous operation to 1940; three southern locals—two at Mobile and one at Charleston—were among them. There were 238 southern locals with 19,918 members in 1916, constituting 7.61 per cent of the UBCJ's United States membership. The number of locals more than doubled, and membership almost tripled during the next four years; there were 58,673 southern members in 502 locals in 1920, constituting 16.6 per cent of the membership. It declined more relatively in the south during the early 1920's, so that the south accounted for only 8.8 per cent of the UBCJ's total membership in 1924. However, the subsequent decline was not as great as that for the United States, and the southern proportion increased to 10.5 per cent in 1928, but the region's 1920 proportion of 16.6 per cent was not regained. This seems to have been the pattern in the south during these years—membership expanded and contracted with the national rates.

Membership in the various states followed the regional and national pattern, peaking in 1920 and declining thereafter, except for Kentucky and Florida, where top membership was not reached until 1924; however, these figures were from the UBCJ's quadrennial conventions, so membership in Florida might actually have peaked before 1924. The reason for Kentucky's atypical experience is not known, but the Florida case is probably explained by the boom during the 1920's. Moreover, UBCJ membership declines were especially severe in the textile states of Georgia, North Carolina, South Carolina, Alabama, Tennessee and Virginia between 1920 and 1924, which probably reflects depressed economic conditions in textiles.

Race problems. Building trades unions faced considerable difficulty with racial problems. The older trades like carpentry and bricklaying had numerous Negroes, and they were forced to orgnize them (although the carpenters usually formed segregated locals). The carpenters had 12 Negro locals in the south in 1886 and 25 in 1912.[24]

The bricklayers had Negroes in both segregated and integrated locals. The bricklayers were organized in New Orleans before the Civil War and faced crucial racial difficulties immediately after the war because of the number of slaves who had been trained for this craft. However, an amicable settlement of their differences was achieved immediately after the war.

In 1901 the bricklayers in Nashville, Tennessee, were reported "in first class condition, as they have taken all the colored men working at the trade into their union, and are thereby enabled to control the entire situation." Before 1903, the bricklayers' international permitted the existing local union in an area to decide if another local would be established there, and the bricklayers' locals at Washington, D.C. and Richmond refused to permit the international to issue separate charters to Negroes. However, white bricklayers at Charleston consented to the formation of a colored local because Negroes were "too numerous to be ignored . . . they stood two to one over whites since the colored bricklayers didn't regulate apprenticeships." The bricklayers' 1903 convention at Memphis permitted the international executive board to issue charters to Negroes where white locals refused to consent, provided the colored bricklayers could demand the same wages.

Most building trades locals including the plumbers, electricians, sheet metal workers, elevator constructors, and iron workers, barred Negroes by control of licensing boards; control of apprenticeship training; boycotting employers who used Negroes; refusing to work with Negroes, and striking against the use of Negroes on traditionally unionized projects. Except for the trowel trades, hod carriers, and common laborers, building trades unions usually restricted Negro employment to nonunion house or repair work.

Although the pattern of union discrimination against Negroes is relatively clear, we know less about the extent to which unions influenced Negro employment opportunities in these trades. Racial employment patterns are influenced by community sentiment as well as by union and employer attitudes. Moreover, unions might have inadvertently created job opportunities for Negroes by reserving certain nonunion sectors for them.

Our statistics on Negro employment before 1890 do not reveal much about colored craftsmen before that date. The Census of Manufactures conducted in 1865 cites 120,000 mechanics in the south, 100,000 of whom were Negroes. It would not be evidence of discrimination, however, if Negroes failed to retain this proportion. In the first place, unions were not very important before 1890, and there is no indication that the proportion of Negroes in the various organized crafts declined until 1920, when southern unions reached their peak strength before the 1930's. The statistics on the leading organized crafts in which Negroes were engaged before 1920 indicate that they actually increased in importance during the 1890-1920 period for every major craft except blacksmiths: carpenters from 3.6 per cent to 3.8 per cent; masons from 6.0 per cent to 8.0 per cent; painters, 2.0 per cent to 2.9 per cent; plasterers from 10.0 per cent to 15.2 per cent; plumbers from 1.1 per cent to 1.7 per cent; blacksmiths, 5.0 per cent to 4.3 per cent; machinists, 0.4 per cent to 1.1 per cent; and printers, 0.5 percent to 1.1 per cent.

What undoubtedly happened in the south after the Civil War was a change in the jobs performed by Negroes. Building trades unions, for example, were able to control the better commercial jobs, and Negroes were relegated to house work and work in Negro sections. They suffered a marked disadvantage because employers preferred white workers. They were thus able to get work only if they were willing to accept lower wages, or if they were numerous enough to supply the employer with labor if white workers boycotted him.

Thus, while Negroes were forced out of some good jobs, they were not forced out of their crafts, and the feeling against Negroes probably would have been enforced by southern communities, whether or not unions existed. There is no evidence that Negroes were able to enter nonunion industries with any greater ease; indeed, as we have seen, textiles, the south's leading industry has generally been regarded as "white" work.

In the north, Negroes were able to break into a number of industries by strikebreaking, but, for the most part, northern unions, which were stronger than those in the south, barred them from the crafts. They were thus forced to enter as strikebreakers, to practice their crafts in nonunion areas, or enter other occupations. Resistance to Negroes in the north was so intense that the great Negro leader Frederick Douglass advised colored workers to return to the south where the skilled crafts were still open to them.[25]

CHAPTER IV

Railroad Workers and Longshoremen

RAILROAD UNIONS

Railroad building in the south was interrupted by the Civil War, but was renewed during Reconstruction and greatly accelerated during the 1800's; the region's rail mileage increased by 136 per cent between 1880 and 1890 as compared with about 87 per cent for the United States (expansion being particularly rapid in the southwest[1]). The railroads were the first large-scale capitalist ventures witnessed by many southerners and became even larger because of consolidations and mergers accompanying the boom of the 1880's.[2]

In the south, railway workers have been relatively well organized, and the strongest organizations were formed by the operating unions: the Brotherhood of Locomotive Engineers (BLE), the Order of Railroad Conductors (ORC), the Brotherhood of Locomotive Firemen and Enginemen (BLF), and the Brotherhood of Railroad Trainmen (BRT). The operating unions started organizing in the south almost as soon as they were formed. The BLE, BLF and ORC started during the 1860's and 1870's, and the BRT during the 1880's.[3] Because of their members' mobility, the railroad operating brotherhoods were motivated to organize the south and all other competitive areas in order to eliminate wage competition. During the 1890's the operating unions succeeded in stabilizing wages throughout the territory of a carrier or system. And in the first decade of the twentieth century, they succeeded in negotiating contracts covering broad geographic areas, including the south. The following shopmen's union had more difficulties but were also active at an early date: the blacksmiths, drop forgers, and helpers; the railway carmen of America; the sheet metal workers; the boilermakers; and the electrical workers. A third group includes the Brotherhood of Railway Clerks, the Order of Railway Telegraphers (organized in Augusta, Georgia, in 1863), the Switchmen's Union of North America, the International Brotherhood of Railway Signalmen, and the Brotherhood of Maintenance of Way Employees (organized at Demopolis, Alabama).

Machinists, blacksmiths, and boilermakers. Although it would be interesting to know why the national unions of the machinists, blacksmiths, and boilermakers were formed in Atlanta around 1888, we have insufficient information to permit a definite answer to this question. Among the factors that probably contributed to their formation, however, were the following: Atlanta was the south's most important railroad center at a time when it was experiencing much more rapid growth in railroad mileage than any other area; the preceding ten-year period had been one of great social ferment, labor agitation and strikes; the defeat of the Knights of Labor in the Great Southwest Strike of 1886 suggested the need to form railroad unions along different structural lines; and a desire by railroad workers to disassociate themselves both from the "radical" image which the Knights had acquired as a result of their racial policies and their (unwarranted) association with the Haymarket riots, and from the damage done the reputations of machinists in general by the undesirables in their ranks. In addition, there were specific grievances, the most important being the steady decline of shopmen's wages. According to Tom Talbot, first leader of the United Machinists and Mechanical Engineers of America (as the IAM was originally called), machinists' wages had declined from $3.50 to $4.00 a day when he started his apprenticeship[4] to $1.80 to $2.50 a day in 1888. In order to build an image of quality, the machinists, like most other railroad shop organizations excluded Negroes. Their initial objectives included the promotion of "harmonious relations by settling grievances through arbitration instead of strikes, between employees and employers," the provision of sickness, accident and, later, life insurance, the publication of a journal, and facilities to find jobs for unemployed members.[5]

Within a few months they had established lodges in Georgia,

Alabama, and North and South Carolina; the new organization established 104 locals in the United States during the first year—at least
one in every southern state by that time.[6]

In spite of its southern origin, the Machinists Union soon had more
members in other areas. In 1890, only 41 of the machinists' 101 lodges
were in the south, and 40 were in the midwest; the following year there
were 189 lodges, 54 in the south, and 76 in the midwest. This expansion produced an internal conflict over union policies, particularly
racial exclusion. In 1895, as a price of admission to the AFL, the IAM
transferred the racial exclusion provision to the ritual where it stayed
until 1948.[7]

The Boilermakers' Union apparently originated at Atlanta in 1888
in response to the same forces which produced the machinists. Boilermakers' Local 1 was in Atlanta in 1901, though it apparently went out
of existence shortly after the 1901 convention.[8] (The pattern of growth
of the blacksmiths was similar to that of the boilermakers.) The International Brotherhood of Boilermakers and Iron Shipbuilders, which
absorbed the Boilermakers' Union in 1951, also was active.

The early strength of the railroad unions came from a number of
factors. For one thing, the size of the railroad work forces made
organization relatively easy and produced sufficiently complex organizational structures within the companies to require workers to
organize as a means of presenting their grievances. Also, workers in
the industry were mobile. Since many of the earliest organizations
were fraternal societies, they apparently were not too difficult in dealings with their employers. The oldest brotherhood was the BLE
organized in 1863. One of the reasons for the acceptance of this
organization was indicated by the attitude of its president, Charles
Wilson, who made an organizing trip into the south in 1869. When
advised that New Orleans employers opposed unions, Wilson advised
the engineers not to organize until "the prejudice has been removed."[9]
As we shall see, the Illinois Central, one of the south's main railroads,
accepted the principle of collective bargaining before the 1911 strike.

But when they were forced to strike, the railroad brotherhoods
were strengthened by their strategic positions. In addition, the importance of railroad transportation caused the federal government to
pass special legislation for railroad workers. Another important factor
was that many southern roads were in receivership during the 1890's,
and some courts settled strikes in the workers' favor.

As a result, unions were comparatively strong on the south's railroads by 1900. In Georgia, for example, the conductors and engineers
gained almost complete collective bargaining rights on all important

roads during the early nineties; telegraphers, firemen and trainmen gained strength during the late nineties, but did not gain recognition of many of the major roads until the First World War.[10]

The 1911 Illinois Central strike. The organizing problems of the nonoperating railway unions are demonstrated by their experience with the Illinois Central, the main railroad extending from Illinois through Kentucky, Tennessee, Mississippi, Arkansas, and Louisiana to the Gulf of Mexico. In 1910, the machinists, steamfitters, sheet metal workers, railway carmen, blacksmiths, bricklayes, and painters all had contracts with the railroad.[11] The main grievances were wage inequities between the operating and nonoperating unions, piece rates, and hours of work. Although journeymen rates in the south were as high or higher than those in Chicago, the rates for clerks were $10 to $30 a week lower in the south; helpers' rates generally were about five cents an hour lower. The Federal Labor Union (FLU) representing helpers and the Brotherhood of Railway Clerks (BRSC) were unable to gain recognition from the Illinois Central (IC), and were especially dissatisfied with the differential between the IC's rates in its southern and northern shops. The company's stated reason for refusing to bargain with the BRSC was that the clerks occupied a position of confidence and therefore should not be a part of the labor movement.

In order to present a united front, all the shop crafts, the BRSC, and the FLU met at Memphis May 1, 1911 and formed a system federation coalition to bargain for all the unions on the IC system. However, the IC refused to recognize the system federation because of the BRSC and because it opposed dealing with one organization encompassing all these crafts, although it said it had no objection to bargaining with the unions individually. The company believed that the problems of each craft could best be handled separately and that disputes with one would lead to walkouts by the others. In addition, it argued that the system federation combined railroad employees' unions with others from other industries, and would therefore cause disputes outside the industry to extend to the railroads. The company also pointed out that the shop craft unions would violate their contracts if they struck to support the system federation without giving the required notice.

As a result of management's refusal to bargain, a strike began on September 25, 1911, which spread to include about 9000 workers and affected all Harriman lines. The strike was almost 100 per cent effective throughout the IC system. On September 30, mechanics in other locations struck—some 8587 in all.

IC management complained of violence. A particularly important problem for the railroad, according to management testimony before the Commission on Industrial Relations, was the concealment or destruction of records by the clerks, making it difficult for the trains to move to the right places. The IC secured federal court injunctions against the clerks, and against the destruction of property and interference with strikebreakers (many of whom were Negroes) by other strikers. Although management had no trouble finding strikebreakers, it had difficulty protecting them, especially in McComb, and Water Valley, Mississippi, where the railroad shops constituted the main source of employment and almost every worker was unionized. The company recruited the almost 9000 men it needed mainly through detective agencies. Because of high turnover and the incompetence of strikebreakers, however, management representatives said they had to hire 15,000 workers to get necessary replacements. These strikebreakers commonly were placed behind stockades, and commissaries were provided for them.

The most serious clash occurred at McComb, Mississippi, where two Negro strikebreakers were killed and three were wounded. Six strikers were arrested but were not convicted. In addition, a train loaded with strikebreakers was attacked by about 250 men at McComb on October 11. These disturbances caused local officials to ask the governor to send in troops, and "modified martial law" was imposed in McComb. Troops also were sent to Water Valley after the shops there were attacked in October.

The IC strikers were completely defeated by the middle of March 1912, although the strike continued until June 1915. The reason was not lack of unity among the strikers, but the ease with which the company recruited strikebreakers and its willingness to spend the "several million" dollars required to break the unions. When the strike was over the company took back about 2000 of the shopmen and announced that it would rehire the others when places were available. The strike had a profound impact because it caused unionism to be equated with violence and the loss of jobs. In McComb, for instance, it was reported that of 800 strikers only 10 were still living there by 1915. A McComb labor leader said that practically every workingman in town had belonged to the union before the strike because "it was the thing to do," and because workers felt a need for the protection afforded by the unions.

Union strength in the 1920's. As a result of the favorable attitude of the federal government, which operated the railroads during World

War I, and continued to regulate them when the war was over, most of the south's railroad workers were organized by 1920.

For the United States in 1920, unions had organized 39.6 per cent of the transportation industry and 19.4 per cent of all nonagricultural workers.[12]

However, some railroads continued their defiance of unions. One of the most obstinate was the Atlanta, Birmingham and Atlantic, which, in 1921:

> . . . threatened to lower wages in the face of orders from the Railroad Labor Board to the contrary. Legal complications developed to the great embarrassment of the unions, and a federal court and federal district attorney gave moral support to the management, with the result that the railroad locked out all of the union employees. Despite a terrific fight, the railroad maintained its position, and it is now [1928] the only Class I railroad in the United States which is entirely anti-union, refusing to employ or to retain in employment any member of any union.[13]

In 1925 and 1926 the telegraphers struck the Atlantic Coast Line for an improved contract, and were defeated and locked out. This railroad and the Atlanta, Birmingham and Atlantic were the only first-class lines in the United States with which the telegraphers did not have a contract.

The nonoperating unions generally had much more difficulty. During the government's operation of the railroads during World War I, recognition was extended to nearly all roads in the south, but, following the war, private employers were able to destroy nearly all the unions' gains. The strike on the Atlanta, Birmingham and Atlantic in 1921 caused the disintegration of the unions on that road. A defeat of the shopmen in a 1922 national strike over wage reductions ordered by the Railway Labor Board routed many of the unions in the region. The shop strike of 1922 coincided with a revival of the Ku Klux Klan and other antiunion organizations.[14] Perhaps the most violent opposition occurred in Arkansas. During the 1922 strike against the Missouri and North Arkansas Railroad, a "citizens' committee" of 12 men led an organization of some 1000 members. In a number of communities the committee forced the resignation of civil authorities, and in others dictated the policies to be followed by local officials. One union man was lynched when he refused to permit a mob to enter his home.[15]

The citizens' committee put out a circular entitled "Come to the Rescue—our Country is in Danger" which alleged that the M & NA strikers were burning bridges and threatening to halt railroad service into the area. The committee called meetings in Harrison, Arkansas at which it was declared that any striker who would "pledge himself to 100% support of our city, and to an absoulte abandonment of all active participation in or support of the strike . . . is welcome here"; those who would not give such a pledge were "not desired as a resi- dent . . . and this shall apply without further investigation to any and all of such strikers or union members whose residence in any town along the line of the railway has been determined to be undesirable by the local committee of such town or by the committee of 12 of Harrison."[16]

Those unionists "who would not forsake allegience to the union were ordered deported. Deportees were given clearance cards which would enable them to pass the guards on the way out. Many whole families were thus compelled to leave their homes. In numerous cases summary punishment was meted out by mob authorities in the form of whippings . . . The situation is one of the most important and serious of its kind with which the country has been faced."[17]

The committee of twelve adopted a statement which left no doubt about their attitude toward the strike: "First . . . we endorse the efforts of . . . the management of the Missouri and North Arkansas Railroad and the service they have given us in the face of the opposi- tion of the so-called strikers, and we pledge . . . that we will give [the M & NA management] every effort in our power to bring to justice the criminals who have been destroying the property of said railroad, and to assist the management in resuming service on the railroad and keeping it in operation."[18]

The national shopman's strike was called after 75 days. Because of a sweeping injunction against the shop crafts and vigorous opposition by the carriers, the strike is generally conceded to have been lost by the unions. Although the shop crafts maintained some strength on northern railroads, in the south apparently only the southern and sea- board railroads recognized nonoperating unions after the 1922 strikes, and during the open-shop period of the 1920's the railroad formed "company unions" and adopted other tactics to keep unions out. As to the estimated percentages of the nonoperating unions organized in Georgia during this period, in 1920: "The whole group . . . appears to have been about 38% organized. Assuming no change in the total number of workers, the group would have been 18% organized in 1928."[19] Evans estimated that Georgia maintenance-of-waymen were about 11 per cent organized in 1928. Table 2 gives the estimated membership of all railroad unions in Georgia during this period. These figures reveal that the more highly skilled declined only slightly from the 1920 peak to 1928, whereas membership in other railroad unions declined greatly in the same period. Table 3 shows a similar pattern for some nonoperating unions in Louisiana.

The Race Problem. Many Negroes were employed on southern railroads either because the jobs were classified as "Negro work" by the

Table 2.   Membership of railway operating unions in Georgia, 1890–1928.

Unions	1928	1925	1920	1910	1900	1890
Operating Unions						
Conductors	1130	1130	1265	985	410	370
Sleeping car conductors	65	65	65	—	—	—
Engineers	1500	1570	1635	1350	530	570
Firemen	770	830	925	400	275	320
Trainmen	2275	2190	2325	1135	315	50
Porters, etc.	565	510	225	—	—	—
Total operating	6305	6295	6440	3870	1530	1310
Total railroad maintenance	3400	2450	5750	1000	—	—
Total metal trades	1300	1250	3330	2050	550	200

Source: M. G. Evans, "History of the Organized Labor Movement in Georgia," unpub. diss., University of Chicago, August 1929, pp. 36, 122.

Table 3.   Membership in railroad unions affiliated with the Louisiana Federation of Labor, 1912, 1920, 1928

Unions	1912		1920		1928	
	Locals	Members	Locals	Members	Locals	Members
Blacksmith	0	0	2	178	0	0
Boilermakers	0	0	2	200	0	0
Maintenance-of-way employees	0	0	1	214	0	0
Railway carmen	3	176	8	444	1	47
Railway clerks	0	0	2	322	0	0
Machinists	2	69	5	187	3	66
Totals	5	245	20	1,645	4	113

Source: Louisiana Federation of Labor *Convention Proceedings,* various years.

southern community or because Negroes acted as strikebreakers or were forced to accept lower wages. Negroes apparently had even greater difficulty breaking into railroad jobs outside the south and were restricted primarily to menial jobs even in that region; of 136,065 Negro railroad workers in the United States in 1924, 115,937 were in the laborer and porter categories, and 86,262 were in the south.

The extent to which racial conflict weakened unions was determined largely by the strength of the union and the ease with which Negroes could replace its members. The conductors and engineers were strong enough at the time of the Emancipation Proclamation to prevent the use of Negroes on southern railroads.

Trouble came when the jobs Negroes held became desirable and when unions extended their jurisdictions to include the jobs held by Negroes, especially after the government began to encourage railroad unions. The firemen and trainmen had special problems because of the number of Negroes in their jurisdictions. When locomotive firemen's work was hot and dirty it was generally considered "Negro" work, but when the automatic stoker and Diesel engine were invented it became more attractive to whites. Moreover, with collective bargaining, it became customary for workers to be promoted to engineers' and conductors' jobs on the basis of seniority. But is was unthinkable that Negroes would hold these status positions.

These developments created a real dilemma for the railroad unions. Most of them, including Eugene Debs' American Railway Union, restricted membership to whites. If Negroes had acquired conductors' jobs, they might have had positions of authority over whites which would have been considered improper in the south.

But the problem for the unions was that they were weakened by their unwillingness to admit Negroes. For one thing, employers were able to defeat strikes by hiring the Negroes who were excluded from the unions, and white firemen and trainmen were forced to accept lower wages and inferior contract terms in so-called "Negro territory."[20] In 1909, for example, the Georgia Railroad replaced several white BLF members being paid $1.75 a day with Negroes paid $1.25 a day.[21] The unions' failure to admit Negroes also made it difficult for them to use seniority as a means of promotion or to impose union security provisions. White firemen, for example, found that the increasing number of Negroes who could not become engineers limited the whites' opportunities to serve the necesary time as firemen in order to be promoted to engineering jobs.

White railroad employees realized that their greatest weakness in the south was competition from Negroes,[22] and sought desparately to overcome this difficulty. At first the unions struck in an effort to prevent the use of Negroes.[23] As a general rule, the strikes failed because Negroes and employers had the support of government officials. In some cases, however, local law enforcement officials did not interfere with the strikers for fear of being branded as integrationists. In a

Georgia railroad strike of 1909, for example, Governor Smith, who had previously been attacked as a "nigger lover," refused to intervene with strikers who were seeking the removal of Negro firemen. During the strike the company sought to turn the public against the strikers by pointing out that BLF President Ball was a Canadian, but "This appeal was quickly met and outdone by Ball, who issued a statement admitting that he was a Canadian, but added that he was a white man and stood 'for a white man's country.' He charged Manager Scott as being the only one who doubted that a white man was better than a negro. 'I stand for white superiority,' said Ball, 'and Mr. Scott stands for negro superiority; let the south judge between us.' "[24] The Georgia railroad strike was settled by an agreement that: the ten white firemen who had been replaced would be rehired, the Negro workers would be retained, and the dispute would be submitted to arbitration. The board of arbitration decided that the road could hire Negroes if it would give them the same wages as white workers.

In addition to strikes, white railroad workers sought to remove Negroes from the railroads by contract provisions limiting their employment. After a 1911 strike against granting equal seniority to Negro firemen on the New Orleans and Texas Pacific Railroad, which resulted in the killing of ten Negro firemen, the company agreed that Negroes would be limited to a certain geographic area, and that their proportion would remain as it had been on January 1, 1911. The firemen on the Southern Railroad of Georgia immediately demanded and received a similar contract provision.[25] The most important of these agreements, however, was the so-called Southeastern Carriers' Agreement of 1941 which limited Negro employment to 50 per cent of the firemen's jobs on any railroad or class of service and which caused the federal courts to intervene and prohibit the white unions' attempt to displace Negro workers.[26]

In an effort to protect their jobs, Negro railroad workers also formed their own unions. The first organization, the Colored Locomotive Firemen's Association, was formed in Georgia in the early 1900's. In 1913 another was formed "to guard against attacks upon colored railway employees."[27] The Railwaymen's International Benevolent and Industrial Association, a colored workers' organization formed in 1915, had about 15,000 workers at its peak in 1920. The other important Negro railroad workers organizations included: the Association of Train Porters, Brakemen and Switchmen; the Brotherhood of Sleeping Car Porters; the Protective Order of Railway Trainmen; the Association of Colored Railway Trainmen; and the Interstate Order of Colored Locomotive Firemen, Engine Helpers, Yard and Train Service Employees and Railway Mechanics. All these organizations probably had less than 10,000 members in 1931.[28]

LONGSHOREMEN

Before the 1920's, some southern longshoremen, the screwmen, who stowed cotton and tobacco aboard ship with jackscrews, formed strong unions.[29] They occupied an important position in the economy because much of the south's foreign and coastal shipping consisted of the two staple crops, cotton and tobacco, which had to be carefully packed aboard ship if their export were to be profitable. The space required to ship cotton was considerably reduced around World War I by the invention of the power compress which pressed bales of cotton to less than half their former size—a function formerly performed by the screwmen.

New Orleans and the race problem. Their strategic position in the shipping industry made it possible to form relatively strong labor organizations very early in ports like Charleston, Savannah, New Orleans, Mobile, and Galveston. In New Orleans, for example, the screwmen, many of whom were Irish immigrants, had informal organizations before 1850. At that time they formed the Screwmen's Benevolent Association (NOSBA).[30] The NOSBA originally was created as a mutual benefit society to provide sickness and death benefits, but soon turned to collective bargaining and strikes as a means of improving wages and working conditions. An indication of its strength is the fact that it successfully struck for higher wages in 1851, 1854, 1858, and 1866.[31] Wages were $2.50 a day in 1850 but increased to $3.00 in 1854, $4.00 in 1858, and $6.00 in 1866.[32] In 1866 the NOSBA demanded $5.00 a day but raised its demand to $6.00 after it was forced to strike; the employers granted the $6.00 two hours after the strike started. These collective bargaining successes were accompanied by equally significant membership increases. Membership, which was 121 in 1850, had tripled by 1853.[33] By 1860 the NOSBA had 600 members and had organized virtually every screwman on the New Orleans docks. But membership was reduce to 100 in 1861 by enlistments in the army.

Following the Civil War the New Orleans longshoremen were confronted with a serious racial problem because of the use of slaves on the docks during the war and the great increase in the number of Negro workers, especially in longshoremen's jobs, after the war. If matters had been left to the workers, Negro and white longshoremen might have cooperated peacefully during Reconstruction, but community sentiment opposed unity between Negro and white workers, and politicians incited racial conflict among New Orleans longshoremen throughout the period before World War II. An 1865 longshoremen's strike by both races in New Orleans was broken when police arrested Negro longshoremen who had attempted to halt Negro strikebreakers. After this 1865 strike, the skilled screwmen were strong enough to maintain their organization, but the general longshoremen's unions seem to have been relatively weak. There were not many Negro screwmen immediately after the war, but their numbers increased as some colored longshoremen learned the "mysteries" of the trade and taught it to others.

Following the 1865 strike the white workers were supported by politicians who wanted their help in reestablishing white control. The Negroes were supported by the carpetbag administration of Governor Henry Clay Warmoth and Negro Lieutenant Governor P. B. S. Pinchback. It was during this administration, in 1872, that the Labor's Protective Benevolent Mutual Aid Association was incorporated as an organization of Negro longshoremen.[34] This organization was described in 1931 as being "still alive and kicking and... the oldest Negro labor organization in the country."[35]

Racial tension among New Orleans longshoremen was aggravated by competition for jobs during the recession of 1873, when a bloody race riot erupted on the New Orleans docks and levees. Although white workers, with the aid of the politicians, gradually took over an increasing number of longshoring jobs, they were able to do so only by agreeing to accept the same low wages paid to Negroes. And the Negroes who were barred from these jobs stood ready to undercut wage rates.

As a result of this competition, even the white screwmen felt that their positions were in jeopardy and in order to protect their conditions organized the Screwmen's Benevolent Association Number 2 for Negroes in 1875.[36] These organizations and their employers worked out an agreement whereby wages were equalized, and Negroes agreed to supply no more than 100 men to work at any one time. Cooperation between the screwmen's associations did not solve the racial problem on the New Orleans docks, but it was a force for racial stability. Moreover, the screwmen aided the organization of other white and Negro workers, particularly the teamsters and workers engaged in the transport and processing of cotton.[37] Although Negro screwmen were not entirely satisfied with the racial quota system worked out with the whites and the employers in 1875, this arrangement prevailed until 1902, in spite of waves of race riots during the 1880's and 1890's.

Racial unity was sufficient to make it possible for Negro and white screwmen to participate in the leadership of the 1892 New Orleans general strike, which was one of the most important events in early southern labor history.

The stage for the 1892 strike was set by a rapid increase in membership brought about by the AFL's southern organizing campaign, which found rapid response in New Orleans, where 30 new locals were charted between 1891 and 1892.[38] The 1892 strike, which has been described as "The first general strike in American history to enlist both skilled and unskilled labor, black and white, and to paralyze the life of a great city,"[39] also was foreshadowed in the spring of 1892 by a successful strike by 728 street car drivers to reduce hours from 16 to 12 with no loss in pay and to obtain the "preferential union shop."[40] After the streetcar strike, 49 AFL unions representing 20,000 members formed a Workingmen's Amalgamated Council, consisting of two delegates from each of the affiliated unions. Three of the newly organized unions—the teamsters, packers, and scalesmen—formed a so-called Triple Alliance to pursue common objectives; a large number of the members in the Triple Alliance were Negro laborers.

The general strike was precipitated October 24, 1892, by between two and three thousand workers represented by the Triple Alliance; the unions demanded a ten-hour day, overtime pay and the preferential closed shop from the board of trade, representing the employers. The Triple Alliance relied on aid from the Workingmen's Amalgamated Council, which appointed a committee of five, including one Negro, to conduct the strike. The board of trade at first refused to meet with union representatives and, when it did meet, refused to restore all strikers to their jobs. As a result, 24,100 workers answered a general strike call on November 8.

The walkout was called off after three days when the governor issued a proclamation ordering citizens not to congregate in crowds and implying that the militia would be called if the strike continued.[41] A prominent citizen effected a final settlement which amounted to defeat for the strikers. It gave the workers a ten-hour day, overtime pay and an adjusted wage scale, but not the closed shop.

> Workers were to be restored to all jobs which remained open. Employers asserted their customary right to deal directly with individuals, and to hire and fire as they pleased. It was, in short, an open shop victory for the Board of Trade, and the report of the Labor Committee to the union could scarcely gloss the fact. The merchants organized on a stronger and permanent basis; the Working Men's Amalgamated Council

carried on; and never again . . . would business fear a general strike . . .
The principal mission of the Labor Committee was henceforth to try in
vain to find work for many black-listed strikers.[42]

The New Orleans general strike weakened unions in that city
for many years. The U.S. Commissioner of Labor reports no strikes for
Louisiana in 1893 and 1894, and two years later there were many
fewer unions in New Orleans than when the 1892 strike started, although a survey found that there were still 54 local unions and one
district Assembly of the Knights of Labor in 1894.[43]

Following the 1892 strike, the racial quota system worked out by
the New Orleans screwmen began to weaken under the pressure of
increasing numbers of Negroes whose competence caused employers
to hire more than the prescribed 100. In 1894, when white screwmen
decided to strike to enforce the quota system, there were about as
many Negroes as whites. When the white screwmen struck they were
joined by white longshoremen, and racial trouble erupted when the
whites resorted to violence to prevent the employment of Negroes.[44]
Employers responded to the walk-out by having each experienced
Negro screwmen instruct four "green hands." During the initial stages
of the strike the police, some of whom were members of the white
NOSBA, refused to protect the colored workers. And when criticism
of the police and pressure from employers forced the law officers to
protect the Negroes, the white workers attacked the employers. The
employers therefore obtained a federal injunction to stop the strike,
and the white screwmen returned to work on the basis of the 1875 job
quota system, which the Negroes agreed to accept.[45]

By 1901 the racial cleavage between New Orleans longshoremen
was sufficiently healed to permit the formation of the New Orleans
Dock and Cotton Council, which included unions of screwmen, general longshoremen, teamsters, yard men, cotton classers, scalehands,
and cotton weighers. The screwmen dominated the council, and an
arrangement was agreed to whereby the president was from the white
NOSBA and the secretary was from the colored longshoremen's
union. Also in 1901, when there were about 2000 longshoremen in
New Orleans, the New Orleans unions affiliated with the newly organized International Longshoremen's Association and won an important strike for higher pay, which, according to an AFL organizer,
"strengthened the interest of organized labor and restored a friendly
feeling between the white and colored members of this city. They
have gone into local combinations and are dividing the work

equally."[46] In 1902 the Negro and white screwmen agreed to change the quota system to permit an equal sharing of the work between the races.[47]

Following this agreement, however, the New Orleans longshoremen were forced to contend with another problem: technological changes, which greatly increased the amount of cotton each worker could load. For many years the screwmen successfully resisted these developments and enforced rules which limited the number of bales loaded aboard ship to 160 a day, even though the system, called the "shoot-the-chute," made it possible to load at least twice that amount.

During the 1907 negotiations, employers demanded that the screwmen load 200 bales a day, and the Negroes demanded that the racial quota system be extended to foremen's jobs. The whites rejected both proposals, and the Negroes dropped their demand when whites adamantly refused to work under colored foremen.[48] In an effort to force an agreement on the number of bales to be loaded, the screwmen struck and were joined by the longshoremen. However, after eleven days the longshoremen went back to work under a three-year contract. During the twenty-first day of the strike, when the employers put sailors to work, the teamsters and longshoremen walked out to support the screwmen, and other union members refused to handle cotton off-loaded by the sailors. After one month, when it was learned that strikebreakers were being imported, the Dock and Cotton Council called a general strike of 10,000 men. However, the council called the strike off when the parties, under pressure from the mayor, agreed to arbitrate. But the strike almost broke out again because employer representatives refused to meet with the Negroes who, along with whites, were delegated from the screwmen's organizations. When the Dock and Cotton Council backed the Negroes, the employers appointed new delegates who were willing to meet with colored men, and an agreement was reached.

In spite of this agreement, however, technological changes continued to undermine the power of the screwmen, who had been the key to unionization of southern longshoremen. As Miller observed:

> In the old days when ships carried around 7,000 bales of cotton it had been profitable to spend a few extra days in port to allow the screwmen to tightly compress the cotton aboard. Now the ships were much larger and with ships carrying as many as 20,000 bales, it was no longer profitable to spend the time in port that would be required to screw in this many bales. Finally, just prior to the war, the high density cotton press was perfected. Now, with only unskilled labor, the cotton could be compressed and stowed aboard the ships.[49]

As we shall see after examining the early activities of longshoremen elsewhere in the south, in an effort to preserve their positions, the New Orleans screwmen took action after World War I which led to the destruction of the New Orleans unions.

The first Texas longshoremen's union was formed in 1866 and received a state charter of incorporation as the Galveston Screwman's Benevolent Association (GSBA). The GSBA cooperated with and was inspired by the New Orleans Screwmen's Association after which it modeled its constitution and bylaws.[50] The GSBA's membership was about one-third German, one-third Irish, and one-third native whites It had 60 members shortly after its formation and attempted to be a relatively exclusive organization. In 1875 for instance, it was necessary to increase the number of blackballs—to exclude a prospective member—from seven to fifteen because the organization's leaders thought blackballs were being used too freely to exclude competent screwmen (members voted for applicants with white balls and against them with black balls). Until the First World War, prospective members were required to reside in Galveston for at least six months. The GSBA also adopted rules designed to protect the jobs of its members. Foremen members of the organization agreed to hire not only GSBA members, and all members agreed not to work with screwmen who had been expelled from the organization. Efforts also were made to prevent sailors from performing screwmen's work.

The GSBA was quite successful in preserving its organization, in spite of constant difficulties enforcing its rules because of the large number of nonmembers. It was incorporated by the state of Texas in 1870 and accumulated a sufficient surplus in its treasury after 1872 to invest in a building. By 1875, the organization was strong enough to enforce the closed shop. The GSBA remained independent until 1914 when it affiliated with the International Longshoremen's Association as Local 329, which was still active in 1965.

The Galveston screwmen's success came from its efforts to present moral, competent, and physically qualified workers and by policing their job performance; to provide sickness and funeral benefits; and to conduct social and fraternal services. (The elaborate funeral ceremonies were particularly significant.)

One of the greatest problems confronting the exclusive GSBA was competition from Negroes. In 1869 the organization adopted a resolution not to work for anyone "who shall employ to work on shipboard persons of color." A Negro Longshoremen's Benevolent Association was formed in 1870, but restricted its activities to the docks, while the GSBA worked aboard ship. Until 1918, members of the white screwmen's union could not serve as foremen over Negroes.[51] Relations between the Negroes and whites apparently were peaceful during the 1870's when agreements to share the work were enforced. However, trouble erupted during the 1880's as whites attempted to bar Negroes from longshoring jobs, and Negroes sought to increase their job opportunities.

A particularly significant strike occurred in Galveston in 1883, which involved Norris Wright Cuney, a Negro longshoremen's leader. Cuney had gained favor with the white community in Galveston as a result of his opposition to an 1877 strike by Negro laborers, led by Irish immigrants, against a cut in wages from $2.00 to $1.50 a day. The Galveston strike was inspired by news of the violent 1877 railroad strikes which swept into the south from the north.[52] Although there was much militant talk by the Negroes during the 1877 strike in Galveston, they policed their demonstrations remarkably well as they moved from job to job, asking all workers who made less than $2.00 a day to join them. However, tension mounted after a Negro striker was shot by a policeman. It happened when a mob of Negro strikers sought to take a white man involved in a fight with a Negro away from the policeman, and lynch him. An alarm was sounded, rallying the "citizen soldiery" at Artillery Hall. This show of force convinced Cuney that Negroes had little chance of achieving their objectives through strikes and demonstrations. Although the strike caused a number of employers to agree to pay $2.00, Cuney told a crowd of 250 strikers that their action was unwise because:

> . . . the most respectable number the strikers had ever been able to muster did not equal 300 men, and as there were 1,500 laborers in the city, he asked what that handful of malcontents hoped to accomplish by their turbulent demonstrations, except riots and bloodshed, and the destruction of their own best interests. He . . . told them that there were over 700 armed men—trained soldiers—in the city, who could annihilate them all in an hour; and if they could not . . . in the city of Houston there were 1,000 men under arms, who could be brought to this city in two hours to accomplish that bloody work. He deprecated in the severest terms the follies into which the colored men had fallen, and said they were not supported by the white men, nor by the full strength of their own color . . . and in an eloquent and forcible manner appealed to his countrymen to heed his warning and go peacefully to their homes and stay there.

Cuney was "treated with contempt by the rabid faction in the crowd," but he was hailed by the *Galveston Daily News,* in an editorial, as "one of the most intelligent of his race in the State." The *News* added: "Mr. Cuney knows but too well that the poor, deluded colored men who are now on strike in this city are but the tools of some few designing white men who have aspirations—political and otherwise." Cuney's advice apparently was heeded by the strikers.

In 1883, Cuney hired 500 Negroes to unload ships in Galveston, organized his men into an association of longshoremen, and approached the Mallory Steamship Company for a contract. According to Cuney's daughter:

> Not long after father's attempt, the white longshoremen launched a strike against the Mallory Steamship Company. Captain Sawyer of the Mallory Line called father into consultation with a view of engaging colored labor. Father promised to furnish the workmen, but stipulated that before doing so, he must have a guarantee that his men would not be "catspaws to pull the chestnuts out of the fire." The condition was that the colored men would go to work, but must be retained on good behavior, and that in the future they have an equal showing with white laborers. . . .[53]

The 1883 Galveston strike, involving 1500 longshoremen, was broken when Cuney's men went to work under police protection. The agreement concluding this strike provided for a sharing of work between colored and white workers. After this strike, two colored unions, a screwmen's organization, and the other longshoremen's union were admitted to the Galveston Trades Assembly.[54]

Other Gulf ports and the race problem. The position of colored workers in southern longshoremen's organizations was solidified around the time of the First World War, when labor shortages brought large numbers of Negroes into southern ports. The abundance of colored labor had forced white unions to make agreements with Negro unions; sharing the work had become quite general by the time of the war. In 1914, white longshoremen along the waterfront at Mobile, Alabama, where a Colored Longshoremen's Benevolent Association had been formed in 1894, quit work in order to support a strike by 2000 colored longshoremen for higher wages.[55] In 1917, after the Port of Houston was opened, the Negro local of the ILA consented to the formation of a white local and entered into a 99-year compact with them to divide all work equally.

South Atlantic and the race problem. Longshoremen on the South Atlantic also were among the earliest southern workers to form unions. In 1867, for example, Negro longshoremen at Charleston formed a Longshoreman's Protective Union Association, whose record of vigorously conducted strikes caused the Charleston *Daily News* to describe it as the most powerful organization of colored workers in South Carolina.[56] The Knights of Labor organized longshoremen in this area in the 1890's, and in 1910 the colored longshoremen of Norfolk formed the Transportation Workers' Association of Virginia. This organization joined the ILA during the First World War, when the United States Shipping Board gave the international exclusive jurisdiction in Norfolk.

Virginia coal trimmers, a craft under ILA jurisdiction, organized and struck in 1914. The immediate cause of the strike was the firing of George Millner, a Negro, who later became a vice-president of the ILA. The Coal Trimmers' Union was at first chartered as a federal labor union, but was absorbed by the ILA in 1917.

The ILA organized a Negro local at Hampton, Virginia in 1921 and won a strike for higher wages despite opposition from influential Negro leaders and the importation of strikebreakers.

> As a result of the government's support, the International Longshoremen's Association was able, during the war, to organize the entire Hampton Roads waterfront of between eight and nine thousand men. Fully six thousand of these were Negroes. After the war union strength declined rapidly . . . Today [1931] of about six thousand men employed in the district, 2,200 are organized. Of approximately 4,000 unorganized workers, about 500 are white and 3,500 black. Of the organized workers about 200 are white and about 2,000 colored. The colored worker thus dominates union affairs in the district. Of the nine locals seven are black and two white. There are no mixed locals due, first, to the strength of the southern tradition of racial separation and, second, to the preference of the Negroes themselves for their own organizations.

In 1928, ILA Local 978 in the Hampton Roads district owned about $40,000 worth of property; Local 1221 owned a building bought for $17,000; and Locals 846 and 944 jointly owned a building valued at $10,000.

One reason for the relative success of the South Atlantic longshoremen in suggested by Millner's description of a strike around 1928 in the Hampton Roads area: "The longshoremen of this vicinity . . . deported themselves like men. Membership roll was called each morning and afternoon. Those failing to answer were sent for by detachments. This strike lasted 4 weeks and 3 days. Not a man deserted the ranks. No picketing was done. When the strike was ended each man went back to his former position and the employers were just as glad to have the men back as the men were themselves."

Destruction of the Gulf longshoremen's unions. Although it was strengthened by the federal government's control of the docks during World War I, national unionism among longshoremen on the Gulf

Coast was almost completely destroyed by a series of strikes in the early 1920's. The militia was sent to Galveston to break a 1920 strike; the ILA locals at Galveston surrendered their charters in 1922, and company unions were chartered in 1924. The beginning of the end for unionism on the New Orleans docks came with a strike in 1921, precipitated by the screwmen and joined by over 12,000 men from 24 unions in the Dock and Cotton Council.[57] Though the employers hired strikebreakers from among the large number of men who had been trained during the war, the unions survived the strike, which lasted about a week; however, they had to accept a basic wage scale of 65 cents an hour and $1.00 for overtime, which was lower than the basic rate of 80 cents established by the National Adjustment Commission in 1919. In addition, the screwmen were forced to increase the number of bales of cotton loaded from 200 to 225 a day. Several large companies, including United Fruit and Southern Pacific Lines, broke with the union after this strike and began hiring nonunion labor.[58] The situation was complicated by the IWW which sought to organize longshoremen on the basis of solidarity between white and colored workers. It was unsuccessful, however, because the colored and white workers gave their allegiance to the ILA.

The other complicating factor was agitation by the white screwmen's union for a showdown because it feared the continued use of nonunion men by the companies would jeopardize its position. Though screwmen had been reduced in importance by the high-powered compress, they continued to hold the better jobs, and insisted upon storing all tobacco and cotton in ships. Some of them actually became "doubleheaders," storing cotton and tobacco so long as the work was plentiful, and at other times shifting to work reserved for longshoremen. Realizing that their tasks could be done quite readily by unskilled workers, with the assistance of nonunion men who had been trained earlier, the screwmen pressed for a strike. The longshoremen, realizing the difficulty of winning a strike in the face of abundant strikebreakers, argued against it.

In 1923 the screwmen finally forced a strike vote, after their demands for higher pay and shorter hours had been rejected. The companies had no trouble obtaining strikebreakers, and indeed, apparently welcomed the strike as an opportunity to rid themselves of the troublesome work rules imposed upon them by the unions, particularly the screwmen. ILA locals at Gulfport, Mississippi and Mobile, Alabama also were destroyed when they struck in sympathy with the New Orleans longshoremen.

The ease with which the companies were able to break the strike was not entirely becaue of the supply of unskilled nonunion labor. Other reasons included the split within union ranks between the screwmen and general longshoremen and dissatisfaction by colored longshoremen over the 50-50 work sharing arrangements. After the 1923 strike, the New Orleans Steamship Association ceased dealing with the union and placed hiring of longshoremen in the hands of Alvin E. Harris, a Negro, and "white longshoremen were gradually driven off the docks."[59]

Defeat had disastrous consequences for the New Orleans longshoremen. The membership of the colored union at the time of the strike has been placed at 1956 members; afterwards the number fell to 300 (though it had again risen to 1500 by about 1930). The loss of this strike reduced the Negro union to a position of unimportance.

The Dock and Cotton Council was saved from complete destruction by a "gentlemen's agreement" with the United States Shipping Board, which dealt with the union, but refused to give special consideration to the screwmen. In 1931, however, the last remaining unionized longshoremen in New Orleans were locked out when the U.S. Shipping Board leased its ships to private employers.[60]

CHAPTER V

Coal Miners and Textile Workers

COAL MINERS

The largest and the most bitter of the early labor conflicts in the south involved coal miners. Statistics show that in the 1887-1894 period, about 12 per cent of all coal strikes in the United States were in the south, and approximately one third of all southern strikers during that period were in the coal mines. Most of this activity was in Alabama, Kentucky, and Tennessee, though Virginia became more important in the 1901-1905 period.

Miners were among the first southern noncraft workers to attempt unionization. The Knights of Labor were active in the Texas, Tennessee, Kentucky and Alabama coal fields.[1] The Knights of Labor National Trade Assembly 135 and the National Progressive Union merged in 1890 to form the United Mine Workers. However, some southern miners formed independent unions.

The workers in early southern mining camps were good targets for union organizers because of their many grievances: the use of convict labor; payment in scrip; high prices at company stores; unfair weighing of the coal produced by each worker; low wages and poor working conditions; and autocratic control of company towns by mine guards.

Tennessee. According to reports by the U.S. Commissioner of Labor, a large proportion of the strikes during the 1887-1894 period were spontaneous and not called by formal labor organizations. Of five coal strikes in 1890, for example, only two were called formally, and

71

neither was successful. There were seven strikes in 1891, only three of which were called by unions. Neither of the 1892 strikes was called by labor organizations, but unions had grown in importance in the Tennessee mines by 1893 and 1894; of seven strikes in 1893, for example, three were called by unions, as were three of the four the following year.

The use of convicts was one of the most serious complaints of Tennessee miners. In 1883, the Tennessee Coal, Iron, and Railroad Company's general counsel explained: "For some years after we began the convict labor system, we found that we were right in calculating that free laborers would be loath to enter upon strikes when they saw that the company was amply provided with convict labor."[2]

There were frequent clashes during these early years between militia and Tennessee miners. In 1891, when Anderson County operators rejected a contract calling for an end to scrip pay and a no-strike pledge, management ordered convicts to tear down company houses and to erect stockades to quarter themselves. The armed miners removed the convicts from the mines at Coal Creek and marched them back to jail at Knoxville. On other occasions the strikers freed convicts and burned their stockades; in 1892 they actually laid siege to Fort Anderson. Their dramatic demonstrations caused the Tennessee legislature to abolish the convict lease system in 1893.[3]

Alabama. Judging from the proportion of strikes called by formal labor organizations, Alabama miners were well organized during the early years. As it had been in Tennessee, the convict lease system was a great impediment to unionization. As early as 1882, 200 convicts and other strikebreakers were used at Pratt Mines, and, in 1885, Alabama miners organized an anticonvict league, but the operators continued to use convicts during strikes.

A particularly significant event occurred in April 1894 when the independent United Mine Workers of Alabama struck against a 10 per cent wage cut.[4] The walkout was followed a week later by a national coal strike under the direction of the United Mine Workers. Although the operators could use convicts and strikebreakers, they apparently were unable to resume full operations in the face of the workers' solidarity and threats of violence. The depression in the industry, however, reduced pressure on the employers to settle. In August, after troops were sent in to keep order, an agreement was reached which was a partial victory for the union. It signed a two-year contract with the Tennessee Coal, Iron and Railroad Company, granting the miners reductions in the cost of supplies, rent, and wage payments every two

COAL AND TEXTILE WORKERS

weeks for the following three months. The miners' protest also served to publicize conditions, resulting in legislation for mine inspection, checkweighmen, and safety and health regulations. Perhaps the most important effect was the stimulus it gave to strengthening the miners' organization.

There were many independent local unions, some of them secret, in the Alabama mine fields before the 1893 recession, though the Knights of Labor were apparently dominant there before 1890. When the United Mine Workers were established in 1890, they set up District 20 to cover Alabama and Georgia. However, many of the Alabama miners, especially the Negroes, remained loyal to the Knights of Labor, and a majority supported the United Mine Workers of Alabama, which represented about 5000 workers and was formed during the 1893 recession. The UMW of Alabama was a secret organization with one open branch and, realizing the need for Negro-white unity, proclaimed its intention to protect the job rights of Negroes. The union was strengthened during the 1894 general strike and the subsequent agreement with Tennessee Coal and Iron.

Four years later, after much indecision, Alabama miners decided to cast their lot with the UMW. UMW District 20 signed a contract with Tennessee Coal and Iron in July 1898 which fixed minimum wages and provided for no discrimination against Negroes.[5] Wages improved markedly with economic conditions the following year, and by 1899 42 locals were affiliated with District 20.[6] The proportion of organized Alabama miners increased from about one fourth in 1899, to nearly two thirds in 1902. The Knights of Labor disintegrated rapidly after 1899.

District 20 began to lose ground after reaching its highwater mark around 1902. Many Alabama coal operators began to oppose the union as a result of depressed business conditions in 1904, when some large coal companies provoked a strike by announcing that they would not operate under the 1900 agreement. With the management front broken, other employers decided not to renew their contracts when they expired in 1907. The UMW National Executive Board threw its resources into a strike called for July 6, 1908. Within ten days, 18,000 Negro and white miners were on strike, and almost every mine in the state, except those operated with convicts, was closed. The companies countered in characteristic fashion by importing strikebreakers, evicting workers from company houses, and calling in troops to protect company property. The strike was finally defeated when the governor ordered militiamen to tear down the tent colony, in which evicted

Negro and white families lived, on the grounds that racial mixing could not be permitted in Alabama. The UMW spent $407,500 on relief, but the defeat brought union membership from 18,000 to 700.[7]

The racial composition of Alabama miners changed considerably after the 1908 strikes. Employers blacklisted white miners, and about three fourths[8] of Alabama miners were colored in the years immediately after 1908. Thereafter, employers apparently hired additional whites because Negroes constituted only 54 per cent of Alabama miners in 1920.[9] The companies also launched elaborate welfare programs to keep Negroes out of unions; these programs were in line with the teachings of the Negro leaders who cautioned colored workers to avoid unions, white workers, and the Democratic Party and ally themselves with employers and Republicans. A DeBardeleben Coal Company vice-president told the Alabama Mining Institute in 1922: "The Alabama coal operator has the cooperation and active support of the Negro. The Negro is primarily a free agent and hence a nonunion man ... You appreciate, I am sure, the measure of the Negro's contribution to nonunion Alabama ... We should carry our welfare work for the Negro beyond the confines of any single mining village and apply such principles to all deserving Negroes wherever found, and thus have the Negro understand that he is to have justice and opportunity.[10]

Negro leaders hailed the advent of welfare capitalism as a boon to their race. The *Southern Industrial-Fraternal Review,* a Birmingham weekly circulated among Negro secret societies said: "It is a great thing to realize that at last the Southern Negro miner has awakened ... and ... has decided a long time ago that he was through looking for the 'End of the Rainbow' through the ranks of the United Mine Workers, and that he was going to remain right down here in Dixie." The *Southern Workman,* official publication of Hampton Institute, greatly influenced by Booker T. Washington's philosophy, commented upon welfare capitalism in the Alabama coal fields: "Welfare work of the Tennessee Coal, Iron and Railroad Company ... is an outstanding example of what can be done to improve the living and social status of the Negro industrial worker ... Leadership of their people in this field opens up a new opportunity for Hampton and Tuskegee graduates."

The UMW did not completely disappear from the Alabama coal fields after the 1908 strike, however, and experienced a revival around the time of World War I, when about a fourth of the miners were organized. A 1917 strike succeeded in obtaining wage increases, but the UMW did not achieve recognition because the union agreed, in the interest of the war, not to press its advantage. Another strike occurred in 1919, but the real showdown came the following year when 12,000 of the 27,000 Alabama miners responded to a strike call on September 8.[11] The employers responded characteristically. For seven months during this strike the UMW fed some 48,000 men, women and children. The union finally agreed to arbitrate the dispute in February 1921, with the governor as the sole arbitrator; the governor decided against the union on every point,[12] and the UMW declined to insignificance in the Alabama coal fields until the 1930's.

The UMW's national officers devoted considerable attention to organizing southern districts during these years because the south's increasing share of the nation's coal production threatened union conditions elsewhere. A 1925 study concluded: "With due allowance for . . . other factors . . . it is still true that the nonunion fields have been greatly encouraged by the mere fact that they could keep their labor costs below the costs of the union shippers and that they were free to operate during strikes."[13] Coal production in Kentucky increased by 95.83 per cent in the 1921-1928 period, which was the highest rate in the country; coal production in West Virginia increased by 82.65 per cent, replacing Pennsylvania as the leading coal-producing state.[14]

The southwest. By 1900, the UMW had established five locals in Texas (where the Knights had been defeated in a mine strike in 1889) and had a strong union movement in Oklahoma, then the Indian territory.[15] It organized 1600 workers at Thurber, Texas, in 1889 and conducted a successful strike which greatly increased its prestige. By the winter of 1904, UMW membership in Arkansas, the Indian territory, and Texas was 13,000; at its peak in 1912, membership in southwestern District 21 of the UMW was approximately 16,000. Between 1900 and 1925, however, southwestern railroads changed from coal to oil, reducing membership in Texas and Oklahoma. Texas workers lost a 1926 strike against a 25 per cent wage cut, and the UMW disappeared from that state. Martial law was declared in Oklahoma during 1926 in a strike following the operators' repudiation of the Jacksonville agreement.

West Virginia and Kentucky. Because of the size of its coal fields, the easier access to its seams, its thicker veins, and lower wages, no area posed a more serious threat to the UMW during its early days than West Virginia. The UMW became established in the Northern Central Competitive Field (Pennsylvania, Illinois, Indiana, and Ohio), where it signed an agreement in 1898 following a strike the previous year, but was unsuccesful in its efforts to extend unionism to West Virginia. The UMW consequently launched a new and more vigorous organizing campaign in 1902. It was under the general direction of

Thomas Haggerty, a member of the UMW Executive Board, who dispatched one of his most colorful representatives, "Mother" Mary Jones, together with a contingent of organizers. This resulted in strikes in the Kanawha and New River fields, accompanied by violence, the use of injunctions against the strikers, and the deportation of "Mother" Jones and Thomas Haggerty. Although the union succeeded in signing an agreement with the Kanawha operators, it failed to organize the New River fields.

Another wave of strikes and violence swept West Virginia in 1912, when, at the expiration of their contract, the Kanawha operators refused the UMW's demands for wage increases, the eight-hour day, the check-off, and an end to discrimination against union men. During these strikes, which started at Paint Creek and spread to Cabin Creek and New River, the union set up a tent colony at Holly Grove. Martial law was established in September following a pitched battle at Mucklow between miners and guards. Although the dispute was settled in April 1913 by a compromise proposed by the governor, the strike was defeated, and the union failed again.[16]

Despite these setbacks, the mine workers maintained some membership in West Virginia from 1902 through the First World War. The UMW represented 53,000 of West Virginia's 110,00 in 1917,[17] and, although it still had 46,000 members in West Virginia in 1920, it had only 40 dues-paying members there in 1931.[18] UMW membership in Kentucky declined almost as dramatically from 19,000 in 1912 to 1000 in 1931.

During the early 1920's, the UMW engaged in a long and bitter series of strikes in an effort to organize a tier of counties south of the Kanawha river. During the 1920[19] strike in Mingo, where 40,000 men were employed,[20] Baldwin-Felts guards were brought in. A tragic fight occurred in August 1921 when Albert Felts, wearing a deputy sheriff's badge, became involved in a dispute with the chief of police, Sid Hatfield, at Matewan where the Baldwin-Felts agents had evicted some strikers from their homes.[21] Twelve people, including Albert Felts, were killed in this fight. Hatfield was tried and acquitted for murder, but was later killed by a Baldwin-Felts gunman and two others. Hatfield's killers pleaded self-defense and were acquitted.

Violence continued sporadically from 1920 to 1921. President Warren Harding sent federal troops in 1920 and again in 1921 when the armed miners threatened to invade Logan County and the sheriff and his deputies were just as determined to repel the invasion. Although the strike was not officially settled until October 1922, it was over for all practical purposes when the federal troops came in in 1921.[22]

Employers in the Central Competitive Field claimed that their refusal to sign a contract with the UMW was because they were afraid of being prosecuted for conspiracy in restraint of trade.[23] The check-off provision in the UMW contract was the basis for the conspiracy charge, which resulted in the indictment of 226 operators and all the union officials by a federal grand jury at Indianapolis in April 1922. "The operators are no fools," a spokesman declared, "Already under indictment for a conspiracy in restraint of trade in making the 1920 agreement, they are not going to stick their heads in the same noose again." It was apparent, however, that the operators thought wages were too high:

> Under the present scale a practical miner can earn fully $5,000 a year, though miners know they dare not earn all the scale allows. The coal operator stands at a point where he must see the cause on one side and effect on the other. He has to turn about and fight. He has decided to strike at the real cause and he is going into the wage battle to clean the mines of the shirkers and the pay roll padders . . . let it be a fair fight to the finish and refrain from prodding the government until it steps in.[24]

During the nationwide strike of 1922, UMW officials in Kentucky and Tennessee signed agreements with the operators to continue on the old terms.

In the face of this nonunion competition, organized West Virginia operators agreed to pay ten cents above the nonunion scale, but the UMW refused because it would have meant a wage cut.[25] West Virginia and Kentucky operators also refused to sign the Jacksonville agreement in 1924, causing employers of the Central Competitive Field and elsewhere to decline to sign the contract in 1927. John L. Lewis later described the tragic difficulties encountered by Kentucky workers after they struck in a vain effort to save the union in that district.

The AFL Executive Council was drawn into a study of the economic situation confronting the United Mine Workers when it was rumored that 70 per cent of the stock in one of the companies that refused to sign the Jacksonville agreement, the Coal River Collieries, with properties in Kentucky and West Virginia, was owned by the Brotherhood of Locomotive Engineers, and that an official of the brotherhood was chairman of the board of directors of the company. The UMW struck Coal River on April 1, 1924; the company was accused of discharging and evicting workers from company houses because they joined the union. The AFL Executive Council appointed a joint committee to attempt a settlement; after studying the situation, the committee was unable to reach an agreement, but issued a report June 9, 1925 which set forth both the union and company positions.[26]

The UMW said that it could not accept the company's proposal, which would have caused about a 35 per cent wage cut, because the Jacksonville agreement was the union's national policy and the West Virginia operators already enjoyed a differential over the Central Competitive Field. The UMW also cited figures to show that union miners were more productive than nonunion miners and that the company should not try to make a profit on wages since it was in the development stage.

The company said that it "opposed the closed shop, but naturally leaned toward organization;" however, the UMW's insistence on the Jacksonville agreement would not permit Coal River to operate in competition with nonunion mines and continue to develop its properties. "We were placed in a position that in justice to our stockholders, we had to refuse to sign an agreement, which we knew would close our mines during the life of same."

The company argued that in 1922 the whole Kanawha district had been under UMW contract, but in April 1923, 50 per cent of the operators refused to sign the union agreement, and by March 1924, before the Coal Creek company started operations on October 1, 1924, 95 per cent of the mines were operating on a nonunion basis at the 1917 wage rates. At the time of the company's report (June 6, 1925) only two mines in the Kanawha district were reported operating on a union-shop basis and these were expected to go open shop shortly. Coal Creek's manager concluded: "The enforcement of the Jacksonville agreement has practically closed down 50 per cent of the mines of the Central Competitive Field. And bear in mind that they have a decided advantage over the operators in the Kanawha Field, in the matter of freight rates."

The UMW continued to lose ground until the 1930's as new nonunion southern operators replaced bankrupt unionized companies.[27] Besides the growth of nonunion competition in the south, a declining demand for coal cut into UMW membership, which was further reduced by the union's refusal to accept a wage cut during the depression of 1929. In 1922, approximately 70 per cent of the nation's coal was produced in unionized mines; by 1932 this proportion had declined to 20 per cent.[28]

Conclusions. We have seen many reasons for the defeat of unionism in the southern coal fields during this period. The basic factors were the highly competitive nature of the industry and the abundance of strikebreakers. The UMW also faced hostile courts, injunctions, yellow-dog contracts, well-guarded company towns, and the evictions of strikers. There was also considerable debate in the 1930's as to whether union officers should have permitted wage reductions to meet non-union competition (though John L. Lewis and Philip Murray insisted that the organization's wage policy had been correct[29]).

According to Lewis, inadequate leadership also contributed to the UMW's problems in the south and elsewhere during these years. For example, Tennessee and Kentucky District 19 became well organized and accumulated a treasury of $100,000 under international control during World War I. Thereafter, according to Lewis, the district acquired local autonomy and elected inexperienced men who spent the money and incurred debts. District 19 then lost its contracts and was destroyed. Lewis claimed, "The effects of that action unfortunately were not confined only to the men of District 19, but the effect of that debacle in that district, brought about only through stupidity of administration, affected the men of West Virginia and Kentucky, Indiana and Pennsylvania, Virginia, and elsewhere."[30]

Lewis told of similar difficulties in other southern districts. The UMW had tried for forty years to complete organization in West Virginia, but time after time the international had to straighten out the district's affairs. After considerable progress during World War I, a dishonest, incompetent president was elected. Lewis described him as a man with a "big mouth and a small brain and a selfish heart who wrecked the organization by his stupid policies." He told the 1936 and 1942 conventions that the International had to pay back $10,000 borrowed from a coal operator by the West Virginia district president who signed a confession of failure and neglect and asked the UMW to come in and salvage the operation. District officers had also clipped coupons from bonds bought by the union during the war:

> When they had clipped all the coupons off they thought the bonds were worthless and threw them away . . . the ignoramuses that the people elected to office did not have sense enough not to throw away the money of the members of our Union.
>
> Well, these affairs in West Virginia had their repercussions elsewhere. Who can say how many years it delayed the organization of the mine workers in Kentucky, and in Virginia, and in Tennessee and in Alabama?

Although Lewis' statements were made in defense of his centralized control of the UMW, and perhaps do not reflect the realities of the situation, there can be little question that these experiences, and the union's external organizing problems, convinced him and other international officers that authority would have to be centralized in the UMW before the southern coal fields could be organized.

TEXTILE WORKERS

Before 1928, textile manufacturing became the south's leading manufacturing industry, and the south became the nation's main textile producing area. Between 1899 and 1929 the south increased its share of the country's cotton textile spindles from 21.8 per cent to 56.5 per cent, surpassing the New England states in 1925.[31] The bulk of its cotton textile industry was in the Carolinas, with Virginia, Georgia, and Alabama accounting for most of the remainder. The south initially produced only the coarser cotton textile goods but gradually took over finer productions.

The main reason for the shift of the textile industry from New England was lower costs. Costs were important because the demand for textiles is highly elastic. Labor costs are particularly important because they form a large proportion of the total.[32] Transportation costs were also lower in the south because cotton had to be moved a shorter distance to the mills.[33] In addition, taxes were lower, and the mills had more modern equipment than those in New England.[34] Employers also apparently were attracted because unions were weaker and workers were relatively more satisfied. Although wages were lower, southerners worked as a family, acquired most of their supplies from company stores, and lived in company houses. Moreover, the southern farmer or mountaineer found that his lot improved considerably when he moved into a mill village. In 1909, for example, a tenant family of three workers could expect to earn an average of $375 a year, and the mountaineer, who was largely self-sufficient, could expect to earn even less. In the Piedmont mills, on the other hand, a family of three workers could earn $900 a year in 1909.[35]

Increasing competition from the south forced the AFL to turn its attention to unionizing southern textile workers. Around 1898, for example, New England textile workers struck because of a 10 per cent wage reduction, which employers said was necessary. Gompers took this as his cue to write an editorial on the situation.[36] He spoke of the competition from southern workers as "chineising [sic] our people, our institutions and our civilizations." "It cannnot be disputed," Gompers wrote, "that because of the industrial conditions and the development of the spirit of organized labor among the New England wage earners, the spirit of resistance of its textile operatives is much further and higher developed than that of their Southern fellowcraftspeople." Gompers added that the wage reduction of the New England employers "may well prove a blessing in disguise. It has already accomplished three unlooked for things, one to arouse the inactive spirit of the textile workers which has lain dormant so long; second, the agitation which soon must be again prosecuted for the organization of the textile workers of the South; and third, the agitation for a reduction of their hours of labor."

Gompers also called upon the New England textile employers to help correct the disparity between the north and the south. Gompers and other AFL leaders repeated this at the AFL convention later that year. In discussing the Augusta, Georgia, textile strike then in progress, Gompers told the convention that "a better [opportunity] for organizing American textile workers of the South prevails than at any time heretofore."[37]

The organizing movement in southern textiles did not originate in AFL headquarters, however. In 1896, Columbus, Georgia, textile workers organized and struck unsuccessfully against a wage cut.[38]

Also in 1896, the workers at Rome, Georgia, struck against the replacement of a white worker with a Negro, and succeeded in having the white man reinstated.[39]

Another strike against the hiring of Negroes occurred the next year at the Fulton Bag and Cotton Mill in Atlanta. "The strike was a spontaneous protest against the employment of twenty negro women spinners, who were to work alongside white women. Fourteen hundred workers quit, and formed a union that afternoon. The strike lasted only a day. The employers agreed to discharge the negroes, and the employees agreed to work overtime when necessary."[40]

Another dispute occurred at this mill when the returning strikers presented an ultimatum to the manager to discharge all Negroes, with the exception of janitors and scrubbers. The manager refused, and the workers went out again. This strike also lasted only one day because the manager agreed to segregate all Negro employees.

The partial success of the workers gave impetus to a local union, and another strike took place later that year against the Fulton Bag and Cotton Mill Company, which the union learned was discriminating against its members. On the second day of the strike the company began to evict workers from company-owned houses and to hire strikebreakers. "The strike continued actively for more than a month, but the aggressiveness of the management, the lack of unanimity among the strikers, and the availability of many strikebreakers, made it possible for the company to overcome its inconvenience in a few days." The strikers were left without employment, and the union disappeared.

A very important strike occurred in 1898 against all the mills in Augusta, Georgia. The Augusta unions were independent locals but were affiliated with the Augusta Federation of Trades. The workers walked out to protest wage reductions, and the employers countered with a lockout. The mill owners were able to defeat the strikers by the use of strikebreakers, agreements to rehire all the strikers except the leaders, and evictions of workers from company-owned houses. Since the industry was depressed, the strike caused the mills only limited inconvenience.

The publicity accompanying the strike activated textile organizations throughout the region for the next four years. The workers in Augusta managed to keep their organizations alive, and they, together with other southern operatives, under the leadership of Prince W. Greene, of Columbus, Georgia, applied for affiliation in the American Federation of Labor. The AFL enrolled them in the ineffectual National Union of Textile Workers (NUTW), and sent in organizers.[41] The NUTW played a minor role in the organizing campaign, since it was extremely weak financially and had little northern membership. The union was so weak, in fact, that the newly affiliated southern workers were in the majority, and Prince W. Greene was elected president from 1898 to 1900.

Danville, Virginia textile workers began agitating in 1900 for a reduction in hours from the prevailing twelve to ten. The union gained prestige and membership when the Riverside Mills established a ten-hour day on a temporary basis between January and March 1901. But the union struck in April 1901 when the company adopted the eleven-hour day.[42] Realizing the importance of the Danville strike for the textile organizing campaign, the AFL gave the strikers moral and financial help, and Gompers visited Danville.[43]

The Danville strike was defeated—halting the attempt to organize the mills in the upper Piedmont—because, according to Gompers, the workers "dabbled in politics." "After the politicians used them on election day and told them to return to work under the 11-hour system, they realized who their true friends were, but too late." The union seems to have had support from local politicians and citizens, but the mill claimed that it could not grant the workers' concessions because it faced stiff competition and was already paying higher wages than other mills in the south.[44] The local continued in Danville some months after the strike, but it had only a few unemployed members.

The 1902 Augusta strike was an organized conflict between the Augusta Cotton Manufacturers' Association and the textile workers, representing some 7000. The managers of the big King Mills responded to the workers' demand for a 10 per cent wage increase with a lockout; the cotton manufacturers' association followed a few days later with a lockout of every mill in the city. The strike was defeated, despite union solidarity for six weeks, because the company was able to obtain strikebreakers and evict workers from company houses.[45]

There seems to have been very little union activity in the southern textile industry for ten years after the Augusta strike except for some weak locals in North and South Carolina. There was a revival of activity around 1912, however, when textile locals were formed at Danville and Lynchburg, Virginia, and Knoxville, Tennessee. These southern locals prevailed upon the 1913 UTW convention to join with them in a renewed effort to organize. The timeliness of this new effort was exemplified by an important strike in Atlanta at the Fulton Bag and Cotton Mill. The Atlanta strike was a spontaneous walkout to protest poor working conditions. This strike lasted for about nine months, but the company was little affected by it.[46]

The beginning of World War I in Europe greatly stimulated the industry and raised labor's hopes. There were numerous unsuccessful textile strikes in Columbus, Georgia, and at various places in North and South Carolina during 1918 and 1919.[47] In Charlotte, North Carolina, however, textile workers won a partial victory when their strike caused management to reduce hours from 60 to 55 a week, with no reduction in pay, and to grant other concessions; it was also stipulated that strikers would be reinstated without discrimination, but that open-shop conditions would be observed.

This relatively successful settlement caused requests for organizers to come to the region and both the UTWA and the AFL enrolled large numbers of workers.

The 1920-1921 textile recession in the south caused wage cuts, widespread unrest and many requests to the AFL for help. President Gompers met with a group of workers in 1920 but told them that the federation had no money to send organizers, though he assigned two AFL representatives to work in the industry.[48]

Wage cuts were being made throughout the industry during these years, but reductions in the south appear to have been greater than elsewhere; in 1921, for example, southern reductions are reported to have averaged about 40 per cent as compared with 22 per cent in New England.[49] The UTWA locals in the upper Piedmont made urgent requests to national headquarters to take action to save the organization in that area. The northern leaders called upon the AFL for help.

UTWA's President T. A. McMahon and Vice-President McKoskey appeared before the August 1920 AFL Executive Council meeting with a request for assistance from AFL and international union organizers with an organizing campaign in Alabama, Georgia, North and

South Carolina. The council seemed reluctant to support the UTWA's efforts, questioning the advisability of a campaign when there was so much unemployment. McMahon replied that the southern mills were operating at practically 100 per cent capacity.

Gompers told the UTWA leaders that he had recently had some success in conferences with southern labor men and that he would go to Atlanta. He then met with UTWA leaders to agree on the cities and states to include in the campaign. The federation agreed to designate an AFL organizer, from those already employed, for each of the areas. President Gompers also agreed to ask each international union to assist the textile workers with their campaign.

The organizing campaign came to a climax during 1921, when thousands of workers in the south flocked to the UTWA's banners. On June 1, 1921, about 9000 North Carolina workers struck mills belonging to three large companies and a chain of independents. The nature of some of the difficulties in the south during these years is suggested by a report on the strike at Concord, North Carolina in 1921.[50] The UTW had called strikes against strings of mills in the area to protest reductions which brought wages down to within an average of 10 per cent above prewar rates. The UTWA had hoped with the meager resources at its command, "that by successfully opposing the reduction in sections where resistance is possible, they may raise the general standard." Troops were sent into the area, and on the roof of the largest mill at Kannapolis, North Carolina, "they had a machine gun trained upon the town." The Concord City Council passed an antipicketing ordinance, which the governor of North Carolina said "was in contradiction to the laws of the state and nation. But he insisted that he had no right to insist or even persuade employers that they must contract with their employees if they did not choose to do so."

The *Southern Textile Bulletin* instigated a newspaper campaign to convince the workers that the "Northern" union had not dealt in good faith with the southerners; the *Bulletin* argued that the cost of living had fallen by as much as the wage cuts and asked union leaders what had happened to the funds paid in by the southerners for so long. Union leaders knew, according to this argument, that they had insufficient funds when they launched the strike.[51]

The strike finally collapsed late in August 1921, when the mills at Concord and Kannapolis resumed operation with protection from national guardsmen. The leaders were refused employment, and long after the strike was over, hundreds of workers had not been reemployed. These events, and the antiunion newspaper campaign, soured worker attitude toward the union, and the feeling lasted for years in the area.

In November 1921, it was announced that the textile workers' campaign had been officially "abandoned for the present" and the AFL organizers withdrawn.[52] The decision was made because of financial difficulties encountered by the AFL as a result of the recession. The UTWA continued to call upon the AFL for aid during the following year, but the federation could only issue appeals to the nationals for help.

The textile workers were also active in eastern Tennessee during these years. Knoxville textile workers had organized as early as 1900 and are reported to have had 1200 members between 1912 and 1921.[53] The workers exerted considerable leadership in the area until the union was destroyed in 1921 when it lost a strike against a wage cut.

Conclusions. Thus, after 1921, there was little textile union activity in the south, though the American Federation of Full-Fashioned Hosiery Workers entered the region around 1924. Although a relatively small proportion of the full-fashioned hosiery industry was in the south in 1919 (only 17 of the nation's 92 mills were there),[54] the hosiery workers were concerned about the expanding proportion of the industry in the south.

It is not difficult to understand why strikes were unsuccessful during the recession, but the fact that employers defeated unions even during relative prosperity indicates that the southern textile industry faced fundamental obstacles.

One was the weakness of the UTW. The national organization's frail nonsouthern base made it impossible to launch a vigorous campaign in the south. The UTW's strategy was to concentrate its activities in areas where spontaneous strikes had taken place. Consequently, the UTW took over strikes which frequently had not been strategically called, and which the UTW was not strong enough to support adequately; the union was therefore frequently blamed for the failure of these strikes. The UTW's position also was lessened by the fact that the strikes occurred during recession when workers were protesting wage cuts which economic conditions made the companies powerless to remedy.

CHAPTER VI

Agricultural and Lumber Workers

AGRICULTURAL ORGANIZATIONS

Industrialization and Commercialization. Industrialization produced much more unrest in the rural south than it did among urban workers. Although we noted in Chapter II that there were many strikes in the south during the period of rapid industrialization following Reconstruction, most of these were either in the coal mines or the building trades and not attributable to the industrializing process itself. Protest movements were noticeably absent among workers in the textile industry, which spearheaded industrialization in the region. The ease with which southern agrarians adjusted to urban jobs was undoubtedly due to their poverty before industrialization. They "were dispossessed, not only of progressive occupation, but of participation in the larger life of the section. From the time cotton began to control until after the period of Reconstruction, these people lapsed into the background."[1] The main economic activity associated with the "new south" grew up outside the cotton belts and therefore drew some of these workers into the factories, where conditions usually were so much better than they were in rural areas that there were usually many applicants for each job. Discontent among southern nonagricultural workers also was lessened by the prevailing ideology that industrialists were benefactors. While this "new South" idea originated in the north, was popularized by southern newspapers, and was espoused by local economic groups who had much to gain from industrialization, the illusion was prevalent. Moreover, in spite of the rapid growth of industry during the 1880's, which caused one southern economic historian to observe that "It is probable that never before or since has an agricultural population been so suddenly drawn into industry," the transition was apparently neither drastic nor onerous to these workers. For one thing, most southern factories were located in relatively rural areas,[2] and most of the labor was drawn from the surrounding countryside. The former agricultural workers also found many familiar practices in the factories: most of their fellow workers and even their employers were from similar agricultural and ethnic backgrounds; the houses in the company towns were (improved) versions of their own farm houses; the paternalism of mill villages resembled that of the plantations; company stores and payment in scrip were common both on plantations and in mill villages; whole families worked in the mills as they had on the farms; and the church remained the principal social institution.[3] Those who had been left out of the slave economy undoubtedly felt a special satisfaction with the new system. The Negro was "put in his place" in the economic as well as political system which emerged following Reconstruction, and racial solidarity undoubtedly muted some worker protest which whites might have directed at employers.

As a result, the most radical protest movements in the south before the First World War were found among agricultural workers. Although industrialization greatly improved the lot of poor whites, it produced serious problems for southern agrarians. This situation gave Socialists, Syndicalists, and other radicals considerable support. Industrialization made agricultural workers increasingly dependent on unstable markets and subjected them to forces which they could not control and sometimes could not understand. In addition to fluctuations in cotton prices, farmers suffered from monopoly prices established by local merchants who furnished supplies on credit secured by cotton crops,[4] what they considered to be unfair railroad rates, high interest rates and poor credit facilities. The frequently perverse relations between their costs and their prices persuaded many southern farmers that mysterious forces in the cities, particularly in the north, were manipulating money and prices to defraud them. There was also a strong suspicion, particularly in the southwest, that too much land had been taken over by railroads, absentee landlords, and land speculators, limiting the supply available to independent farmers. Indeed, in the years between 1890 and 1930, many farmers lost the land they had homesteaded.[5] In Texas, for example, 55 per cent of the farmers were tenants in 1920 as contrasted with 41 per cent in 1890.[6] Conditions in the rural south were made worse by the depletion of the soil caused by excessive reliance on cotton, the low level of skill required to produce it, high rates of population growth, and the migration of people from the worn-out lands of the old south.

The low levels of literacy and the poor education system made it difficult for these southerners either to understand the reasons for their difficulties or to provide the leadership to correct them. And the region's political, economic and social structure, particularly the race problem, made it difficult to improve the educational system. Southern education suffered not only from the burden of having to support a segregated school system at a time when the region could scarcely afford a single good system, but also because the presence of Negroes made southern whites reluctant to support any educational system at all. Josephus Daniels observed in 1903 that the greatest obstacle to educational progress in the south was "The negro—enfranchised against the protest of the people, who were forced against their will to pay a tax to educate him."[7]

The Grange with its emphasis on regulation of the railroads, educational programs for farmers, control of interest rates, cooperatives, and even farmer-owned manufacturing activities to eliminate "middlemen profits" had much appeal for southern farmers during Reconstruction.[8] With the worsening of agricultural conditions in the 1880's, however, southern farmers turned to the more radical Farmers' Alliance (FA) formed in Texas in 1872.

After 1887 the Alliance shifted its emphasis more to political action in cooperation with other groups, particularly the Knights of Labor. In 1887 it established headquarters in Washington, D.C., and reached its first formal agreement with the Knights of Labor in 1889. T. V. Powderly and other KL leaders were present at the FA's 1887 convention in St. Louis, and endorsed the program. It was agreed that the "legislative committees of both organizations will act in concert before Congress for the purpose of securing the enactment of laws mutually agreed. And it is further agreed, in order to carry out these objects, we will support for office only such men as can be depended on to enact these principles in statute law, uninfluenced by party caucus."[9]

The Knights and the Alliance agreed upon the abolition of national banks and the issuance of treasury notes in lieu of national bank notes on a per capita basis; the prohibition of dealings in commodity futures; free and unlimited coinage of silver; the prohibition of land ownership by aliens and the reclamation of unused land granted to railroads; equitable and just taxation and economy in government; the issuance of paper money to facilitate mail-order transactions; government ownership of transportation and communications facilities; and the mutual recognition of union labels. These demands obviously were more heavily weighted by agricultural than urban labor objectives, and probably reflected the fact that the Knights' membership had become more rural and small town as the national craft organizations joined the AFL.

The Alliance, working with the Knights of Labor, achieved important, though temporary, political successes in the south. In 1890 it sought to gain control of southern governments by working from within the state Democratic conventions. These efforts led to election of Alliancemen and their supporters to majority control of the legislatures in North Carolina, Alabama, and Florida. The Alliance also gained a strong minority of the Tennessee legislature. In addition, it elected governors in Tennessee and Georgia and congressmen in Virginia and Kentucky. In Arkansas, the Alliance supported the Union Labor Party, "which ran a strong race but lost."[10]

The Alliance's demonstration of political power produced demands for the establishment of a third party. At the 1890 convention in Ocala, Florida, the organization was urged by Terence V. Powderly and other leaders of the Knights of Labor, the Colored Alliance, and Populist delegates from the west, to bolt the Democratic Party and support the Populists. While the Ocala convention refused to follow the suggestion, subsequent events forced the Alliance out of the Democratic Party and into a coalition with the Populists. The public officials elected with Alliance support usually proved to be only slightly less conservative than their fellow Democrats and generally refused to support Alliance demands. Alliance support for the Populists also increased when the Democrats nominated ultraconservative Grover Cleveland for the presidency in 1892.

Though many Populist leaders were upper-class "intellectuals," they supported programs which were designed to appeal to small farmers and laborers. Some Populists were even so bold as to challenge racism openly in favor of common action by all farmers. And, emphasizing their continuity with southern tradition, Populists based their ideas on the revolutionary writings of Jefferson and other eighteenth-century southerners. The Populists also attacked those political and business leaders who wanted to form alliances with eastern monopolists in order to industrialize the south at the expense of the workers and farmers, and adopted a platform in 1892 which closely resembled the 1887 program agreed to by the Knights of Labor and the Farmers' Alliance. The official paper of the Texas Alliance called on every "wage earner to combine and march shoulder to shoulder to the ballot box and by their suffrage overthrow the capitalist class."[11]

The Alliance's economic program included the establishment of cooperatives, the most important of which was the Farmers' Alliance Exchange, organized in Dallas for selling cotton. It also rendered valuable consumer education service to its members. But the organization's rapid growth was due as much to the social outlet for southern farmers and their families as to its impressive economic objectives. Especially popular were the week-long meetings resembling religious revivals which were held each year after the crops had been gathered.

In spite of its large membership and optimistic beginnings, the Alliance movement was unable to survive. Its political program was vigorously opposed by conservative Democratic leaders in the south because its support of the Populists threatened to split the white vote and give Negroes greater political power. The economic programs were also opposed by southerners as being "socialistic" and under-mining the free enterprise system. Opposition was so strong in some areas that Alliancemen were physically abused.[12] But the chief economic weakness of the Alliance appears to have been its attempt to conduct too much business for its limited capital.

The organizational demise of populism did not eliminate its influence from the south, however, because many of its basic ideas became a part of the southern ideology. The Socialists gained considerable support in areas where the Populists had thrived, and southerners who found kinship with the liberal ideas of the New Deal often came from areas where populism had been strong. Populist influence also survived in the efforts to organize agricultural workers between 1900 and the 1930's.

The Farmers' Union. The Farmers' Educational and Cooperative Union of America (FU) was formed in Rains County, Texas, in 1902. Rains County had been a Populist stronghold and had very small farms and relatively few Negroes. The Farmers' Union, like the Farmers' Alliance, limited its membership to whites but also admitted country teachers, mechanics, physicians, ministers of the gospel and publishers. Membership spread rapidly from Texas to other southern states, and by 1905 the union reported 200,000 members—with 120,000 in Texas, and others in Indian Territory, Oklahoma Territory, Louisiana, Georgia, Missouri, Tennessee, Mississippi, South Carolina, North Carolina, Alabama and Kentucky.[13] By 1908, the FU is reported to have had 1,200,000 members in Texas and other southern states.[14]

The union's rapid growth came from many of the same factors which caused such flourishing among previous farmers' organizations, and it, like the Alliance, formed a close working relationship with organized labor. In 1905, when the Farmers' Union became a national organization, it adopted a program which included many of organized labor's objectives, including an endorsement of the cigarmakers' label and a resolution which resolved that, since "the city labor unions have a tendency to increase consumption of the products of the farm, . . . wherever possible to do so, members of the Farmers' Union cooperate with trade unions in their efforts."[15] The FU also cooperated with the Joint Labor Legislative Board of Texas, formed in 1903 by the Texas State Federation of Labor (TSFL), the Brotherhood of Railroad Trainmen, the Brotherhood of Locomotive Firemen, the Order of Railway Conductors, the Brotherhood of Locomotive Engineers and the Order of Railway Telegraphers.[16] TSFL representatives attended the open meetings of the FU, and the 1906 meeting of the Texas Farmers' Union adopted resolutions against the employment of convict labor; recommending an eight-hour day for workers in public enterprises; and demanding laws to make employers who import labor admit if the laborers are to be used as strikebreakers.[17] The FU observed union boycotts, made contributions to unions during strikes, and adopted a union label for farm products which the TSFL asked its members to honor.[18] Although we noted in Chapter II that the period of cooperation between the FU and the urban unions caused the passage of several laws favorable to organized labor in Texas, the alliance began to weaken around 1911. The reasons were: the farmers supported some important legislation which the urban unions opposed, the Texas Joint Labor Legislative Board was infiltrated by members of the Commercial Secretaries' Association, an antilabor organization of businessmen formed in 1907 to oppose progressive labor legislation, and there were differences between the railway brotherhoods and the TSFL.[19]

The economic program of the Farmers' Union included: agreements to withhold cotton from the market until a certain price was reached; acreage limitations to reduce the supply of cotton; establishing cooperative warehouses with schools to teach farmers to grade cotton;[20] the creation of buying and credit cooperatives; and the operation of some factories, especially for the production of cottonseed oil. The FU was reported by the U.S. Commissioner of Corporations to have represented "the most comprehensive movement ever undertaken by farmers to control the production and marketing of their crops."[21]

While the FU's economic activities served useful educational functions, they suffered from some of the same weaknesses as those of the Alliance. The efforts to reduce the supply of cotton were partially successful, but the FU could not control enough of the total supply to have a significant influence on prices. The buying cooperatives fre-

quently failed because of poor management, and, where they succeeded, they ceased to be cooperatives and became profit-making
organizations. By 1919 the Farmers' Union had virtually gone out of
existence.

The agrarian Socialists. The ideas sustained and strengthened by the
Populists, the Alliance, and the Farmers' Union were continued in the
south by the Socialists. Indeed Socialists existed contemporaneously
with the Populists. The Texas Socialist party for example, was a
member of the radical wing of the national party. E. O. Meitzen, of
Hallettsville, a member of the Grange, who helped organize the
Farmers' Alliance in Fayette County, and edited a German Populist
paper *(Der Anzeiger)* during the 1890's, was an active Socialist, and
was secretary of the Renters' Union, formed by Texas Socialists around
1909. Meitzen's activities were continued by Thomas Hickey, a lecturer
for the Social-Democratic Party in the south during the early 1900's.
Hickey published a magazine, *The Rebel* form Hallettsville for many
years.[22] The leaders of the Socialist Party in Oklahoma were Otto
Branstetter, later national secretary of the party, and Oscar Ameringer,
who published a number of papers, including the *American Guardian*
and served as an organizer and lecturer for the party in Oklahoma between 1907 and 1922.[23] Some Socialists also migrated to the southwest
after the defeat of the Pullman strike led by Eugene Debs in 1894, the
same year the Cherokee Strip in Oklahoma was opened for settlement.
Debs and ex-American Railway Union members held frequent re-
unions in the southwest. Other radicals migrated into the south,
particularly in north Texas, Oklahoma and Arkansas, from western
mining areas after the defeat of strikes or loss of jobs for other reasons.

There was also a direct relationship between populism—which was
uniquely American—and the kind of socialism which flourished in the
southwest between 1900 and World War I.

At its peak, the Socialist Party commanded close to a third of the
vote in Oklahoma and elected six legislators and a number of county
officers. In 1912 E. V. Debs, the Socialist candidate for President of the
United States, got a higher proportion of the votes in Oklahoma than
he did in any other state. Debs got 7 per cent of the vote in Louisiana
and Arkansas that year, 10 per cent of the Florida vote, and about 9
per cent of the Texas vote. In Louisiana the Socialists were strong in
1912 in almost exactly the same areas as the Populists in the 1890's.[24]

During these years southern Socialists were most active in the rural
areas of the southwest and, like previous agrarian movements, their
methods and appeal resembled the religious revival meetings characteristic of the rural south today. Indeed, Socialists were frequently

mistaken for "preachers" by southerners. Oscar Ameringer's descriptions demonstrate this similarity:

> Our meetings were usually held in schoolhouses which also served as churches . . . These frontier people constituted the most satisfactory audience of my long experience in "riling up the people." They were grateful for anything that broke the monotony of their lonesome lives . . . As the movement developed, we added summer encampments to schoolhouse meetings. These encampments were lineal descendants of the religious and Populist camp meetings of former days. They usually lasted a full week. The audience came in covered wagons from as far as seventy miles around . . . Expenses were defrayed from collections taken at meetings and funds raised by the chambers of commerce in the nearest trading centers, the local bankers usually heading the list.
>
> These encampments were attended by an average of five thousand people . . . they were welcome because they brought customers together and stimulated business.

The gospel preached at these meetings would perhaps have seemed as strange to northern Socialists as the settings in which they took place. The speech delivered by Thomas Hickey at the West Texas Encampment at Ellison Springs in 1912 was a blend of socialism and homilies familiar to rural southerners. Hickey's theme was "The Moral Teaching of the Good Book Insofar as it Applies to the Land."[25] "Turn we then to the Good Book," Hickey said, and "you cannot find anywhere that the Lord ordains that the earth—his gift to all mankind—should ever fall into private hands and be fenced in for the benefit of the few." Hickey also quoted passages from the Bible and from the treatises of various philosophers.

While socialism ceased to be an active force in the south after the First World War, its ideology survived, especially in the rural areas and gave rise to the Farm-Labor Union of America in the 1920's and the Southern Tenant Farmers' Union (STFU) in the 1930's. The Socialists also sponsored a number of short-lived organizations among agricultural workers in the southwest during the 1920's. Moreover, we shall see a continuity of method and even membership between the STFU and these earlier farm organizations.

LUMBER WORKERS

Lumber workers, many of whom were sharecroppers, small farmers, and agricultural laborers who worked in the lumber camps and saw mills during off-seasons in agriculture, allied themselves with the Industrial Workers of the World (IWW) shortly before the First World War. These workers gave the Syndicalistic IWW its most important southern base, though it also had scattered support in other industries throughout the region. It is significant that both the Socialists and Syndicalists had their greatest southern support among agricultural workers.

As noted in Chapter I, the southern timber reserves were rapidly exploited by large operators in the years between Reconstruction and World War I.[26] When the larger companies depleted the timber reserves, production was left to the smaller "peckerwood" mills which were predominant by 1930. As might be expected, the period of greatest union activity coincided with the predominance of the large mills.

The main grievances which prompted the unionization of southern lumber workers were poor housing (most of which was designed to last only until the mills exhausted the timber resources and moved to other areas), isolation, low wages, infrequent wage payments, payment of wages in scrip, peonage, and the convict lease system. As compared with other regions, the south was unique in having larger proportions of Negroes and married men in its lumber work force.[27]

Although the Knights of Labor were active among southern lumber workers during the 1890's,[28] the period of greatest union activity came between 1910 and 1912. The only event of more than local significance before 1910 was a large-scale strike by lumber workers in eastern Texas and western Louisiana called in 1907 to protest wage cuts. The Southern Lumber Operators' Association was formed at this time as an antiunion organization, but it soon became inactive because union agitation failed to survive.

In 1910, however, some IWW supporters organized the Brotherhood of Timber Workers (BTW) which affiliated with the IWW two years later. The founder of the BTW was Arthur Lee Emerson, who had worked in the lumber camps of the northwest, where he had found higher wages and better working conditions and where he learned about unions, particularly the IWW.

Upon returning to Louisiana in 1910, he formed the BTW.[29] The brotherhood grew to 30,000 Negro and white members mainly in Texas and Louisiana, but it also had members in Arkansas and Mississippi. The union's rapid growth was attributable to a combination of factors: it was a mass organization, admitting Negroes and whites and requiring very small dues; there was intense unrest among these workers; and the union employed successful organizing techniques. Membership meetings were held at night, and members went from camp to camp holding demonstrations on Sunday. The BTW's liberal racial policies were important because the larger companies had high proportions of Negro employees.

The employers' attitude toward the BTW is reflected in a comment from the *Saint Louis Lumberman:*

> Neither in the matter of its so-called principles nor in its disregard of the color line does the B.T.W. appeal to Southern sentiment, business or social. Moreover, it appears to accept for membership not only those who labor more or less in the saw mill industry but the rag-tag bob-tail of almost any old line of employment or business. . . . Still, the activity of the organizers is such, and membership is made so easy, that the order continues to make numerical headway—in new places especially—notwithstanding that the better class of workmen, both white and black, is openly opposed to it. Indeed, at many sawmilling points counter organizations have been formed to prevent the Brotherhood from making inroads among those who desire to work rather than agitate.[30]

The activities of the brotherhood also stirred several dormant employers' groups to action, including the Southern Lumber Operator's Association, (SLOA) headed by John H. Kirby, former president of the National Association of Manufacturers, and reportedly the largest lumber operator in Texas.

The SLOA attempted to destroy the BTW by reducing working time to four days a week, but in July 1911, resorted to a lockout when the earlier tactic failed. At a New Orleans SLOA meeting, between eight and ten Louisiana mills employing 1000 workers voted to close "until the labor situation is settled satisfactorily to the mill owners."[31] It was explained that "a satisfactory settlement will mean nothing more or less than the disruption of the National Brotherhood of Timber Workers in the territory where the Southern Lumber Operators Association does business. We will operate only with non-union labor." SLOA's executive committee was given power to close any or all of its 300 affiliated mills.

The SLOA ultimately was forced to use an almost complete lockout for as long as seven months in many mills in order to subdue the BTW; and employers sometimes had to go as far as Kentucky and Tennessee for nonunion labor. "According to the sworn testimony of several of these workers, they were virtually stockaded on the mill premises. Armed guards were posted at all gates, and passes had to be obtained before passage was allowed."[32]

Kirby brought 1000 "friends" from east Texas to troubled De Ridder, Louisiana, August 1, 1911, where he made an impassioned speech against unions.[33] Three weeks later, the employers' association became alarmed at the rapid spread of union membership and extended its lockout against the BTW; over twenty-five of the largest sawmills in western Louisiana and east Texas immediately participated in the lockout, which spread to thirty large plants employing 10,000 workers by the middle of September.

The employers were not alone in their opposition to the Brotherhood of Timber Workers. Some workers formed counter organizations. On September 2, 1911, the white and colored workers of the Enterprise Lumber Company of Alexandria, Louisiana drafted resolutions calling for the discharge of all who joined the organization.

The companies instituted a campaign of blacklisting active BTW members. The *Saint Louis Lumberman* reported on October 1, 1911:

> The operators are discharging every man whom they find has joined the order, and they . . . are open in their declaration that they are going to kill the Brotherhood in its incipiency, and that they are going to take every action that they consider necessary to arrive at that end. The number of mills that will close in the future depends entirely on the action of the Brotherhood. If they keep up their work as they have been doing, there will be twice as many mills down thirty days hence, as there are now. The leaders of that organization say that they are making good headway and are going to fight the thing to the finish and win, so there are chances for long curtailment and a hot fight.

The companies were aided by a surplus of lumber, which put them under no pressure to resume operations; however, the workers were also under little pressure until after cotton-picking season. They accordingly began leaving the union in the winter of 1911, and by February 1912 the lockout had ended.

In May 1912 the Brotherhood of Timber Workers affiliated with the IWW's National Industrial Union of Forest and Lumber Workers, and decided to push for more complete organization of southern lumber workers.[34] IWW leader Bill Haywood, was at the meeting in Alexandria, Louisiana, when the brotherhood decided to affiliate with the IWW:

> I knew that the lumber jacks and mill workers of that part of the country were both black and white, and when I went to the convention hall in Alexandria, I was very much surprised to find no Negroes in the session. . . . I was told that it was against the law in Louisiana for black and white men to meet together . . .
>
> I said, you work in the same mills together . . . You are meeting in convention now to discuss the conditions under which you labor. This can't be done intelligently by passing resolutions here and then sending them out to another room for the black men to act upon. Why not be sensible

about this and call the Negroes into this convention? If it is against the law, this is one time when the law should be broken.

The Negroes were called into the session without a murmur of opposition from any one.[35]

Haywood's account was not entirely accurate, however, because, according to Covington Hall, the leading New Orleans Socialist and supporter of the BTW, Negroes were segregated at the convention.[36]

Despite these reports, there were some racial clashes during the lumber strikes. And although Negroes and whites struck together during 1912, most of the strikebreakers were Negroes.[37] Racial trouble erupted in Sabine Parish, Louisiana, early in 1913 after whites ordered Negroes to stop work.[38]

The BTW's most serious trouble came on July 7, 1912, when one company representative and two union men were killed at Graybow, Louisiana. Sixty-four BTW members and four Galloway Lumber Company men were arrested on charges of murder; the situation became so tense that troops were called in to maintain order.

The trial of these men, held at Lake Charles, Louisiana, in October 1912, revealed that one of the prosecution's witnesses who had been a member of the BTW was actually a detective on the payroll of the Kirby Lumber Company. Burns detectives had even become officers in the union; one of them is reported to have stolen union records after he became the BTW's general secretary.[39] The court was packed with unionists who responded to a BTW circular calling on union men to appear "to show that organized labor is opposed to legalized murder."[40]

The owner of the Galloway Lumber Company testified during the trial that BTW leaders told him to either recognize the union or go broke.

The *Southern Lumberman* observed: "The mill men in this section are watching the outcome of the timber workers' trial at Lake Charles, and they do not fear any more labor trouble, no matter which way the matter goes." However, after the BTW men had been acquitted, and after arsonists had burned the mill, the *Southern Lumberman* took a somewhat different position: "The mill owners seem to realize that the union question is in its infancy, and will have to be finally disposed of later. They are laying their plans accordingly . . . Many of the large saw mills in the Lake Charles territory are now having fences built to enclose their plants . . . also signs . . . : 'No trespassing. No admittance to these premises without an order from the manager.'"

The organized employers did not confine their opposition to direct action against union members and organizers for the BTW. Also, pressure was brought against employers who failed to fight the union.

The BTW considered the acquittal of the workers involved in the "Graybow massacre" a victory for the union and, encouraged by this "success," launched a new organizing drive which culminated in a showdown with the employers at Merryville and Sweet Home Front, Louisiana.[41] The BTW called a strike of 1300 men at Merryville in November 1912, in the only mill in the southwest that had recognized the union, because the new owners, the Santa Fe Railroad, announced that no union men would be hired and refused to reinstate men tried for complicity in the Graybow riot.

The *Southern Lumberman* reported that the mills at Merryville "were closed down in an effort to shut out members of the Brotherhood of Timber Workers and the Industrial Workers of the World," adding that after these mills were closed there was not a BTW member known to be employed in the southwest.

A circular distributed by the union to raise funds for the Merryville strikers indicates the general tone of the campaign of the Brotherhood of Timber Workers:

> Labor, the creator of wealth, is entitled to all it creates . . . Out of the attempt of the International Lumber Trust to peonize the men working in the forests . . . sprang the Industrial Union of Forest and Lumber Workers, of which the Brotherhood is now a part, as out of this question and the same attempts and practices on the part of Capitalists in other industries sprang . . . the IWW which movement, meeting and fusing with French Syndicalism has shaken the Industrial Despotism to its foundations and brought into the glare of open day, where all mankind can see it, the inherent hypocracy[sic] and brutality of Capitalist Society.

Community opposition to the BTW intensified during the early months of 1913 as strike activity continued. In February, for example, about 50 "citizens" at Lake Charles, Louisiana, ran four union representatives out of town and removed records and archives from union headquarters.[42] The big mill of the American Lumber Company at Merryville was reported to have been operating full time with "over 50 guards . . . surrounding the plant night and day."

Troops were sent to the Merryville area in March when it was feared that armed conflict would break out again.[43]

Covington Hall wrote to the New Orleans *Daily News* in February 1913, giving the union's view of the "citizens" actions. Hall said the citizens' committee consisted of "officers and gunmen of the American Lumber Company and the Santa Fe Railroad," and denied that the American Lumber Company was operating "full blast" or that it ever had been since the strike.[44]

The BTW ceased to exist after these defeats, but it must not be implied that the brotherhood had no effect on employment relations in the lumber camps of the southwest. It is probably not entirely coincidental that many of the workers' grievances—payment in scrip, forced purchases at company stores, infrequent wage payments—were modified after the BTW became active in the region. The *Southern Lumberman* reported:[45] "Better wages, better working conditions and all that can add to the comfort and satisfaction of their employees are constantly being granted by the big companies to their faithful employees."

Bogalusa episode. The next attempt to organize southern lumber workers of the large companies in the Gulf states was in 1919 when two AFL unions, the International Timber Workers' Union and the United Brotherhood of Carpenters and Joiners of America, centered their activities around Bogalusa, Louisiana, a town owned by the Great Southern Lumber Company, at that time the largest single lumber company in the world. Great Southern was successful in avoiding unions during the first few years of its existence by running union organizers out of town and raising wages to discourage workers from organizing.[46] However, unions made considerable headway during and after World War I, and were stimulated by rising rents during the early months of 1919. The idea of unionization as a protest seems to have originated with the workers on the New Orleans and Great Northern Railroad, which was owned by Great Southern. By September 1919, there were enough union members to have 1200 marchers in the Bogalusa Labor Day parade.

The AFL organized the sawyers and filers of Bogalusa into a federal labor union in the summer of 1919, and the carpenters took this local over two months later. The AFL also had a regular carpenters' local and a timber workers' union, 75 per cent of whose members were colored. These three unions organized a central trades assembly with Lum Williams, president of the local carpenters' union, as president. Williams initiated a campaign to organize all the lumber workers in the area. The organizing activity among the Negroes, who were organized in a segregated local, was undertaken by colored members of the union, most important of whom was Sol Dacus, vice-president of the local.

Local citizens countered with a vigorous antiunion campaign. Members of a local citizens' committee, the Self-preservation and Loyalty League (SPLL), some of whom were made deputy sheriffs, intimidated union members. League members ransacked Dacus' house several times. The company also announced an indefinite layoff in September, ostensibly because of a breakdown in the plant, though union members interpreted the company's action as a lockout. Lum Williams attempted to alleviate hardships among the workers by sending them to work on the levee and turning union headquarters into an employment office.

An editorial in the local paper claimed that SPLL had been formed because the AFL had started organizing Negro workers.

About two months after the plant closed, an incident occurred which sealed the doom of the union in Bogalusa. Sol Dacus, whose life had been threatened, sought protection from Lum Williams, and Williams assigned two armed union men to guard him. Shortly after Dacus left Williams' office, SPLL "Law Enforcement" representatives killed Williams and three other union men. Williams' brother fired at the attackers, wounding one of them. All those charged with the murder of the unionists were subsequently acquitted, though union leaders report that Williams' wife received $4500 in damages from the company nine years later.

CHAPTER VII

Revolt of the Textile Workers

The south industrialized at a relatively rapid rate in the 1919-1929 period; manufacturing employment in the region increased 14.5 per cent during this decade, and the south's proportion of United States manufacturing employment increased from 13.0 per cent to 15.2 per cent. Growth was particularly rapid in the textile industry, which was declining nationally; the south's proportion of total cotton spindles increased from 42.3 per cent in 1919 to 56.5 per cent in 1929, while New England's proportion declined from 52.0 per cent to 38.5 per cent.[1]

Unit costs were 16.8 per cent less in the south than in the typical New England mill, according to a study by the American Society of Mechanical Engineers.[2] The Mitchells estimated that there was a $6.73 per spindle difference between the south and New England, of which $4.53 was due to lower labor costs.[3] The average weekly wage in cotton mills for the four leading New England textile states in 1927 was $19.16 as compared with $12.83 for the four leading southern states (North Carolina, South Carolina, Georgia, and Alabama).[4] Lockwood, Green and Company, textile engineers, reported: "The South is fortunate in having a supply of native American labor which is still satisfied to work at low wages."[5]

UNION REVIVAL

Although union membership in the United States declined between 1924 and 1928,[6] it grew in the textile areas of the southeast and in the

101

southwest. The growth of the industry in the Piedmont area apparently stimulated other unions after 1924—though the United Textile Workers' Union (UTW) was relatively inactive until 1929. In Georgia, for example, membership increased in every building trades union, and all of them taken together increased their membership from 2940 to 3345 in the 1925-1928 period. As noted in Chapter 3, there was a general revival of craft union membership in Georgia during the late 1920's. While total carpenters' (UBCJ) membership in the south declined from 35,317 to 34,462 in the 1924-1928 period, membership increased in the textile states: Alabama, 1605 to 1709; Georgia, 1012 to 1255; North Carolina, 1254 to 1551; South Carolina, 478 to 506; and Virginia, 1657 to 1732. It is significant that UBCJ membership declined in all the other southeastern states—where textiles are relatively unimportant—during this period. In the southwest, however, membership in the UBCJ and other unions increased after 1924, probably reflecting the economic development associated with the petroleum industry in those states after 1926.[7]

Not only did membership in craft unions pick up, but the unions also started organizing central labor organizations throughout the region. As a result of public opposition to unions, the Georgia Federation of Labor started a program in 1926 to educate the citizens to unionism. In April 1928, the AFL took over the program, which was faltering from lack of finances, and put it under the direction of George Googe of the Printing Pressmens' Union; this campaign was strengthened by aid from the reorganized trades and labor assembly of Googe's native Savannah. The number of local unions in Georgia increased by more than 20 per cent in a few months, and many dormant unions and central organizations were revived.

The upsurge in southern union activity in the 1929-1930 period was preceded by the reactivation of craft unions and local federations. The Interstate Virginia-Carolinas Typographical Association was formed in January 1927 at Charlotte, North Carolina. The most famous, however, was the Piedmont Organizing Council (POC) formed at Durham in January 1928. POC, instigated primarily by Alfred Hoffman of the Hosiery Workers' Union, tried to organize all the crafts in the Piedmont section. It held monthly meetings attended by delegates from about twelve cities and crafts. Seventy-two delegates were at the initial meeting, but about 450 attended the June meeting in Winston-Salem. The July meeting, attended by about 175 delegates, was held at Danville, Virginia. Impressed by the activities of the Piedmont Organizing Committee, Virginians formed a similar organization called the Tidewater Labor Conference (TLC). The TLC had 75 unionists at its initial meeting on October 7, 1928; there were 200 unions in Tidewater, Virginia, by the end of 1928.

Strike activity. The nature of the revival in union activity primarily in the textile areas of the southeast is reflected in the strike statistics for these areas. It will be seen, however, that most of the textile strikes were spontaneous and not called by unions. In marked contrast to the virtual absence of textile strikes during the period of early industrialization, 1887-1905, most of the strike activity during the 1929-1930 period was in the Piedmont area, where the southern textile industry was concentrated. For example, 1929 was the peak year in the number of idle man-days due to strikes during the 1929-1931 period in Georgia (10,053 man-days), North Carolina (90,673), South Carolina (302,034) and Tennessee (149,391), all in the Piedmont area. Peak strike activity came later for all non-Piedmont southern states except Louisiana— where 1929 was also the top strike year (201,976 man-days)—because of strikes in other industries, especially a long and violent New Orleans street railway strike.[8]

Although labor activity in the Piedmont during these years was not restricted to textiles, the industry accounted for most of the strikes and idle man-days. For example, 94 of the 134 North Carolina strikes in the 1927-1936 period were in textiles, and so were 81 of the 96 South Carolina strikes. Peak strike activity in Virginia came in 1930— 316, 361 idle man-days—reflecting the choice of that state for the decisive strike in the AFL's 1930 organizing campaign. Over half the man-days lost due to strikes in Tennessee between 1927 and 1936 were in the textile industry, and there were more strikes in textiles in Alabama during that period than in any other industry (37 and 1,331,375 man-days lost); mining had slightly fewer strikes, but more man-days lost (35 and 1,514,372 man-days) due to strikes. There were only four strikes in Alabama in the 1927-1931 period as compared with 161 for the 1932-1936 period, indicating the shift in union activity to the iron and steel industries around Birmingham in the New Deal period.

Efforts to launch a general organizing campaign. As a result of the revival of union activity, the growth of industry, and the many manifestations of unrest among workers in the region, southern union leaders, especially in the Piedmont central labor organizations and state federations, together with the national leaders of the textile and tobacco workers' unions, called upon the AFL for help in launching general southern organizing campaigns. North Carolina unionists launched a campaign in 1925 and were "urging the AFL to use every available means to organize the industrial workers of that state."[9] In the spring of 1928, the tobacco workers (TWIU) started a campaign to organize R. J. Reynolds' 11,000 to 12,000 workers at Winston-Salem, North Carolina, but, when between 3000 and 4000 workers had signed up, the company discharged the union men. The AFL Executive Council responded to the TWIU's request for help by sending Edward F. McGrady to call on the company. Although he was unable to persuade the company to recognize the union, McGrady told the executive council that a strike "would be fatal," and the council decided to put Reynolds' products on the the unfair list.

Other southern unions and union leaders sought the AFL's aid in organizing. North Carolina union leaders obtained a conference with federation leaders in AFL headquarters in April 1928 to discuss a Piedmont campaign. The North Carolina leaders—from the central labor unions in Winston-Salem, Greensboro, Raleigh and Asheville—attempted to impress the AFL officials with the opportunities afforded by the unrest accompanying worsening conditions in the textile industry. The AFL Executive Council left it to Green to assign an organizer "if he could find one" and to communicate with national unions for assistance. Green advised the North Carolina delegation that we were willing to extend all possible assistance, but could not give financial help."

In October 1928, delegates from six southern states met in Chattanooga to discuss a campaign for the industrial workers of the region—especially in the coal and textile industries. And the 1928 AFL Convention at New Orleans adopted a resolution instructing the AFL to call a conference of "organizations interested in organizing in the South and officers of state federations in the South in the near future to work out cooperation on problems in Southern campaigns."[10] However, the February executive council meeting decided to hold this instruction "in abeyance until the time was ripe to hold a conference."[11]

Whatever the attitude of the AFL toward a southern organizing campaign—and the evidence suggests considerable caution by the executive council—dramatic developments in 1929 gave it no choice.

After 1923, the recession in the textile industry put pressure on the United Textile Workers to organize the south and prevent wage cuts and the "stretch-out" in both the north and the south. Although the New England mills were in bad financial condition, many of those in the south were making large profits. For example, the Cleveland Cloth Mills at Shelby, North Carolina earned between $30 and $102 for each $100 share of stock between 1929 and 1933.[12] Between 1923 and 1929, while over a million spindles were being added in the south, New England mills experienced bankruptcy and voluntary liquidation.

Northern owners responded by instituting an industrial rationalization scheme, and, in an effort to hold their share of the market, southern mills attempted to reduce labor costs by introducing the stretch-out, which made it possible to produce more with fewer workers.[13]

The AFL's problems were complicated by the weakness of the United Textile Workers, who had to receive aid from the federation, and the Communists' threat to fill the vacuum in textiles, coal, and other industries by organizing a dual union movement. After the National Textile Workers' Union was formed by the Communists in 1928, the UTW advised William Green that the new textile union was "a dual organization, communistic in character, and detrimental to the welfare of the textile workers as a whole."[14]

As a result of appeals from the south for organizing help, pressure from the Communist organizing campaigns, and criticism of the AFL for its failure to launch a campaign, President Green reported to the executive council in February 1929 that he had made two speaking trips into the south to build a favorable image of the AFL; he contacted outstanding men in an effort to get a publicity statement to "help in developing a healthy public opinion in support of cooperation and would cause a large number of influential men to look with a greater degree of favor upon the AFL." Green's proposed statement expressed the belief that any interruption of industrial production through strikes or lockouts was an economic waste, that every avenue of arbitration and mediation should be explored, and deplored unnecessary government interference in labor relations.

THE REVOLT

While the AFL was considering its future course in the south, a series of bitter strikes swept the industry; the three most important conflicts occurred at Elizabethton, Tennessee, and Marion and Gastonia, North Carolina.

Elizabethton. The Bemberg-Glanzstoff Company's textile plants at Elizabethton, Tennessee, where the first of the strikes started in March 1929, were established in 1926 by a group of German rayon manufacturers, who were granted tax exemption by the city which, unlike many textile villages, was not a company town. Though the rayon industry was in somewhat better economic circumstances than cotton textiles, the company had also felt the pinch of the recession, and countered by introducing the stretch-out.

The immediate cause of the spontaneous March 1929 strike at Elizabethton was the promotion of an unpopular worker, though there also was dissatisfaction over low wages. About 550 workers walked out the first day, but were joined within a week by the entire work force of 5000, approximately three fourths of whom were women and girls. During the first week, management secured an injunction, and national guard troops were sent in to protect company property. Paul Aymon, president of the Tennessee Federation of Labor, arrived in Elizabethton after the strike started and, with the aid of local craft unionists, formed a UTWA local of 2000 members.[15] Although a UTW local had been established at Elizabethton in 1928, it was not active at the time of the strike. A "Loyal Workers Organization" was formed in 1929 and told the company that it opposed outside unions and "at this trying hour for the management we take this opportunity of pledging continued support, loyalty, cooperation, unqualified and unreservedly."[16]

The first Elizabethton strike was settled on March 22 by an agreement between management, union, U. S. Department of Labor, and national guard representatives. The agreement provided for wage increases and for the rehiring of strikers. This agreement did not, however, end the unrest in Elizabethton. About one week after it was consummated, President Green's personal representative Edward F. McGrady, Alfred Hoffman, and a striker, were kidnapped; McGrady and Hoffman were transported out of Tennessee and warned never to return if they valued their lives. Actually, the kidnapping episode unified the workers and gained them some public support.

The companies set the stage for the second strike on April 15 by refusing to pay the wages which the workers thought had been agreed to and by discharging active union members who were presenting grievances in accordance with the March agreement.[17] This strike was contested more vigorously on both sides. After some minor violence, which occurred when the company attempted to reopen with strikebreakers, the governor sent two companies of national guards, who mounted machine guns on the factories. The troops were supported by management.[18] Strikers picketed in defiance of an injunction, resulting in 1250 arrests. The town's main waterline supply was dynamited May 16. The Communist-led NTWU sent agents from nearby Gastonia, North Carolina, to agitate against the UTW.[19] And, according to McGrady, "Sympathizers with mill management have had the union put out of its regular meeting place; young girls and young men were arrested for nonpayment of their board bills while they were on strike. The home of one of the leaders was blown to pieces; barns were burned."[20]

The AFL also sought to help the strikers. President Green addressed a rally at Elizabethton on April 7 and later told the AFL Executive Council that "we have succeeded in having the German President of the company removed and a new man assigned. In addition we have succeeded in having a liberal minded man installed as personnel manager."[21] Green explained that they had also succeeded in having some discharged workers reinstated. These results were achieved by "capitalizing on an inside fight" within the company through Lieutenant Governor Herbert H. Lehman of New York; "Lehman Brothers, Bankers, were represented on this Board."

In spite of this maneuvering in high places, local leaders finally saw the hopelessness of the situation and on May 25 accepted a settlement negotiated by a representative of the U. S. Department of Labor. The terms of this agreement amounted to complete defeat for the union, which was mentioned in only one paragraph: "The companies agree not to discriminate against any former employee because of his or her affiliations with the union provided the employee's activities were legitimate and were not carried on at the plants."[22] In spite of this agreement, hundreds of workers were blacklisted and gradually left the area as the completeness of the union's defeat became obvious.[23]

In March 1930, practically the entire work force struck for a third time because, among other things, of "discrimination against union members by the so-called 'impartial' personnel director."[24] Although the company was forced to go as far away as Kentucky and Georgia for strikebreakers, the strike collapsed after about a week.

Gastonia. The next important strike began at Gastonia, North Carolina, on April 1, 1929, but was conducted by the Communist-led NTWU and was not a spontaneous walkout like the other major southern strikes of this period.[25] The Communists decided to inaugurate their textile campaign by striking the most strategic company in the industry, the Loray Mill, of the Manville-Jenckes Company at Gastonia, the largest mill of its kind in America. North Carolina was the leading textile state in the United States, and Gastonia was the key textile county in North Carolina, making the Loray Mill the logical choice for an organizing campaign in the American textile industry.[26]

In the 1919-1920 textile boom, Gastonia had been very prosperous, at least from the standpoint of the owners of the mills. In this boom, according to Professor B. U. Ratchford, a native of Gastonia, a mill a week was organized in the town. It was also rumored that during this period the construction costs of a mill could be repaid with a year's earnings.

The stretch-out was the major cause of worker discontent at Gastonia, where wages were higher than those generally prevailing in the region. The Loray Mill was the only one in Gaston County to use this system to any appreciable extent, according to Ratchford:

> The result was that the workers rebelled. Far more than low wages and long hours, the easy-going southern worker resented this innovation that disturbed his routine of work, the constant pressure that kept him going at high speed and robbed him of occasional moments of rest . . . We may conclude, then, that the strike was made possible when the attempts to apply New England standards of efficiency to southern conditions, aroused the hostility of the worker.

There had been very little union activity in Gastonia before Fred Beal of the National Textile Workers started secretly organizing there and in the Charlotte area early in 1929, after Communist agents made a survey the previous fall and winter. The UTW had signed up many workers in the Gastonia district in 1920-1921, but withdrew after losing a strike—causing the workers to be bitter toward unions but giving the Communists an excellent propaganda weapon: "The UTW officials, after making many promises and collecting a considerable sum in initiation fees and dues, in the face of the pressure from the mill owners and their government, abandoned the field and left the mill workers to their fate."[27]

In 1929, the company discharged NTWU supporters as soon as it discovered their identities. The company's hostility and the workers' militancy, inculcated no doubt by the Communists' propaganda as well as their grievances, forced Beal to call a strike April 1, before he was ready. The strikers formulated the following demands, which management rejected: a $20 a week minimum wage, better working conditions, a five-day week, an eight-hour day, improvements in company houses, and union recognition. The mill was closed momentarily, but had little difficulty obtaining strikebreakers, and was soon operating at capacity.

There was no doubt that the Communists considered the Gastonia strike a key to their program to organize the industry. Albert Weisbord, NTWU secretary, noted that the strikes at Passaic in 1926-1927, New Bedford in 1928, and North Carolina in 1929, were "Three important steps forward . . . by the left wing forces in the textile industry since we first took upon ourselves the task of organizing the unorganized textile workers."[28] Weisbord also noted some differences in the New Bedford and North Carolina strikes which the Communists would have to understand and exploit: in New Bedford, the strike was restricted to one city, whereas in North Carolina it included a 100-mile area; North Carolina specialized in coarser cotton goods than New

England; New Bedford workers were mostly foreigners, while North Carolina workers "are Americans who could trace their ancestors at least to the Revolutionary War if not beyond"; New Bedford workers were more seasoned industrially than North Carolinians who were "fresh from the farms and mountains near the mills"; unlike New Bedford workers, the North Carolinians "had no property or material reserve power"; in New Bedford, defense work was mainly legal, whereas in North Carolina it "means an armed workers' defense corps ready to defend at any cost the lives and union property of the strikers against the open fascist attacks of the armed thugs of the company"; and, finally, the Negro question was of paramount importance in North Carolina, and "The solution of the Negro question in the South becomes the most difficult and at the same time the most vital and fundamental problem we have to solve. It presents us with an entirely new plane of tasks and difficulties."

Beal faced another unusual situation at Gastonia:

At first, nearly the entire force of 2,500 went out on strike. Then due to meager relief many of them drifted back. Within a few weeks they came out again. So that the scab of today was the striker of tomorrow, this, and the fact that most of the workers were related to each other, established a unique attitude on the part of the strikers toward the scabs. Elsewhere the scab or strikebreaker is regarded by the workers as the most contemptible of creatures; in Gastonia the scab was considered merely as a potential striker. Those that worked on the day shift attended union meetings on the lot in the evening; night shift workers argued strike issues with the strikers in the daytime.

The situation called for a different type of strategy from that usually practiced in strikes. I began to organize the scabs in order to have periodic walkouts to support the regular strike. Sometimes this succeeded. More often it failed because the plans would be betrayed to the bosses and at the crucial moment the mill doors would be locked, armed men would force the workers to remain at their machines, the militant scabs would be beaten up and fired. The rest would be cowed into submission. But not long. Soon another attempt would be under way.[29]

Although the strike was lost almost as soon as it started, the NTWU leaders continued their activities for propaganda purposes and in a desperate effort to realize their ambitious plans for the textile industry, which depended very much upon success at the Loray Mill. The evictions, arrests, refusals of credit and violence called for great expenditures for food, housing, legal and medical payments. The elaborate auxiliary organizations of the Communist Party came to the aid of the Gastonia strikers. The Workers' International Relief sent funds and trained leaders, while the International Labor Defense Press

Service sent well-trained publicity experts. The International Labor Defense sent expert legal assistance, while the Young Communists organized the workers' children for strike activity. Other organizations, such as the non-Communist American Civil Liberties Union, aided the union in its fight for civil rights. The Communists also made the most of their propaganda activity by sending delegations of impoverished, North Carolina workers into northern cities where they were used to demonstrate the effects of "capitalism" and to raise money, which, according to Beal, was used by the Communists for other purposes.

Strike meetings were conducted in open fields, and were addressed by union sympathizers and leaders. The following speech by Albert Weisbord, former leader of a woolen strike at Passaic, New Jersey, was typical:

> This strike is the first shot in a battle which will be heard around the world. It will prove as important in transforming the social and political life of this country as the Civil War itself. These yellow aristocrats have ground you down for centuries. Make this strike a flame that will sweep from Gastonia to Atlanta, and beyond, so that we can have at least 200,000 cotton mill workers on strike. You can't get ahead by yourself. Stick together! Don't listen to the poison of the bosses—extend the strike over the whole country-side. We need mass action![30]

The south responded quickly to the activities of these radical leaders. The *Gastonia Gazette,* and other southern papers, joined in denouncing the union. The radical utterances fed ammunition to this barrage. The conservative labor movement also joined the attack against the NTWU; President Green of the AFL sent a message to the central labor union at nearby Charlotte expressing his opposition to the strike.

The governor sent the national guard to the scene on April 4 after a picket line scuffle. Troops prevented picketing on mill property, but the strikers continued their activities in an area near the mill. Injunctions were secured forbidding all union activities, but these were ignored. Almost all sources report that violence was used against the strikers. Tom Tippett gives the following account:

> I saw a woman striker knocked down and struck with a bayonet until she bled profusely . . . a mob of masked men attacked the union headquarters . . . and destroyed every breakable article in sight . . . destroyed every article of furniture together with all food, and utterly demolished the entire building . . . Such indestructible articles of food as sugar and flour were dumped into the street on the car track. Then kerosene was poured over the mass, . . . While this wrecking was in progress 250 soldiers slept peacefully within 500 feet of the racket . . . When the last

ax fell on the food store the soldiers came running—arrested the strikers who had been guarding their property unarmed and who were being held at bay by the mob.

The leaders of the strike called upon the soldiers to mutiny with the following statement: "Workers of the National Guard! Do not accept the orders of the capitalist murderers . . . Refuse to shoot your fathers and brothers in the picket lines! Don't be a strikebreaking scab! Fight with your class, the strikers, against your common enemy, the textile bosses. Join us on the picket line and help win this strike."

The *Gastonia Gazette* and local citizens countered with equal vigor. An ad paid for by "citizens of Gaston County" in the *Gazette* declared in part: "The strike at Loray is something more than merely a few men striking for better wages. It was started simply for the purpose of overthrowing the Government and destroying property and to kill, kill, kill. The time is at hand for every American to do his duty."[31]

A so-called "committee of 100" was organized as a special police force when the remainder of the militia was removed April 20; many of the "committee of 100" were deputized as sheriffs or policemen.

Union leaders built a tent colony and a frame shack on the outskirts of town to house evicted strikers and serve as union headquarters. Armed guards were posted around this area and on May 16, union leaders informed the governor:

> The textile strikers of Gastonia are building . . . new union head-quarters to take the place of the one demolished by thugs, while the state militiamen were looking on . . . It is rumored around Gastonia that enemies of the workers, inspired by the mill owners, are plotting to wreck our new headquarters
> . . . it is useless to expect the one-sided Manneville [sic] Jenckes law to protect the life and property of the many striking textile workers of Gastonia. Every worker is determined to defend the new union head-quarters at all costs.[32]

The Communist leaders sought to keep the conflict alive, while the enraged community sought to end it. Local business interests ran full page ads in the newspapers, and the *Gastonia Gazette* printed a cartoon of an American flag with a snake coiled at its base and a caption which read: "Communism in the South. Kill it!"[33]

Appeals were also made to the conservative southern community's prejudice against foreigners. A handbill distributed in the area read: "Here are the names of the union leaders: Albert Weisbord, Michael Intrator, Lono Cherenko, Peter Russak, Peter Hegelia, Sonia Kaross. Are these American names?"[34]

Much was made of the fact that the Communists advocated racial equality. According to Paul Blanshard, who visited Gastonia: "The National Textile Workers Union believes in admitting Negroes and whites upon the same basis, and in a few instances Negroes have joined the union, although I have never seen one at a meeting." The strikers at nearby Pineville, who also were led by NTWU, objected to Negroes and whites working under the same roof and meeting in the same hall; employers at Pineville had conducted an unsuccessful "experiment" to replace white workers with Negroes causing almost all the whites to join the NTWU.[35] There is a tradition in the south that textile jobs are for whites, and, according to Blanshard: "The tradition is so strong that any manufacturer who imported Negro strikebreakers would be overwhelmed by community opposition. Incidentally, the Negro strike-breakers would be killed."[36]

Although there were almost no Negroes in the textile mills of the area, the Communists attempted to make the most of the race issue. A Communist publication declared "Special efforts were made, in the Southern textile mills, and successfully, to break down the racial pre-judices of the white workers and establish a solid battleline of black and white workers."[37] The Communist Party gave Beal orders to emphasize the Negro question. Beal "explained that there had only been two Negroes working in the mill and they had fled when the strike started. But Weisbord argued this situation involved other things than a mere strike . . . 'we must prepare the workers for the coming revolution' . . . I failed to understand how it was possible to bring into the strike the question of Negro rights when there were no Negroes involved. It reminded me of the time when the Party made the idiotic mistake in the miners' strike of placing in the demands of 'recognition of Soviet Russia.'"[38] Another Communist spokeman wrote: "Its leadership of the struggles of the Southern textile workers brought our Party for the first time in its history squarely up against the Negro question in its most acute form."[39]

The Communists had a policy of permitting separate unions for Negroes, but "only in those places where the reactionary unions bar Negro membership and we have no left wing unions." They were particularly disturbed because some of their most trusted leaders per-mitted segregation, and they were forced to take action against "comrades" who refused to integrate, especially in social affairs. At Norfolk, most of the whites were expelled from the Communist Party for refusing to admit Negroes.[40] However, the Communist Party later adopted the policy of permitting segregated organizations in the south, where Negroes wanted them, but not in the nonsouth.[41]

It became increasingly unlikely that the Gastonia strike would be settled without some catastrophe. Charles G. Wood of the Federal Conciliation Service investigated the situation, but announced that the only thing that could be done until "the misled workers divorce themselves from their Communistic leaders. . . . is just what is being done now in the way of protecting the rights of organized government by the military power of the community."[42]

The strike was brought to a climax on the night of June 7, when NTWU leaders decided to stage a parade around the mill in an attempt to induce the workers who had not joined the union to come out. The parade was intercepted, however, and many of the demonstrators were beaten. Police Chief Aderholt of Gastonia later arrived with four deputies, reportedly to investigate a fight among the strikers. There was an altercation, during which Chief Aderholt was shot. He died the next day. The outraged community was quick to react to his death. Officers arrested seventy-one persons, including three women, of whom the Gaston County Grand Jury indicted sixteen for murder and seven for assault with deadly weapons. Trial was set for July 29, and State Solicitor J. G. Carpenter announced that he would seek the death penalty against the thirteen male defendants.

On June 8, 1929, the day after the shooting, the *Gastonia Gazette* printed an enraged editorial, suggesting that "the display of gang law must not go unavenged."[43]

While preparations were being made to try the indicted strike leaders, the "Committee of 100," probably incited by the *Gastonia Gazette's* words, started hunting down the strikers. More than a hundred of them were caught and placed in jail. When ILD attorneys moved for a change of venue on the grounds that a fair trial could not be had in Gastonia, Judge M. V. Barnhill granted their motion, and the trial was moved to Charlotte. Although Judge Barnhill was widely acclaimed for his objectivity,[44] the Communists issued a statement proclaiming: "The false show of fairness of repeated hypocrisies about no economic or political beliefs of the strikers being admitted in the court room must be met by mass action of the workers."[45]

When the trial opened August 26 at Charlotte, the attorneys were among the most famous in the United States. Representing the prosecution, besides Solicitor Carpenter, were Clyde Hoey, the governor's brother-in-law; Major A. L. Bulwinkle, special counsel for the Manville-Jenckes Company and former U. S. Congressman, who was reelected after the trial; and R. G. Cherry, state commander of the American Legion. Representing the defense were Dr. John R. Neal, a famous defender of liberal causes who had been chief counsel for the defense in the Scopes trial and Arthur Garfield Hays, general counsel for the American Civil Liberties Union.[46]

The trial took on a theatrical appearance as the prosecution apparently realized that an appeal to the emotions was necessary to bring murder convictions against the sixteen defendants on the evidence available. Tippett describes the scene in the following words:

> Then Solicitor Carpenter arose to play his part. By order of the court he could not mention Communism, but Mr. Carpenter is resourceful. As he spoke there was wheeled into the courtroom a stretcher on which . . . lay Chief of Police Aderholt in effigy . . . The dead policeman's features were molded in wax, and he was dressed in the bloody uniform he wore at the time of the shooting. A juror sat transfixed with fright. In the jury room he went stark mad. His insanity caused a mistrial. With the jury dismissed five of its members told the press they would have voted for acquittal "if the state had no stronger evidence than what we heard."[47]

On September 9, the day of the mistrial, a mob raided union headquarters and kidnapped three men. They then surrounded the Charlotte jail, threatening defense attorneys and others sympathetic with the strikers.[48] On September 14, a mob shot into a truck load of workers killing Ella May Wiggens, twenty-nine-year-old mother of five children, whose name was flashed across the world as a martyr in the Communist cause.[49] Seven men were tried and acquitted for the shooting of Mrs. Wiggens.[50]

Another attempt to try the strike leaders got under way on September 30. Realizing the difficulty in convicting all 16 of the defendants for first degree murder, Solicitor Carpenter nol-prossed the charges against nine of the defendants and reduced the charges against the remaining seven men to conspiracy to murder and assault. During this trial the prosecution was again unable to shake the strikers' plea of self-defense,[51] but introduced the defendants' views regarding atheism, communism and race equality, and on October 18, the defendants were found guilty. The four northern defendants were sentenced to 17 to 20 years in prison; two of the Gastonia men got 12 to 15 years, and the other, five to seven years. In order to avoid serving the sentences, however, all seven defendants jumped bail; two went into hiding in the United States, while Beal and the others fled to Russia.[52]

Fred Beal returned to the United States in 1933. He published a book, *Proletarian Journey*, and a series of articles in the Hearst papers, in which he explained his dissillusionment with the Communists.[53] Beal was arrested in 1939 and sentenced to serve 17 to 20 years in North Carolina prison. He was released in 1942 and died in 1954.

The defeat of the union at Gastonia practically destroyed Communist trade union activity in southern textiles. In the light of subsequent history, the strike probably did the AFL more harm than good. It is true that some southerners began to express a more favorable attitude toward the federation,[54] but employers welcomed the AFL only until the Communist threat subsided. Charles A. Gulick argued that "It is not at all improbable that the Mitchell brothers are entirely justified in suggesting that the Gastonia incident may prove as unfortunate for the progress of unionization in the South as the Haymarket riot was for the labor movement in general."[55]

The workers at Gastonia, for many years afterwards, felt that they had been tricked by the Communists. Future events were to validate the *Gastonia Gazette,* editorial of October 22, 1929: "It will not be safe for any so-called labor agitator to be caught nosing around here any time soon. The folks here are simply not going to put up with it any longer." In the summer of 1930, during a spontaneous strike in Bessemer City, near Gastonia, the workers rejected the NTWU organizers who came in after the strike was called; the Communist leaders were "tied together by a rope and driven out of town by the strikers themselves while their literature was burned."[56]

The NTWU leadership was thoroughly discredited by its handling of the Gastonia episode.

Though one might have expected the Communists to mend their ways in the Gastonia situation with first degree murder charges pending, J. B. S. Hardman observed:

> The group exhibited the most appalling irresponsibility and disregard for the fate of the movement as a whole . . . The International Labor Defense is . . . primarily concerned with manufacturing martyrs in order to raise funds for the defense in order to advertise the revolutionary label of certain party leaders.[57]

Hardman pointed out that the ILD admitted such outside lawyers as Arthur Garfield Hays only under strong pressure.

Although it might have hurt unions, the wide publicity given the Gastonia affair stirred a southern interest in social and economic conditions.[58]

Marion. The third and most disastrous of the strikes occurred at Marion, North Carolina on July 11, 1929. The Gastonia and Elizabethton strike publicity made the Marion workers union-conscious. They accordingly went to Elizabethton, Tennessee, and talked to Alfred Hoffman, who promised to help them. The union was formed in April, and Hoffman took over its direction on July 10, the day before the first strike.[59] By July 11, when 22 workers had been fired for union activity, the workers decided upon a showdown. A local committee was chosen to present a list of demands to the manager of the mill. He rejected them and laughingly offered to pay them to strike.

The committee contacted Hoffman who in turn telephoned President McMahon of the UTWA in New York, and was urged to prevent a walk-out; the UTWA had a policy not to support strikes where unions had not been in existence for at least six months. But 650 workers struck the Marion Manufacturing Company against the UTWA's advice.

Hoffman not only had to conduct the strike at Marion, but was flooded with so many requests for organization from other places in North Carolina that President McMahon of the UTW ordered John A. Peel, one of his two South Carolina organizers, to Marion.[60]

In spite of Hoffman's effort to restrict the strike, because of inadequate relief funds, it spread rapidly as 1300 workers from the Clinchfield mills were locked out. The strikers' morale seems to have been good during the early days of the walkout. Indeed, union meetings took on a religious fervor as church songs and concepts were converted to the cause of unionism.

But as the strike wore on, the union encountered many difficulties. The UTW's inability to furnish adequate aid was a serious problem, even though church and labor groups sent money and other assistance to the workers. The strikers also had legal troubles from the beginning. A sweeping injunction, which the strikers ignored, was issued after the mill's manager claims to have been knocked unconscious in a scuffle between pickets and strikebreakers during the first week of the strike.[61] Some workers were charged with dynamiting a house, and the governor sent in two companies of militia on August 19. On August 28, several men removed a strikebreaker's furniture from the house of an evicted striker, prevented the sheriff from carrying it back in again, drove the officers away, and put the furniture back. Alfred Hoffman and 147 strikers were arrested and charged with "insurrection against the State of North Carolina." This charge was later reduced to "rioting," and on October 1, Hoffman and three strikers were convicted. Hoffman was fined $1000 and sentenced to thirty days in jail, and the three strikers were sentenced to six months on the chain gang.[62]

The antinorthern attitudes expressed during the selection of the jury for Hoffman's trial caused Stark to conclude that if the south were to be organized, it would have to be done by southerners.[63]

The strike was over for all practical purposes when the troops halted union activity, but it was not officially called off until September 11, after a conference between public, labor, and company officials arranged by L. L. Jenkins, banker and textile manufacturer from Asheville. This conference produced an unwritten "gentlemen's agreement" that hours were to be reduced to 55 a week for three weeks, after which the workers would vote on whether or not to return to the 60 to 65-hour week; the workers would accept a corresponding reduction in wages, and all of the strikers would be rehired with the exception of a few. Before the conference was over, Jenkins made a speech attacking the one-sidedness of the agreement.

The mill allegedly violated the contract and refused to rehire 102 of the strikers. Jenkins returned to Marion in an unsuccessful attempt to have the mills abide by the agreement. In the meantime, North Carolina braced for another strike at Marion. Union leaders who had participated in the Elizabethton strike urged another walkout, and management was advised that another strike would be called unless it honored the agreement; Francis J. Gorman, first vice-president of UTWA, and others advised the workers to strike if the company proved obstinate.

The second strike started on October 2, apparently because a twenty-two-year-old worker took a dare from a foreman, and "shut off the power and ran through the factory telling the workers to walk out."[64]

When the sheriff and his deputies, some of whom were petty company officials, attempted to disperse the pickets there occurred one of the most tragic episodes in southern labor history. A witness gives the following account:

> The sheriff immediately released tear gas into the strikers' ranks. George Jonas, a crippled mill worker, 65 years old, was standing right by the sheriff. As the gas burnt the old man's eyes, he, in pain or perhaps anger, began grappling with the sheriff. While the sheriff, who struck Jonas over the head with his gun, was handcuffing the old man, the deputies opened fire . . . Thirty-six strikers were hit by the bullets. Old man Jonas lay in the road, with a bullet in him, his hands locked together. Others lay moaning or dead in the dust. Two died instantly, Jonas and another one on the way to the hospital. Another was dead on the following day, and the sixth died several weeks later. The hospital was full of wounded strikers; 25 of them were seriously injured. Not one deputy sheriff or mill official was hurt. All the dead workers were shot in their backs, like rats, as they tried to escape from the burning gas. The strikers were caught in the narrow street and found escape difficult because of the concrete wall that blocked their way. Many of them were shot as they tried to scramble up that barricade.[65]

The plant manager's reaction to the killing was widely publicized.

Before a group of national newspaper correspondents he is reported to have made the following statement, which appeared in the *Asheville Citizen* on October 5, 1929:

> I understand there were 60 or 75 shots fired in the Wednesday's fight. If this is true there are 30 or 35 of the bullets accounted for. I think the officers are damn good marksmen. If I ever organize an army they can have jobs with me.
>
> I read that the death of each soldier in the World War consumed more than five tons of lead. Here we have less than five pounds and these casualties. A good average I call it.

A little over a week after the union men were sentenced for the "furniture incident," the trial of the seven deputies indicted for the murder of the strikers started in Burnsville with the American Civil Liberties Union assisting the prosecution. The deputies pleaded "self-defense" and were found "not guilty." In all the major strikes during 1929 not one nonunionist was sentenced for violence against union members, whereas in every strike union leaders and members were fined and/or jailed.[66]

The clergy in Marion offered little comfort and aid to the strikers during their difficulties. Union leaders from out of state conducted the funeral of at least one of the dead strikers, and at the mass funeral of another a mountain preacher offered the prayer when no other minister came forward. During the strike the Marion ministers preached against the strikers, and, after the tragedy, the Rev. S. J. McAbee sent letters to more than 100 strikers notifying them that they were dropped from the rolls of the East Marion Missionary Baptist Church.[67] Sixteen of these strikers were reinstated in May 1930, after the Federal Council of Churches exonerated them of any wrong-doing. The pastor of the church was reportedly a strikebreaker from South Carolina, and the clerk of the congregation was a supervisor in the mill.[68]

After the strike, the UTWA almost completely withdrew from Marion, though Tippett believes a stable union could have been built if men and money had been sent.[69] Lawrence Hogan, who had been instrumental in calling in Alfred Hoffman, returned after studying at Brookwood Labor College, and took charge of the situation there, but he was jailed for his part in the "furniture incident," effectively smothering the hope that a permanent union might be established.

Other strikes. These were not the only strikes in 1929. News of the three famous strikes inspired others throughout the south. Probably the most notable were in the important textile areas of South Carolina. There were 84,219 workers involved in 94 North Carolina strikes in 1929, and 1,071,861 man-days lost due to strikes; in South Carolina

79,027 workers were involved in 81 strikes with 1,459,885 idle man-days.[70] The South Carolina strikes were not as widely publicized and almost invariably occurred without union leadership. As a rule, George Googe or some other AFL representative contacted the strikers' grievance committees and capitalized on the unrest wherever large numbers of workers could be signed up easily. Perhaps the attitude of the Forest City, North Carolina, strikers was typical: " 'We don't want a union,' said a spokeman of the men to the writer. 'Some of us have been working for Mr. Little (the treasurer of the mill) for thirty years. We can get along with him. Let him fire that blue-bellied Yankee (the cost accountant, a native of Georgia), abolish the stretch-out system and give us some more money.' "[71]

Perhaps because no unions were usually involved, and because of violence elsewhere in the south, South Carolina officials exhibited considerable sympathy for the workers. About the only case of trouble in South Carolina came during a strike at Ware Shoals by 1000 workers who were protesting the stretch-out and other grievances. George Googe and UTW officials attempted to organize the workers' grievance committee into a local union, but the union leaders were asked to leave town after nonunion men demonstrated against them when they attempted to address a mass meeting.[72]

In other cases, South Carolina officials seemed sympathetic to the workers' grievances. Before the union came in, legislature had addressed the Ware Shoals strikers. A committee of the South Carolina Legislature found "the whole trouble in the textile industry where strikes have occurred has been brought about by putting more work upon the employees than they can do,"[73] and the sheriff at Greenville, South Carolina, said the strikers had "forbidden any bootleggers or liquor dealers of any kind to enter or practice their trade in their midst. They have put down drunkenness and they have established guard systems to protect the mill's property."

There were many leaderless walkouts in the Greenville area, all against the stretch-out and nearly all successful, according to Blanshard:

> Of the fifteen strikes against the system in this region in three weeks all but four have been won, and the leaderless strikers have returned with flying colors. The truth is that not one of these strikes could have been won if conventional strike tactics and union organizers had been used. The presence of an outside labor leader would have challenged that philosophy of class partnership which is the corner-stone of South Carolina life. For the time being the weakness of these leaderless strikers is their strength.

Local union leaders apparently concurred in these sentiments. The president of the South Carolina State Federation of Labor said the strikes were not the fault of the corporations but resulted from the introduction of a new system to South Carolina workers, who were

> . . . for the most part, conservative, almost to the extreme. The situation at Gastonia, N.C., is no indication of the attitude of the workers generally, but simply the first flush of resentment against methods and policies alien to those generally accepted through inertia.[74]

CHAPTER VIII

The 1930 AFL Organizing Campaign

There was mounting criticism of the AFL for its failure to capitalize on the militancy exhibited by southern workers during the 1929 textile strikes. These attacks came not only from the Communists and southerners who had been clamoring for organizing assistance since the middle twenties but included many non-Communist liberals. Norman Thomas and others formed the Emergency Committee for Strikers' Relief to raise funds for the strikers. After Alfred Hoffman appealed to the emergency committee for help with the Marion strike, Thomas wrote AFL President Green that the emergency committee had been an industrial Red Cross without attempting to dictate the conduct of the strikes. "I think you know," Thomas wrote, "that it was a substantial check from us which at a critical moment in Elizabethton helped to save the situation." He added:

> I think this statement of facts warrants my asking certain questions and making certain suggestions The Marion situation illustrates a condition . . . which does not promise well for the best use of the heaven-sent opportunity to organize the textile industry in the South. Here you have a strike against intolerable conditions in a field which is of vital importance to organized labor. The strike is in all respects regular but so far it has got little but kind words from the organized labor movement and other mills have been held back from following the example of the Marion strikers because of lack of relief funds. Thus opportunities are being lost.[1]

121

Thomas conceded that the UTW was weak, but pointed out that the AFL had few extensive strikes on its hands except in the textile area.

A. J. Muste of Brookwood Labor College was "puzzled and disappointed" at the way the strikes had been conducted.[2] It was sad, Muste wrote, if relief money were short when only 600 people at first, and at most 1700 were involved. When the strike was threatening, according to Muste, and the UTW organizer asked the AFL for help, he was told that North Carolina would have to finance its own strikes.

President Green told the executive council, in response to such critics, that there had been numerous strikes in the south, some of which were won and others lost or compromised: "We have been helping in every way. A lot of people think the AFL has not. Some criticize the Council and the AFL for what they alleged is indifference to the southern situation and the lack of support to what they have given the Textile Workers in their fight . . . In addition to the $19,000 which was turned over to President McMahon I have given all the support I could through correspondence and assigned representatives to help him."[3] After some discussion, the executive council passed a resolution pledging the UTW "all support and all assistance possible."

Representatives of southern federations met at Rock Hill, South Carolina, September 29, 1929, and repeated their request to the AFL. The matter came up again at the 1929 AFL convention in Toronto—dramatized by appeals from the Marion and Elizabethton strikers—and it was finally decided that a southern organizing campaign would be launched. President McMahon of the UTW planned to introduce a resolution calling for a levy on the membership of the AFL to support a campaign, but Green advised McMahon that the convention would not approve such an assessment. One week after the burial of the "Marion Massacre" victims, the 1929 convention authorized the federation's executive officers to raise funds to organize the workers and instructed the officers of the federation "to call a conference of all national and international unions for the purpose of devising a policy which will be acceptable to all interested in the proposed campaign of organization among southern workers regardless of craft or calling."[4] The executive council authorized Green to speak for the council, "and to give such confirmation to the action of the Conference as he in his judgment deems best."[5] He suggested that appeals for voluntary help be made.

THE SOUTHERN CAMPAIGN

Proponents of a campaign were encouraged by the militancy of the unorganized workers, the revival of craft union strength, the formation and reactivation of central bodies, and what seemed to be growing liberal sentiment. The Southern Industrial Conference (SIC) was organized in December 1927 to propagandize against low wages and poor working conditions; Bishop James A. Conner was chairman of its executive committee. In 1929, 415 North Carolinians, headed by Dr. Frank Graham, president of the University of North Carolina, adopted a "Statement on North Carolina Industry," approving the principle of collective bargaining. These liberal movements undoubtedly were stimulated by the publicity given the Communist activity at Gastonia and elsewhere.

President Green called a conference in Washington on November 14, 1929. There, UTWA representatives impressed upon the delegates both the impossibility of maintaining favorable labor conditions in the north if the south remained unorganized and the difficulty in carrying through a campaign with the meager finances at their disposal. President Green requested that each of the 105 affiliated unions lend at least one organizer to the campaign, and declared his intention to participate in the drive.

Realizing that they would have to provide most of the money, northern craft unionists at the meeting proposed a quiet campaign and argued against militancy, while all the southerners favored a bold policy.

Campaign headquarters were established at the Bankhead Hotel in Birmingham, and, early in January 1930, the first meeting was held at Charlotte, North Carolina. This organization meeting was attended by 229 southern delegates, organizers from 26 national unions, and representatives from seven state federations, a number of city centrals, and workers from 95 local craft unions.[6]

Besides its appeal to employers—which emphasized the AFL's "cooperativeness" and respectability in contrast with the Communists—the campaign sought to convince southern workers that their hours would be shorter, wages higher, and working conditions better if they organized. The AFL issued a *Southern Workers Handbook* which compared wages, hours, and working conditions in the south and non-south, adding that since "trade unions have set high standards in the North, we need unions here."[7] The AFL also sought to counter the charge that unions were foreign organizations by pointing out that there were 160 central labor unions and 6366 local unions in the south affiliated with the AFL.

Green made two tours during which he sought to project an image of respectability. He was emphatic in his denunciation of communism: "Its purposes are not our purposes. When we find a worker in our ranks subscribing to Communism—out he goes!" He told Mississipians of the American Federation of Labor's approach: "in the South workers are welcomed into the National Federation when they show unmistakable signs of desiring it. We welcome them, but do not force our organization upon them in any sense."[8]

The AFL had decided at the Charlotte conference to convince employers that if they espoused the union, not only would they be free from the evils of communism, but the AFL's efficiency engineer, Geoffery Brown, would show them how to improve their cost-price position.[9] In an attempt to implement this policy, Brown held over 200 conferences with southern managers between March 30 and September 31, 1930. Only three small Columbus, Georgia, firms agreed to try the plan. In return for encouraging their employees to organize, the AFL agreed to push the sale of the firms' products.[10] One firm, a hosiery mill, had a deficit for the two years of its existence; it realized considerable saving from Brown's survey, but not enough to eliminate the deficit. Brown's recommendation that the AFL lend the company some money for capital expansion was declined by President Green.

After Brown and the employers at another firm, a syrup mill, had signed an agreement, all the Negro workers were called together and told to elect officers; their understanding of trade unionism was indicated when they elected the superintendent as vice-president!

Meanwhile, other organizing methods were being tried. The United Textile Workers had five organizers in the south, the AFL had seventeen, and other national unions had thirty; these organizers were also aided by southern unionists. In October 1930, the AFL reported that it had organized 112 new locals, 87 of them in industries other than textiles. The UTWA reported in May that it had organized 29 locals with 10,340 members, but only 2175 were able to pay dues because of unemployment.[11] The membership gain attributed to the campaign through December 1930 was 2909.[12]

Two colored organizers, operating out of the Birmingham office, reported great success. To the AFL, Paul J. Smith, director of the campaign wrote: "The colored labor of the South apparently will be easier to organize than the white, but as a matter of policy we are trying to be careful and not shove the organization work among the colored people out in the spotlight of notoriety ahead of the organization of white labor."[13]

The Danville Strike. The nonmilitant approach was adopted chiefly because of lack of finances to support strikes and the desire to win the south to the idea of unionism. As time went on, however, the futility of this tactic became more obvious, and the AFL had difficulty checking

southern workers who wanted to strike in the face of growing opposition from employers and deteriorating working conditions.[14]

The union averted a showdown at all other places, but decided at
last to stake the 1930 campaign on a strike at the Dan River and
Riverside Cotton Mills at Danville, Virginia. The firm had 5000 workers
and about a dozen plants, one of which was reported to be the largest
cotton factory in the world.[15] Danville seemed a logical target for the
union because there was already a union there among the loom fixers.
The workers, unlike those in the other major strikes of this period, were
not fresh from the farms, many of them being second-generation industrial workers. The union probably launched the campaign at Danville
because the company's importance in the textile industry and its
history of fair labor practices gave the cooperative "no strike" policy
some promise for success. The company had a welfare plan which
included a YMCA, social workers, group life insurance, medical service,
higher than average wages, a 55-hour week, and a company union
patterned after the Leitch System of Industrial Democracy.[16]

The company union was formed after Local No. 1 of the Loom
Fixers' Southern Association had been organized in 1919. The company's president, H. R. Fitzgerald, explained his reasons for adopting
the Industrial Democracy system to his board of directors: "The whole
atmosphere, especially for the past few months [has been] surcharged
with labor troubles. Unions have been organized all over the South, and
with the backing of the Government Labor Departments, all of whom
seem to champion any demands that the Unions make, it has been
extremely difficult to keep our situation here free from complications."
However, the system broke down when the company tried to force a
10 per cent wage cut supposedly to bring its rates of pay in line with
competing mills; the wage cut was put into effect after it was accepted
by the "senate" (supervisors) but rejected by the "house" (workers).
Other grievances included: the stretch-out; the reduction on the
"economy dividend" (a bonus paid for labor saving) which had been
paid for a number of years; and dissatisfaction with the Industrial
Democracy System, which was considered a failure by workers and
management alike. In spite of the grievances, the union challenged a
mill whose workers were relatively well off. "If wages were not higher
at Dan River than at other southern mills, at least they were not lower;
and, with minor exception, labor relations had been conspicuously good
for nearly thirty years."

The Danville workers sent a delegation to Richmond, in January
1930, where President Green was speaking on his first southern tour,
to ask for help; Green sent Francis Gorman, vice-president of the

UTWA. By September, UTWA Local 1685 was formed, and the mills were almost completely organized. Gorman was careful to make the AFL's position clear to the Danville workers; he emphasized "that the union had no intention of stirring up strife. That would benefit no one. He was anxious that a system of cost accounting should be introduced which would help locate avoidable expense and point the way to elimination of waste and more efficient production."[17] Geoffery Brown called on Fitzgerald, Dan River's president, on March 26 to arrange a conference, but the president refused to discuss the matter. The company countered the growth of the union by laying off members and steadfastly refusing to deal with the union; it became clear that the UTW would either have to strike or leave Danville. On September 29, after mediation efforts failed, 4000 workers walked out. Crowds of pickets appeared at the mill gates and persuaded other workers to stay out. This and similar action the following day caused a county court judge to issue a restraining order the second day of the strike.[18] At the same time, William Murdoch, secretary of the Communist-led National Textile Workers' Union, came to Danville and distributed literature attacking UTWA leaders, but was promptly jailed for three months.

Public opinion seemed to favor the strikers:

> In the long months leading up to the strike the union had benefited from the friendly attitude of the public. The union used not only school grounds and the City Park for its meetings, but also the large hall owned by the Ku Klux Klan! Even the chief of police and his force were friendly. The union was allowed to picket all roads leading into Danville and to inform imported mill workers of the significance of the controversy. This they did without being beaten up by the police as happened in the other labor controversies of the South.[19]

The AFL convention met in Boston one week after the strike began and gave its official sanction, but failed to pass a resolution proposed by President McMahon of the United Textile Workers calling for some $300,000 a year to support the southern campaign;[20] this happened despite the realization that defeat at Danville would be fatal to the southern campaign and a serious blow to the labor movement.[21] Actually, the executive council and President Green had advised against the strike.

The UTW trained a corps of girls to tour the country to raise money, and circulars were distributed to central bodies advising against the strike, "though [the workers] were driven to desperation." However, according to the circular, "the company was determined to force the issue . . . The winning of the fight at Danville means permanent organization in the South to us."

There was some violence during October as more and more workers started crossing the picket lines; the tires of a nonstriker's car were reported slashed; a nonstriker's house was stoned; dynamite was thrown into an overseer's yard; and a Negro worker was badly beaten.[22]

Negro employees were ineligible for membership in UTW Local 1685 and remained loyal to the company. The policy of excluding Negroes had been adopted by the Industrial Democracy System in 1919 when a segregation "law" was drawn up restricting colored workers to certain occupations and providing for separate toilets; the "law" was introduced by the workers' representatives, though this had been company policy. A group of colored employees wrote the mill's president in February 1930 that they had confidence in him and their supervisors.

The mill reopened November 24 while police and troops prevented mass picketing, but many acts of violence occurred thereafter. Evictions from company houses were announced in December.

The problem of providing relief for some 12,000 people would have been more desperate if outside organizations had not assisted. The Emergency Committee for Strikers' Relief, church organizations, and other groups contributed thousands of dollars. The significance of relief is illustrated by the fact that: "The breaks in the ranks of the strikers, that is the period when large numbers of them lost hope and began returning to the mill, correspond with the times when union relief was scarce. Had the Danville strike leaders had adequate money to finance their struggle, the solidity of their lines would very likely have remained intact."[23]

In a speech in Danville on December 30, President Green asked that the strikers be allowed to return to their jobs without discrimination, that the issues be submitted to arbitration, and that the governor withdraw the national guard if management refused to comply with his recommendations. Dan River's president refused the request, and the troops stayed. Green's speech proved to be a great mistake because it gave the impression that the strike was over, causing contributions to fall off.[24]

The situation was such by January 1931 that Paul J. Aymon of the Tennessee Federation of Labor recommended to the AFL Executive Council that it call a convention of officers to raise a strike fund to be controlled by the AFL. The council replied, "While we would like to see it realized . . . it is impossible."[25] The AFL had issued two appeals for help since the October, 1930, convention, and $24,716 had been raised by January 15, 1931. Green also told the executive council that he had sent organizers to Danville to help, and he made a heartfelt speech on the futility of the situation.

Touched by Green's picture of the strike, McMahon asked the executive council for a statement emphasizing the need for money.[26] He reported that the UTW had taken $35,000 from its own treasury. At the same time, a strike meeting addressed by Sherwood Anderson in a hall owned by the Ku Klux Klan indicates the morale of the strikers at that late date:

> Fifteen hundred strikers squeezed themselves inside . . . The strike was very much alive and enthusiasm charged the air. Inside the mass sang a strike song to the music of "Jesus Saves." . . The hall resounded with familiar hymn tunes that now accompanied the story of why a union had come to Danville. The leader who directed the singing mass had formerly led the choir in the church at the cotton mill . . . A small boy, not yet in his teens, sang a solo accompanying himself with a guitar swung from his shoulder. It was called "Cotton Mill Colic" and accurately portrayed in comic vein the economics of the textile industry, as well as the tragedy of cotton mill folk, each stanza ended with:
>
> > "I'm going to starve
> > Everybody will
> > Cause you can't make a living
> > in a cotton mill."[27]

President Green received several reports on the Danville strike in mid-January 1931.[28] Matilda Lindsey, a native Virginian representing the Women's Trade Union League, reported that of 4000 strikers only 250 had gone back in four months, and about 2500 workers living in company houses had not received eviction notices. "This goes to substantiate the expression of the company, which is reliable, that they want their old workers back again, and there seems to be a splendid opportunity for us to get an honorable settlement provided we can continue to keep our people out of the mills."[29] The WTUL representative wanted an encouraging telegram from the AFL to offset the impression that the strike was over.

Organizer O. E. Woodbury reported that some of the strikebreakers were paid only half of what they were promised. "From reliable information we have learned that 23 car loads (of cloth) have been sent back to the mills rejected."[30] However, if all was not well with management, Woodbury's report indicated that the situation was infinitely worse among the strikers:

There is very little money coming in for the past two weeks and there is much suffering. Quite a number of the strikers are without food and quite a number are sick or having sickness in the family and we have two deaths this week. Heat has been provided by our men going 12 to 16 miles in the country and chopping wood . . .

With the spirit shown by the men and women engaged in this struggle it appears to me that they are worthy of more help than they are receiving which has been so far below their needs. All they ask is enough to keep body and soul together.

When Green brought these reports to the attention of the executive council, "The situation was discussed in reference to the policy of the Textile Workers in calling the strike against the advice and recommendation of the Executive Committee . . . Upon the conclusion of the discussion it was decided that the correspondence be filed and no action taken."[31]

In spite of these problems, Edward F. McGrady was not completely discouraged. He told the AFL Executive Council in January 1931 that the southern campaign had produced 122 new locals by the middle of November 1930, and that between then and January 14, 1931, five new wage agreements were negotiated, 12 new locals organized, 23 factories canvassed, 188 union meetings and 100 mass meetings held. McGrady had several suggestions for revising the southern organizing campaign: less time should be spent by organizers talking with organized workers and more contacting nonunion workers; organizers should stay in one place "doing personal work" rather than jumping from place to place; the Southern Organizing Committee (SOC) should meet quarterly in order to exchange information and "correct mistakes more quickly." In order to create more interest in the campaign, and "to arouse further activity on the part of the organizers of the International Unions," the SOC "suggested that you might consider calling another 'all Southern Conference.' "[32]

President Green had decided, however, that calling another conference would be "unwise and unnecessary," because some "effective work" was being done, through the traditional craft union approach of appealing to employers, in Augusta and Macon, Georgia, and Greenville, South Carolina, where "It seems there is not so much hostility among the mill owners . . . to the textile workers joining the union as there is in Virginia and North Carolina."

On January 29, 1931, the Danville strike was officially ended. Gorman made the proposal to end the strike at a union meeting on January 28; the next day, before leaving town, he gave the press a statement which said that the original strike was called because of discrimination against union members, but:

> ... during the past weeks it has been increasingly plain . . . by the action of the company in taking old employees back in the mills in considerable numbers without raising the question of union membership, that this principle of labor is being respected . . . With this fundamental principle no longer questioned, those especially charged with the interests of organized labor feel that the necessity for this strike no longer exists, and members of the union are called upon to return to work as promptly as places may be found for them.

A majority of the union members who crowded around the gates the next day to get their jobs back were told that they had been replaced. Whereupon the workers accused the company of betraying them, since the union leaders had led them to believe that there was an agreement with the company. Management vehemently denied any such agreement, and the press ridiculed the union for deceiving the workers.[33]

The Communists immediately attempted to capitalize on the UTW's defeat by "collecting information on everything those jokers did to sell us workers out."[34]

The defeat at Danville was a serious blow to the organizing campaign, though technically it continued until 1935. The Birmingham office was closed in 1932, and campaign headquarters moved to George Googe's home in Savannah until June 1933, when it went to Atlanta. After 1932, the campaign continued with several presidents of state federations of labor as organizers. In late 1934 and early 1935, those state presidents were removed from the AFL payroll for reasons of economy.[35]

Besides the traditional impediments to unionism in the region, the depression, inadequate finances and the weakness of the UTWA were probably the most important reasons for the defeat of the 1930 organizing campaign.

Only the textile workers felt that they had a sufficient stake in the south at this time to make a determined effort, but they lacked the necessary men and money to do the job. Vice-President Gorman told the 1930 UTW convention "This union work has been retarded because we had only three organizers in a territory comprising 1,440 mills and 300,000 workers."[36] Louis Lorwin concluded: "The workers asked why they should join a union that had shown itself incapable of supporting the promising beginnings made by the mill workers themselves. They had expected real aid from the AFL and attributed its failures to extend such aid to weakness and timidity."[37]

The strike at Danville was under the leadership of an organized union representing a vast majority of the employees in the plant, as contrasted with the earlier spontaneous, unorganized walk-outs. Public opinion was also in the workers' favor, though Dan River had been considered a good company and its working conditions above average for the south.

Considering these factors, it must be conceded that this was a test of strength between the union and one of the strongest employers in the south, who apparently had no help from other southern mill owners. It is true that the national guard prevented mass picketing, but only after the company had shown that it could secure sufficient strikebreakers.

Of course, the intransigence of Dan River's president was also a factor in the campaign's failure. The president attributed the workers' actions to the union "agitators and professional propagandists."

Fitzgerald died suddenly February 24, 1931. Robert Smith—who made an exhaustive study of the company—concluded:

> Although he was able to report to the stockholders in January, 1931, that the strike lost the company "but little inconvenience" since "old and loyal employees' reported for work promptly as the company had need for their services, the strain of managing mills surrounded by militia, like an armed encampment, the bitter abuse of those who held him personally responsible for the misery among strikers' families, and the ingratitude of those whom he regarded as the beneficiaries of his enlightened industrial leadership—these and other tensions growing out of the futile attempts to keep peace among laborers and make dividends for stockholders exhausted him.[38]

Other strikes. As the depression deepened and threatened the workers' living standards, many other protest demonstrations were staged throughout the region. A series of strikes which swept North Carolina in 1932 produced a somewhat different approach from that used by the AFL at Danville. During the year over 15,000 workers were out against thirty-five companies in the seamless hosiery, full-fashioned hosiery, silk, cotton mill, and furniture industries. These conflicts ranged in duration from a one-day walk-out to a fifty-eight-day strike.[39]

These strikes were significant for several reasons. In the first place, workers won partial victories in several places. Second, the leaders were southern workers. H. M. Douty believed this to be very important. "If there is ever to be a southern labor movement, southern workers must be largely instrumental in its construction." Third, a number of local organizations grew out of the strikes. The largest was the Industrial Workers of High Point, which had over 4000 members. The constitution of this organization made any industrial worker in the city eligible for membership. "Although the union is not formally recognized by the employers, partial recognition is achieved by the simple device of having the union committee members represent the workers in grievances that come up." The Industrial Workers of High Point planned to make the organization a social center for its members and had secured a large meeting hall. Dues were only fifty cents a month. Arrangements were also made with local merchants to give discounts to union members, and the organization provided aid for its needy.

SUMMARY AND CONCLUSIONS

The spontaneous strikes which swept the south in 1929 were not signs that the southern workers were ready to join unions to improve their conditions; they were acts of desperation to prevent the worsening of conditions which, while perhaps poor by nonsouthern standards, were improvements for workers recently removed from marginal agriculture. Although these spontaneous walkouts might have encouraged unions to come in in the hope of signing up large numbers of workers, they were only evidences of the workers' weakness, since many of them had already lost their jobs and others feared that they or their families would soon be unemployed because of the stretch-out and the recession in the industry.

The AFL was at this time neither financially nor structurally suited to organize the industrial workers, in spite of the pockets of craft union strength throughout the area which might have been used as springboards. The AFL itself was not the main organizing body in the American trade union movement, and the nationals, which were primarily concerned with organizing, were more interested in signing up workers who were within their jurisdictions than helping the weaker unions. The local unions and central bodies were not prepared to give the necessary support.

The AFL's "industrial cooperation" approach in the 1930 organizing campaign was not only poorly conceived, but showed lack of confidence because it indicated that the unions were not willing to undertake the type of campaign that might lead to strikes which would, in turn, have to be supported by sizable financial contributions. Craft unions can organize employers instead of workers because they have considerable control of the supply of labor and can therefore help employers stabilize their industries. Textile unions, on the other hand, were far too weak to protect employers from competition. The unions hurt their organizing chances for years to come by abandoning the workers when the strikes were over; and there was some outright deceit by the unions in their dealing with the workers.

The Communists might have filled the vacuum left by the AFL, but their leaders exhibited little understanding of the situation, and really had no interest in building permanent job-oriented unions; they were much more interested in publicity and sensationalism, and were thoroughly discredited by their activities during this period.

Police, the national guard, and injunctions were frequently blamed for the failure of the unions, but this is obviously superficial. The main reason for the loss of these strikes was the ability of the employers to recruit strikebreakers from the vast pool of unemployed and underemployed workers in the region. When employers could get enough workers to reopen, the strikes were over. Injunctions were frequently issued in this period before the Norris-LaGuardia Act, but the evidence suggests that they were not major impediments to the strikes because they were frequently ignored by the workers.

It is, of course, highly unlikely that the unions could have organized the south even in the absence of these obstacles. A number of other basic impediments were at work: the prevalence of company towns made it easy for employers to defeat strikes by evicting workers and denying unions the use of company property; the competitive nature of the south's leading industries, especially coal and textiles, combined with their chronic overcapacity during this period; and the stretch-out to put the employers under no pressure to deal with unions, particularly in view of the deepening depression.

The period here considered was probably the time of greatest labor unrest for textiles, the south's leading industry. With the coming of the New Deal, the main organizing activity shifted to basic industries outside the textile areas.

PART III
The Depression and the New Deal

CHAPTER IX

Coal Mining

THE UNITED MINE WORKERS

Our discussion of unionism in the coal industry in Chapter V illustrated the impact of unionism in the south on the nonsouth. The United Mine Workers' failure to extend unionism to the south during the 1920's greatly weakened their entire collective bargaining machinery in the United States; as noted earlier, by the time of the depression, the UMW's strength had been reduced to sections of Illinois and Indiana and parts of the southwest. But during the 1929-1941 period the United Mine Workers extended the union shop to virtually every major coal field in the United States and practically eliminated the north-south wage differentials. The UMW's experience is important to an understanding of the factors responsible for the spread of unions, because other industries, like textiles, with many of the same conditions, could not be unionized in the south during this period.

Kentucky. One of the most important coal fields was in Harlan County, Kentucky, which also proved to be one of the most difficult organizing situations ever attempted by the UMW, the Communist-led National Miners' Union, and the Progressive Miners.

With the aid of the federal government, the UMW had established collective bargaining in Harlan County during the First World War, but the union was wiped out during the 1920's. A senate investigating committee found that unions were suppressed in the 1920's by company towns, "policed by large bodies of men, privately paid, many of

137

them clothed with public authority as deputies. Many of them were seasoned criminals who had been released from the State penitentiary."[1] The county acquired such a reputation that even organizers with experience in West Virginia reported Harlan to be "far worse" than anything they had ever witnessed.

The United Mine Workers launched a district-wide organizing campaign in Kentucky May 20, 1929, and enrolled 12,000 workers in a relatively short time.[2] These successes were short-lived, however, and the UMW was defeated and virtually driven out of Kentucky between the summer of 1930 and the spring of 1931. The IWW, the NMU, and other rival organizations attempted to fill the gap between the time the UMW was defeated in 1931 and its return in 1933. The IWW led a strike in Bell County in 1931, but the operators, aided by depressed economic conditions, countered the union's activities with violence and arrests for "criminal syndicalism."

The violence was not limited to the coal operators, however, because the miners armed themselves and fought pitched battles with deputies, strikebreakers, and plant guards. On April 17, 1931, for example, a deputy was killed near Evarts in a battle between Black Mountain Coal Company strikers and deputies, and on May 5, 1931, one striker and three deputies were killed.[3]

Governor Flem D. Sampson of Kentucky appointed a commission on November 7, 1931 to investigate conditions in Harlan county. Referring to one witness, the commission report found "conditions almost too horrible for belief; yet the facts he testifies to are borne out and substantiated by other apparently creditable witnesses who testified before this commission. Here is work for a grand jury not afraid of coal operators, miners or 'the law' that is now in power in Harlan." The commission observed, after another witness told of having been falsely arrested and mistreated by a raiding party which included the city judge: "If this man's statements are true, the law acts rather unlawfully in Harlan County." In another case, Mrs. Harry Appleton was arrested for criminal conspiracy for feeding some 50 children a day from her small store in Evarts; of this, the commission observed: "Here, it seems, the finest trait and virtue, charity, was illy rewarded by the authorities."

After investigating conditions in Harlan and Bell counties during the year following February 1931, the American Civil Liberties Union found: "Eleven people have been killed (five deputies, four miners, one organizer from Connecticut, and one Harlan County storekeeper sympathetic with the miners). . . Scores wounded. . . Men have been taken out and flogged, and deported from the state. . . Buildings have been dynamited. . . Sympathizers have been arrested, beaten or deported. . . Two union leaders have been sentenced to life imprisonment. . . Over one hundred others have been indicted either for criminal syndicalism, banding and confederating, or conspiracy to murder. . . Only one man among the gunmen is held for the shooting of miners."

Nor did conditions in Harlan County improve much in the next few years. In 1932, a subcommittee of the United States Senate held hearings in Harlan, found violations of civil rights and recommended further investigations. In the spring of 1935, a state commission appointed by Governor Ruby Laffoon reported that it was:

> . . . almost unbelievable that anywhere in a free and democratic Nation such as ours, conditions can be found as bad as they are in Harlan County. There exists a virtual reign of terror, financed in general by a group of coal mine operators in collusion with certain public officials; the victims of this reign of terror are the coal miners and their families. In Harlan County we found a monster-like reign of terror . . . whose tentacles reached into the very foundation of the social structure and even into the church of God.[4]

National Miners' Union. The Communist-led National Miners' Union (NMU) sought to take advantage of the widespread unrest resulting from the depression and the blacklisting of miners involved in the 1931 UMW strike. The NMU called a strike for January 1, 1932, which involved Bell, Harlan, Knox, Whatley and other counties, "with at least 10,000 miners answering the call."[5] It soon became apparent, however, that this was less a strike than a relief operation for unemployed or blacklisted miners.[6]

Local officials countered the NMU's activities by raiding union headquarters at Pineville and arresting six men and four women including an ILD defense attorney, on charges of "criminal syndicalism."[7]

The New Deal. As noted in Chapter V, at least partly because of its inability to protect the central competitive field by organizing the south, the UMW's membership declined greatly during the 1920's, and the union was unable to regain its losses before 1933. John L. Lewis' rivals claimed that the UMW had only 84,000 of the 522,000 bituminous coal miners organized in 1930.[8] Alabama District 20 had 23,000 members around 1920 but almost none in 1930. Membership in Kentucky had declined from 19,000 in 1921 to 100 in 1932. Of 112,000 miners in West Virginia in 1932, only 6000 were covered by UMW contracts.[9] The mine workers' membership had shrunk to such an extent that the union was relieved of part of its per capita tax payments by the AFL.

From this low ebb, the UMW's total membership reached 541,000 by April 1935, and membership growth in the south was no less spectacular: membership in southern West Virginia went from seven in June 1933 to 85,764 in June 1935. Membership in Alabama District 20 increased from 225 in June 1933 to 18,000 in July 1933 and 20,000 by the beginning of 1934.[10] By the time of the 1934 UMW convention, every commercial mine in West Virginia had been organized. The miners had 100,000 members in West Virginia and about 90,000 in all other southern states.

Although 95 per cent of the anthracite and bituminous coal workers in the United States were union members in 1934, several major coal operators did not have contracts with the UMW, and most of these were in the south: the captive mines of the United States Steel Company at Gary, West Virginia and Lynch, Kentucky; the Alabama Fuel and Iron Company; the Western Kentucky Coal Company and other companies in western Kentucky; the De Bardeleben mines in Alabama; and the Harlan County fields. The UMW had a contract with the Harlan County Coal Operators' Association in 1933, but the employers refused to renew the agreement in 1935, and signed a contract with the Progressive Miners' Union, which had taken over a "company union."[11]

Rival unions. The major captive mine operators in the south and elsewhere formed company unions in an effort to forestall legitimate unions and meet the requirements of the NIRA. These so-called employee representation plans were formed by southern local subsidiaries of the U.S. Steel and Republic Steel Corporations in June 1933.[12] The following excerpt from a letter of June 15, 1933 (one day before President Roosevelt signed the NIRA) by the president of the Tennessee Coal, Iron, and Railroad Company to its Alabama employees, leaves little doubt as to the company's motive for forming the Employee Representative Plan (ERP):

> The Tennessee Coal, Iron and Railroad Company, adhering to the principles set forth in the 'National Industrial Recovery Act,' has inaugurated a plan of Employee Representation under the provisions of which the employees of our various plants and operations will have a voice in matters pertaining to industrial relations.
>
> It is hoped that you will secure a copy of the Plan, read it carefully, and give it your hearty support. We would suggest that arrangements be made promptly to have this Plan become effective by nomination and election of representatives as provided under the Plan.[13]

The UMW also faced competition from a number of rival unions, the most important of which was the Progressive Miners of America

(PMA), whose main strength was in the nonsouth, virtually all of which was in former UMWA District 12 in Illinois. Although the PMA was also active in Kentucky and in West Virginia, it was never able successfully to challenge the UMW. The UMW also had competition from the Independent Miners' Union in western Kentucky, and the West Virginia Miners' Union.[14] In addition, we saw that the UMW had minor difficulties because of the activities of the Communist-led National Miners' Union.

Employer attitudes. But neither rival unions nor employers caused the UMW much trouble. In view of the past opposition from coal operators, it is perhaps surprising to see how rapidly the UMW's whirlwind organizing campaign in the summer of 1933 resulted in the unionization of 95 per cent of the industry. Although a great majority of the workers undoubtedly were ready for unionization, as they apparently always had been, the unique thing about the 1933 campaign was the limited amount of employer opposition, particularly outside the south. It might be argued that the NIRA made the difference, but this is hardly an acceptable explanation in view of the successful resistance of the captive mine operators and the major Alabama producers. The apparent explanation is that the majority of northern mine operators were willing to deal with the UMW because the industry needed stabilizing, and because production in the southern nonunion fields had grown impressively. The situation in the industry was such in 1933 that some coal operators suggested a federal coal dictator and even told the secretary of labor that they would "sell the mines to the government at any price fixed by the government. Anything so we can get out of it."[15] A group of operators from western Pennsylvania called on Secretary of the Interior Harold Ickes in April 1933, and asked:

> for a bill setting up what amounts to a Federal coal dictator. They want the Federal Government to take over the industry, establish minimum wages, regulate output, and set a minimum price . . . F. E. Taplin, president of the North American Coal Company, who operates in three states, and who is the president of a railroad . . . advanced exactly the same position.[16]

In May, a group of coal operators from Illinois and Indiana made the same proposal to Ickes, who wrote:

> They lay most of their ills to differentials in wages between their fields and other fields. In Illinois and Indiana the basic wage is $5 a day, while in other competitive fields as low as $1 a day is paid, with the result that outside coal can undersell Illinois coal even in the Chicago market, in spite of the advantage Illinois has in freight rates.

However, many southern coal operators were opposed to a coal code. Ickes noted on May 11, 1933:

> A. Mitchell Palmer, who was Attorney General in the Wilson administration, came in on behalf of clients who are coal operators, protesting against any special legislation dealing with the coal industry. He plainly represents that group from West Virginia and one or two southern states that are reputed to be paying their labor a dollar a day.

Citizens in the coal districts were also calling for unionization. Conditions were so bad in West Virginia in 1930 that coal was selling at below cost, wages were extremely low, and some companies were bankrupt. Resolutions were adopted at public mass meetings in Morgantown and Fairmont:

> We believe the United Mine Workers of America is the only stabilizing influence in the coal mining industry . . . therefore . . . this public mass meeting . . . goes on record as unqualifiedly asking the coal operators to meet the representatives of the United Mine Workers . . . for the purpose of negotiating a uniform wage scale . . . and consider and act on such matters as will stabilize the coal mining industry and be for the best interests of all concerned.[17]

The UMW's importance as a stabilizing influence was magnified by the uncertain legality of collusive measures by the operators themselves, the absence of a dominant firm or group of firms in a highly competitive industry, and the importance of labor costs. They varied greatly as a proportion of total cost—depending upon general technical and geological conditions—but in 1945 constituted about half of total costs in strip mining to over three fourths for hand mines; the average for all mines was about 63 per cent.[18]

The history of wage negotiations in the next few years reveals the main conflict to have been as much between northern and southern operators as between the UMW and the operators. Indeed, the question of north-south wage differentials was the subject of "bitter debate and heated squabbles," which, according to UMW's officers, had come up at every Appalachian joint conference in the 50 years before 1936.[19] By 1934, the old central competitive field had been surpassed by the Appalachian region as the main coal producing area in the United States. Operators in this region, representing about 70 per cent of the nation's bituminous coal production, formed the Appalachian Joint Conference (Ohio, Central and Western Pennsylvania, West Virginia, Eastern Kentucky, Tennessee and Virginia) and entered into an agreement with the UMW under the auspices of the NRA on September 21, 1933. This agreement established a basic wage of $4.60

a day south of the Ohio River and $5.00 a day in the north. Wage agreements had been signed by the time of the 1934 UMW convention in all districts except Alabama—"due to peculiar conditions there not yet overcome"—and some companies in western Kentucky.

Alabama. The "peculiar conditions" in Alabama were the number of companies that refused to deal with the UMW, the nature of the market, and the narrow coal seam which was relatively expensive to mine.

William Mitch and William Dalrymple came to Birmingham early in June 1933 to reorganize Alabama miners.[20] There were at that time only about 225 UMW members in two locals, but the response to unionism was so rapid that by July 23, 1933, 18,000 miners had been enrolled in 85 local unions.[21] These successes contrasted with the UMW's failures during the preceding ten years, when the international had spent $2,000,000 in unsuccessful efforts to organize Alabama.[22] But, as noted earlier, in spite of these membership gains, a number of Alabama coal producers refused to deal with the UMW, and the signing of the coal code on October 2 did not bring peace to the coal fields. There were strikes throughout the state in 1933 and early 1934, mainly for union recognition and the check-off. They were particularly violent in the Cahaba field which supplied about half the domestic coal for the Birmingham market. The national guard was sent in February after pickets at the Piper mine of the Little Cahaba Coal Company and the Coleanor mine of the Blackton-Cahaba Coal Company prevented workers from returning to work and disarmed 15 guards. The strike spread to include 7000 miners in seven companies by the end of February. The companies said they were willing to bargain but refused to check off union dues. Union leaders announced that 16,000 Alabama miners would strike unless the coal board acceded their demands for the check-off. The unions' ability to strike was strengthened considerably when Mitch had the international union apply pressure in Washington to require the local relief administrator to allow the distribution of relief to strikers.[23]

The divisional coal board sought to end the walkout March 7 by ruling that the miners had violated the code by striking and that collective bargaining could not be resumed while the strikers were out; the board said that the workers would forfeit their rights unless they returned to work by March 12 at noon. However, some 11,000 strikers refused to return, and armed Negro and white miners sought to close additional mines. On March 13, the national guard was increased from 80 to 320 troops at the request of a local sheriff who claimed: "It's a question of bloodshed or backing down. I have temporized a week with them in the face of strong pressure to call out the troops. This morning the pickets absolutely refused to obey the orders of my men."[24] There appear to have been no significant clashes between the troops and the strikers. Indeed the UMW commended the national guard commander, "not alone for his services in bringing about mediation, but also for the consideration he and his officers and men under him had shown in the field."

An agreement was finally signed on March 14 between the UMW and 38 companies, representing 90 per cent of the operators and 85 per cent of the commercial coal tonnage in the district; the captive mine operators in the district had already signed the standard captive mine contract with the UMW. The agreement increased the basic wage from $3.40 to $3.60 a day, and granted the check-off and other features.[25] However, Alabama operators still had lower basic daily wages than other southern areas.[26]

Missouri, Arkansas, Kansas	$4.60
Southern Tennessee	4.44
Western Kentucky	4.60
Southern Appalachian	4.60
Fairmont, West Virginia	5.00

Two large Alabama operators—the De Bardeleben Coal Corporation and the Alabama Fuel and Iron Company with 800 and 1200 employees, respectively, refused to sign an agreement with the UMW. Henry De Bardeleben, head of De Bardeleben, said his company had an agreement with a company union; Charles F. De Bardeleben, Sr., head of Alabama Fuel and Iron also dealt with a company union.

The antiunion attitude of the De Bardelebens was a tradition handed down from father to son, and it continued to guide the company's policy.[27] The De Bardelebens were also willing to help other firms resist unionization. In 1934, for instance, De Bardeleben is reported by the La Follette Committee to have lent three machine guns to the West Point Manufacturing Company of West Point, Georgia, which was resisting a textile workers' organizing drive.[28]

After some violence, De Bardeleben and the UMW signed an "understanding" on April 2, 1934, worked out by a federal investigator, whereby the company agreed to withdraw a temporary injunction against the union, cancelling a hearing to make the injunction permanent scheduled for April 17. The UMW agreed to hold no meetings on company property without the latter's consent; to have circulars and other literature signed by the district president or his assistants;

to make every effort to prevent marches against the company's property by workers from other mines; to make every effort to prevent the gathering of armed groups near the company's property; and to prevent the intimidation of the company's workers. The company agreed to prevent the intimidation of workers; to reduce the number of deputy sheriffs; and to reinstate the workers who went out during the general strike of March 1934. It was understood that no new men would be employed until all those desiring employment were reinstated and that persons discharged after October 2, 1933 could have their cases reviewed by the Divisional Coal Labor Board if they so desired. De Bardeleben agreed to notify its employees that they were free to join or refrain from joining any labor organization.[29]

This understanding did not, however, restore peace to the Alabama coal fields, and there was considerable violence and destruction of property in subsequent months as company officials resisted the miners' organizing activities. In December, a U.S. Department of Labor investigator upheld the union's charges that the company had sponsored a company union in its mines and had coerced and intimidated its employees against affiliating with an independent union. According to the investigator, "A situation at the company's Margaret and Acmar mines is extremely dangerous and may at any time result in wholesale bloodshed."[30] This was prophetic, because one worker was killed and ten wounded the following October when 1500 strikers engaged in a pitched battle with company guards.

In spite of much agitation, most of the mines of the De Bardeleben interests remained unorganized, except for one at Overton, which Alabama Fuel and Iron promptly closed when the workers voted for the union in August 1934. A management spokesman said:

> To us this matter is a tragedy. These men have switched their allegiance. It is up to them to shift for themselves. They have found an arrangement that suits them better.
> Our relations, until recently have been entirely amiable. Never has there been a sack of Red Cross flour or a pound of relief food at Overton. We have given these people all the land they could cultivate. We have built them community houses, furnished them mules and cows free and seed at cost. They pay 90 cents a month for hospitalization which included all their medical and surgical fees, dentistry excepted. Charles De Bardeleben has danced at their weddings and wept at their funerals. He has encouraged and aided them to become self sustaining . . . what other answer could we give to such an apparent repudiation of what we had come to cherish as an unwrittten law of allegiance one to the other?[31]

The Overton workers naturally had a different story; they issued a statement saying the UMW had opened their eyes to the fact that the union had been responsible for their short hours and good wages.

'We know that the miners have not received the full provisions of the coal code or the same wages and conditions that the miners in other sections . . . of Alabama now receive and we have had to work . . . overtime without pay and have had to go back on idle days to timber and move rock and do dead work without pay.

When we organized into the UMW of A, this Alabama Fuel and Iron Company told us that if as many as 15 men joined the UMW of A, that they would shut the mines down. This shows how much they regard the bituminous coal code.

All we want is a square deal that the President of the United States promised us and the bituminous coal code and the industrial recovery act guarantee us, that is the right to join an organization of our own choosing and the right of collective bargaining. We are only asking our God-given right to live in decency the same as the coal miners of all other sections are now enjoying.'[32]

The unionization of Harlan County. The other major nonunion area was the Harlan County Coal Operators' Association (HCCOA). The UMW launched a new organizing drive in Harlan when the Wagner Act was passed in 1935, but was defeated by the same tactics of violence and intimidation as in the past. In another organizing effort in January 1937, the UMW held a convention in Harlan attended by delegates from other districts, and again the HCCOA resisted. According to a report to the 1938 UMW convention: "Our men were followed. Their rooms were gassed with tear-gas bombs. Organizers' cars were shot into the representative that president Owens sent in [was] shot from ambush." The father of three boys who witnessed the ambush of the UMW organizers' car was shot and killed when his sons were subpoenaed by the La Follette Committee; the small son of a UMW organizer was killed by shots fired into his home—the organizer had left the area on the advice of friends who feared for his safety; a deputy sheriff who became concerned about these atrocities was shot and left for dead by fellow deputies.[33]

When its direct efforts to organize the Harlan operators were repulsed, the UMW attacked them indirectly through the federal government. The La Follette hearings March 22-May 5, 1937 focused worldwide attention on the county, and the HCCOA seems to have been overcome by this adverse publicity as well as by the Supreme Court's decision in May 1937, upholding the constitutionality of the Wagner Act; the new Kentucky law making it illegal to deputize guards, company officials, and deputy sheriffs; and an indictment by a federal grand jury in September for conspiracy to deprive the miners of their rights under the Wagner Act. Though the jury deadlocked in the conspiracy case, company officials, who had suffered considerable embarrassment because of the publicity given the trial, capitulated and signed a contract with the UMW on August 19, 1938, covering 13,500 miners.[34]

The indictments against the Harlan operators were not dismissed, however, and served the UMW to advantage in 1939, when six southern coal associations, including the HCCOA, refused to accept the Appalachian Joint Conference's recommendation for the union shop. Although the Harlan County operators sought to remain non-union, the other five associations—Big Sandy Elkhorn Coal operators, Hazard Coal operators, Kanawha Coal operators, Southern Appalachian Coal operators, and Virginia Coal operators—signed the Appalachian agreement with the respective UMW district organizations. The HCCOA's action produced new violence in Harlan, forcing Governor Chandler to send in the militia. Two strikers were killed by militiamen on July 12 when they and other pickets attempted to keep strikebreakers from going to work.[35] Approximately 300 strikers had been arrested by the time a settlement was finally reached on July 19, 1939.

The Harlan County operators agreed to the settlement in July 1939, after special agents of the Department of Justice came to Kentucky to prepare for a retrial of the conspiracy indictments, which were dismissed in September 1939. Although the HCCOA did not grant the union shop until 1941, the 1939 agreement caused membership in the Harlan County area, which had been around 5000 in May 1937, to rise to 15,000 in 1940. UMW membership in Kentucky was about 38,500 in 1939.

Thus, after years of conflict almost all the major southern operators—with the exception of the De Bardeleben interests in Alabama—were organized by the UMW. The UMW hailed the signing of the Harlan contract.

Wage developments. The UMW's experience with the north-south wage differential was similar to its efforts to obtain the union shop: the greatest resistance to wage equalization came from the south, and again the Alabama operators remained the major exception to the union's success. The UMW's experiences during the 1920's demonstrated the problems for the union in the north unless it equalized wages. The UMW, with considerable pressure from northern operators, sought the NRA's help in abolishing the regional wage differential.

But NRA Administrator Hugh Johnson elicited bitter protest from

southern employers with an order of March 31, 1934, which attempted
to establish a daily wage of $4.60 for the bituminous coal industry and
reduce hours from eight to seven. The average daily rate in Alabama would have increased from the $3.60 established the previous
month to $4.60, and the differential between northern and southern
fields would almost have been eliminated. Since 40 cents a day
represented about 3.6 cents per ton, more than offsetting usual profit
margins of between 2 cents and 3 cents a ton, this equalization order
naturally evoked bitter opposition from the south, especially from
Alabama, where operators obtained a federal district court injunction
against the NRA and launched a campaign of political pressure and
publicity against the NRA's effort to abolish north-south wage differentials.[36] The Alabama producers argued that "very much lower"
production costs made it possible for northern operators "to ship coal
into . . . Alabama at a lower price than Alabama coal can be delivered,"
and that many markets, "including Memphis, have been entirely lost
to the Alabama mines." The Alabama operators also pointed out that
the northern mines had a freight rate advantage because the Interstate Commerce Commission required the southern operators to pay
35 cents a ton more for coal shipped above the Ohio River, while
northern and southern operators paid the same rate on coal shipped
into Memphis.[37] The Alabama employers' resistance movement was
joined by others throughout the south, and by April 5, 40,000 miners
were locked out or on strike in southern Tennessee, western Kentucky
and northern Georgia. In Alabama, the only major mines remaining in
operation were those of De Bardeleben, and even these mines were
closed temporarily when they were marched on in April by a large
number of strikers.[38]

While NRA hearings were going on in Washington under the federal
district court injunction, and thousands of miners were on strike or
locked out, Alabama operators instigated a meeting of the Southern
Industrial Council in Birmingham to discuss the fight against the
NRA.[39] The Southern Industrial Council meeting was attended by
300 operators, from a variety of southern industries, who were told by
a Tennessee woolen manufacturer that the "fight against the Alabama
coal interests is but the entering wedge of a broader and more disastrous program against the entire South." The NRA's order was said
to have caused serious disaffection "everywhere except in Pennsylvania,
which would profit from the proposal." The industrialists were also
given a report from the strike in the coal fields which "presented an
alarming picture of conditions there with groups of armed Negroes
moving over the countryside."

The NRA hearing opened in Washington on April 9, 1934. Birmingham attorney Forney Johnston presented the Alabama operator's argument that special conditions made it difficult for them to pay the same wages as the northern operators. John L. Lewis answered the Alabama operators' defiance of the coal code with: "If they feel that way, the United Mine Workers are ready within fifteen days to furnish the President with twenty army divisions to force them to comply with the law." As Johnston sought to answer, Lewis continued in his inimitable fashion:

> The chief dissenter to this order is representative of a group in the state of Alabama . . . They seek to make a virtue of the fact that they were able in the precode days, to impose upon the workers in the coal industry in Alabama more degrading working conditions and a greater degree of medieval barbarism . . . than was the case in any other group of the coal industry of the country . . .
>
> Mr. Johnston's opinion of this hearing is that it is largely stage play for publicity purposes. I assume Mr. Johnston, when he said that, was somewhat inebriated by the exuberance of his own verbosity . . .
>
> And be it said to their dishonor, the Alabama operators are reneging on [their] agreement, which is not an honorable thing to do.[40]

However, Lewis' oratory and political strength were not enough to overcome the opposition of politicians, industrialists and others from the south. The NRA was forced to revoke the order of March 31, and President Roosevelt issued a statement requesting that the southern coal strikers return to their jobs peacefully; he said the Recovery Act recognized geographical differentials.

The new wage scale was announced April 23, 1934, and provided for an increase of 40 cents a day as compared with the $1.20 ordered earlier. The new daily rates for southern areas became:

Alabama	$3.80
Missouri, Arkansas, Kansas	4.35
Southern Tennessee	4.24
Western Kentucky	4.60
Southern Appalachian	4.60
Fairmont	5.00

Under the new agreement, Alabama operators agreed not to sell coal in other areas at less than the established price.

The major conflicts over wage differentials after 1934 involved disputes between northern and southern coal operators, with the United Mine Workers allied with the northerners in an effort to eliminate the differentials, to close "uneconomical" mines, and to stabilize the industry. The UMW remained the main "stabilizing" force when the NIRA and the Guffey-Snyder Act, which sought to achieve that objective, were declared unconstitutional in 1935 and 1936 respectively.

On July 5, 1941, after President Roosevelt and the NDMB intervened to halt a coal strike, the UMW signed an agreement with southern coal operators which eliminated the 40-cent north-south wage differential. The basic daily wage became $7.00 a day, and the union shop became universal in the commercial mines, even in Harlan County. The UMW thus claimed to be "the first union to wipe out the wage differential between North and South."[41]

It is not entirely accurate to say, however, that the UMW eliminated the north-south wage differential, because wages in Alabama were still lower than those of other areas. Also, while the day rates were equalized between regions, the differential rate per ton remained. In 1941, for example, the rate per ton for pick mining was $1.10 in central Pennsylvania, $.96 in northern West Virginia, $.87 in the Kanawha area, $.752 in the Hazard Kentucky area and $.75 for the southern Appalachian area.[42]

Racial practices. The racial policy of the United Mine Workers was another factor making it possible for them to organize southern miners. The union had been weakened in the past by racial dissension in the south, though the international union seems consistently to have followed a policy of organizing all miners regardless of race or national origin.

This does not mean, however, that Negro members of the UMW had no grievances against their union. There were some complaints, for example, concerning the absence of Negro representation in official positions, and discrimination against Negroes in some mines.[43]

As compared with most other unions at the time, however, Negroes had few significant complaints against the mine workers. The UMW's racial approach was particularly important in Alabama where almost half the miners were Negroes, and where racial divisions had hampered unionization during the 1930 AFL southern campaign because segregationist organizations like the Ku Klux Klan refused to permit Negroes and whites to join the same unions. Because of the number of Negro workers and the traditional alliance between Negroes and employers, the UMW knew that it stood little chance of organizing Alabama unless the colored miners were won over. Of the approximately 23,000 UMW members in Alabama in 1935, fully 60 per cent were estimated to have been Negroes.[44] Although complete unity between the races could not be achieved in such short order, the following description of an Alabama union meeting during the 1930's indicates the progress that had been made in this direction:

> The conduct of the mixed meetings is a most interesting study in shifting patterns of behavior. Neither race shows distaste for being present together in the same hall, but each preserves a plain if unspoken racial distance. Almost without exception the two races sit in segregated parts . . . Quickly the custom was established to have a White president, a Negro vice-president, a White secretary and treasurer, and minor offices nearly all Negro . . .
>
> Negroes are never Mister, and are seldom Brother . . . But the Negroes do not protest the absence of marks of social recognition; they agree with the Whites that the unon is an association for economic purposes only.[45]

The custom of having a white president, Negro vice-president, white secretary and treasurer, and Negro minor officers was called the "UMW formula" and was adopted by other basic industries around Birmingham with large proportions of Negroes. The "UMW formula" permitted white men to negotiate with the operators at first, gave Negroes union experience, as well as let white workers and bosses get accustomed to the idea of dealing with Negroes. However, Negroes continued segregating themselves in union meetings, and the UMW's racial policies—which were carried over into the Alabama State Federation of Labor—did not go unchallenged.

When William Mitch started reorganizing Alabama coal miners in 1933, he was assisted by Walter Jones, a Negro miner who joined the UMW in 1891. (After serving in various official positions in Alabama, Jones was commissioned an international organizer in 1918, but when the 1922 strike was defeated, he was blacklisted and went to Ohio to get work. He returned to Alabama in 1933 and joined as a field worker in the UMW organizing campaign.) The UMW's efforts in organizing Negroes caused little attention until the 1934 strikes when Alabama whites became alarmed at the aggressiveness of Negro strikers, especially when it became generally known that the Communists were concentrating on organized Negroes in Birmingham and surrounding areas. For example, an editorial in the Birmingham *Age-Herald* noted:

> The wholesale unionizing that has taken place in recent months has included Negro as well as white miners. As a matter of organizing strategy, that was a shrewd step, although it does run counter to the practice of the AF of L in the past. But as things have worked out, Negroes have been conspicuous in demonstrations and other activities. What the arming of people who nurse their own racial grievances could lead to must be left to the imagination. This is another reason for a balanced and creative policy on the part of union leaders.[46]

A 1936 dispute within the Alabama State Federation of Labor demonstrated the racial attitude of Alabama white workers during these years. John W. Altman, General Counsel of the ASFL for twenty years led an attack on the racial policies of the UMW and the state federation, especially its president, William Mitch, who was also president of UMW District 20.

At the Alabama state federation, Altman accused "Mitch of Indiana" of practicing "what the Communists preach on Negro equality in the ranks of the United Mine Workers and in Organized Labor." Altman concluded:

> Organized labor in Alabama will not tolerate social equality between the whites and the blacks as advocated by the Communists or by any other[s] . . . These Communist papers praise the UMW very highly because there is no discrimination between the whites and the blacks in the UMW . . . They have many local unions wherein the President is a Negro and the Vice-President is a White man. I do not stand for that. I oppose that. It will be the ruination of Organized Labor if carried into effect.[47]

Several white UMW members answered Altman by saying that he did not object to Negro members so long as he could take their money. While these charges and counter charges were undoubtedly based on political considerations, they motivated the *Union News* to make its position clear:

> The *Union News* will oppose any attempt to place the negro and white upon social equality. We do not hesitate in pointing out the importance of educating the negro and helping him secure a decent wage for his work . . .
>
> Walter Jones is a negro. He represents the negro side of the organization's activities and as such representative takes up their problems, both with the district office and with employers. Walter Jones respects the white man for his color . . .
>
> If the negro is ignored by the white miners the companies will use them to further their own selfish end and bring both down to the utter depths of starvation and long hours.[48]

Thus, the UMW's racial policy did not go unchallenged. Alabama workers were not prepared to accept racial equality, but the policy of stressing the economic need for cooperation within the labor movement succeeded in unifying the Negro and white workers in industries like coal mining.

The autonomy question. Another factor which undoubtedly influenced the UMW's ability to organize the coal fields of the south was centralized control within the international union. As noted in Chapter

5, the organizing situation confronting the UMW required centralized direction and fiscal responsibility because of the different conditions and large geographic area to be covered. History had also convinced John L. Lewis and the international's officers that a single wage scale had to be established to prevent the weaker districts from cutting wages and destroying the scale as they had done during the 1920's. It was obvious that the organizing task would be lessened considerably if a sizable number of employers were willing to cooperate with the union in return for its stabilizing influence: this was considered by Lewis to be an impossible task without centralized direction.

District autonomy was one of the most debated questions at the UMW conventions during the 1930's. John L. Lewis had used his power to revoke district charters and appoint provisional officers to gain almost complete control of the international union by 1932; by the time of the 1934 convention only 10 of the union's 30 districts had autonomy, and two thirds of the convention delegates came from the provisional districts. The southern districts were singled out by Lewis as illustrations of what would come of autonomy; he repeatedly recounted the international's troubles in the south where the districts "went down because of excessive democracy" during the 1920's.[49] Shortly before the 1938 convention, the *United Mine Workers Journal* told how the Baldwin-Felts detective agency had been hired to agitate the autonomy question, claiming that "Autonomy in West Virginia at the present time would turn the whole organization of the United Mine Workers of America into the hands of certain labor-hating coal companies and their Baldwin-Felts thugs."[50] These sentiments were echoed by John L. Lewis who told the convention: "Now there are two sides to this autonomy question. A child can only be given so much responsibility, and if we sometimes elect men to office who are either inexperienced or not sufficiently equipped and not sufficiently honest to be true to their membership, someone has to pay the fiddler."[51]

CHAPTER X

Communists, Socialists, and Sharecroppers

ECONOMIC CONDITIONS

The efforts to organize southern agricultural workers during the 1929-1941 period attracted worldwide attention because of the publicity given their abject poverty at a time when industrial workers were being exhorted to organize. Their poverty and the fact that a large proportion of them were Negroes created ideal conditions for the Communists.

In 1929, 57.1 per cent of the farms and 54.1 per cent of the crop land in the south were harvested by 1,762,000 tenants. Of this number, 773,000 were sharecroppers[1] who harvested 25 per cent of the farms, but only 15 per cent of the crop land; the Agricultural Adjustment Administration (AAA) program contributed to a decline in the number of sharecroppers to 540,000 in 1939, at which time croppers cultivated only 18.9 per cent of the farms and 12.7 per cent of the land.[2] The proportion of farms operated and acreage harvested by tenants increased after 1890, reaching a peak in 1929 and declining thereafter, but the absolute number of tenants reached a peak in 1935.

The economic condition of these workers was much worse relatively than that of nonagricultural workers with similar skills. For example, average hourly earnings of agricultural laborers in 1929 were about

154

17 cents an hour, while common laborers in road building earned an average of 28 cents.[3] A WPA study in 1934 found that the average family income for sharecroppers was $363, which rose to $400 in 1937, a relatively good year for southern agriculture.[4] Gunnar Myrdal and associates reported a net cash income of $300 for the average tenant family in 1937.[5]

The President's Committee on the Economic Conditions of the South reported in 1938: "Of the 1,831,000 tenant families in the region, about 66 per cent are white. Approximately half of the sharecroppers are white, living under economic conditions almost identical with those of Negro sharecroppers."[6] Economic conditions in the region prompted President Roosevelt to declare: "It is my conviction that the South presents right now the Nation's No. 1 economic problem—the Nation's problem, not merely the South's. For we have an economic unbalance in the Nation as a whole, due to this very condition of the South."

COMMUNISTS

For the Communist Party, agricultural labor activities were a part of the larger program of organizing those industrial workers who had not been approached by the American Federation of Labor.

The pre-1928 Communist policy of "boring from within" did not succeed with Negroes in the south because Communist leaders, failing to understand the importance of the church as an opinion-molding institution, alienated church leaders; they also approached the Negro race as if it were a class, whereas Negroes have a class structure reflecting that of the whites.[7]

From 1928 until the "united front" movement against fascism in in 1935, Communists organized dual unions, and the fifth point in the seven-point program adopted at the Sixth World Congress of the Comintern in 1928 called for the development of "A Solid Communist Party and revolutionary trade union movement among workers, Negro and White in the South."[8] The southern activities of the National Miners' Union and the National Textile Union were a part of this program, though the theory of "self-determination" for Negroes which occupied a central place in Communist plans,[9] was directed mainly at agricultural workers.

The Communist theory was that a separate Negro "nation" would be formed in a "Black Belt" extending from the Potomac into Texas, which contained a continuous area of counties with Negro majorities.[10] The Communists thought that the Black Belt met Stalin's definition of a nation as "an historically developed lasting identity of language, territory, economic life and psychology."[11] They later attempted to clarify the theory, which appeared to be a segregation policy, by explaining that, although this was to be their main program for the south, in the north they were to promote a slogan of "equal rights." They emphasized that the "Northern struggle was linked with that of the South in order to endow the Negro movement throughout the U. S. with the necessary effective strength."[12] The program also called for the "confiscation of the landed property of the white landowners and capitalists for the benefit of the Negro farmers," and provided that the Negro "nation" thus established in the Black Belt "would be free to secede from the U. S."

The program first called for organizing industrial workers around the basic industries in Birmingham, which had a high proportion of Negroes. Industrial unions would form a base from which to organize the Black Belt of Alabama, and from there organization would spread throughout the southern states.

Probably the most effective agency for these goals was the International Labor Defense (ILD) organized in 1925. We have noted the ILD's activities in the southern coal mining and textile industries, but it gained most of its publicity in the famous Scottsboro case in which nine Negro boys were indicted for raping two white women in March 1931. The widespread coverage of the Scottsboro trial helped Communist fund-raising activities and strengthened the Party among Negroes.[13] The widespread publicity given the trial brought funds into the Communist treasury, caused greater disrespect for the law, in accordance with the Communist plan for "mass pressure," and angered the southern white population, but did little to insure that justice would be done. After the 1934 party line change, the ILD allowed the NAACP, the ACLU, and other less radical organizations to handle the case; only then was a compromise reached which resulted in the release of four of the accused.

The Sharecroppers' Union of Alabama. The Communists started their southern organizing activities after the 1928 Cleveland meeting of the Trade Union Unity League (TUUL), but it was not until after 1931 that they exerted their major effort. The Sharecroppers' Union of Alabama (SUA) was organized that year, its growth coinciding with the Scottsboro case. Although the Sharecroppers' Union also had some membership in Louisiana and other southern states,[14] apparently the Communists were principally interested in Alabama.

The SUA's activities were vigorously resisted by rioting and mob action. Beginning in 1934 the SUA conducted a number of strikes in an effort to raise the price for picking cotton from the prevailing 40 cents a hundred pounds. Although these strikes persuaded some planters to raise wages,[15] they were usually violently suppressed and ineffective except for their propaganda value.[16] One of the largest, involving 3000 cotton pickers on a plantation in Lowndes County, resulted in the death of one SUA member.[17] This strike was almost completely undermined by September when most of the pickers returned to work for the same pay.[18] In 1935 the SUA shifted its headquarters to Montgomery to take advantage of the unrest among sharecroppers who were being displaced by mechanization and the New Deal's agricultural policies. Although the union enrolled many workers in the area, its 1935 strikes were no more successful than those the previous year. The union claimed some concessions in a month-long strike in the spring, but the community countered with a "great wave of terror."

The union claimed 12,000 members by the end of 1935, 2500 of whom were in Mississippi, Louisiana, Georgia, and North Carolina. At that time it proposed a general strike throughout the south, and sought a unity agreement with the Southern Tenant Farmers' Union (STFU), formed in Arkansas in 1934, which was preparing for a similar strike. The Communists invited H. L. Mitchell, Socialist leader of the STFU, to Montgomery to discuss the possibility of unity. But Mitchell told the writer: "I found out this was a Communist underground movement among Negroes and suggested to our board that we have nothing to do with them."[19]

After the Communist Party-line change dictated that member organizations join with other groups, the Alabama Sharecroppers' Union was taken over by the Farmers' Union of Alabama, an organization of small operators formed in 1930, and others went into the Alabama Agricultural Workers' Union chartered by the AFL in 1937 as the Farm Laborers' and Cotton Field Workers' Union No. 20471. The latter claimed 10,000 members in the spring of 1937, shortly before it was absorbed by the United Cannery, Agricultural, Packing and Allied Workers of America, CIO (UCAPAWA).[20]

The Communists thus had relatively little success with their program for "self-determination," though they succeeded in establishing a base in the Birmingham area among Negroes in the iron ore mines organized by the Mine, Mill and Smelter Workers. In spite of their difficulties in attracting Negroes and building stable organizations in the Negro community, the Communists had nevertheless acquired some influence in the Negro world by 1935, especially among intellectuals. Their failure was mainly in terms of their inability to gain a mass following.

SOUTHERN TENANT FARMERS' UNION

While the Communists were attempting to carry out their program in Alabama, tenant farmers and sharecroppers in other areas of the south were seeking organized help to redress their grievances. One of the most lasting of these organizations was the STFU. The STFU's primary objective was to eliminate what the tenant farmers, wage hands, and Socialists considered inequities in the New Deal agricultural program, but their plans subsequently expanded to encompass other goals, including collective bargaining and legislation to improve the desperate conditions under which the workers lived.[21]

The conditions of Arkansas tenants, sharecroppers and agricultural laborers were so bad by 1930 and 1931 that bread riots were staged in a number of places.

Although the croppers were encouraged at first by the Roosevelt administration's promise to do something to improve their conditions, they were bitterly disappointed by the New Deal. Indeed, conditions were frequently worsened because the production limitations imposed by the plan caused the displacement of many croppers. When the AAA program went into effect in 1933, it was on the basis of a land rental contract between landowners and the government whereby the land was taken out of production. Since tenants and sharecroppers were not landowners, they were not parties to the contracts, and the only benefit they received was a possible increase in cotton prices and half of any "parity" payments on cotton produced on land still cultivated. The planters consequently received about 90 per cent of the government payments.[22] The government sought to prevent this by requiring provisions in contracts to protect tenants, but these were often breached by the planters or their representatives, who were usually the local administrators of the program. The relief measures given destitute farmers and workers overcame whatever paternalistic inclinations many planters had to protect their workers, while mechanization and production controls threatened to displace tenants and turn them into wage hands.[23]

During the early days of the depression, some citizens of Tyronza, particularly Clay East, a service station operator, and H. L. Mitchell, a former sharecropper and owner of a pressing establishment, met frequently to discuss solutions to the economic conditions. Some of Huey P. Long's "Share the Wealth" clubs were established in the area, but Mitchell and East rejected Long's ideas of solving the farmers' problems by state legislation to halt agricultural production.

Mitchell, East and others were attracted to Socialist ideas by the writings of Upton Sinclair and by Oscar Ameringer's *American Guardian,* a weekly published at Oklahoma City; they were also greatly impressed by Norman Thomas when he came south during the 1932 presidential campaign. Consequently, a Socialist organization was started in Tyronza which many Negro and white sharecroppers joined.

An absentee owner from Kansas City produced the "cause célèbre" when he decided to evict some sharecroppers in 1934. Planters in the Tyronza area commonly allocated land and supplies to their croppers on the basis of the number of workers in a family, but paternalism and loose business practices frequently permitted exceptions to this formula by giving more land to families with unusual need. The Kansas City planter discovered that the ratio between people and land was too great; he also advocated that the customary share going to croppers be reduced from one half of the total crop to one third because of production limitations imposed by the New Deal program.

A number of Negro and white croppers from his land started holding meetings. Some of the Socialists suggested joining the Farmers' Union, but the croppers were not interested because it was made up of workers in better circumstances.

The immediate impetus to the formation of the STFU came from Norman Thomas. The Socialist League for Industrial Democracy also financed a survey, headed by a University of Tennessee professor, which substantiated the charge that sharecroppers were being evicted in spite of the alleged AAA guarantees.

The first local of the Southern Tenant Farmers' Union was formed at an abandoned school on the land owned by the Kansas City planter. A white chairman and a Negro vice-chairman were elected, establishing the pattern subsequently followed by the STFU of having white presidents and secretaries and Negro vice-presidents. Although the STFU held integrated conventions, some of its locals were segregated, and it conducted some segregated educational meetings.[24]

The organization's constitution was modeled after that of the Renters' Union of Oklahoma. The STFU was incorporated under an Arkansas law providing for the chartering of farmers' unions, granges and cooperatives. The initiation fee was set at 25 cents and dues at 10 cents a month or $1.00 a year. The initial program adopted by the organization was limited to securing a share of the government crop restriction money for sharecroppers.

Because of the popularity of its program, and because Clay East was elected constable of Tyronza and deputy sheriff of Poinsett county, the STFU's membership grew rapidly. East's presence gave the STFU a cloak of legality and overcame the workers' fear of opposing the powerful planters.

The early activities of the union gained some publicity and ultimately attracted considerable help throughout the country. In addition to financial contributions, many people volunteered their services.

STFU's racial practices and its program to challenge the planters brought about considerable opposition. Union meetings were frequently interrupted, and organizers and members beaten.

Attitude of the New Deal. In keeping with its primary objective of securing part of the crop reduction payments for croppers, the union challenged the Kansas City planter in U. S. District Court after he had served eviction notices on between 30 and 40 tenants. The court decided in 1935 that the croppers had no legal right to bring action against planters because they were not parties to the rental agreements; only the secretary of agriculture and the planters could sue under these agreements.

After some difficulty, the secretary of agriculture, Henry Wallace, promised to send a representative to Arkansas to investigate the complaints.

Chester Davis, administrator of the AAA in the Department of Agriculture, considered the sharecroppers' problems but saw little the AAA could do for them. He felt a surplus of labor in the cotton belt to be the basic problem, but thought the sharecroppers would have been displaced by day laborers if the federal government required cash payments to croppers. Davis nevertheless held up the 1934-1935 cotton contract for several weeks in order to insert a clause, over strong planter opposition, requiring the retention of the same number of tenants that existed in 1933.

However, this did not prevent the displacement of tenants, because there was no way to force employers to keep the same tenants and bcause the planters had considerable control over the local administration of the AAA program. The STFU was therefore forced to resort to publicity to get the the Department of Agriculture to do something to help the sharecroppers.

The croppers also had friends within the department, especially Gardner Jackson (who acted as Washington representative for the STFU), Jerome Frank, later a judge of the U.S. Court of Appeals (USDA General Counsel), Lee Pressman, the chief counsel for the CIO in 1935-1948, and, in 1937-1938, lawyer for SWOC, Alger Hiss, and Frederic Howe, a progressive with service under the Wilson administration. A scheme devised by this group to help the share-croppers precipitated a crisis within the department. Alger Hiss wrote a reinterpretation of the AAA contract requiring the landlords to permit every individual tenant to remain in his place during the life of the agreement. This reinterpretation was sent out in 1935 as a directive, while Davis was away from Washington.

When Davis returned, he revoked it, fearing that it would lead to outbreaks of violence in the south, and prevailed upon Wallace to remove Frank. Wallace agreed that the liberal group had "allowed their social preconceptions to lead them into something which was not only indefensible from a practical agricultural point of view but also bad law."[25] Davis prevailed upon Wallace to get rid of the liberal group except for Hiss, who Davis believed was misled by the others.

The STFU was thus disappointed in the federal government's approach to its problems, but the union profited from the publicity. Rockwell Kent designed a stamp to "End Peonage in Arkansas," the American Civil Liberties Union posted a $1000 reward for anyone giving information leading to the arrest and conviction of persons abridging the civil liberties of sharecroppers, and many distinguished visiters came to see the conditions of the Arkansas tenant farmers. Henry Wallace made a southern trip in 1936.

Communist efforts to capture STFU. The Communists, having failed to effect a merger between the SUA and the STFU, sought to influence the latter organization from within. One of their main techniques was to have Communists join wherever possible. Sometimes STFU leaders were known Communists. They also sought to gain control through the Commonwealth Labor College at Mena, Arkansas. Commonwealth had been established by a group of Socialists in the early 1920's as a labor training school; the president of the student association in 1935 was a young Arkansan named Orval E. Faubus. Until about 1938, when the school was reorganized, the Communists apparently were not in control of Commonwealth, and the school contained all shades of political opinion.

Harry Bridges, president of the International Longshoremen and Warehousemen's Union on the West Coast, and Donald Henderson, former assistant professor of economics at Columbia (who claimed his dismissal was because of Communist affiliation) were interested in forming an agricultural and cannery workers union at a meeting in Denver, July 9-11, 1937, at which the STFU was represented. The president of the STFU, J. R. Bulter, became vice-president of the United Canning, Agricultural, Packinghouse and Allied Workers of

America (UCAPAWA) formed as a result. When the STFU became a part of UCAPAWA it claimed 50,000 followers and 4000 to 5000 dues payers on an irregular basis.

The merger with UCAPAWA was never very firm, however, because Mitchell and other STFU leaders felt that the Communists were attempting to destroy their autonomy. After the Denver convention, the STFU convention met in Memphis to decide its relationship with UCAPAWA. Because of his fear of the Communists' designs, Mitchell had attempted to get John L. Lewis' agreement for a separate charter, but Henderson told the delegates that the only way STFU could become a part of the CIO was through UCAPAWA. STFU leaders had given the CIO such a buildup with their members, and the CIO was so popular with Negroes at the time, that it was impossible for Mitchell and his followers to block the alliance. The STFU thus became the southern division of the UCAPAWA.

During 1937-1938, however, the Communists spent considerable time attempting to gain control of the STFU. Because the STFU had a small minority on the UCAPAWA Executive Board, it was ineffective in opposing the Communists within the organization. An appeal was made to John L. Lewis, but Lewis told the organization to exhaust all possibilities within the UCAPAWA before calling on him.

In the summer of 1938, while H. L. Mitchell was on an assignment for the National Youth Administration, STFU's president, J. R. Butler, uncovered evidence that the Communists were attempting to take over the union. A leader of the plot, a member of STFU's executive board, left his coat containing some Communist literature in Bulter's home. One of the documents was addressed to the Central Committee of the Communist Party of the USA and outlined the importance of Commonwealth College and the STFU for the Communist program.

The executive board member denied that the document was really a report to the Communist Party, claiming that it was written by one of the students at Commonwealth College. The STFU Executive Board expelled him. He appealed to the 1939 convention, but the executive council's action was sustained.[26]

After this, Donald Henderson precipitated a complete break between the STFU and UCAPAWA in 1939 by attempting to reorganize the southern union in such a way as to destroy its autonomy. A CIO spokesman defended Henderson by saying that he had tried to bring order into a maladministered union, and that Butler and Mitchell had fooled themselves into thinking they could pull out of UCAPAWA and stay in the CIO.[27]

Strikes. While the STFU's main activities before World War II were political, it conducted a number of unique strikes and demonstrations. The first occurred in the fall of 1935 when the union demanded an increase in cotton-picking wages from the prevailing 30 to 35 cents to 65 cents a hundredweight.[28] The union did not attempt to bargain with the planters, who were not organized at this time, but covered the countryside with handbills calling on the workers to stay out of the fields. The strike's effectiveness was strengthened by a rumor that a strikebreaker had been killed when he attempted to go to work. The strike was so complete that an investigation by an Arkansas deputy labor commissioner found only five people working in three counties. Though the STFU offered to meet with any representative group of planters, the planters refused. However, when some of the employers granted compromise wage increases, the STFU called off the strike and held a victory celebration.

The STFU received support during the 1935 strike from various sources. President Green of the AFL, who had expressed interest and sympathy, sent a letter to AFL affiliates asking them to help; this appeal raised nearly $1000 for the tenant farmers. Local AFL unions, especially in Memphis, took a dim view of the STFU's activities, especially its racial practices. However, the 1935 AFL convention adopted a resolution supporting it, and the January 1936 AFL Executive Council meeting directed an investigation "to determine the facts in the case and maybe extend aid to them."[29]

The 1935 strike "victory" brought STFU membership to about 30,000. Locals were organized in neighboring states; especially Oklahoma, where between 75 and 80 were established. Mitchell estimated that three or four East Arkansas counties were 50 to 60 per cent organized after the strike, though not many of these "members" paid union dues.

The feeling of invincibility was shattered the following year after STFU members voted 6457 to 804 to strike unless the planters raised wages to $1.00 from the prevailing average of 70 cents a day for weeding, chopping, and plowing. The planters, who were given until May 18, 1936, to meet this demand, ignored the union's ultimatum. When the strike started, the strikers marched through the plantations calling on workers to join them.[30] The strike was reported to have been 80 per cent effective.

The governor sent troops into the strike zone, and strikebreakers were imported from Memphis. Many strikers were beaten, and "Rev. Wm. Bennett, of Wyne, died of injuries inflicted by floggers." A picket line was broken up near Earle, Arkansas, and two strikers seriously injured. One of them, a Negro, was reported killed. Reaction to the strike was so strong that it was virtually impossible for the STFU to hold a meeting until the strike had been called off in July 1936.

The strike was not a complete loss for the STFU. The "March of Time" made a movie, giving the union valuable publicity and focusing attention on the plight of the sharecroppers. Publicity given the beating of Clay East and an investigation by Spencer McCullogh of the St. Louis *Post Dispatch* led to the conviction of an Arkansas planter for peonage. Dr. Sherwood Eddy established the biracial Delta Cooperative Farm near Clarksdale, Mississippi to care for evicted strikers. This publicity was also instrumental in bringing about an investigation by the President's Committee on Farm Tenancy and similar state commissions in Arkansas and Oklahoma.

Relations with the AFL. After it broke with UCAPAWA in 1939, the STFU received some support from the International Ladies' Garment Workers Union (ILGWU), which put H. L. Mitchell on its payroll as an organizer. ILGWU was conducting an organizing drive in the south in 1940 and was interested in organizing agricultural workers as a union education venture; this objective was explained to the 1940 STFU convention by an ILGWU spokeman.

> In Texas, Arkansas, Mississippi, etc., there are garment shops opening up. We are trying to organize them. There is no region where it is easier to organize our union than where miners have been organized for instance. In these places the people know about unions already. In districts where unions have never been heard of, we can't organize the girls in the garment factories. If you understand unionism you can help us. You can tell your daughters, wives and friends that the union is a good thing.[31]

In 1940, when it had 4500 to 5000 members, of whom 2189 were paid up, the STFU attempted to affiliate with the AFL. In its application, the STFU reported that it had nine employees and a budget of $750 a month; dues of 25 cents a month, 15 cents of which went to the national organization; and 138 locals, 35 in Arkansas, 23 in Mississippi, 17 in Missouri, and the others in Oklahoma and Tennessee.[32] The AFL Executive Council denied the STFU's application for a charter in 1940 but promised to help in any other way possible.

The STFU launched an organizing drive in the TVA area in 1941. An arrangement was worked out with the business agent of the Hod Carriers and Common Laborers' Union (HCL) whereby STFU members were given perference for jobs; this program was so successful that the HCL business agent was elected president of the STFU in 1941, and the annual convention was held in Sheffield, Alabama. During World War II, the STFU kept up its membership by serving as an agricultural labor recruiting agency; it signed up over 10,000 workers for Seabrook Farms in New Jersey. On August 14, 1946, the STFU was chartered by the AFL as the National Farm Labor Union; at that time the organization had 6151 paid-up members in 204 locals.

Conclusions. The reasons for the STFU's failure as a trade union are not difficult to find. Most important were: the depression; opposition from planters who considered the union a threat to the plantation system and white supremacy; the workers' poverty, which made it difficult for them either to support a union or to refrain from working for more than a few days during picking and chopping seasons; an uneducated membership; lack of cooperative habits among southern agricultural workers; the paternalism of the plantation system; lack of legal status by croppers and tenants; the political power of agricultural interests which made it difficult for the New Deal to help these workers; the more traditional impediments to agricultural unionism of individualism and spatial separateness; and the economic condition of the industry which made it difficult for planters to pay much more than prevailing wages. Of course, because of their low levels of skill and the economic conditions in the industry, agricultural workers have had difficulties organizing everywhere in the United States. But the conditions in southern agriculture during the 1930's made unionization even more difficult.

The STFU's efforts were not entirely in vain. Its activities focused attention on the plight of southern agriculture, giving support to such programs as the Farm Security Administration, Soil Conservation Service, the Agricultural Extension Service, the Tennessee Valley Authority and the Rural Electrification Administration, all of which greatly benefited southern tenants and sharecroppers.

CHAPTER XI

Textile and Clothing Workers

TEXTILE WORKERS

The United Textile Workers (UTW) also tried to take advantage of the friendly political atmosphere of the Roosevelt administration to organize, but it had neither the membership nor the money.

The unions in the textile and garment industries were unhappy about several features of the NRA, especially the reduced work week, a ruling that the stretch-out did not violate the cotton textile code (adopted in July 1933), and the code's inadequate enforcement machinery. Textile employers frequently ignored the NIRA's collective bargaining provisions and countered the UTW's organizing activities with antiunion tactics. Unlike some other unions, the UTW was too weak to enforce the collective bargaining features of the act, even though it was supported by the ACWA and the ILGWU.[1]

As a result of dissatisfaction with the NIRA and the persistent refusal of textile employers to recognize the union or to permit it to speak for employees in the industry, the delegates to the August 1934 UTWA convention authorized the calling of a strike if the following demands were not met: elimination of the stretch-out, establishment of a thirty-hour and five-day work week, recognition of the union as bargaining agent for the industry, and the creation of an arbitration board to adjust disputes. When these demands were not met, the union called a strike for September 1, 1934.

166

Even before the UTWA convention, however, some textile workers in the south, where two thirds of the industry's employment was located, were prepared to strike obstinate employers. On July 18, 1934, for example, 40 of 42 textile locals in Alabama representing 20,000 workers called a general strike to support demands for a $12.00 minimum weekly wage, 30-hour week and union recognition.[2] The Alabama strikers' ranks held firm, but the many unorganized mills in central Alabama continued to operate, reducing the strike's effectiveness; the union had its main strength in the Birmingham area and had hoped the unorganized mills would join the walkout.

The September 1 general strike is reported to have affected 450,000[3] workers at its peak, 170,000 of whom were in the south.[4] Obviously, however, the union had nowhere near that many members north or south in 1934, and since the UTW had a minority of the mills organized, it formed "flying squads" of strikers to close mills whose workers did not join the walkout. This tactic, which had been used by the coal miners, led to several deaths and much bloodshed as local law enforcement officials, national guardsmen and strikers clashed. At Augusta, Georgia, two Enterprise Mill pickets were wounded and another killed when a policeman who was being trampled by the pickets fired from the ground. At Greenville, South Carolina, one man and four women were beaten by deputies and at Trion, Georgia, a deputy sheriff and a nonunion man were killed and 15 persons were injured in a battle between deputy sheriffs and strikers. In numerous skirmishes on a front between Gastonia, North Carolina, and Greenville, South Carolina, 300 mills were closed by flying squads traveling from mill to mill by automobile, sometimes forcing workers to quit and destroying company property. National guardsmen were called out in North and South Carolina, but they were not successful in preventing a tragedy at Honea Path, a mill town in South Carolina where six strikers were killed and fifteen wounded.[5]

Perhaps the strike was most forcefully suppressed in Georgia where Governor Eugene Talmadge declared martial law and had troops place strikers and their families in concentration camps surrounded by barbed wire. Talmadge had been considered friendly to organized labor during the 1920's but he broke with the unions during the New Deal over the question of paying WPA wage rates on all state work in Georgia.

Talmadge declared martial law during the 1934 general strike, sending some 4000 national guardsmen into practically every textile mill village in Georgia. It turned out that one employer had hired

Pearl Bergoff, a notorious strikebreaker, who came with about 200 hired gunmen from New York, to help break the strike, but Talmadge had them deported.[6]

While such vigorous opposition from local officials undoubtedly contributed to the defeat of the 1934 strike, it is by no means certain that the strike would have been won in the absence of such tactics. It could not be expected that local officials would remain aloof from the conflict in view of the methods of some of the flying squads which could not even be controlled by union officials. The mine workers had been able to use the same practices, but they had a much larger organized base from which to operate and were relatively isolated geographically.

The UTW's handling of the strike suggests that it was not well planned and certainly inadequately financed. Before it started, UTW officials asked William Green for aid from other unions. When the UTW leaders told the AFL president that they had no money, he informed them that if they were in desperate circumstances "there was no chance" and that it was too late to get help because most union leaders had started for the AFL convention in San Francisco. Green hurriedly helped the UTW raise some money—$5000 from the hatters, $10,000 from the ILGWU and $5000 from the UMW—and helped secure a settlement.[7]

Realizing the need for government intervention if the strike were to be even partially successful, Green and other union officials prevailed upon President Roosevelt to appoint a board of inquiry. The board recommended: the appointment of a new textile labor relations board; a Federal Trade Commission investigation of the industry's ability to pay higher wages; amendment of existing textile codes to permit regulation of the stretch-out; and a United States Department of Labor study of the wage rates in the industry.

On September 22, 1934, the UTWA called off the strike on the basis of these recommendations. The president then appointed a board to investigate violations of the NIRA, to arbitrate disputes where requested to do so by both parties, and to carry on various other minor regulatory functions. This board also appointed a committee to study the stretch-out.

The strike did very little to improve the workers' conditions. The companies did not recognize the union; wages were not increased; and the new textile board was no more effective than the old. Although the stretch-out was modified, the workers generally regarded the strike settlement as a defeat for the union. Employers refused to rehire many strikers, and union membership declined sharply.[8] The

UTW maintained a few locals in the region and had a few oral agreements, but in 1937 there appears to have been only one written contract in the southern textile industry.[9]

The 1937 campaign. The formation of the CIO (which was supported by the UTW's executive council and 1936 convention, and of which UTW President McMahon was a charter member) and its successes in other industries, especially coal, automobiles and steel, gave textile union leaders new hope. UTW officials presented to the CIO a plan to organize the industry in the summer of 1936 and in March 1937, and a committee met in Washington and approved a contract between the UTWA and the CIO for an organizing campaign to be conducted by the Textile Workers' Organizing Committee (TWOC).

> The South held the key to the success of the C.I.O. in welding together the elements of a permanent union of textile workers. It has for years been an axiom that the awakening of Southern labor and its organization will be a landmark in the history of the states, bringing a shifting of political and economic influence.[10]

When the campaign started, however, the TWOC had only 15,000 employees under contract, and only 800 of these, at the Louisville Textile Company, were in the south.[11]

The TWOC attempted to overcome some of the major impediments to past organizing campaigns—inadequate finances, poor planning and strategy, and the use of nonsouthern organizers. The agreement with the UTW stipulated that the TWOC would assume complete control of the campaign; this was done partly because the UTW had been discredited in the 1934 general textile strike.

Some of the most experienced union leaders in the CIO served on the TWOC. Sidney Hillman president of the ACWA became chairman, and Thomas Kennedy of the UMW became treasurer; other members were Francis J. Gorman, who succeeded McMahon as president of the UTW in February 1937; Emil Rieve of the hosiery workers, Charles Zimmerman, a vice-president of the ILGWU, and Thomas F. Burns of the United Rubber Workers.

Over $2,000,000 were spent during the campaign. It was raised[12] principally from the Amalgamated Clothing Workers ($523,000); TWOC locals and joint boards (442,000); United Mine Workers (198,000); American Federation of Hosiery Workers (183,000); United Textile Workers (126,000); International Ladies' Garment Workers (110,000); and the CIO (85,000).

In addition to this, various unions, especially the ACWA, spent large sums directly to support the campaign. Hillman exhorted his union to make the heavy commitment in the TWOC because of the close relationship between garment and textile wages and of the importance of organizing the south for all unions.[13] According to *Advance*, the ACWA's official organ:

> Cotton garment factories have sprung up under the protecting wing of the powerful open-shopism of the South. A whole area of our country has been turned into a swamp of exploitation by the arbitrary rule of the textile kings . . . This area has been a threat to unionized workers in the wearing apparel industries. Organization of the textile workers will clean it out. For our own sakes, as well as for the sake of the laboring people of the country, this textile drive must go over the top.[14]

The TWOC used southern organizers wherever possible. Steve Nance, ex-president of the Georgia Federation of Labor, who was impeached by the AFL for supporting the CIO, was placed in charge of the lower south with headquarters in Atlanta, and John A. Peel, also a southerner, directed the campaign in the upper south. Nance was very popular with the southern labor leaders and was also highly regarded by some employers and state officials. In addition to Nance and Peel, the TWOC employed 160 southern organizers, including such non-working-class intellectuals as Witherspoon Dodge, Franz Daniel, and Lucy Randolph Mason.

The 1937 drive was undoubtedly the best-planned textile organizing campaign ever undertaken. Hillman and his lieutenants spent weeks in TWOC's New York headquarters planning the strategy. It was decided that the first phase would be educational, stressing the "respectability" of unions and their value to workers and the community alike. The TWOC *Parade*, southern organ of the textile drive, had a special issue on labor and religion. During this time, Hillman decided to avoid strikes and show employers the value of unions, a program which had brought some success in the garment industry where the unions had helped employers by stabilizing the industry and promoting industrial efficiency. The southern regional organizers sought to project an image of strength and confidence in order to overcome the textile workers' fears that the union was too weak to oppose management successfully. The TWOC sought to create this image of strength through a widespread publicity campaign which included mass meetings, pamphleteering, house-to-house canvassing and speeches in favor of unionism by prominent southerners. The plan also called for full use of the facilities of the federal government in order to overcome the workers' fears of employer retaliation.

This was followed by a movement to stimulate demands for NLRB representation elections and the negotiation of contracts. These contracts were to be promoted by political pressure on the employers wherever possible and by strikes only where absolutely necessary.[15]

The TWOC had some immediate success during the spring and summer of 1937. By August 1937, for example, the committee and ACWA had negotiated 29 agreements, covering 23,000 workers, 17,000 of whom were in the textile industry.[16] Resistance to unionism stiffened during the winter, however, and in spite of some successes elsewhere the TWOC reported only about 25,000 workers under contract by the spring of 1938.[17]

In addition to the usual employer opposition, the TWOC faced the beating and kidnapping of organizers, antiunion citizens' committees, the Ku Klux Klan, antiunion religious revivalists and the AFL. The AFL was offering itself to employers and workers as a more respectable alternative.[18] And the TWOC campaign, like almost every effort to unionize the southern textile industry, was interrupted by a recession.

When the TWOC became the Textile Workers' Union of America-CIO in May 1939, it had 858 contracts covering 235,000 workers. A management evaluation in 1939 placed the TWOC's card-carrying membership in the south at about 20 per cent of the region's 350,000 cotton workers, and only 15 per cent paid dues regularly. The union was able to get contracts covering many fewer than this; only 5 per cent of the south's spindles were estimated to have been affected by union contracts, and a third of these were no longer in force by April 1939.[19] An examination of TWUA records reveals an average of about 10,000 members in the south in 1939. The union encountered much more opposition in the south than in the north. Though the southern unions won more elections, the northern locals had many more closed shops, more active contracts, and fewer antiunion complaint cases filed with the NLRB. Herbert J. Lahne said:

> In the South, by the end of 1939, there were indications (such as a falling off in the number of NLRB elections held) that the union had reached the end of the more readily organizable sections of this traditionally difficult territory . . . If the T.W.U.A. fails in the Southern cotton mills it cannot really succeed elsewhere.[20]

Reorganization. In 1939, the AFL reconstituted the UTW around several federal labor unions and some dissident groups from the CIO. Southerners were prominent in its reorganization, and efforts to reorganize the south played an important part in its plans. In January 1939, for example, a month before the UTW's AFL charter was restored, a meeting in Washington, D.C. recommended that a cotton federation be created with a southern branch under George Googe's direction.[21]

The first convention of the reconstituted UTW was held May 8-10, 1939, with 126 delegates, 63 of whom were from the south: 21 from South Carolina, 15 from North Carolina, 15 from Alabama, five from Georgia, four from Mississippi and three from Tennessee. The Southern Cotton Textile Federation had been formed, according to Googe, because of the conviction that:

> the only way we could organize the Textile industry in the South permanently was to organize it through the workers in the southern plants themselves and let them elect their own officers and run their own organizations. After all the heartaches and disappointments, I am confident with the experience of the last few years, that it is possible for the American Federation of Labor to let the southern textile workers have their own organization and run it.[22]

C. M. Fox of Atlanta was elected president of the UTW at the 1939 special convention; John W. Pollard and Gordon L. Chastain of Spartanburg, South Carolina were elected first and fourth vice-presidents respectively. This convention also was told that the CIO had fewer southern members than at any time since the first months of the TWOC.

> Hundreds of thousands of pledge cards in the South have been torn up and hundreds of thousands of workers have become dissillusioned in organization due to the fact that elections have been won in mills in which little or no effort has been made to consolidate and recruit active membership. Also, because organizers were sent in with their usual tales about how low the U.T.W. was, and have offered absolutely nothing in its place.

The delegates were also told that before the TWOC was formed, the UTW had "organizations in every state . . . we had federations containing three or four or five hundred delegates, today we have not over 2,500 people paying dues."

The UTW was relatively insignificant in the south before World War II, having contracts in only nine mills covering 6000 workers by November 1942, though it gained more members and contracts during the war.[23] (Of special importance for the UTW was the unionization of the American Bemberg and North American Rayon Corporation at Elizabethton, Tennessee, where it lost the 1929 textile strike.[24]) First Vice-President Pollard told the 1941 UTW convention that the union had comparatively little organization in the south because, while the workers wanted organization, "our organizers have been subject to brutal attacks, have been escorted by representatives of the government in those areas where we were organizing." Pollard added that while contracts were being negotiated, "The kind of contract we are getting in the South . . . is not particularly the kind of contract we desire." It was now easier for the UTW-AFL to sell a contract to employers after representation elections, but according to Pollard:

> These contracts have to be competitive, which is the unfortunate part about it. The cotton textile industry is probably one of the most competitive branches of the industry, and if we get wage clauses, work load clauses, we have simply got to make them competititve, at least until we get the major part of the industry organized.

1940 CIO campaign. After the reactivation of the UTW, the CIO launched a 1940 organizing campaign under the direction of Emil Rieve, president of the TWUA. This campaign encountered stiff opposition, produced some important results and offers some insights into the nature of union organizing in the face of vigorous employer resistance. The TWOC won an important election victory at the Marshall Field Company's five mills in the Leaksville, Draper and Spray, North Carolina area involving 3000 workers in cotton goods, blankets, rugs, and woolens. The contract at Marshall Field came after the company was charged with failing to bargain in good faith and after national officials joined the negotiations; this contract caused other textile workers in the area to join the union, resulting in almost complete unionization of the Tri-Cities area. The union reported that it was making progress organizing the important Irwin Mills of North Carolina by the time of the 1941 convention.

Frequently, however, companies refused to sign contracts with the TWUA after representation elections were won. For example, the Nashua Manufacturing Company's plant in Cordova, Alabama, and Profile Mills at Jacksonville, Alabama, were closed by strikes for seven months and two years respectively, before contracts were signed. The TWOC won an election in 1937 at the Lane Cotton Mills in New Orleans, but the company refused to sign a contract. The union relied on federal legislation and litigation to get an agreement with Lane in 1940. The company was forced by the Circuit Court of Appeals to reinstate 50 workers and to disband a company union. The TWUA brought further action against Lane for violation of the Walsh-Healey Act. "The company was finally deprived of government orders for three years and it was only then that it yielded to the workers' demand for recognition and signed a contract."[25]

Between 1939 and 1941, the TWUA won bargaining rights at 31 mills at which no contracts were signed. At the Vance Knitting Mills in Kernersville, North Carolina, for example, the union won an election in June 1939, 366 to 66. Negotiations began immediately, but no contract was signed. At the Union Manufacturing Company of Union Point, Georgia, and at the Scottdale and Whittier Mills in Georgia, company lawyers practiced various stalling tactics to avoid a contract. At Union Point, the company said the contract had to be ratified by each individual employee in order to be effective. The union was forced to start a new campaign and to strike various departments in order to correct grievances and forestall dismissals for union activity; the NLRB could not be used "because of the delay involved in such proceedings." The union had similar experiences elsewhere. In the hosiery industry, "prolonged strikes at southern mills were necessary in order to obtain any hearing at all. . . The most significant experience during this period was the relatively restricted nature of these strikes. They were for the most part in the South and among smaller concerns. Both groups represent some of the more backward industrial areas in American industry."

The southern textile industry thus remained largely unorganized by the beginning of World War II. It is interesting to contrast these failures with the success of the UMW which faced similar problems in the bituminous coal mining industry. Probably the most important factors causing the textile unions to fail were: the weakness of the UTWA and the TWUA which, unlike the UMW, had no strong non-southern base from which to organize; the dispersion of the textile workers in the United States, making it more difficult for them to be reached by organizers; the much greater opposition from employers; the lack of leadership in the UTW to stabilize the industry; the psychological barriers of past failures in textile unions; the lack of incentive of local government officials to deal with the TWOC, the UTWA or the TWUA. Thus, while unions were too weak to overcome the traditional economic, political and social impediments to unions in the south, they did have a base in that industry which was enlarged considerably during the war. The textile experience also indicates that more than NLRB elections were necessary to secure collective bargaining contracts in the southern textile industry. In spite of the Wagner Act, strikes were still necessary to get contracts because nothing in the law required employers to sign agreements with unions; and, after a little experience, it was an unimaginative lawyer indeed who could not "bargain in good faith" as required by the law and never sign a contract.

MEN'S CLOTHING

The principal union in the men's clothing industry is the Amalgamated Clothing Workers of America (ACWA), though the Amalgamated also organizes workers in laundries and cleaning and dying establishments. The men's clothing industry had many of the same organizing problems as coal mining: a highly competitive industry, many small employers, high ratio of labor cost to total cost, and the effects of the depression. Like the coal operators, clothing employers felt that the NRA and the union could stabilize the industry. Between 1933 and 1940, employers and the Amalgamated succeeded in stabilizing wage costs.

The Amalgamated was similar to the UMW in giving full support to the CIO organizing campaigns and, as we have seen, was deeply involved in the Textile Workers' Organizing Committee. The UMW, the ACWA, and the International Ladies' Garment Workers' Union probably benefited from the NRA more than any other unions; the ACWA added between 40,000 and 50,000 new members between 1930 and 1934, half of which came in the 1933 period.[26] By the beginning of 1936, the ACWA claimed 150,000 members; the union had organized 80 per cent of the men's clothing and 50 per cent of the shirt industry by that date.[27] By the end of 1937 the Amalgamated had organized 90 per cent of the men's clothing industry, "and only half a dozen firms of any consequence were not unionized."

The most important difference between the UMW and the ACWA was the geographic concentration of the industry by the time of the NRA. While the coal industry was widely scattered, the men's clothing industry was concentrated in New York City and other northern centers. The Amalgamated's only southern local before the NRA was at Louisville, Kentucky.[28] The Louisville contract with Sherman and Sons, the largest firm in the market, had been in force for many years, but was broken during the depression because the firm wanted "extreme concessions" which the members would not grant. "Sherman soon reopened its factory with scabs, shielding them behind a union label." ACWA continued its efforts to renew the contract with Sherman and Sons, but the company was able to operate with little difficulty, especially after it got an injunction against picketing; arrangements were made for some of ACWA's members to work for other firms in Louisville with which the union had contracts, but this was not enough to absorb the Sherman workers. Thus, while the Louisville local did not fail completely, in 1934, the ACWA described it as "small and weak."

When the NIRA was declared unconstitutional in 1935, the ACWA starting organizing in the south "determined that work standards in the few southern clothing plants would be maintained at code levels."[29] The two main firms in the region in 1934 were Sam Finkelstein & Sons of Norfolk, Virginia, and Friedman-Harry Marks of Richmond. The ACWA therefore formed locals at Norfolk and Richmond in 1934 and launched a campaign to organize these firms, which the union claimed were "run-aways" from New York. The company countered by forming a company union. The Amalgamated enlisted the aid of the Norfolk Central Labor Union and sent an organizer to help reach the colored workers in the plant. ACWA Vice-President Jacob Potofsky took charge of the campaign in June 1935, when the company discharged two union members. After unsuccessful mediation efforts, the union struck the plant August 15, 1935. On August 20, the company obtained a sweeping injunction limiting pickets to two at each gate; one of the arguments used to get the injunction was that the strike was "fomenting intermingling of races." In spite of this, the union held firm and strike activity was described as being well organized, well financed and almost festive.

The strike was settled November 20, after unsuccessful mediation efforts by the U.S. Department of Labor, and amounted to only partial defeat in the sense that: "The over one hundred strikers who braved a fight of several months duration, under most trying circumstances have won the right to return to their jobs."[30] While the settlement was not satisfactory from the Amalgamated's point of view, it obligated the firm to operate at the NRA minima, providing some protection to the union's wage stabilization efforts. Moreover, "It was the first serious labor strike in Norfolk in Heaven knows how many years which did not result in frustrating labor's hopes."[31] The ACWA said it had impressed other unions in the south because "it was properly financed, was directed in an organized way, and had punch, daring and appeal."

The Amalgamated also formed a local in Richmond during 1934 to organize the over 1000 workers at Friedman-Harry Marks. The company responded in July 1935 by discharging four union members; this was later increased to 19. The NLRB found the company guilty of unfair labor practices, but the employers refused to reinstate the workers and give them back pay on the grounds that the Wagner Act was unconstitutional.

In all its activities in the south, the ACWA was most successful in those areas which had other unions, especially if the other union was the United Mine Workers, as demonstrated by the union's struggle to organize the Atlas and Reade Shirt companies of La Follette, Tennessee. These firms were owned by a New York firm, and the Atlas plant had about 400 employees, while Reade had 600. The United Mine Workers, with locals in Coal Creek, Jellicoe, and other places, supported the ACWA. The workers in the garment plants were mostly women from the miners' families.

The ACWA struck the Atlas plant in January 1937, and shortly thereafter the workers at the Reade plant followed.[32] The ACWA won the strike at the Atlas plant, and signed a contract on February 17 which granted a closed shop, the check-off, shorter hours and a wage increase.[33] The strike continued at the Reade plant until March 13, 1937, at which time the plant signed an agreement providing for a closed shop, a wage increase, the return of strikers without discrimination, and an arbitration provision.[34]

After seven weeks of the strike, "not a single striker had broken ranks" at the Reade plant, but, the union said, the company was convinced that the workers did not really want the union; it asked that ratification of the agreement be delayed until April 17, hoping that the workers would desert the ACWA. The company also wanted the union to agree to keep the terms of the contract secret, which it refused to do. On April 17, the workers voted 4 to 1 for the ACWA.

The Atlas Shirt Company continued to fight the union, however, and on February 17, 1938, the ACWA called a strike to prevent further contract violations. The company was accused of threatening workers and seeking injunctions against the collection of dues. At the beginning of the strike, the local police prohibited strikers from picketing in front of the plant and escorted strikebreakers in. UMW members from the surrounding coal towns came to La Follette—700 strong—to support the strikers. No strikebreakers tried to enter the factory after lunch on the day the miners came to town. By Saturday there were 1500 miners supporting the strike.

The police withdrew, and the town people persuaded the company to close down until an agreement could be reached. On March 5, after a week of negotiations, a contract was signed which provided for the closed shop, check-off, and 5 per cent wage increases.

The ACWA won another important victory in 1937 when it succeeded in organizing Friedman-Harry Marks at Richmond. The union was assisted by Richmond carpenters and longshoremen, "friends of the Amalgamated from the time the Amalgamated had helped them two years ago—and friends in spite of anything William Green or the American Federation of Labor may say about it."

But the immediate reason for the Richmond contract was the U.S. Supreme Court's decision upholding the Wagner Act; ACWA's case against Friedman-Harry Marks was one involved in the decision. AWCA organizers were at the plant gates in Richmond the day following this, and, in a whirlwind campaign lasting a month, on May 15 the union secured a three-year contract providing for "complete union recognition, a 36-hour week, with a 12 per cent wage increase and a minimum wage of $14.00. In addition, 4 per cent of the weekly pay roll is set aside for lifting up underpaid operations, the revision in rates to be decided through subsequent negotiations." The contract also carried with it the restoration of jobs to a number of those previously discharged for union activity.[35] A meeting was held to discuss the provision of the agreement at which the workers sang "Glory, Glory, Amalgamated." The Richmond ACWA local became strong and active and helped to organize other Virginia plants, including Finkelstein at Norfolk in 1941.

After the Supreme Court decision, ACWA instituted a drive against the Washington Manufacturing Company in seven Kentucky and Tennessee towns; this drive came as a result of hundreds of requests by workers because of the TWOC campaign. At one of Washington's plants in Cookeville, Tennessee, two organizers were arrested and fined $25.00 under a five-day old ordinance forbidding distribution of leaflets at the plant gate.[36] The company also locked out 400 workers in three Nashville plants, and the union filed charges with the NLRB. During the NLRB hearing:

> Efforts of the company's lawyers to draw a red herring across the path met with no success. Each attempt to raise a Communist scare made them look more and more ridiculous. When organizer Elaine Wright was on the stand, Armistead, chief counsel for the company asked, "Don't you know that he (Hillman) is one of the leading Communists in the country?"
>
> "No," she replied.
>
> "Did you ever hear of the 'Red Network?'"
>
> "Yes, I believe that is the book that lists Mrs. Roosevelt as a Communist."

Workers present at the hearing laughed, and the union read a letter from the President of the United States to Sidney Hillman, whereupon the company's lawyers took another approach:

With a great show of proving that the union had nothing to do with the South, he asked, "Now this Amalgamated Union takes in members whether they are white or black, natives or what not?"

"It does."

"Can a Negro be a member, and if elected, can he attend conventions as a member?"

"He can," Miss Dickason replied, "just as if one were elected he may sit in the Congress of the United States."

In June 1937, the NLRB ordered the company to cease violating the act and to give back pay to the discharged workers. The company refused, however, and the NLRB was forced to get a court order to enforce its award. In the meantime the company changed ownership, but the new management was related to the old and still bound by the decision.[37] This case was further complicated by the formation of an independent union. By 1940, three years after the NLRB complaint, and faced with further litigation, the ACWA agreed to reduce some $200,000 in back pay against the company to $20,000 and the reinstatement of most of its members.[38]

The NLRB aided the ACWA in its southern drive when it ordered the S and K Kneepants Company of Lynchburg, Virginia, to rehire Lynchburg workers who lost their jobs when the company closed down and moved to Culpepper, Virginia. Before it moved, it offered to rehire the workers if they would "forget about the union." The workers refused, the company moved to Culpepper, and the union filed charges with NLRB. The board held that the company had to rehire these workers and pay their expenses to the town to which it had moved unless they had found "regular and substantially equivalent" employment elsewhere.[39]

The Amalgamated also made a strong effort to unionize the 10,000 men's garment workers in Texas, but encountered stiff opposition, especially in Dallas, which ACWA officials described as "the citadel of the open shop in the Southwest, and has come to be known as the worst open shop city in the U.S."[40] By 1940 the union was organizing in Waco, Fort Worth, Dallas, San Antonio and Houston.

The ACWA won another important victory when it organized the Atlanta plants of Cluett-Peabody—the largest shirt firm in the industry. The Amalgamated organized the Troy, New York, plant of this firm and in 1939 enrolled the pressers in the Atlanta plant. Some of the workers had joined an independent union, which collapsed when the ACWA filed charges with the NLRB that it was a company union. The United Garment Workers established some membership among the

Atlanta workers, but, starting from the pressers, the ACWA expanded until it represented a substantial majority of the employees by 1941.

The Atlanta workers struck over a wage dispute February 17, 1941, and were joined by workers at the firm's plant in Troy, New York, February 20, and Leominster, Massachusetts, February 21. The Amalgamated planned relief, recreation and other activities at these three plants while the strike was in progress. A joint committee from the three plants began negotiations February 23 and on February 28 signed a "full fledged union agreement" with wage increases, arbitration and other features. "All complications were finally removed in Atlanta only after a NLRB election in May, 1941."[41] This agreement was extended in 1944 to plants in Bremen, Georgia, Lexington, Kentucky, and Fleetwood, Pennsylvania, which were operated by Cluett-Peabody. In 1941, before the Cluett-Peabody agreement, the Amalgamated signed a contract with the Manhattan Shirt Company of Americus, Georgia.

Another 1941 victory for the ACWA was the contract with the Finkelstein company at Norfolk, Virginia, after 15 years of effort. The Amalgamated held separate ratification meetings for Negro and white employees.

Despite these successes, ACWA found its organizing activities in the south blocked by many obstacles. Organizers encountered community opposition throughout the area and were sometimes beaten and driven out of town. In an attempt to strengthen its own southern campaign, the ACWA decided to sever its affiliation with the TWOC. The Amalgamated met in a joint conference with leaders of the textile workers at Charlotte, North Carolina, July 11, and 12, 1938. With President Hillman present, "the progress and problems of the organizing work in the South was carefully reviewed. It was decided that the time had come to separate the textile and clothing organizing work, and soon after, a Southern Regional Office of the Amalgamated with Clyde Mills as Director was opened in Atlanta."[42]

The newly established regional office organized locals throughout the south by 1941, and gained a firm footing in the region, but realized that the expansion of its southern membership was an uphill struggle. At that time, the ACWA had about 3200 members in the south; over half of whom were in Virginia and Tennessee.

Although the ACWA's major activity in the south did not take place until World War II, the union sought to organize the major firms in the industry as soon as they moved there. The union's success came of its willingness and ability to pay the cost of organizing. Its stabilization program reduced employer opposition in the coat and suit branch of the industry, and its geographic concentration in the east gave the

Amalgamated a strong base from which to operate. Compared with textiles, the Amalgamated's organizing task was also reduced by the relative insignificance of the south in the men's clothing industry; the ACWA could organize plants as they went south, while the textile unions had to organize the major part of the industry already there.

OTHER UNIONS

The other major unions in the clothing industry are the United Garment Workers and the International Ladies' Garment Workers' Union (ILGWU). However the ILGWU's southern activity was restricted almost entirely to the period during and after World War II. The ILGWU organized Petrillo and Company in Dallas peacefully in 1937, but three other firms there had signed agreements only after bitter strikes following the ILGWU's campaign in the fall of 1936.[43] The Ladies' Garment Workers had about 3100 southern members in 1939, 2100 of whom were in Texas.

The UGW was active in the south long before 1932, though it relied heavily on organizing employers through the union label and, in contrast with the ACWA, did not conduct aggressive campaigns to organize employees. As early as 1927, UGW had locals in Atlanta, Georgia; Houston, Texas; Denison, Texas; Danville, Virginia; Covington, Kentucky; Oklahoma City, Oklahoma; Birmingham, Alabama; Sherman, Texas; New Orleans, Louisiana; San Antonio, Texas; Fort Worth, Texas; Mobile, Alabama; Jeffersonville, Kentucky; Lynchburg, Virginia; Shawnee, Oklahoma; and Dallas, Texas.[44]

In 1937, the UGW had only nine locals in the south: Atlanta, Houston, Denison (Texas), Mobile, Birmingham, Newport (Kentucky), and Fort Worth. The 1937 UGW Convention was the first held in ten years, and complaints were aired that only three of the 500 garment manufacturers in the south used the UGW label.

> [The convention resolved to] instruct the incoming General Executive Board to place one of its members or International Representatives in the Southern District to look after the interest of the members of the United Garment Workers, to help organize the non-organized Garment Workers and help check the C.I.O. movement in the industry of the Southern States. [These] representatives to be given authority to appoint as many assistants and place them in localities where they are needed to carry on the work and that special attention be given to the following states: Tennessee, Georgia, Alabama, and Mississippi, as conditions are worse in the Garment Industry in those States than any other.[45]

In 1939, the UGW had about 3300 members in the south, giving it slightly more members than the ACWA, and 1000 more than the ILGWU.

CHAPTER XII

Growth of CIO Unions

IRON AND STEEL

In 1939 the iron and steel industry accounted for about 5 per cent of the south's total manufacturing employment. If iron and steel products are included, the percentage rises to 11.6 per cent. Of the nation's 1,171,000 workers in this industry, 85,000 were concentrated in the south, primarily in the states of Alabama, Kentucky, Tennessee and Texas. Alabama had 35,700 workers—42 per cent of the total.[1]

Before the NRA there had been several unsuccessful attempts to organize the Birmingham workers. The Sons of Vulcan had been active there in 1876, and the Amalgamated Association of Iron, Steel and Tin Workers had contracts until 1909, at which time its strength was greatly weakened by a series of strikes which began back in 1901. One of the reasons the Amalgamated was unsuccessful was that it did not encourage the organization of Negroes. In 1918, the Mine, Mill and Smelter Workers' Union organized a few Negro workers in the area, but after the union had lost one strike the workers refused to participate in another one in 1919. After this, there was little unionism before the NRA.

As we have noted, because of the high proportion of Negro workers, Communists attempted to organize them in Alabama as a base for their program to create a "Negro nation." In June 1930, the Communists started a small paper called the *Southern Worker* in Birmingham. While they organized many unemployed workers, at no time did they have much strength among employed industrial workers. However, the group was active despite its size, and drew strong opposition.

> This general agitation in the region has been met with almost ruthless resistance by the police, by vigilante bands and by the trade unions. The police have raided Negro homes by the score, sometimes brutally beating occupants of the houses, and searching at will for literature which could be in any way labeled revolutionary . . . Detective agencies have made a business of spying and informing upon every type of Communist activity.[2]

The Communists also were vigorously opposed by the American Legion, the White Legion, the Ku Klux Klan, and the Alabama Blackshirts. Overt Communist activity declined in Birmingham after 1935 because of the rise of CIO unions and the change in the party line from "dual unionism" to the "popular front" with other antifascist groups.

The CIO's policies were particularly important to Negroes, who comprised a majority of the employees in the Alabama iron and steel industry, but whose employment declined considerably during the 1930-1940 period (probably because the equalization of wages under the NRA permitted employers to use white workers).

Stimulated by the UMW's successes, the Mine, Mill and Smelter Workers started an organizing campaign among the 8000 ore miners in Birmingham in 1933. Eighty per cent of them were Negroes, as were a large proportion of the smelter workers in Bessemer, where the MMSW also was active during the NRA period. Probably because of the Negro members and its identification with communism, the MMSW was vigorously resisted. In a two-month strike in 1934, for example, two Negro strikers were killed, many others were injured, and Negro homes were bombed or burned.

There also were some AFL federal labor unions (FLU) at four out of the eight cast-iron pipe shops by the middle of 1934. In these shops, 70 per cent of the between 1000 and 1200 members were Negroes.

The union's failure in the basic iron and steel industry came from the depressed conditions in the industry—only about 8 or 10 of the 18 furnaces in the area were in operation—and the inability of the NRA Labor Board to enforce its decisions. The specific instance that disillusioned local workers occurred at the East Thomas blast furnace, which employed 500 men, 40 per cent of whom were colored. Many of these workers joined the MMSW when it stepped up its activities in the fall of 1933, and the union won an election 290 to 8. But management rejected a committee which called upon it to negotiate. The

MMSW then called a strike which drew 475 men out of the plant, but "In spite of prolonged and vigorous picketing by both races, the company slowly filled with unorganized labor, some of it conveyed in under cover of machine guns."

This episode had harmful effects. According to Mitchell: "Smelters and other blast furnace men held back partly because the government failed wretchedly in its guarantee of collective bargaining to the first group of furnace men who organized and struck."[3]

The Amalgamated Association formed five unions after July 1933, with about 2000 members, many of whom did not pay dues, but membership was reduced to only a few hundred by the spring of 1934.

Another obstacle faced by Birmingham unions was the attempt by many companies to form unions. W. H. Crawford, one of the first to start organizing steel workers in the area, explained the difficulties at the Tennessee Coal and Iron Company:

> Having nothing to turn to in the way of real collective bargaining the men seized upon the "Employee Representation Plan" offered them by the employers. The unions hoped that they could use this plan as a means of turning the workers' minds to genuine collective bargaining. Indeed, they felt that there was a mandate from the New Deal for them to utilize this means of building unions. But the promise of help in bringing about genuine collective bargaining through company unions was a vain shadow. The big corporations, including the Tenneessee Coal and Iron Company, moved in adroitly and began to capture this opportunity to plant company unions among their employees.[4]

After the company union was declared illegal because "it was imposed on the workers rather than chosen by them," the company revised the plan for union membership and gave the employees the choice of either voting for the new plan or the old plan. The workers accepted the new plan by an overwhelming majority.

Other Birmingham unions grew under the NRA despite the steel industry's failure. Mitchell and Cayton report an increase of 48,600 members in Jefferson County between 1933 and 1934 (17,400 white, and 31,200 colored). Labor officials also estimated 50,000 trade union members in the area by the end of 1934, 30 per cent of whom were Negroes. If these estimates are correct, there were only about 1400 union members in the Birmingham area when the NRA was established, most of them white. Estimated union membership in Alabama late in 1934 was 125,000.[5] Except for the activities of the United Mine Workers, there apparently was little additional union growth until 1937, when the steel workers organized several major companies.

Steel Workers' Organizing Committee. The CIO finally signed a contract with the United States Steel Corporation in 1937 which paved the way for the unionization of other major companies by 1941. The CIO took over the weak and ineffective Amalgamated Association of Iron, Steel, and Tin Workers in June 1936, and established the Steel Workers' Organizing Committee (SWOC) with UMW Vice-President Philip Murray as chairman and William Mitch of the UMW in charge of the southern region. The SWOC was led and financed largely by the United Mine Workers.

The SWOC's first objective was to organize U.S. Steel by infiltrating the company's employee representation plan. In a surprising move, Myron C. Taylor, chairman of the board of directors of the U.S. Steel Corporation, signed agreements with John L. Lewis and the SWOC in March 1937. Walter Galenson gives us the following reasons: 1) The company wished to avoid disruption because it was earning substantial profits for the first time since 1930. 2) It also wished to avoid the costs of a strike, though "It was by no means a foregone conclusion, as some contemporary observers implied, that victory for the union was inevitable or even likely. Little Steel, after all, was able to battle SWOC to a standstill even after the latter had acquired the funds and prestige that went with recognition by U.S. Steel."[6] 3) The political atmosphere in the wake of the 1936 reelection of President Roosevelt favored the union. 4) The corporation probably preferred to deal with an industrial union. There can be little doubt that the SWOC would have had much greater difficulty if Taylor had not decided to deal with it.

After the SWOC was organized, 4000 employees at the Republic Steel's Thomas works, the Bessemer Rolling Mill group and the Fairfield Steel Works of the Tennessee Coal and Iron Company adopted resolutions that they would not become parties to the CIO campaign. In a statement to the public, 13 members of a white committee and seven members of a Negro committee, representing 3000 workers at the Fairfield Steel Works, said, "we are going to continue free and independent workers . . . and we are going to continue to deal with the management of our company through men of our own choosing, and not through any outsiders who would charge us tribute for the privilege of working."[7]

In October 1936, when the company union employees at Tennessee Coal and Iron demanded wage increases of between 5 and 15 per cent for 17,000 employees, management announced that it was approaching the demands with an open mind.[8] In November it was announced that the workers in all U.S. Steel subsidiaries would receive wage hikes equal to 10 per cent in order to offset increases in cost of living and increased production; similar increases were given within a week to employees in the Republic, Sloss-Sheffield, and to those in Woodward Iron in the Birmingham area.[9]

In January 1937, before the Taylor-Lewis talks, Tennessee Coal and Iron management announced that it would not recognize an outside union and planned to continue operating on an open-shop basis. The company's president, mindful of the importance of industrialization to southern leaders, had announced the previous July that peace and harmonious labor relations would determine the investment future of U.S. Steel, "which may spend millions in the district." He warned that four strikes at the company in the past three years had all been caused by "paid and trained labor organizers," and "We have one of John L. Lewis' chief lieutenants [William Mitch] in the Birmingham district attempting to take over power in the district."

Tennessee Coal and Iron signed a contract with SWOC on March 17, following the settlement between Lewis and Taylor at Carnegie-Illinois Steel on March 10. Membership lagged at the company during the next four years, but renewed efforts by the union resulted in an overwhelming election victory in 1942. After this election, many of the small companies also signed contracts.

Other companies refused to follow U.S. Steel's lead in recognizing the union despite vigorous organizing efforts by the SWOC. In March, following the signing of the U.S. Steel contracts, the SWOC demanded recognition from the Little Steel companies. When they refused, the SWOC called a series of generally unsuccessful strikes; in the 1937 strike against Republic, the company's Alabama affiliates continued to operate. It was not until May 1941 that SWOC was able to achieve a significant breakthrough with the Little Steel companies by winning a representation election covering the workers at Bethlehem's Lacka-wanna plant. In July 1941, Republic, Inland and Youngstown Sheet and Tube agreed to recognize SWOC after an NLRB check of membership cards, thus avoiding an election.[10]

The SWOC regional office at Birmingham was established July 1, 1936, and in November 1937, had 11 full-time field workers, four part-time workers, and five office workers.[11] Subregional offices were established in Chattanooga and Nashville. Regional Director N. R. Beddow, who had been Alabama director of the NRA, announced that he had "tried to conform to well understood southern psychology in making selections for organizers."

When the SWOC started in the south, the only plant organized was the Kilby Car Manufacturing Company at Anniston, Alabama, but by the time of the 1937 wage and policy convention it had contracts with 18 steel mills, blast furnaces, foundries and fabricating plants, including Tennessee Coal and Iron, the major company in the region.

The former general superintendent at Atlantic Steel in Atlanta was Tom Girdler, who was president of Republic Steel in 1937.[12] It was reported that when he had been general superintendent at Atlantic his attitude "was about the same as his attitude today. Fear was instilled in the minds of the workers to prevent them from organizing."[13] The main support for the SWOC at Atlantic was the mechanical department, which contained most of the highly skilled workers in the plant. This group started a petition in 1940 to get a 10 cent wage increase; management caused the resentment which probably led to victory in the representation election by granting an increase only to the skilled workers. Workers also voted for the SWOC because the company attempted to break the local by declaring "its intention to keep the plant open if the union won and a strike resulted; it had gone so far as to say that food would be brought into the plant, and that those employees who elected to stay with the company could remain inside the gate around the clock and receive pay for 24 hours a day for the duration of strike." This caused many workers to join the union because "they were actually hoping for a strike, and an opportunity to cash in as strikebreakers."[14] Although the SWOC won the election overwhelmingly, in the early fall of 1941 there were only 114 dues-paying members in a bargaining unit of 1102 employees. Membership did not increase very greatly until after World War II, in spite of a contract following an October 1941 strike.

The SWOC won a representation election at the Woodward Iron Company 327 to 17 by the end of 1937, and was also negotiating a contract with Sloss-Sheffield.

There was stormy opposition elsewhere in the south. At Gadsden, union meetings were broken up because they violated the city ordinance prohibiting Negroes and whites from meeting together. At Nashville, Tennessee, the mayor, city council and American Legion openly defied the SWOC, and vigilantes escorted negotiators and L. J. Smith, a conciliator for the U.S. Department of Labor, out of Cleveland, Tennessee, where they were negotiating with the Brown Foundry Company. The Ku Klux Klan was revived, especially in Birmingham and Atlanta.

In spite of these obstacles, by the time of the second wage and policy convention in 1940, SWOC reported 33 lodges in the south, about half of which were in the Birmingham area and the others in Texas, Tennessee, Georgia and Kentucky.[15] The steelworkers had about 9800 southern members at that time, almost 5700 of whom were in Alabama.

Thus, by the beginning of World War II, the steel workers had established a major base of operations especially in the Birmingham iron and steel complex. While much of the union growth was an extension of unionism from nonsouthern companies with branches in the area, the SWOC was also active in the south.

It is probable that the steelworkers would have retained their independent unions if U.S. Steel had not capitulated. The employers found that the Wagner Act NLRB had more power than its predecessor, though one federal agency head is reported to have said in 1937 "that 30 per cent of the southern corporations involved were disregarding rulings of the agencies dealing with such cases."[16]

Just as the inability of the old NLRB to enforce its ruling had impeded unionism, the new board was instrumental in the SWOC's success in the area by backing its vigorous drive, particularly among Negroes. The SWOC also adopted the "UMW formula" of having integrated unions with Negro and white officers and Negro leaders. The influential bishop of the Methodist Church made radio broadcasts in its support, telling workers that the union was sent from almighty God to help them.[17]

However, there has never been as much racial unity among steelworkers as among coal miners. Reasons include: the greater segregation in the steel industry jobs; the wider wage spread between jobs, with Negroes concentrated in the lower-paying category. Coal miners also are more likely to live in isolated villages, making them less vulnerable to community pressures.

Organized Negro steel workers were dissatisfied because they found that the best jobs still went to the white workers. This caused the steel workers to lose two Birmingham plants of the Ingalls Company to the Bridge, Structural Steel and Ornamental Iron Workers-AFL in 1942. The company promised a job reclassification to give Negroes opportunities for advancement.[18]

RUBBER WORKERS

Before the decentralization movement which started after the 1937 recession, the only significant rubber plant in the south was at Gadsden, Alabama, where Goodyear had about 1500 employees. After 1937, a number of plants of the major firms went south to take advantage of cheaper transportation, taxes, power and labor costs.[19] A Bureau of Labor Statistics study revealed that southern rubber workers' wages were concentrated much more in the lower categories and that average hourly earnings in the Akron-Detroit area stood at $1.063 as compared with $0.607 in the south.

Unions attempted to organize Goodyear early in the NRA period, although they encountered considerable opposition. The AFL chartered a federal local for Gadsden rubber workers in 1933, and the United Rubber Workers (URW) chartered Local 12 in Gadsden in October 1935, and made a determined effort to organize there in 1935 and 1936. On June 6, 1936, URW President Sherman Dalrymple was severely beaten when he attempted to address a crowd.[20] Three other unionists were later beaten, and on June 25 between 200 and 300 Goodyear employees descended on union headquarters and drove the organizers out of town.[21] This ended the Gadsden campaign until the Wagner Act was upheld by the U.S. Supreme Court in 1937.

Gadsden's opposition to unions was undoubtedly influenced by its industrialization drive. Its plan to attract industry by giving tax inducements and pledges of ample and "reasonable" labor was so successful that it had been copied by other communities. With a population of about 40,000 in 1937, Gadsden had 75 industries including the Goodyear plant, Gulf States (Republic) Steel, and Dwight Manufacturing Company, a large textile mill; there were 15,388 industrial workers there in 1937.[22] A pamphlet issued by the Gadsden Chamber of Commerce about this time declared:

> Having a large rural population on which to draw, industry of the Gadsden district is assured of a practically inexhaustible supply of native-born labor that is loyal, capable, entirely trained and willing to work for reasonable wages. American-plan open shop conditions prevail in this district and the community is definitely pledged to support this policy.[23]

The feeling of the citizens was expressed by John Temple Graves in the Birmingham *News* of July 1, 1936. However, he felt that the mob action in Gadsden was "bitterly wrong . . . It has made a national incident out of what might otherwise have been a local one. It has made martyrs of the union organizers against whom it was directed. It has obscured a debatable economic issue with an undebatable moral issue." While he was in sympathy with collective bargaining, he expressed the belief that union policies formulated outside the south might be harmful to that region and that "unionization of the South may require a more Southern point of view if it is to be of real value to those it enlists."

Goodyear workers attacked the union organizers after a Gadsden native—identified only as Charley—had been beaten and knifed in Akron when he refused to join the union.

Last year there was trouble in Gadsden. Union and non-union men were involved. As to who started it, or who was to blame, or what weapons, if any, were used, that's still a matter of controversy; but in the clash downtown there suddenly rang out the cry: "Hit him one for Charley." Charley's friends felt that they had a debt to pay back to union organizers.[24]

City officials also attempted to defeat unions through racial divisions. A city ordinance was passed in July 1936, making it unlawful for "three or more persons, some of whom are white and some Negroes to hold either a public or secret meeting in which is advocated a movement looking toward destruction of the governments of the United States, the State of Alabama or the city." Violation of this statute was punishable by a fine of between $10.00 and $100 and up to six months' imprisonment. Local CIO leaders tried to test it by publicizing mixed meetings; they were arrested but acquitted by the local authorities, making it impossible to take the case to the U.S. Supreme Court.[25]

Union organizers continued to receive hostile receptions in Gadsden in subsequent years.[26] In 1943, however, the URW won a representative election at Goodyear by 1144 to 327,[27] and, as has frequently happened in cases where unions have been violently resisted, Gadsden eventually became one of the strongest union towns in the south. The wartime growth of unionism came about largely because city officials agreed to cease their hostility in exchange for Sidney Hillman's agreement to support the establishment of a large war plant in Gadsden. Hillman was at that time director of the Office of Production Management in the defense program.

Memphis. The Firestone plant at Memphis was established as a result of the decentralization movement. Although the new Memphis Ford plant undoubtedly contributed, an important reason for Firestone's location in Memphis was low wages. About 40 per cent of the plant's over 2000 employees were Negroes, and wages for unskilled labor were reported to be "in the vicinity of 30 to 40 cents."[28] Straight-time hourly earnings in the Memphis plant were 50 cents an hour in January 1941. In 1943, "a comparison of the occupational rates of the Firestone Company with those of other rubber plants in the South showed this company with rates from 8 to 18 cents lower than those of its competitors." Another factor in the Memphis situation, according to Lucy R. Mason was AFL-CIO rivalry and the area's industrialization plans.[29]

As they had at Gadsden, URW organizers encountered violence. In 1941, for example, URW organizer George Bass and others were severely beaten when they attempted to pass out leaflets at the plant gates.[30] The Memphis contest also involved a racial division, with Negroes generally supporting the CIO, and the whites the AFL. The AFL established a separate local for Negroes, and it was reported that a meeting of 300 was attended by only six Negroes, and only 35 whites attended a CIO meeting of 350. The AFL won the 1941 election 1008 to 805.[31] However, the URW won bargaining rights at the plant a year later.[32] The rubber workers also won bargaining rights at the B. F. Goodrich plant in Clarksville, Tennessee, in 1941 by a vote of 179 to 176[33] and established Local Union No. 181 at the Reed Rubber Company in Atlanta in June 1940.[34]

Thus, despite heated opposition, the rubber workers had established a base in the south which they consolidated during the war. The factors favoring their organization were: relatively large plant size; branches of plants with headquarters elsewhere; a concentrated base of operations of the union in Akron (which had about a third of its membership in 1940); and lower wages than elsewhere.

UNITED AUTOMOBILE WORKERS

Although the south's automobile plants were organized as extensions of companywide contracts signed by the UAW and the companies in Detroit, unionization of the southern plants was a part of the over-all campaign. The Ford Motor Company's vicious drive against the union in Dallas was a part of the NLRB case which finally brought Ford to terms with the union. Ford's campaign was carefully documented by the NLRB,[35] with details of union organizers or sympathizers being kidnapped and beaten by company employees, workers discharged for union activity, and numerous other violations of the act. The Board ordered the company to change its tactics.

The United Automobile Workers also encountered hostility elsewhere in the south. In Memphis, for example, Mayor Watkins Overton told newsmen on September 18, 1937, that CIO agitators would not be tolerated there.

The UAW filed unfair labor practice charges with the NLRB against Ford in Dallas during 1939 and 1940; the intermediate report on these cases accused company officials of "brutality unknown in the history of the Board."[36]

The UAW was more successful at Atlanta's Fisher Body and Chevrolet plants. The employees in the two General Motors plants had been organized under the NRA, but could not get recognition. Management started a company union, and, according to Tom Starling, an organizer of the UAW local and later UAW regional director, "The company didn't do anything it said it would. The guys expected something and didn't get it, so they joined our union."[37] The workers started with the AFL and later went into the CIO, because "local AFL leaders seemed afraid of General Motors and had no place to put the auto workers."

The first sit-down strike in the auto industry started at Atlanta in November 1936, when the company fired a worker for wearing a CIO button. According to Charlie Gillman, union leader at Atlanta: "We were the only local on strike in Atlanta. We surely felt lonely. When General Motors reached a national agreement with the United Automobile Workers of America, the obligation to bargain collectively came with the national contract. After that we had a good strong union—born on the picket line."[38]

The UAW won bargaining rights in the Atlanta General Motors plants April 17, 1940, in companywide voting. It secured a contract with Ford on April 20, 1941, after a vigorous drive masterminded by John L. Lewis, and after findings of unfair labor practices against the company had been sustained by the U.S. Court of Appeals. In the NLRB election following the signing of the contract, the UAW got 70 per cent of the vote.[39] This agreement automatically extended the union to the south, and, by August 1941, the UAW had contracts with 11 southern plants with 9377 employees.

THE AMERICAN NEWSPAPER GUILD

The first union of white-collar workers to be active in the south was the American Newspaper Guild (ANG), which had affiliates in the south when it was organized in December 1933. The grievances which led to the formation of the guild had existed for many years, but its founding was inspired by an editorial by Heywood Broun in the New York *World-Telegram*, August 7, 1933. Broun had learned that "a number of publishers are planning to cheat NRA re-employment aims" by "reclassifying their editorial staff as 'professional men.' Since NRA regulations do not cover professionals, newspapermen, therefore, would continue in many instances to work all hours of the day and any number of hours of the week."[40] Broun noted that newspaper men had regarded unions as "all right for dopes like printers, not for smart guys like newspaper men," but that "the printers because of their union, are getting 30 per cent more than the smart fourth estaters. And . . . the printers, because of their union and because they don't permit themselves to be called high-faluting names, will now benefit by the new NRA regulations." Broun concluded that there should be a newspaper writers' union, adding: "I am going to do the best I can to help get one up."

The conditions of newspaper workers were very bad when Broun made his decision. Hours were long and irregular. There had been a period of job insecurity and unemployment as a result of newspaper mergers during the 1920's and the depression of the 1930's, and many newspapers were autocratic in the treatment of their employees.[41] There was therefore considerable enthusiasm for the guild, which was formally organized in December 1933, affiliated with the AFL in 1936, and joined the CIO the following year.

It was particularly active in the southwest. Tulsa, Oklahoma, started a movement to organize newspaper workers even before the ANG was formally created.[42] At about the same time, the editorial workers of three Birmingham newspapers were discussing the formation of a local guild, and one was organized at Richmond, Virginia, on December 5, 1933. Editorial writers at Austin had formed the first Texas ANG local by January 1934. In May it was reported that the first contract had been negotiated with the Austin *American-Statesman,* and "The three Austin newspapers report 100 per cent membership." At the founding convention of the ANG, Monroe, Louisiana, and Tulsa, Richmond, and Norfolk were represented. By proxies, El Paso, San Antonio, Austin, Dallas, Birmingham and Columbia, South Carolina were included. By 1941, the ANG had chartered 28 locals in the south, but only six of them remained in 1965. Although 42 ANG charters had been issued in the south by 1965, there were only seven guild locals in the region at that time.[43] The guild's relatively high attrition rate can be attributed to a high turnover of members, mergers of newspapers, the unwise policy of issuing charters during the union's early days, and vigorous employer opposition.

The first ANG strike in the south was against the Chattanooga *Evening News,* from May 22 to May 26, 1939.[44] This involved 25 employees in the editorial and commercial departments who struck "over a series of contract violations and other anti-labor practices." This strike was won by the Chattanooga Guild, and "the *Chattanooga News* reinstated two persons fired . . . and signed a year's industrial contract prohibiting economy dismissals and allowing the guild grievance committee to review firings for other causes."

The second ANG strike was against the Monroe, Louisiana, *World and News-Star* over the discharge of Harold Breard, secretary of the Monroe Guild, who had protested the publisher's antiunion activities. Eighteen strikers, including eight women, were involved in this walkout, which lasted until December 18. (Information on this strike is from the *The Monroe Guild Striker* and flyers released daily by the strikers.) The Monroe strikers' effort to urge advertisers to cease dealing with the paper caused the Monroe Chamber of Commerce to obtain an injunction against the guild. The settlement was finally reached in December, after an NLRB trial examiner recommended that the publisher stop interfering with the union, reinstate the union official, and grant the strikers back pay. Under the terms of the settlement reached before the NLRB issued an order, the strikers were paid $11,000 in full back pay, improved wages, seniority in layoffs, and arbitration. Although the settlement failed to provide for recognition of the guild or reinstatement of Harold Breard, "The strikers by unanimous vote pooled their checks for back pay and divided $10,000 between Breard and two other strikers who, with their consent and approval, were not reinstated. The amounts approximated two years pay for each of the three strikers."[45] After this strike was settled, the Monroe Guild dwindled to a few members by 1943, and its charter was revoked in 1944. It was announced in June 1941 that Harold Breard had become an organizer for the ANG in Kansas City.[46]

The third strike, against the *Birmingham Post*, September 5 to December 18, 1941, is significant because it was "The Guild's first strike against a Scripps-Howard newspaper and launched what appeared to be the long-expected finish fight against Scripps-Howard anti-Guild policies." This strike involved 30 workers and came with the expiration of a contract when the company refused to grant the union shop and a wage increase. The strike forced the *Post* to suspend operations and was settled on December 18, by a contract that recognized the union as exclusive bargaining agent in the editorial and circulation departments, provided substantial wage gains, and included improved overtime, holiday, severance pay, and the voluntary check-off. Thus, although the ANG's membership in the south was highly unstable, it acquired a strong base in several major cities; in 1939, the guild had about 1200 members in the south. In addition, the labor movement acquired many articulate spokesmen through members of the southern guilds, some of whom joined the CIO and other union staffs in the region.

OIL WORKERS

The Oil Workers' International Union made an unsuccessful effort to organize the workers in its jurisdiction in the southwest during the 1930's. OWIU's predecessor, the Oil Field, Gas Well, and Refinery Workers' Union, was active in the southwest during the First World War, but almost completely disappeared between 1922 and 1929. The union maintained some strength in California and in 1929 initiated a campaign in the mid-continent field because it feared that competition from that area would jeopardize working conditions in California. During this drive, the union organized twelve locals in Oklahoma and Texas.

The drive was brought to an end by the depression and the adamant refusal of the employers, most of whom had company unions, to bargain with the oil workers. Membership declined to about 300 in 1931 but was revived somewhat by the NRA. A real boost was Sinclair's recognition of the union in 1934, probably because of the pro-New Deal attitude of Harry F. Sinclair. The Sinclair local in Houston, Texas, had 1157 members in 1939—the largest local in the south; total southern membership was only 6206 that year.[47] The local was the OWIU's main base for organization on the Gulf Coast, and Sinclair was the only major refinery to sign a nationwide agreement with the oil workers.

Unlike the ACWA and the UMW, the oil workers were not strong enough either to increase membership under the NRA or to enforce the petroleum code after the NIRA was declared unconstitutional. Moreover, unlike the clothing and coal industries, petroleum employers did not look to the union to stabilize the industry.

The oil workers experienced their greatest pre-World War II southern growth in 1933 and 1934. The union chartered 32 locals in the south during 1933; 18 in Texas, 12 in Oklahoma, and one each in Louisiana and Kentucky. In 1934 it chartered 29 locals; 14 in Oklahoma, nine in Texas, two each in Arkansas and Georgia, and one each in Kentucky and Louisiana. The union's expansion in the south almost ceased in the following years, however; it chartered only two locals in 1935, none in 1936, seven in 1937, three in 1938, two in 1939, one in 1940 and eight in 1941. In 1939, the oil workers had about 22,960 members in the United States, 6206 (27.03 per cent) of whom were in the south; the 1941 membership was 19,270 in the United States and 6115 in the south (31.73 per cent).[48]

The first major oil workers' local in the Gulf Coast area was Local 227 at Sinclair in Houston. Local 227 replaced a company union at Sinclair and attracted members from the Gulf Coast Metal Trades Council formed during 1933-1934, and, with the aid of pro-union ministers and other unions (especially the National Maritime Union) established other locals at nearby Pasadena and Baytown, Texas; the Pasadena local had an average membership of 677 during 1939. The oil workers established Local 229 for Negroes and Local 243 for whites at the Magnolia refinery at Beaumont, Texas, in 1933, but they did not win bargaining rights from an independent local until 1944, when 500 Negro votes provided the margin of victory.[49] Local 23 at Port

Arthur, Texas, was reorganized in 1933 and attempted to win contracts from Gulf and Texaco, but the oil workers' activities in Port Arthur were impeded by conflicts between craft and industrial unions within the refineries. The union lost an election at Gulf in 1938 by 1468 to 1211. The first major election won in the Sabine area was at Pure Oil's Port Neches refinery by 152 to 110 in 1938; this was followed by a victory at the Texas Company refinery at Port Neches in March 1941, where it received 299 of 414 votes. The Texas Company's independent union at Port Arthur was declared illegal by the NLRB, and the board's ruling was upheld by the U.S. Circuit Court in March 1941. But the oil workers did not succeed in winning an election at the important Texas Company and Gulf refineries until 1942.[50]

In 1936, the Oil Field, Gas Well, and Refinery Workers participated in the formation of the CIO, and the name was later changed to the Oil Workers' International Union (OWIU). In March 1937, the CIO created the Petroleum Workers' Organizing Committee (PWOC), which put 21 organizers in the field. The PWOC planned to organize 1,000,000 oil workers.[51] Of these, an estimated 37,000 were in refining, 102,000 in the production of oil, 320,000 in marketing, 500,000 in the distribution of refined products.

Companies in the Gulf Coast area countered the organizing drive by raising wages, and the local communities attacked the CIO for being Communist. In addition, the Metal Trades Council of the AFL launched a competitive organizing drive with a mass meeting in Houston on April 15, 1937.

In spite of the activity of the PWOC, the oil workers actually gained very few members until they were aided by the War Labor Board. Because of poor results and financial difficulties, the PWOC reduced the number of organizers from 21 to two in June 1938. Actually, the 21 organizers were in the field for only about six months.[52]

By 1939, the OWIU and its AFL competitors had organized only about 15 to 20 per cent of the total refinery workers. A survey of 14 major companies by the Temporary National Economic Committee in 1939 revealed:

> Of 66,657 employees in these refineries, some 80 per cent of the national refinery employment of wage earners, 9054 in 20 refineries were covered by CIO agreements and 4116 in 7 refineries by AFL agreements, 13.6 per cent and 6.1 per cent, respectively, of the total employment. Since June, 1935, the two organizations had secured agreements in only six refineries of the larger companies, representing less than 3000 workers. In addition, the CIO or AFL was recognized as collective bargaining agency, but without contracts in 10 refineries employing 4023 employees.

On the other hand, independent unions represented 34,100 employees in 53 refineries under formal agreement. It was also brought out that from 1936 to 1939 the CIO had raised its percentage of representation in refineries from about 10 per cent to the current 13.6 per cent; that of the AFL had increased by a few percentage points; while the share of the independent unions had risen from 20 to 47.8 per cent.[53]

The OWIU's experience suggests that the unions which were most successful during the New Deal period were those strong enough to enforce the NRA and the Wagner Act with strikes. This had become clear to the OWIU Executive Board by 1939 when it reported to the annual convention that the NLRB was a "major disappointment" because it had inadequate staff, and was opposed by employers, who were openly violating the act, "realizing that they had little to fear from the union even when found guilty." The OWIU had filed many complaints, but the board had issued few orders, though some of the cases were tried "a year or two ago."

The Mid-Continent strike. Another factor crippling the oil workers in the southwest, and indeed throughout the country, was the disastrous 15-month strike against the Mid-Continent Petroleum Corporation at Tulsa, Oklahoma, beginning December 22, 1938. This strike cost the international union $324,925.41[54] by June 30, 1943, and local unions and individuals undetermined amounts; the international paid for the strike until as late as 1950.[55] The executive council, in explaining the failure of organizing efforts in the east Texas and Gulf areas to the 1939 convention, said: "There can be little organization work sufficiently done until the present Mid-Continent strike is concluded." The executive council considered the strike a test between the Oil Workers' International and the oil industry; it told the convention: "The story of this strike marks one of the outstanding pages in the struggle between capital and labor in the Southwest. In fact, it is probably one of the outstanding strikes in the history of the Oil Workers International Union."[56]

The psychological and human effects of the strike were probably more important for union growth than the financial costs. Union members committed illegal acts because they considered this a deliberate effort by Mid-Continent to break the union. During the 1937 negotiations, which culminated in a contract, union leaders accused management of attempting to destroy interest in the union by posting the points agreed to on the bulletin board as if they were gifts from management. After the 1937 agreement, the union complained that it was unable to adjust grievances with management and that there would be a strike if the grievances could not be adjusted.

When the strike started in 1938, about 150 men occupied the turbo-electric plant for over six hours, and the plant was blockaded for two days during which time airplanes brought food and supplies to non-strikers in the plant. Before the plant reopened with the help of the national guard, Tulsa police used tear gas to break up crowds in front of the refinery.[57] After the plant resumed operations, some of Mid-Continent's pipe lines were dynamited, and 106 strikers were indicted for unlawful assembly. These charges were dropped in May 1939, but 17 of the men were indicted on the more serious charge of inciting to riot.

The men involved in the strike during most of the fifteen months suffered real hardship. They were paid $10.00 a week strike benefits until February 1939, when this was reduced to $5.00. By September 1939, strike benefits had been reduced to $5.00 every two weeks. An international representative told the 1939 convention that the union would have spent some $237,000 on the strike in the eight months since it started if it had been adequately financed and that if the union "had had $237,000 in the defense fund in December 1938, we would not have had a strike."

The representative said that new members told him the union had tricked them into joining because it could not continue paying strike benefits; he said the average striker had not received over $110 or $115. "They don't mind when they lose an automobile. Lot's of them have lost that. They don't even mind when they take their furniture, when they lost their homes that kinda get them blue."

When the plant reopened, the oil workers resorted to a boycott of the company's products. Strikers went before an average of 47 unions a week throughout the trade area and sent out thousands of letters to unions and editors of labor papers. The boycott was handicapped by inadequate finances, and the union was urged to give it greater publicity "as being a national strike and a threat to either destroy the OWIU or make it."

The strike was officially terminated in March 1940, and the company agreed to rehire all strikers with seniority rights except 247 who were accused of having sabotaged the company's property. However, only about 40 men were rehired immediately, and a year later this number had only increased to 200, leaving some 600 strikers out of work; many of them did not find employment until the beginning of World War II. The executive council member from the Tulsa district told the 1940 convention, "we have suffered ignominious defeat, as judged by the public in the settlement of the Mid-Continent strike, and we have only the mutitude of N.L.R.B. cases as evidence of the justice and rectitude of our cause."[58] OWIU officers told the convention, "Organizing has been conducted under a tremendous handicap since the last convention. The Mid-Continent strike situation has blocked any appreciative headway being made in the Southwestern states, while opposition of the companies, company unions and general apathy of the workers has presented a general problem which we have been unable to successfully overcome."

The union's total membership had declined from about 30,000 in May 1938, to around 21,000 in 1940, and the 1938 total was not regained until late in 1943 under the stimulus of the War Labor Board and improving economic conditions associated with the war.

Standard of New Jersey and the independent unions. The dominant position of the Standard Oil Company of New Jersey strongly influenced the labor relations policies of other firms in the industry.[59] OWIU President O. A. Knight told the 1941 convention that it had become increasingly obvious that the union could not attain proper effectiveness in the oil industry without organizing Standard Oil, and that the CIO was being urged to undertake this task.[60]

A device which helped Esso and other Standard of New Jersey affiliates avoid outside unions before the 1930's was the company union system devised by Mackenzie King—later Canadian prime minister—around the time of World War I. When the Wagner Act outlawed "company" unions, Standard affiliates severed their formal ties with these organizations but continued to deal with them as independent unaffiliated local unions. No significant breach in Standard's system occurred until 1942 when the workers at the Ingleside (Texas) Refinery of Humble Oil and Refining Company (a Standard of New Jersey subsidiary) rejected the employees federation in an NLRB election (212 to 69) in favor of the oil workers. However, Humble sealed this breach in November 1945 by closing the Ingleside refinery. The refinery probably would have been closed whether or not the workers voted for the OWIU, but management was "obviously annoyed with a group that had broken through the wall of its resistance to outside unionism."

The Industrial Representation Plan (IRP) adopted by Standard Oil of New Jersey grew out of the "bloody" Bayonne, New Jersey, strikes against that company in 1914-1916. The IRP was installed by Clarence J. Hicks, who had gained experience with a similar program in another Rockefeller interest—the Colorado Fuel and Iron Company—after the disastrous "Ludlow massacre."[61]

Company officials labeled the IRP "'The Square Deal'—with Emphasis on the Individual."[62] The plan provided for: elected employee representatives, an elaborate welfare program, and the creation of a personnel and training department to administer the plan.

The IRP was ratified by 98 per cent of the workers at the Baton Rouge, Louisiana, refinery (the largest in the United States) late in 1919, but not all the workers considered the plan ideal. In the summer of 1920, for example, boilermakers' Lodge 582 struck after the company refused to recognize it as bargaining agent for the 300-member unit. The boilermakers' strike halted production at the 3200-man refinery for three weeks but was completely defeated.

The company refused to recognize an outside union. D. R. Weller, vice-president of Standard Oil of Louisiana, announced:

> The Company insists upon dealing with its own employees, either directly or through committees of their fellow employees which have been hertofore voluntarily selected in accordance with the company's Industrial Representation Plan which most fairly and fully carries into effect the principle of just and collective bargaining.

After the boilermakers' strike—which was the only serious trouble management had with the IRP—the company sought to improve the plan as a means of handling grievances, providing for labor-management communications, and implementing the "square deal" program.

Jersey Standard officials were obviously unhappy when the Wagner Act "challenged the company's traditional methods of collective bargaining." According to a company publication, "this law was based on the tacit assumption that 'capital' is the enemy of 'labor,' a conflict concept directly opposed to the cooperation concept that had been successfully promoted in Jersey."

After the Wagner Act was upheld in the spring of 1937, the workers at the Baton Rouge refinery voted overwhelmingly to retain a legalized version of the IRP, and management signed a contract with the new union, called the Independent Industrial Workers Association (IIWA), in 1937.

When the IIWA was first established, Negroes and whites were in the same union, but the Negroes formed a separate organization because they wanted control of their own affairs. For all practical purposes, IIWA Section I (white) and Section II (Negro) were separate locals, though a joint bargaining committee gave the Negroes a sort of veto on the contract; Negroes and whites negotiated separate supplementary agreements pertaining to their sections.

Each section of IIWA elected representatives who made up two separate plant councils, which met monthly; union members did not participate in these monthly meetings, though they were permitted to attend.

The basic provisions of the 1937 Esso contract, covering production and maintenance workers in a plantwide unit, remained almost unchanged until 1953. The contract was subject to amendment at any time, though management generally reserved the right to determine if requests were justified.[63] Management was able to make many decisions unilaterally because union and management officials felt that IIWA could not have conducted a successful strike; the memory of the 1920 boilermakers strike and fear that their positions and benefits might be lost served to dampen rank-and-file enthusiasm for strikes.

Esso's wage policy was to meet prevailing adjustments on the Gulf Coast, but not to be a pattern-setter. For example, the 1937 agreement provided that wages would be based on the average of eight other Gulf Coast refineries, most of which were subsequently organized by the Oil Workers' International Union; the practice of naming these refineries in the contract was discontinued in 1946, though their contracts continued to influence Esso wage decisions.

CHAPTER XIII

Growth of AFL Unions

REORGANIZATION OF THE LONGSHOREMEN

As we have noted, the longshoremen had been quite well organized in the south until the 1920's when they were weakened by the open-shop movement. At the time of the 1923 strike in New Orleans, there were two ILA locals—Local 231 for Negroes (with 2700 members), and Local 1226 for whites (with 125 members). Although they continued until their charters were revoked by the international union in 1936, their bargaining strength was restricted to three companies controlled by the United States Shipping Board.

After the strike, general longshoremen in New Orleans were hired through A. E. Harris, a Negro, who gave preferential treatment to his own race. The whites responded by attacking the Steamship Association politically. In 1927, for example, a candidate for mayor denounced the association for having "Africanized" the waterfront.[1] At the same time, the ILA white local was reactivated by a man who campaigned for the local's presidency on the platform of more jobs for whites. To achieve this, he organized an informal club of Negro and white longshoremen outside the ILA. He then admitted the whites to Local 1226 and, through pressure on the international, forced Local 231 to accept the Negroes. Once in the local, the new Negro members provoked a strike. The apparent plan was to have whites and new Negro members force some of the older Negroes out of their jobs.[2] His plan failed, however, because the employers saw through the scheme and because they were eager to preserve their alliance with the Negroes. Although the strike failed, many of the older Negro members of Local 321 left the union and went into nonunion work. The colored local was then taken over by a Negro who was controlled by the president of the white local. This maneuvering meant very little, however, because in 1933 the United States Shipping Board leased its facilities to independent operators, and the ILA locals lost their last contracts on the New Orleans waterfront. Without the protection of these contracts, the Negro members of Local 231 felt compelled to accept lower wages. They voted to accept a pay cut to 65 cents an hour. The white local struck for 80 cents, and its members were promptly replaced by Negroes.[3]

Low wages and nonunion conditions in New Orleans made it difficult for the ILA to hold its position in the Texas Gulf ports, where it maintained some strength throughout the 1920's. In October 1931, the ILA was defeated in a west Gulf strike against a wage cut from 80 to 70 cents an hour and from 18 to 13 cents a bale for cotton work. Since the companies had no trouble importing strikebreakers, the Texas longshoremen were forced to return to work at the lower rates, which prevailed throughout 1933 and 1934 because, as a union leader put it, the union "didn't have the strength to do anything about it."[4]

With the passage of the NIRA in 1933, the New Orleans Steamship Association and other Gulf Coast employees recognized company unions. The Independent White Longshoremen's Association and the Independent Colored Longshoremen's Association were formed in New Orleans under the leadership of former members of the moribund ILA locals. The New Orleans association entered into two-year contracts with these independents which provided for wage increases to 75 cents an hour and grievance procedures. But several important employers, including the Morgan Line, the United Fruit Company, and the Standard Fruit and Steamship Company, refused to sign the agreement.[5]

With the passage of the NIRA, therefore, the ILA was confronted with a difficult situation in the south, where the independents blocked its further expansion and threatened its strength in the north Atlantic ports. These problems were aggravated by the ease with which ships could be diverted from unionized areas and by the growing importance of the southern ports.[6] The international therefore sought to strengthen its position by taking over the independent unions. In New Orleans, in February 1934, ILA president Joseph Ryan invited the two independents to affiliate with the international, and sought to revoke the charters of ILA Local 231 and Local 1226. He was prevented when the locals secured a court order to restrain him.[7]

Although the independents remained in control, the ILA was able to maintain its contracts with employers in the western Gulf ports by threatening to have federal subsidies withdrawn,[8] and by putting pressure on a "shipping association with interests in the south to see that contracts were signed there."[9] On May 1, 1934, when these tactics failed to bring employers on the eastern Gulf to terms, the ILA called a strike of those ports. But it was called off on May 12, when it became obvious that the union was too weak to extend the strike to all Gulf ports.

As a result of the ILA's inability to organize the eastern Gulf, Texas and Lake Charles employers balked at paying higher rates when their contract expired June 30, 1935. The Lake Charles employers imported strikebreakers and attempted to operate on a nonunion basis, but, when a clash between strikers and strikebreakers resulted in the wounding of eight ILA members on July 15, they decided to "go along with the ILA." Their decision apparently was influenced by a warning from William Green to Louisiana Senators Long and Overton that there "would be trouble in other ports" unless the Lake Charles companies remained in the Texas agreement.[10]

After this settlement, the ILA attempted to equalize wages on the Gulf by striking 23 large east Gulf companies on October 1, 1935. It also demanded recognition in the New Orleans and east Gulf ports and the termination of contracts in September 1936 to coincide with the termination of its other contracts. Because of the ineffectiveness of the strike, the ILA extended the walkout to all Gulf ports on October 10, involving 7500 workers from Pensacola to Corpus Christi.[11]

Perhaps because of its importance to all parties concerned, the strike was hard fought and resulted in much bloodshed. The board of commissioners of Lake Charles Harbor had prepared for a showdown with the ILA by purchasing four submachine guns and importing professional strikebreakers, or "guards," from the Railway Audit and Inspection Company. These guards were deputized by the port commission, which also recognized a company union—the Louisiana Longshoremen's Association. However, the Lake Charles port was closed by Governor O. K. Allen after three of the guards had been killed and eight wounded when they attempted to bring 300 members of the company union onto the Lake Charles docks. Some of the violence on the Gulf Coast was too much even for professional strikebreaking agencies. The Burns Detective Agency at Houston refused to cooperate with a company which wanted guards with sawed-off shotguns "to blast their way through the line of pickets on the docks, to kill if necessary and would not in any respect assume any responsibility or liability."[12] The Houston representative of the Burns agency was concerned because it was an election year in Houston, and his guards could not get special commissions from the Houston police. These commissions would have legalized their activities and protected them from damage suits.

At New Orleans, three deaths occurred[13] despite police protection for strikebreakers. The violence ceased, however, when a federal district court enjoined the ILA locals. The union leaders spent their time attempting to have the injunction reconsidered as contrary to the anti-injunction provisions of the Norris-La Guardia Act. With the injunction in force, business was above normal in New Orleans, and the ILA's strike elsewhere was weakened as ships were diverted to New Orleans.[14]

The strike was more effective in the Texas ports, but even some Texas companies reopened with strikebreakers, many of whom were lodged in warehouses. In Houston, Negro and white longshoremen organized independent unions and signed a contract with the Houston Maritime Committee, which divided work equally among Negro and white longshoremen. The employers at Beaumont offered to settle with the ILA, but the union refused because it wanted a Gulf-wide agreement.

The situation became so grave by the last week in October that Joseph Ryan came to Texas and threatened a general shipping boycott of all cargo handled by strikebreakers and independents on the Atlantic and Pacific coasts if the strike were not settled. As a result, a mediation board was appointed by President Roosevelt on November 23 to end the dispute. Though some employers refused to meet with the board, an agreement was finally reached to permit representation elections between the ILA and the independents. It was agreed, however, that the victorious bargaining agent would be open to all applicants. On December 2, 1935, several intercoastal steamship companies with offices in New York notified their Houston representatives to bargain with the ILA and to abide by the decision of the mediation board with respect to the east Gulf ports. A number of companies, including two large New Orleans shippers, signed agreements. The ILA won an election from the independent union at Mobile by 961 to 19, and took over the contract with the Mobile Maritime Committee members; since the members of this committee were also the leading operators in Gulfport, Mississippi, and Pensacola, Florida, the Mobile agreement was extended to these ports. Although the ILA did not succeed in equalizing wages or getting a coastwide agreement, it did establish a strong beachhead, which it later consolidated to gain bargaining rights for the longshoremen in every major southern port.

After the 1935 strike, the ILA revoked the charters of its locals in New Orleans and chartered the former independent unions as ILA Local 1418 (white) and Local 1919 (colored). The old ILA Local 231 (colored) continued as the Longshoremen Protective Union Benevolent Association, but with little strength because the new ILA locals took over the contracts which the independents had had with the companies. The ILA also organized a banana handlers' local which entered into an agreement with the United Fruit and Standard Steamship companies.

ILA-ILWU contest for control of the Gulf ports. No sooner had the ILA established itself on the Gulf ports than it was challenged by the International Longshoremen and Warehousemen's Union (ILWU), led by a group of left-wing West Coast longshoremen who seceded from the ILA in 1937. The ILA's position on the Gulf was rendered increasingly vulnerable by mounting dissatisfaction with some of its policies. The prevailing feeling among New Orleans longshoremen was that their ILA leaders were in collusion with employers, a feeling that was intensified in 1938 when the New Orleans unions agreed to continue working at the old wage rates of 60 cents an hour when ILA locals on the south Atlantic ports had struck successfully for 90 cents. Although Mobile and New Orleans longshoremen voted to accept an increase to 75 cents following the south Atlantic settlement, the suspicion remained. In addition, many New Orleans longshoremen were dissatisfied with the "shape-up" hiring system which gave a little employment to many workers and steady jobs to very few. There also had long been rumors that local ILA leaders were corrupt.

The ILWU capitalized on this unrest by moving into New Orleans and Mobile in 1937 and challenging the ILA's position. In November 1937, the West Coast union won bargaining rights and a contract covering employees of the Morgan (Southern Pacific) Lines at New Orleans, and signed up large numbers of Mobile and New Orleans longshoremen.

There can be little doubt that the ILWU's presence excited New Orleans stevedores who granted a wage increase after the union began organizing. Employers apparently were very satisfied with the shape-up which gave them a steady supply of labor at all times. The importance of the Gulf Coast for the AFL and the CIO is indicated by the fact that "At one time practically the whole machinery of the CIO setup was moved to New Orleans and Mobile and Harry Bridges in person journeyed from the Pacific coast to these cities to direct the CIO campaign," while the AFL spent over $80,000 in an equally vigorous effort.[15]

In addition to their dissatisfaction with the ILA's collective bargaining policies, some colored longshoremen favored the ILWU because it emphasized equalitarian racial policies at a time when the ILA's practice of maintaining segregated locals was under attack in the Negro community. As it turned out, however, the ILA's policies—which provided for racial job quotas and segregated locals—probably helped its position because it gave some Negroes powerful positions on the southern docks. Indeed, the AFL's southern representative in charge of reorganizing the ILA locals reported that "whites couldn't get jobs in longshoring" between Baltimore and Mobile.[16] As a result, Negro leaders fought to retain the ILA. For example, Ed Rhone, president of the Mobile colored local, told Negro longshoremen, "Anyone voting for the C.I.O. tomorrow is a traitor to his race. With the help of the good white people of Mobile we hope to stay on the waterfront honorably."[17]

Because of its ideology and racial position, the ILWU was opposed by the community as well as by most employers and the ILA. During the 1937-1938 election campaign, for example, the Louisiana legislature adopted a resolution condemning the ILWU as "Communistic" and calling the unionization of Negroes a threat to white supremacy.[18] The New Orleans police raided CIO headquarters, arrested union leaders and destroyed membership cards.[19] The day before the election, William Mitch, president of the Alabama State Industrial Union Council–CIO, told an all-Negro crowd, "The only social equality I ever heard a negro ask about is the same amount of money for the same amount of labor." And another Alabama CIO official, Noel Beddow, told the same audience that "Negroes are beginning to believe in Santa Claus again with John L. Lewis."[20]

In spite of this opposition, the ILWU had a number of apparent advantages. For one thing, the CIO union consistently attracted bigger crowds, especially Negroes. And many of these longshoremen signed up with the ILWU, prompting Harry Bridges to claim that 90 per cent of the longshoremen held membership cards and to predict that his union would win with 80 per cent of the vote.[21] Although the local white communities and employers favored the AFL, the CIO had some powerful friends in Washington. For example, George Googe charged the NLRB with having sided with the CIO in this contest by taking unusual procedural steps to circumvent the New Orleans regional NLRB director; he implied that the CIO was given "inside" information concerning the board's proposed actions and that the special representative of the NLRB who came to New Orleans to "investigate" the case sat on the platform with Harry Bridges, and addressed a CIO mass meeting.[22] This and other testimony persuaded a congressional investigating committee that the NLRB had "pronounced pro-CIO sympathies."[23]

However, the NLRB's decision concerning the appropriate bargaining unit and employee eligibility to vote in the election favored the ILA. The board rejected the ILWU's request for a single unit covering all employees in favor of a company-by-company election favored by the ILA and the employers. The board's eligibility ruling favored employees with steady employment so that only 3308 of 6403 men in the 20 companies met the requirements.[24]

In addition to general longshoremen, the clerks and checkers and banana handlers voted in the October 14, 1937 balloting, and a simultaneous election was held at Mobile for 1300 longshoremen, 200 barge operators, 100 clerks and checkers, 350 warehousemen and 700 banana handlers.

The ILA won the elections by wide margins. Some 3500 longshoremen, banana handlers and clerks and checkers voted for the ILA in New Orleans, and 874 for the ILWU; the ILA general longshoremen won bargaining rights in 18 companies; the ILA banana handlers in United Fruit and Standard Fruit; and the ILA clerks and checkers in 12 companies.[25]

Though they did not achieve the results they expected on the Gulf Coast, ILWU officials felt that the organizing campaign

> ... was a long ways from being a failure or unsatisfactory. The obstacles and circumstances that surrounded the duties of the organizers were innumerable and the mere fact that we were able to obtain a foothold and remain in the South despite the terror and the use of organized political and economic forces brought to bear against them alone demonstrates the stamina, courage and ability of our elected organizers . . . workers who were intimidated beyond belief because of corrupt political and trade union machines and have to choose between joining our organization and their very lives are not lost to us.[26]

The ILWU officers claimed their organizers were "hunted like dogs by state and local authorities" and were beaten when found. Harry Bridges reported to CIO President Philip Murray: "we expended a large sum of money, sent our best men into the field, two of whom were beaten so severely they have never recovered physically."[27]

With the defeat of the ILWU, the ILA became firmly entrenched on Gulf Coast ports. In New Orleans, the white general longshoremen's local elected a "rank-and-file" candidate after the ILWU was defeated in 1937 and instituted a "share-the-work" program which gave white longshoremen fairly stable employment.[28]

The Negro local became less powerful in subsequent years, and there were a number of court cases and congressional investigations into charges of corruption.[29] There was also much internal dissension until after World War II when the local's affairs were stabilized.[30] Although Local 1419 was probably the strongest Negro local union in the United States, employment of Negro longshoremen remained on the average much less regular than that of the whites. Moreover, the racial division of labor remained.

The ILWU. After its 1937 defeat for bargaining rights for New Orleans longshoremen, the ILWU continued its activities mainly among warehousemen. ILWU Local 207 under the leadership of Willie Dorsey, a Negro who had supported the ILWU in 1937, succeeded in organizing five companies with 18 warehouses in New Orleans and four in Baton Rouge. Although the work force in the companies was about 2100 at the busiest time of the year, Local 207's average membership was only about 800 in 1943, when the members of the local, almost all of whom were Negroes, withdrew from the ILWU and joined the Retail, Wholesale, and Department Store Union (RWDSU).

The immediate cause of the loss of the ILWU's last stronghold in New Orleans was an attempt by the international to oust Willie Dorsey. The ILWU sent a vice-president, J. R. Robertson, and an international representative, Howard Goddard, in September 1942 to investigate charges that Dorsey had misused the local's funds. Father Jerome A. Drolet, a local priest, came to Dorsey's aid and led a fight against the ILWU. The international was accused of having taken over the local and attempting to make it "follow the Communist Party line."[31] The international also was charged with having installed and retained, over objections from the local's membership, a Communist sympathizer as office assistant; taken over the operation of the grievance procedure; forced the local to subscribe to the *Daily Worker*; and suspended Dorsey and four other local officers.[32]

Supporters of the ILWU responded by attacking Dorsey and accusing Father Drolet of:

> using the raiment of a priest to disguise his activities and his objectives . . . Drolet apparently desires to capture the leadership of the ILWU in order that he may use the union to sell out the workers . . . to red bait and urge the deportation of our beloved leader and President, Harry Bridges, and to deliver us over to the anti-war pro-nazi camp . . . who

advocate strikes during the war and are out to wreck labor and the new deal and put over a Fascist form of slavery in America . . . Father Drolet is not a good Catholic. He has proven himself to be an enemy of the working class.[33]

Harry Bridges complained to Philip Murray concerning Father Drolet's attacks on the ILWU, "especially [his attacks on ILWU's] policy towards the Negro people." According to Bridges:

> Dorsey had . . . performed very well in the early days of building the union . . . There is . . . no question of his theft of the union's funds. The International union attempted to do all in its power to straighten out the situation in a quiet way in view of the fact that we were operating in a Negro community . . .
> The local is largely a Negro local and . . . the whole matter is being watched with interest by Negroes and Negro groups the country over.[34]

Except for a few members of the Transport Workers Union (TWU) and the National Maritime Union (NMU) in New Orleans, the labor movement supported Father Drolet. He had gained respect for his fearless and tireless efforts in behalf of the workers' right to organize. Philip Murray told Father Drolet, "We have a wholesome appreciation of the creditable work you have been doing for the CIO and labor generally."[35] Local CIO leaders also rallied to his defense.

Although its membership was mainly colored, the ILWU failed to gain the support of the Negro press in New Orleans, which admired Father Drolet. The Communists had little support among New Orleans Negroes because they had minimized the drive for fair employment practices in the interest of supporting the war. A local union suspected of being controlled by the Communists was criticized for having put a white man in charge in spite of the fact that its membership was 89 per cent Negro. And the man was accused of having voted with the Communists at a New Orleans NAACP meeting against any assistance to Negroes in ILWU Local 207.[36]

Despite Harry Bridges' personal effort to save the ILWU's beachhead, the overwhelming majority of Local 207's membership seceded to the RWDSU, and, though the ILWU retained the right to put Local 207 under trusteeship, a New Orleans court exonerated Dorsey of any wrongdoing.

The ILWU and the RWDSU under the leadership of Samuel Wolchok had been engaged in a bitter jurisdictional dispute for many years. John L. Lewis had attempted to settle it in 1937 by ruling that "Bridges stays west of the Mississippi and Wolchok east of it." As it turned out, however, New Orleans was not covered by this agreement because the Mississippi almost encircles the city; if anything, New Orleans is north of the river. The outcome of this conflict "showed Wolchok with the members, Bridges with the books, stationery five-and-dime petty cash box of Local 207."[37]

Conclusions. By 1939, the ILA had a southern membership of about 16,611 and had organized every major port in the south; seven of its seventeen vice-presidents were from that region. In addition, wages in the Norfolk area were equalized with those of the north Atlantic,[38] and New Orleans wages and conditions had been equalized, under pressure from the ILWU, with those of Lake Charles and the Texas Ports.[39] However, conditions on the south Atlantic below the Norfolk area "vary from port to port and are inferior to the north Atlantic standards."[40]

The ILA's southern organizing feat nevertheless ranks along with that of the UMW in thoroughness, and it had an important psychological effect on other AFL organizations. In 1939, George Googe called the organization of southern longshoremen the "greatest labor accomplishment in recent years," adding: "The accomplishments for the longshoremen in the South Atlantic and Gulf did more to charge the batteries of the general labor movement in the interior of the South than anything else that has ever occurred."[41]

The AFL and ILA, for one thing, were willing to "disregard expenses" in order to organize the workers. Also, competition with the CIO and the southern ports' threat to conditions in other places gave the AFL and the ILA strong motivation to organize; the union was able to apply pressure to employers in other ports; the workers needed organization in view of the casual nature of longshore employment and the union's demonstrated ability to maintain higher than prevailing wages for similar work. Finally, the ILA understood the racial power relationship in the southern ports. It was willing to give Negro leaders important positions in the international union and considerable local power and prestige. As it had elsewhere, the experience of the 1920's had shown how racial conflict can split a union.

PULP AND PAPER WORKERS

An examination of early convention proceedings of the International Brotherhood of Paper Makers (IBPM), formed in 1893, shows almost no mention of southern activity. The IBPM was controlled primarily by skilled workers. The less skilled workers withdrew in 1906 and established the International Brotherhood of Pulp, Sulphite and Paper Mill Workers (IBPSW). After jurisdictional strife weakened both unions, they entered into an agreement in 1909 defining the IBPM's jurisdiction as the paper machine operators and the beater engineers; the IBPSW handled all other workers in the mills except mechanics who were already members of AFL unions. While there have been occasional jurisdictional clashes, the IBPSW and the UPP, as the IBPM became when it merged with the CIO Paper Worker's Union in 1957, have had fairly close relations.

The first significant mention of the south was in 1931 when President John P. Burke of the IBPSW told his convention that a large number of modern Kraft mills had recently been built and that Kraft paper was so cheap that "it is almost impossible for Northern mills to compete."[42] Moreover, Burke added, the union had lost some locals because northern mills had closed when they were unable to meet this southern competition. For instance, when the IBPSW was negotiating with Advance Bag and Paper Company of Howland, Maine, and the Alliance Paper Company, Merritown, Ontario, the company officials said that southern Kraft competition was so serious that the unions would have to accept a 15 per cent wage cut. Though the union workers voted to accept the cut, the Howland Mill closed and moved its largest machine to its mill at Hodge, Louisiana. Similarly, the Union Bag and Paper Mill Number 5 moved from Hudson Falls, New York, to Bogalusa, Louisiana. Most serious for the union was the number of mills being built in the south by International Paper, the largest company in the industry; Burke thought International Paper might try to make newsprint and told the convention: "The task of organizing these mills will, no doubt, be a herculean one, but the attempt will have to be made in the near future."

The IBPSW's relations with the International Paper Company during the 1920's had important consequences for its future organizing activities. In 1920 the company was completely organized, but in 1921 the union called a strike against International Paper and other companies because they insisted on a 30 per cent wage cut. The IBPSW settled with a group headed by Floyd L. Carlisle, president of the St. Regis Paper Company, but the International Paper strike lasted about five years, and the company operated on an open-shop basis until the New Deal period. The paper makers concluded an agreement with International Paper in 1922 which made no mention of the IBPSW. The 1921 strike was disastrous for the union because it involved two thirds of its membership and lasted for such a long time. The lesson learned by the IBPSW was that a "no-backward-step" wage policy like that followed by the United Mine Workers in the 1920's could ruin a union. Consequently, the organization accepted wage cuts totaling about 20 per cent on the average during the early 1930's.

Both the IBPSW and the Paper Makers entered the south for the first time during the NRA period. One of the first locals established in that region was at Bogalusa, where the paper makers established Local 189 and Local 189-A (colored). According to Luther H. Simmons, the first president of Local 189, "when FDR told us the government was protecting the right to join a union, that's when we signed up."[43] The Bogalusa union was organized around key men at the Great Southern Lumber Company (where, as related earlier, four men were killed in a 1919 organizing effort), followed by a mass enrollment at a public meeting. In spite of its initial support from the workers, membership declined from over 600 to 18 when Great Southern refused to grant formal recognition; the most the company was willing to concede was the union's right to settle grievances on an informal basis.

When the plant was taken over by the Gaylord Corporation in 1938, a formal NLRB election was held, and the union won its first written agreement. This move, according to members of Local 189, came because of Gaylord's more favorable attitude toward unions. Bogalusa subsequently became one of the strongest union towns in the south, and members of Local 189 have played important roles in state and local politics. According to the UPP's official paper, "From the very first, Gaylord management saw to it that the 'company side' abided by the spirit as well as the letter of the agreement. Union leaders will be among the first to acknowledge the contributions of the enlightened Gaylord mill management to industrial progress and building a better Bogalusa community."

The UPP experienced similar results at other places. In 1933, locals were established at Moss Point, Mississippi; Chattanooga, Tennessee; Mobile, Alabama; Panama City, Florida; Bastrop, Louisiana; Camden, Arkansas; and Chrichton, Alabama. The following year the UPP spread to Elizabeth, Louisiana (but the local lasted less than a year), and Tuscaloosa, Alabama, where two locals were established. In 1935, it had some 12,000 members in the international union, and 4000 in the south. However, continued employer opposition reduced membership to 200 by 1937 (this was rebuilt to 3700 by 1939, most of which was in Louisiana, Alabama, and Florida, when the union had 25,000 members).[44] At that time, the IBPSW had about 1700 members, over half of whom were in North Carolina.

Thus, by the time of World War II, the paper makers and the IBPSW had established a firm base of operations in the south. This was extended during the war and consolidated in the postwar period, when the pulp and paper industry became one of the most completely organized industries in the region. The reasons are not hard to find: the pulp and paper industry is a low labor-cost industry with few employees relative to size; while the industry is fairly competitive, there are few firms to be organized; the firms are usually branches from the nonsouth; the attitudes of the unions in this industry have been such since the 1921 strike that they have not been vigorously opposed by the major companies. The history of industrial relations in the pulp and paper industry makes the importance of unionization quite clear to the employer. For instance, the Bogalusa unions were practically impotent, despite support from the workers, until the Gaylord Corporation ended a long period of opposition to collective bargaining. It is also undoubtedly significant that the only important mill organized by the CIO paper workers in the south was a branch of the West Virginia Paper Company, with which the CIO had a contract in West Virginia (an area which the mine workers made very strong).[45]

TOBACCO WORKERS

The south held the key to successful organization of the tobacco industry, because in 1939 the 46,900 tobacco workers—concentrated largely in Virginia, Kentucky, North Carolina, and Florida—constituted about 45 per cent of total employment in the industry.[46]

The Tobacco Workers International Union (TWIU) organized several plants in the south during and after World War I, including the important R. J. Reynolds Company at Winston-Salem, North Carolina. At its peak southern membership in 1920, the TWIU had six locals in the Winston-Salem area, but the last of these disappeared in 1923 after R. J. Reynolds refused to renew its contract. The TWIU started an organizing campaign in the spring of 1928, and, after between 4000 and 5000 of R. J. Reynolds' 12,000 employees had been signed up, the company began discharging union members. After E. Lewis Evans, TWIU president, called on the AFL Executive Council for help in organizing Reynolds, William Green sent E. F. McGrady to confer with the company. Although McGrady was unable to get Reynolds to do business with the TWIU, he advised the executive council that a strike would be disastrous. The company's products were therefore placed on the AFL's unfair list, and the council instructed Green to take the matter up with Evans "as judiciously as possible."[47]

The executive council thought the TWIU was too weak to regain its position in the industry, so, in 1929, it recommended a merger of the tobacco workers and cigar makers. Since the TWIU would have been absorbed by the cigar makers and prohibited from selling employers the union label, it rejected the suggestion.

Failing to organize Reynolds, the TWIU retained only one contract in the south by 1929, and that was with the Axton-Fisher Company at Louisville, Kentucky, which supported the TWIU in exchange for the union label. In 1933, Brown and Williamson absorbed the Axton-Fisher Company and, in exchange for the union label, gave the TWIU a closed shop, the check-off, and a 1 per cent wage increase. This contract covered some 4600 workers in three plants, the largest being at Louisville with 2600 workers (who were surprised to find dues withheld from their wages); an additional 1000 were in the Winston-Salem plant, where the union had a majority, and the remainder were in Petersburg, Virginia.[48]

There was considerable unrest within the TWIU because of its inability to get more favorable contracts under the NRA. Its failure was attributed to President Evans and the absence of democratic procedures within the organization. Evans had almost complete control of the union because he could only be voted out by convention, and he had the power to prevent the calling of a convention. Strikes were also practically impossible because they required the approval of a majority of the locals and the international executive committee.

Impetus was given the TWIU organizing activities when the Supreme Court upheld the Wagner Act in 1937, and CIO unions turned their attention to the tobacco industry. The CIO made a particularly strong effort to organize the many Negro workers in the industry, who had either been neglected or organized into segregated locals by the TWIU.[49] As a result, in 1937, Liggett and Myers, Philip Morris, and the American Tobacco Company all recognized the TWIU and granted it contracts containing wage increases of between 5 and 7 per cent. But it was not until June 1941, when the P. Lorillard Company signed for its Louisville plant, that another important contract was secured by TWIU.

In the meantime, other groups were trying to organize the south's tobacco workers. In May 1937, a strike by 400 Negro women against the I. N. Vaughn Company of Richmond, Virginia, was taken over by the Southern Negro Youth Congress (SNYC), controlled by the Communist Party. Within two days the Youth Congress leaders formed an independent union, and secured its recognition together with a wage increase and a forty-hour week. The success of this strike caused a similar walkout and settlement at the nearby Carrington-Michaux plant. The independent unions affiliated with the CIO, which hired the SNYC leaders as organizers, and secured three other contracts in Richmond within a year. These strikes were the first in the Richmond tobacco industry since 1905, and the first of any kind in the city since

1922. "What is more remarkable," according to Northrup, "is that the strikers were considered absolutely unorganizable before they walked out. Yet this all-Negro union continued to progress, thanks to powerful outside assistance." Although these successes spurred the TWIU to action among Negroes for the first time in many years, the union's reputation failed to attract many colored tobacco workers.

Meanwhile, the rebellion against Lewis Evans within the TWIU was growing. It was stimulated by a five-day strike against Liggett and Meyers in April 1939. The strike, by 4000 workers in Durham and Richmond, came after five months of fruitless negotiations, and was settled by a contract granting a 5 per cent wage increase and a statement from the company saying, "it approved of its employees joining the union and wished them to do so." Although they disregarded the international's ban on strikes, the five locals involved in the walkout were not forced to have a showdown with the TWIU's leadership because the strike did not last long enough to require international strike benefits. At a time when the TWIU was making little progress by other methods, the Liggett and Meyers victory, together with the CIO's earlier successes in Richmond, indicated the efficacy of the strike as a means of organizing and improving contracts.

Although they had little voice in their own international, local tobacco workers were able to use their influence in the various state labor organizations to gain a greater measure of democracy in the TWIU. For example, they pressed the 1938 Kentucky Federation of Labor (KFL) Convention into adopting a resolution urging to the TWIU to call a convention. When the tobacco workers' leaders refused, Edward Wyler, secretary of the KFL, was given power of attorney by a majority of the TWIU's locals to secure a court order instructing Evans to hold a convention in Louisville the fourth week in October 1939.[50] Although Evans attended the convention, he withdrew after two days and got an injunction to prevent the insurgents from taking over the union. After much expensive litigation and a threat by the AFL to revoke the TWIU's charter if it refused to permit the members "greater voice" in the TWIU's affairs, the convention ousted Evans and all but one of his executive board members.[51]

The new leadership inaugurated an aggressive organizing campaign and instituted other reforms. The union label was abandoned as the exclusive weapon and was revoked where it did the membership little or no good. And the strike was used wherever necessary. Negro organizers were hired, and for the first time in many years the union elected a Negro vice-president, George Benjamin. But Negro and white locals remained and usually reinforced job segregation. At Liggett and Meyers, Negroes were hired into stemmery and product departments, each of which had an all-Negro local, while whites were hired in the manufacturing department, represented by another local.

Where locals were not racially integrated, the TWIU attempted to coordinate their activities through allied shop committees. For example, the three colored and two white locals of the Liggett and Myers Company at Durham and Richmond formed a committee, which negotiated a master contract with the company. Other locals, such as those of the American Tobacco plants at Durham and Richmond, had allied councils but did not negotiate master contracts. There was, however, only limited cooperation between the white and colored locals in the American Tobacco plants. "A consequence is that neither in Durham nor in Richmond are the Negroes in the American Tobacco factories as completely organized as their fellow workers in Liggett and Meyers plants."[52]

Racial problems continued to plague TWIU's organizing efforts. Even after the reforms instituted by Evans' successors, the TWIU hired only two Negro organizers to work among a sizeable, potential membership, and, according to Northrup: "Both the Liggett and Meyers and the American Tobacco companies have refused the T.W.I.U closed shop contracts on the grounds that the Negro workers are not well organized. The white organizers charged with altering this condition have not shown either the persistence or the understanding which is required for a successful campaign."

By the end of 1941, all the major tobacco companies in the south, with the exception of R. J. Reynolds' 15,000 workers, were organized. In 1941, the CIO's tobacco workers were taken over by the United Cannery, Agricultural, Packing and Allied Workers of America (UCAPAWA) which started an organizing campaign at Reynolds. In 1944, after it took over the UCAPAWA's campaign, the Food, Tobacco, Agricultural and Allied Workers' Union (FTA), CIO, won bargaining rights at Reynolds. At this time the tobacco industry was 90 per cent organized.[53] About one half of the industry was organized by the Cigar Makers' International Union-AFL which had most of its southern strength in Florida. Although the FTA succeeded in organizing R. J. Reynolds, it lost the contract as a result of an unsuccessful strike in 1946. The TWIU and the AFL-CIO subsequently made several fruitless efforts to organize Reynolds. After it expelled the FTA in 1950 for being dominated by Communists, the CIO sought to organize Reynolds through the all-Negro United Transport Service Employees. All these efforts failed in part because of Reynolds' personnel policies but also because Negroes and whites would not support the same union, giving the nonunion workers the balance of power.

TENNESSEE VALLEY AUTHORITY

The Tennessee Valley Authority's experience is important not only because of its impact on employment and union growth, but also because it demonstrates that effective collective bargaining can be undertaken with an agency of the federal government. Since the TVA's directors were dedicated to this principle, 40,000 workers at the Authority were covered by contracts with AFL affiliates.[54] The TVA was particularly beneficial to the hod carriers and common laborers, who rarely had written contracts before 1933.[55] The TVA's wage rates, which were initially higher than those prevailing in the area, were used by unions to raise wages of other workers. The TVA Act prescribed that "the authority pay the prevailing rates of pay with due regard for those arrived at through collective bargaining."[56]

Because there were no precedents to follow, a number of problems were involved in the establishment of collective bargaining at TVA. One of the first was its legality. Although fourteen AFL metal and building trades crafts and an independent welders' union were involved in the construction of the TVA, the Authority did not immediately recognize these unions as bargaining agents, in spite of the pro-union attitudes of TVA's directors. It was decided, however, that since the act creating the Authority referred to it as a corporation, it had the right to sue and be sued as well as to enter into contracts with unions.[57]

Another problem was the appropriate unit to be recognized for bargaining purposes. Since the unions involved came from an independent union and both the metal trades and building trades departments of the AFL, there was no appropriate structure to take them all in. In addition, the TVA chairman was opposed to negotiating separate agreements with all the crafts and felt that an industrial structure would be more appropriate. After the AFL finally agreed to grant a charter which cut across jurisdictional lines, the Tennessee Valley Trades and Labor Council (TVTLC) was established as bargaining agent for the AFL crafts.[58] This was worked out by TVA's industrial relations representative, Otto Beyer, and provided for one representative from each of the fourteen crafts. Jurisdictional problems were settled by a majority vote of the TVTLC. Although the TVTLC was recognized as exclusive bargaining agent, and refused to permit the independent welders' union to participate in negotiations, management agreed to meet separately with the independent. Sam Roper, president of the Alabama Federation of Labor, became the council's first president, and Gordon Freeman, IBEW representative from Chattanooga, became its first secretary-treasurer.

The success of industrial relations at TVA was probably the result of the philosophy with which the directors approached the problem. The initial plan was discussed at six conferences, at each major project throughout the valley, before it was finally drafted. The union was made to feel that it had a definite stake in the success of the venture. As David E. Lilienthal, chairman of TVA, pointed out:

> Our approach to the question of its relationship with labor was founded on the belief—long since justified—that the workers through their organization have a great deal to contribute to the success of an enterprise. In other words, we in TVA's management refused to follow the all-too-general idea that labor unions are necessary evils, to be dealt with by giving in only as far as necessary to demands for higher wages, improved working conditions and so on. We proceeded instead on the basis that the workers were genuinely interested in seeing that TVA's job was well done.[59]

In spite of the attitude by top management, however, the antiunion feeling of many supervisors, whose experience mainly had been with nonunion public utilities, caused trouble. Many of the supervisors thought that the union idea was "lip service to FDR's union 'monkey business' and had nothing to do with building a dam."[60] This issue was settled during the construction of Wheeler Dam, the first of the TVA dams, when the Chief engineer discharged John Turner for passing out union literature during working hours. Because this was such an important point for TVTLC's organizing campaign, union representatives demanded a hearing before the TVA board of directors. At the hearing, George Googe argued that a decision against Turner would be discriminatory because the board itself had helped unions organize during working hours. It also was established that Turner's union activities had not interfered with his work. The board members therefore reinstated him and told the chief engineer that he had misconstrued and violated TVA policy, because workers had a right to join the union, hold meetings on government property, and had as much right to enroll workers in the union as in the community chest or the church.

Compensation matters at the Authority were settled by an annual wage conference which drew up a general agreement with the TVTLC and supplemental agreements with the various crafts. The wage conference was preceded by a preliminary conference to handle problems such as schedules of wage requests and definitions of procedures for determining prevailing wages. After the preliminary conference, a Joint

Classification Committee—a continuing body to handle classification problems—adopted schedules of classifications for wage negotiations. The classification schedules are subject to review by the president of the TVTLC and the director of personnel. Although TVA's wage rates were supposed to have been based on prevailing rates,[61] they were usually higher and were used by unions in the area as bargaining standards to raise other rates.[62] In December 1950, the collective bargaining procedure was extended to 5100 white-collar and professional employees represented by the Salary Policy Employee Panel.[63]

THE AFL IN 1940

Although the AFL continued to be the main labor federation in the south, the CIO disrupted the AFL's activities in the late 1930's. Because it had a heavy concentration in Alabama, the UMW's withdrawal from the Alabama Federation of Labor was particularly disrupting. Steve Nance caused a split in the Georgia State Federation of Labor (GSFL) by supporting the CIO and taking a job in the southern drive of the textile workers' organizing committee. Nance was so popular in Georgia that the state federation's executive board ignored William Green's orders to remove him as president.[64] When this dispute was aired before the AFL Executive Council in May 1937, Nance did not appear but was represented by O. E. Petry, a member of the GSFL Executive Board. Petry denied that Nance had taken a salaried position with CIO—he was, Petry said, southern director for the ACWA, ILGWU, and Hat, Cap, and Millinery Workers' Union, and his position with the textile workers' organizing campaign was advisory. Green said Nance had a right to "go with the enemy," but he should resign as president of the GSFL. Petry replied that Nance had organized and represented workers for these three organizations, adding:

> Now what magic wand did this Board wave over him in reference to these people in the shops, and to tell them that he cannot represent them any more? . . . You did not set up any place to take them to. There was nothing else for them to do . . . we have a common enemy down in Georgia. It is the boss . . . The boss gains when we fight one another.

Green asked: "Do you think that this Federation could maintain its dignity by standing by and permitting a man to be re-elected as President of the Georgia Federation of Labor and still be in the employ of organizations that have been suspended by the AFL?" On May 28, 1937, the executive council ordered Nance and others to return the property of the GSFL and stop using the name.

The CIO's influence on the AFL was not entirely negative. While it is true that the federations dissipated much of their resources fighting each other, competition spurred both unions to organize more vigorously. The CIO's threat also caused the AFL to modify its racial policies. The federation discontinued the practice of chartering segregated central bodies in the south in 1939, and many of its affiliates amended their discriminatory practices in order to compete with CIO unions. At the same time, the CIO undoubtedly did much to make the more conservative AFL more acceptable in the south. That the AFL sought to publicize this contrast is demonstrated by the 1940 AFL Southern Labor Conference.

Southern Labor Conference. In order to stimulate its organizing activity in the region, the AFL held a Southern Labor Conference in Atlanta on March 2 and 3, 1940,[65] which was hailed as "The largest assemblage of members of organized labor ever to meet in the south, or in the entire United States,"[66] and was attended by all the executive officers of the AFL and by "more than three score national and international unions and railroad organizations." When President Green came to Atlanta, he was officially greeted by Georgia's Governor E. D. Rivers; Atlanta's Mayor William B. Hartsfield, and many union officials. According to the *American Federationist*:

> It was an auspicious moment when President Green, walking between the Governor of Georgia and the Mayor of Atlanta, and flanked on both sides by thousands of cheering men and women, traversed the long corridor of the Terminal Section and passed through the spacious waiting room to enter the Mayor's automobile in waiting to bear him to his hotel. Adding to the scene was the uniformed official escort of six men who had been named by the state and city to be at the service of President Green during his stay in Atlanta.[67]

The conference was addressed by the governor and mayor and by Preston S. Arkwright, president of the Georgia Power Company, and the "largest employer of union labor in Georgia," who gave a luncheon for Green, attended by 100 of the most influential men in the state. Green delivered a nationwide address over the National Broadcasting Company and preached at the Druid Hills Baptist Church at the invitation of the pastor, the Rev. Dr. Louie D. Newton.

President Green set the tone for the AFL's campaign in the south in his radio broadcast. He stressed the value of the AFL's brand of unionism for the industrialization of the south. Green said that unions could stimulate industrialization by bringing higher wages.

> This is the patriotic goal of the American Federation of Labor . . . We do not propose to accomplish our ends by revolution . . . We do not propose to create industrial turmoil . . . We propose to help the workers

of the South, to stimulate industry in the South and to benefit all the people of the South by applying, through organization, the principles of union-management cooperation . . .

The American Federation of Labor is a truly American organization. Its members are loyal, honest, devoted Americans.

The American Federation believes in the institution of private property . . . We have never engaged in sit-down strikes, stay-in strikes, slow-down strikes or other revolutionary techniques. We freely concede the right of capital to a fair return on investments.

We have not sent in outsiders to tell the workers of the South how to run their business. In accordance with our principles of democracy and local autonomy, we have let the Southern workers run their own unions . . . There has been a tendency in our nation to place ever increasing authority and power in the central Government in Washington. That, we believe, is . . . dangerous . . .[68]

These attitudes, as contrasted with the more liberal racial and political views of the CIO, helped to bring about a more acceptable attitude of employers and community officials in the south toward the AFL.

In conclusion, in spite of considerable ferment during the 1930's, southern union membership was concentrated mainly in the older AFL unions and the railway brotherhoods. There were in 1939 about 627,000 union members in the south: 102,000 were in the building trades; 146,100 were in the railroad and related unions; about 13,000 were in the printing trades; 23,700 in the food and tobacco industry; 21,700 were in major government employees unions; 30,200 were in the longshoring, trucking, and streetcar and bus industries. The AFL had about 388,700 members in the south in 1939. The CIO had only about 143,600 members at that time, and about 90,000 of these were in the United Mine Workers, not including 100,000 UMW members in West Virginia. There were only about 25,000 southern members in the newer automobile, rubber, textile and petroleum industries, all of which experienced their most significant expansion during World War II.

PART IV
War and Postwar Development

CHAPTER XIV

World War II

World War II greatly stimulated the southern economy. War plants and army camps created employment for many people directly and affected other industries indirectly.[1] Southern manufacturing employment rose from 1,657,000 before the war to a peak of 2,836,100 in November 1943.[2] By August 1945, total manufacturing employment in the south had declined to 2,462,800, but was still about 50 per cent above the prewar level. Wartime production changed the composition of manufacturing output from the nondurables group—which furnished over two thirds of the south's prewar employment—to the durables group which made up about 46 per cent of the total in 1943; however, by 1946, employment in most manufacturing sectors continued the growth which had been started by the war. The main exceptions were transportation equipment (except automobiles) and durable goods, which experienced great expansion during the war and great contraction when the war ended.

Unionism benefited from the favorable attitude of the federal government and the shortage of manpower, and many unions which started organizing before the war became well organized in its midst. For example, the south's mass transportation systems became almost completely organized by 1944. Of the 66 systems under the jurisdiction of the Fourth Regional War Labor Board, only ten relatively small ones remained unorganized by that date.[3]

By the summer of 1943, the AFL reported organization of the giant

Aluminum Company of America plant at Baton Rouge, Louisiana, as well as the telephone workers, the Copolymer Company (synthetic rubber) and the Du Pont Chemical plant in that city. It had also organized the 9000 employees of the Ingalls Shipbuilding Company at Pascagoula, Mississippi, where it reported a total of 18,000 members. Bogalusa, Louisiana was reported to be "100 per cent organized."[4]

In addition to the longshoremen, AFL unions secured union-shop contracts covering 10,000 metal trades workers in the marine repair shops in New Orleans. The unions also had union-shop contracts with the Delta Shipyard including 20,000 workers, and a closed shop with the Higgens Company covering 15,000 workers. An office workers' local of 500 members, and a new teamsters' local with 300 had also been organized.

In Florida there were eighteen new locals in Panama City with 20,000 members, and "at Tampa all industries are unionized and American Federation of Labor membership totals more than 40,000. The CIO has been defeated in every contest and today not a single dual union is left in the city." At Brunswick, Georgia, the AFL reported all industries under contract and "every industrial employer in the city of Savannah except one." It also claimed approximately 35,000 members in Savannah, 15,000 of whom were in the building trades.

By 1943, the AFL metal trades unions had organized all but three of the shipyards south of Baltimore engaged in the production of seagoing vessels. Five labor temples had been constructed in New Orleans, and three in Tampa. The cities of Charleston, Savannah, Brunswick, Augusta and Jacksonville also erected new temples.

By the end of the war, the federation reported a 100 per cent increase in membership in the southern state federations of labor. Between 1936 and 1946, George Googe claimed an increase from 430,000 to 1,800,000, despite the formation of a "dual movement" which "attempted to destroy the federation."[5]

The CIO also enjoyed great membership gains in the south, although they were achieved with greater difficulty because of community and employer hostility. In Texas, for example, it gained "nearly 40,000" members in four years.[6] Particularly important membership expansion occurred in petroleum refining, and in the Dallas-Forth Worth area, where, in 1943, the CIO claimed 25,000 new members in one year.[7] Important victories there included the organization of the huge North American Aviation Company by the UAW, the Armour plant by the packinghouse workers, Conroe Manufacturing Company by the ACWA, and several steel fabricators by the steelworkers. PWOC Local 54 and stockhandlers' Local 59 acquired bargaining rights under a master agreement with Armour. During the war, the packinghouse workers' strength in Texas was confined largely to this plant. The CIO had 115 locals in Texas in March 1944, the most numerous of which were: auto workers, eight locals; oil workers, 30 locals; and steel-workers, with 12 locals.[8] The textile workers had only two locals in Texas in 1944.

In Gadsden, Alabama, which had been such an obstacle to unionization, one sixth of the city's population were members of the CIO by the end of the war.[9] In 1944, the United Rubber Workers' Union reported nine locals and eleven contracts in the region.[10] By 1946, the revitalized Oil Workers' International Union had organized an estimated 60 per cent of the workers in the refining branch.[11] R. J. Thomas reported that the United Automobile Workers' Union had contracts covering 31 plants by 1944.[12] The CIO probably had some 400,000 members in the south at the end of the war.

THE WAR LABOR BOARD

The National War Labor Board, established in January 1942 to settle disputes and stabilize wages, adopted policies which encouraged union membership in the south, although its avowed purpose was to be neutral in labor-management relations. Since unions and management made no-strike, no-lockout pledges for the duration of the war, the board adopted the maintenance-of-membership provision with the check-off and fifteen-day "escape" period so that unions could keep their membership.[13] This provision, and the board's practice of requiring unions and management to adopt specific contract terms, brought about many agreements that could not otherwise have been written; unlike the NLRB, the NWLB could translate representation elections into contracts.

Regional war labor boards were established in 1943, and a procedure was adopted whereby cases not settled at the regional level went to the NWLB, which could appeal to the president. Besides moral power, the NWLB had certain sanctions such as the power to deny income tax exemptions for employers on wages granted in excess of those allowed by the board, denial of union security provisions to unions, and recommendations that government contracts be cancelled or plants seized; the board also had the right to request subpoenas, though this was rarely used. The main southern regional boards were numbers IV and VIII at Atlanta and Dallas, though Arkansas was in region VII and Kentucky in region V. In the south, the unions used the WLB to such advantage that employers raised money to keep full-time representatives in the various regional headquarters. In 1944, for example, the

Texas State Manufacturers' Association sought to raise between $30,000 and $40,000 because: "It is apparently the purpose of the labor unions to organize every group in this state. They are concentrating on making such a showing with the War Labor Board as to convince all employees they should join the Unions. We on the other hand propose to make such a showing that employees will think otherwise."[14]

The board's policy of equal pay for equal work tended to reduce racial wage differentials. In 1943, for example, the board ordered the Southport Petroleum Corporation, Texas City, Texas, to abolish wage classifications based solely on race; this plant was organized by the OWIU.[15] It also ordered nondiscrimination clauses to be included in some contracts, though it later ruled that the clauses need not be included because the question was covered by the wartime Fair Employment Practices Committee.[16] In his decision in the Southport case, Dr. Frank Graham said: "Economic and political discrimination on account of race or creed, is in line with the Nazi program . . . The American answer to differences in color and creed is not a concentration camp, but cooperation."[17]

The south was also affected by the board's substandards-of-living rulings. The NWLB issued an order in February 1943 permitting wage increases up to 40 cents an hour if this would not cause price increases. The following month it issued an order permitting regional boards to increase wages to 50 cents an hour pending NWLB approval, and in November 1944 the regional boards were allowed to grant a minimum wage of 50 cents an hour. The board ordered a minimum of 55 cents in 23 southern cotton textile cases in March 1945, and later adopted the policy that a minimum of 55 cents could be granted generally if no price increases were required; finally, on August 30, 1945, the NWLB permitted 55 cent minima even if price relief were involved. These increases were not automatic, however, because the board proceeded on an *ad hoc* basis.

One of the most significant cases handled by the War Labor Board in the south involved 23 textile mills. The board created a Southern Textile Commission, with Professor Richard Lester of Duke University as chairman, to carry out its decision involving the textile mills and to handle other textile cases. In February 1945, it ordered the 23 southern mills to establish a 55-cent minimum wage, grant a general wage increase of five cents, pay a premium for shift work, and grant one week's paid vacation. In April, the fourth regional WLB ordered 12 other companies with 20,000 workers to grant these contract terms. In addition, some 400 other southern textile companies filed applications to be allowed to inaugurate portions of the NWLB directive; in all, between 350,000 and 400,000 workers were involved in these changes. In each of the twelve cases in April, "the company and the Textile Workers Union (CIO) were ordered to negotiate a more balanced wage structure and guaranteed minima for piece workers."

However, the board's orders were not always obeyed, and the army was forced to seize a number of firms. The Ingleside refinery of the Humble Oil Company was seized in 1944 in a dispute involving the board's order to grant the OWIU maintenance of membership. The army seized four southern firms within a ten-day period during May 1945, as a result of the companies' refusal to comply with orders; another plant, the American Enka Corporation of Asheville, N.C., was seized in February 1945. The Enka dispute, involving 3000 workers, resulted from the company's refusal to obey the board's order to submit the language of its contract to arbitration. The United Textile Workers-AFL struck to enforce the WLB's order, and the army seized the plant. It was returned to Enka in June 1945, when the company agreed to grant a five-cent an hour across-the-board wage increase. Other companies were also seized by the army in 1945.

Not all the cases of defiance of the WLB involved companies, however. One of the most significant concerned the CIO steelworkers who "failed to abide by a WLB order to end a strike which closed down war essential steel production" at Tennessee Coal and Iron. The union had, according to the chairman of the fourth regional War Labor Board, "failed to live up to their responsibilities" and thus "may have jeopardized the entire issue of union security in the South." Under pressure from regional and national leaders, the Birmingham workers voted two to one to return to work.

The board's ability to grant maintenance-of-membership or other union security provisions was sufficient, however, to secure compliance from most unions. During its first year of operation, the fourth regional WLB dealt with 137 issues involving union security: it granted maintenance of membership in 67 cases and denied it in three. The Atlanta board also granted 45 check-offs, two union shops, and one modified union shop. It denied union shop in one case. In its first nine months of operation, the Dallas WLB office handled 34 labor dispute cases involving union security. The board had denied maintenance of membership if "a union's record has been marred by a wartime strike, or if a union has shown lack of proper responsibility and leadership, or if a union is not well-established and no antiunion attitude of the company involved is shown." For example, Goodyear at Gadsden, Alabama, asked the fourth regional board to rescind maintenance of membership from a rubber workers' local of 3000, which had struck three times in May 1945; public and union members refused this request on the ground that the strikes were spontaneous and that the union had acted quickly to get the workers back. Toward the end of the WLB's experience, the chairman of the fourth regional board challenged unions to assume greater responsibility for efficient production and said that one of the main complaints against unions was that they "work harder for union security than for better production."[18]

Toward the end of the war in Europe, however, there was a growing tendency for southern employers to disregard the board's orders. The fourth regional WLB announced in February 1945 that, because of "an ever increasing number of employers who refuse to abide by its war-time dispute decisions," the board would not order striking workers back.[19] At that time there were 36 cases in the southeast where employers refused to abide by its orders; 15 of these cases had been transmitted to Washington. The fourth regional board considered this high proportion of refusals "serious" and added: "If there were 36 uncontrollable strikes we would see a tremendous clamor of public opinion."

The conclusion drawn from the WLB's experience in the eighth region was that the 950 dispute cases educated unions and employers to collective bargaining, especially on balanced wage structures, job classifications, job descriptions and good industrial relations practices. "Much that was formerly regarded as exclusively the prerogative of management . . . has now been brought within the province of collective bargaining. And the constant emphasis of the board and its representatives upon discussions and negotiations between parties and with the board has tended to break down the emotional obstacles to effective collective bargaining."[20] Both the eighth and fourth regional boards thought that the NWLB's activities unquestionably resulted in more collective agreements than there otherwise would have been.

THE UNIONS

Amalgamated Clothing Workers (ACWA). The ACWA had a southern organizing drive underway when the United States entered World War II. With the aid of the WLB, the Amalgamated organized "well over 10,000 new members in the South" between 1940 and 1944.[21]

It concentrated on organizing multiple-plant concerns. Its techniques included: joint campaigns conducted at several plants of one company; mailing programs to all employees; and joint conferences of representatives from the plants.

The Oil Workers (OWIU). Few unions experienced greater union growth during the war than the OWIU, whose membership more than doubled during the 1941-1946 period. Statistics indicate that the bulk of the oil workers' southern membership came in locals chartered in 1933 and 1934, and that membership expanded during World War II. In most cases, the locals were chartered before the war and existed many years before winning bargaining rights.

In 1940, the OWIU was too weak financially to assign full-time organizers, and the men in the field were busy servicing existing locals.[22] Union officials also were hampered by internal dissension, the vast territory to be covered, and the drain of the 1938 Mid-Continent strike.[23]

However, things started improving in 1941, and the convention of that year approved a special levy of 50 cents a month per member for a concerted organizing drive. Edwin Smith, former member of the NLRB, was hired to head the drive, and four organizers were furnished by the CIO.[24]

By the 1942 convention, the oil worker's organizing committee had achieved significant results. The most important victory was the Texas Company at Port Arthur, Texas, which the union's historian described as "the biggest single refinery victory the union had ever won up to that time." The union won this election in January 1942 over the AFL operating engineers 1351 to 67; the company's independent union had been declared illegal by the NLRB, and "no union" got 781 votes. In March 1942, the OWIU won an election at the Southport refinery in Texas City 105 to 21. It also signed up 84 per cent of the workers at Standard of New Jersey's Humble Oil refinery at Ingleside, Texas, and reported progress at the large Humble refinery at Baytown, Texas, which was described by OWIU officials as the "key to the organization of the Gulf territory." President Knight told the 1942 convention that the OWIU had "launched many campaigns in the last few years and all of them have collapsed for lack of funds. As a result our present drive is handicapped by the belief, on the part of the unorganized workers, that we will again fold up and leave the task half finished."[25] Knight reported, however, that the OWIU could expect continued help from the CIO if necessary and that there was a substantial fund to provide for expansion. Knight said that the union's growth was due to "closing the door to escapes by better service," the check-off, union maintenance and union-shop provisions (the union had been plagued with relatively high membership turnover). The organizing campaign had not been responsible for gaining many new members because it was launched "under the impetus of a strong convention personality without thorough planning." The campaign had, however, caused some momentum to be built up, according to Knight.

Between the 1941 and 1942 conventions, membership in the OWIU increased by some 8000, but southern membership actually declined from 6115 to 4552. The main weak spot in the OWIU's activities was in District 5, which included Tulsa, the scene of the 1938 Mid-Continent strike. It was reported that this area had not benefited directly from the OWOC but that "even in the wake of the torturous D-X strike (Mid-Continent) a renewed vigor is overshadowing the shambles of what was once designed to be the burial ground of the Oil Workers Union."

It was still too early in 1942 to determine the effects of the War Labor Board on the oil workers; the union had filed many cases, but they had not all been settled by the 1942 convention. However, the maintenance-of-membership provisions—which had become the WLB's method of maintaining the status quo—had obviously stabilized the union's membership.

In the year ending June 30, 1943, the OWIU had achieved additional membership results with the aid of the WLB. The most significant victories during this period were Gulf at Port Arthur and the Humble refinery at Ingleside. The OWIU won the Gulf election 1629 to 1096 for no union; this victory was due to the 1000 votes cast by Negroes as most of the "no-union" votes were cast by whites. The Ingleside victory was the first election won at a Standard of New Jersey refinery, but did not result in a contract because Humble later closed the refinery, after it twice had been seized by the federal government, once in 1944 for disobeying a War Labor Board order to grant maintenance of membership and again in the nationwide oil strike of 1945.

The OWIU gained 22,885 new members during the 1942-1943 period, but some of this had been offset by military leaves and delinquency. The OWOC was reorganized and put under the direction of W. B. Taylor of the United Auto Workers. Knight told the OWIU international executive council meeting March 1, 1943, that the union had spent $156,000 in eighteen months trying to organize Standard Oil refineries, and he was obviously dissatisfied with the results achieved. There was also some question of Communist infiltration into the OWIU during the campaign. The international executive council therefore met with CIO officers and Edwin Smith. Taylor replaced Smith, and the campaign was placed under the direction of the OWIU instead of the CIO, though the CIO agreed to continue making financial contributions.

The OWIU increased its collective agreements from 125 to 319 during the year ending July 1, 1944, as the union consolidated some of the gains made during the preceding years with the aid of the War Labor Board. Knight told the 1944 convention that "Almost all negotiations, and a large percentage of our serious disputes, eventually are referred to the WLB for final settlement and the officers and representatives must devote many hours to the preparation and prosecution of such cases."[26] The first major trouble in a petroleum refinery during the war came in June 1943 when the workers at Shell in Pasadena, Texas, struck spontaneously to secure the reinstatement of a discharged union member.[27] Since Taylor had taken charge of the organizing campaign, 88 NLRB elections had been held, of which the OWIU won 67 covering 13,312 workers and lost 21 covering 6121 workers. The expenditures for the organizing campaign averaged $20,000 a month, $5000 of which was contributed by the CIO, and, in July 1944, the OWIU had 40 employees in the field and six in national headquarters.

With the victory at Magnolia Petroleum Corporation in November 1943, the OWIU completed unionization of the major refineries on the Texas Gulf Coast except for the large Humble refinery at Baytown and the nation's largest refinery, Esso at Baton Rouge, a subsidiary of Standard of New Jersey. The OWIU's expansion was much faster in the south during the 1943-1944 period, causing that region to increase its proportion of OWIU's membership from about 22 to over 38 per cent; District 4, centered in east Texas and Louisiana, became the largest district in the union.

One of the OWIU's most serious disputes of the war occurred in February 1944, as a result of a strike at the B. F. Goodrich Company, where an election was won by 219 to 19 in December 1943. After weeks of futile negotiations, the union struck over what it alleged was the company's "intention to stall as long as possible." The Texas Rangers were called into this strike. The strike was also condemned by the regional director of the WLB. The workers went back on March 1, after being urged to do so by the WLB, which conducted hearings on the case. Concerning its no-strike pledge, oil workers' officials declared, "situations sometimes develop which force workers to strike."

The oil workers' experience demonstrated rather conclusively the value of the War Labor Board in encouraging the growth of unions. From a weak organization with little money and few members when the war started, the OWIU emerged in 1946 as an important international union with a strong base in the south and in the oil industry. However, as will be shown, it still faced vigorous competition from the independents and the operating engineers; and the Standard of New Jersey complex continued to defy unionization.

Textile Workers' Union of America (TWUA). The TWUA's progress in the south was relatively slow in the 1941-1943 period. The union reported 408 new contracts, covering 120,387 workers. Of these, it had

71 contracts including 38,387 workers in the south, midwest and far west.[28] The most important gain in the south during these years was the unionization of the Riverside and Dan River mills in Danville, Virginia, the largest cotton mill in the country. With 13,470 workers in the bargaining unit, and 11,920 valid ballots cast, TWUA Local 452 received 7204, and "no union" 4716.[29] This victory was significant not only because of the size of the firm but also because the disastrous 1930 strike at Danville practically ended the 1930 AFL southern organizing campaign; a "workers' anti-CIO association" sought to defeat TWUA with the slogan, "Remember 1930! Vote No."

The Danville election victory did not lead to an immediate contract, however. After the June 26 election, negotiations continued throughout the summer, and, on September 26, the case was referred to the WLB. After a hearing, a contract was signed in June 1943 on all issues except wages and work loads, but containing maintenance-of-membership and check-off provisions. The WLB also succeeded in having the company initiate more systematic job classifications and submit disputes to arbitration. The contract was renewed thereafter, but the maintenance-of-membership provision was dropped in 1948.[30]

The TWUA also won a contract with the Erwin mill chain in North Carolina after a strike threat, and other important contracts. It also won an NLRB election at the Harriet Mills in Henderson, N. C., and representation elections or new contracts at many plants in the south during the 1943-1946 period. While most of the union's southern gains were in the North Carolina and Georgia areas, gains were also made in other states. Texas, for example, was penetrated by the TWUA for the first time when the union started campaigns in Dallas, Waco, Hillsboro, Mexia, and Itasca.

As we have noted, there was growing defiance of the board in the south during the last years of the war. This was particularly true in the textile industry. One of the most antiunion employers in the United States has been the Deering-Milliken chain. During the war, the TWUA struck Deering-Milliken's Gaffney Manufacturing Company at Gaffney, South Carolina, because the company disregarded a WLB directive. The TWUA reported that production went up at Gaffney and the Mary-Leila mill in Greensboro, Georgia, when they were seized by the army because the army, "quite unlike the private operators . . . took interest and action in social and community factors which had an important bearing upon production." When Gaffney resumed operations after the war, the company offered old employees their jobs back on terms different from the WLB directive and disregarded new employees hired by the army. Many other textile plants were struck for refusing to obey WLB orders.

After 1946, the TWUA's major effort was involved with "Operation Dixie," the CIO's greatest organizing effort in the south.

United Textile Workers-AFL. The UTW was much less successful than the TWUA-CIO in organizing in the south or in the United States. In fact, the union's total membership actually decreased during the early years of the war; the UTW claimed an average paid-up membership in March 1944, of 40,915 as compared with 42,608 in November 1941.[31] The union had more success during the last years of the war, however, and reported 60,331 members in March 1946.[32] Judging from representation at the 1939 UTW convention, there were approximately 12,000 members in the south at that time; in April 1944, the union reported 33 active southern locals and 9000 members, and in March 1946 44 locals with 13,000 dues-paying members.

The UTW blamed its failure during the early years of the war on: intra-union national unions; unwise affiliation agreements with independent unions; lack of centralized direction; and failure to use the best organizing personnel.[33] At the 1939 special convention, the UTW had permitted several federations within the union. After the convention, however, the Woolen and Worsted Federation precipitated an internal conflict by attempting to become autonomous. This action diverted the attention of international officers from organizing, as well as cost the union some members through withdrawals. While most of the conflict was in New England, it weakened the union's ability to organize in the south.

Other problems faced by the UTW in the south inhibited union expansion. A southern UTW vice-president reported to the 1944 convention that "Our Southern staff is insufficient and, in some cases, inefficient. The old custom of selecting organizers and representatives because of personal friendship, political reasons, or local union control will have to cease." It was also recommended that the Southern Cotton Textile Federation created after the 1939 convention be abolished as "isolationism itself."

Inadequate finances caused many members to be lost to the UTW even after they were organized. The UTW's major loss was Local 2596 at Memphis, which went over to the TWUA-CIO because it was "(1) not properly serviced due to our limited force and the geographical location. (2) The C.I.O. in their unscrupulous way of making wild promises were able to play up the racial element between the colored and whites inasmuch as well over 60 per cent of the Local was colored. (3) Our inability to develop local leadership in a mixed local."

The TWUA and the UTW achieved their greatest strength in the south by 1946, although the great bulk of industry, including the leading Burlington, J. P. Stevens, Cannon, and Deering-Milliken chains remained unorganized.

International Ladies' Garment Workers' Union (ILGWU). The ILGWU established its first southern local during the NRA period with Local 122 at Atlanta. By 1940, however, locals had been established at Ponca City, Oklahoma; Memphis and Chattanooga, Tennessee; Henderson, Kentucky; Dallas, Houston and Laredo, Texas. In all, the ILGWU had only 1521 members in the south in 1940. Its activities in the important Dallas, Texas, area had been damaged by an unsuccessful strike against several firms in the city in 1935.

During the war, ILGWU leaders became concerned about competition in the south. The southern garment industry not only grew very rapidly during these years, but it was feared that many of the war plants "located in the deep South where unionism is weak and labor standards traditionally low" would flood the market after the war. The ILGWU therefore stepped up its organizing activities, and the union's president, David Dubinsky, was optimistic about success at the 1944 convention.

The most important locals established by the ILGWU during the 1940-1944 period were Local 377 at Knoxville with 2843 members in 1944 and Local 378 at Florence, Alabama, with 1321 members in 1944. Indeed, these two locals had over half of ILGWU's 7429 southern members in that year. From information in the ILGWU's *Report of Proceedings* for various conventions, we can calculate that between 1940 and 1944 the union gained 5908 members in the south, and spent $236,014.31, making the average cost per net member $39.95. The ILGWU has never collected as much in dues and initiation fees in the south as it has spent. That organizing was easier during the war than afterward is suggested by comparing the cost of $209.13 per net member in 1947-1950, $1,261.30 in 1950-1953, and $623.47 in 1953-1956; of course, the relatively low costs are due in part to the organization of a few large knitting mills, whereas after the war the union had the task of organizing small garment plants in isolated areas. ILGWU leaders believed, however, that despite its costliness, the southern effort was worthwhile as an educational effort and a means of protecting their nonsouthern members from southern competition.

The war apparently had different effects on high- and low-wage industries. The high-wage industries like pulp and paper and petroleum refining benefited from the WLB's orders to grant maintenance of membership and the check-off. But the low-wage industries like textiles and garments suffered because many workers took advantage of the tight labor market to move into higher-paying jobs. The wage stabilization program of the WLB made it difficult to hold these workers by raising wages. In fact, the ILGWU regional director in the southeast complained that the WLB aided the employers' antiunion activities by permitting voluntary increases to a minimum of 50 cents an hour without the board's approval. Since many unorganized plants in the garment industry paid less than 50 cents, employers would frequently counter union organizing activities by raising wages to that level, a practice prohibited as unfair by the NLRB before the war.[34]

Pulp and Paper Workers (UPP). Membership in the paper makers more than doubled during the war.[35] Figures are not available for 1941, but in 1939 the international had 25,000 workers, with some 2500 in the south. By 1944, membership was 38,000, and the ten southern states comprising the southern district had 6480 members in 37 locals. In December 1945, the paper makers had 48,000 members and the southern district had 8242 in 53 locals; by November 1946, these figures were 53,000 and 8688 respectively. Membership figures for the pulp-sulphite workers (IBPSW) in the south are not available, but probably bear much the same relation to total membership as the paper makers. In 1941, IBPSW had 60,000 members, in 1944 it had 74,000, and in 1947 it had 115,000 members.

In 1947, the paper makers and the IBPSW reported that their potential membership was 100 per cent organized in Arkansas, 75 per cent in Alabama, 50 to 75 per cent in Texas, Louisiana, Florida, and South Carolina; Tennessee was less than 25 per cent organized, the smallest percentage in the southern states. It should be noted, however, that the south was much better organized by these unions than the midwestern states which were generally less than the 25 per cent figure. In the postwar period, the IBPSW and UPP had the pulp and paper industry tied up in the south, since the only unorganized mills of any significance were Champion in Canton, North Carolina, and Houston, Texas, and the Calcasieu Paper Company at Elizabeth, La. Most of the unorganized mills were in the converted paper products industry.

UCAPAWA-FTA, CIO. The Cannery, Agricultural, Packing and Allied Workers (UCAPAWA), which changed its name to the Food, Tobacco, Agricultural, and Allied Workers' Union of America (FTA) in 1944 and was expelled from the CIO for being Communist-dominated in 1949, had already organized some workers in the southern tobacco and food industries before the war. The union's main targets included: cotton oil mills, cotton compresses, flour and feed mills, food-processing plants, and agricultural field workers. Its strategy was to organize workers in the more permanent and stable operations, and to use them as leverage in organizing agricultural field workers. The processing, cannery, and compress workers were covered by the Wagner Act, while the field workers were not.

In order to establish a stronger base, UCAPAWA sought to take over all CIO local unions of workers in the occupations related to agriculture. This was not always easy, either because workers could see little advantage in it or because other unions already claimed jurisdiction over them. In 1939, for example, when UCAPAWA sought to establish a base in Houston, Texas, the international president, Donald Henderson, demanded that LIU 917 at the Imperial Sugar refinery in Sugarland, Texas, which had been organized by a Negro and the executive secretary of the Texas Industrial Union Council, CIO, be transferred to his union "regardless of how the sugar refinery workers . . . feel."[36] Henderson said that it was obvious that the UCAPAWA could not organize agricultural workers unless groups like the sugar refinery workers were organized into the same union. However, Local 917 was "emphatically opposed," and, though UCAPAWA established a local at the Marshall Canning Company in Sugarland, it failed to acquire Local 917. In addition to resistance from the local industrial unions, the UCAPAWA also faced jurisdictional conflicts with the ILA-AFL, the ILWU-CIO, and United Mine Workers' District 50.

In spite of these problems, the UCAPAWA succeeded in organizing some scattered locals in the south, especially in the tobacco industry of North and South Carolina and Virginia, and among compress and food-processing workers in Arkansas, Tennessee, and Texas. One of UCAPAWA's earliest Texas locals was a shrimp peelers' union at Aransas Pass, but the local went out of existence after its president, Christopher Clarich, was sentenced to 20 years in prison for killing a strikebreaker during a picket line fight in 1938.

The UCAPAWA's greatest activity in the south did not come until the war, when it organized a number of tobacco plants, including R. J. Reynolds' 12,000 employees at Winston-Salem, North Carolina, a plant of the American Tobacco Company at Charleston, South Carolina, and a number of compresses, cotton oil mills, food-processing plants, feed and fertilizer mills, and agricultural workers in the lower south. The union's first contract in Arkansas was signed in February 1942 with the Arkansas Fertilizer Company, at Little Rock, and provided for an increase in wages from 30 cents to 40 cents an hour, the check-off, a closed shop, and seven paid holidays (one of which was June 19, Emancipation Day).

The UCAPAWA's strongest base in Texas was in Houston, where it had five contracts covering over 600 Negro and Mexican-American workers, organized by March 1942. Donald Kobler, UCAPAWA's Texas representative, estimated that there were 400 unorganized compress workers in Houston and 450 additional workers who could be raided from the ILA.[37] Compress workers were considered by UCAPAWA to be relatively easy to organize, apparently because most of them were Negroes and because they, like the pre-World War I jack-screwmen whom they replaced, occupied a strategic position in the cotton industry. UCAPAWA contracts in Houston covered about 150 employees at the Houston Milling Company and 400 Negro and Spanish-speaking workers in four cotton compresses, three of which were owned by the Anderson Clayton company, "the world's biggest and richest cotton business."[38] The president of the Houston Milling Company local was appointed to the industry committee to set a minimum wage for the flour and grain industry under the Wage-Hour Board. UCAPAWA seems to have used its ability to argue wage cases before these boards and the War Labor Board as a means of organizing. In addition, UCAPAWA had locals among pecan workers at San Antonio, spinach workers at Mathis, and cannery workers at Sugarland. During the later years of the war, UCAPAWA or FTA organized fruit and vegetable workers in the Rio Grande Valley of Texas, where its contracts covered 1000 employees during peak seasons but almost none when its Mexican-American members migrated out of the valley to do agricultural work throughout the United States.[39]

The UCAPAWA's activities were aided during the war by its good reputation in the Negro and Mexican-American communities. It also paid particular attention in its contracts to holidays of special interest to Negroes and Mexicans, and maintained contact with the National Negro Congress. The UCAPAWA's representatives also participated in such interracial organizations as the Southern Negro Youth Conference and the Southern Conference for Human Welfare. The union's image in the Negro community was particularly important because the Negroes were much more easily organized in the south than whites. And so long as the wartime no-strike policy made it unnecessary for Negro strikers to confront white strikebreakers, no problem was created by UCAPAWA's virtually all Negro or Mexican membership.

The UCAPAWA also benefited from the activities of the War Labor Board. Donald Henderson declared in 1942:

> As a matter of general procedure, may I emphasize that the War Labor Board is acting in a very friendly manner and if negotiations drag on too long in any of your plants, you should develop a threat of a strike, call in the Department of Conciliation, if that fails, immediately notify us to get the thing certified before the War Labor Board. Their decisions, so far as we are concerned, are excellent. We shouldn't waste too much time when a company stalls. We can get more from the War Labor Board than we used to get in the old days of a strike.[40]

In spite of this favorable action by the WLB, the UCAPAWA was unhappy because the board declined jurisdiction over agricultural labor and because the federal government established no agencies to handle disputes in this industry after southern cotton planters defied the Bureau of Conciliation.[41]

But the greatest impediment to the UCAPAWA's activities in the south during the war was the union's lack of financial strength. This weakness was in turn caused by the low incomes and unstable employment of its members. In July 1942, for example, the UCAPAWA had 40,000 workers under contract but only 16,000 dues-paying members.[42] Inadequate finances also made it impossible for UCAPAWA to protect its jurisdiction from raids by the ILWU and UMW District 50 and to raid compresses organized by the ILA.

The UCAPAWA attempted to make up for its financial weakness by a special assessment of $2.00 per member, levied in June 1941, to be used for organizing. However, the international had difficulties collecting it.

Toward the end of the war, when it was forced to strike in order to defend its position, the FTA had difficulties because of its racial composition and because of its reputation for being Communist-dominated. It succeeded in organizing the important R. J. Reynolds Tobacco Company in 1944 but was unable to keep the plant organized mainly because it did not have the support of whites during strikes. The FTA also organized the American Tobacco Company at Charleston, S. C. in 1945, but was forced into an unsuccessful strike when the company refused to negotiate.

The FTA, like other southern unions, also had problems when the protection of the WLB was withdrawn and it was left to the mercies of state courts. In 1945, it organized a number of cotton-seed oil mills in the Little Rock area and went through its usual procedure of having the cases certified to the WLB. When the war was over, however, the

WLB returned the cases, forcing FTA to strike. In one such case involving the Southern Cotton Oil Company at Little Rock, an FTA Negro striker was killed. A strikebreaker was arrested and released under $1000 bond, but seven FTA Local 98 members were arrested and put under bonds ranging from $1000 to $2500 for violating the newly passed Arkansas Antiviolence Law of 1943 (inspired by activities of the Christian Front).

As we have seen, there was considerable organizing potential in the south during the war, but no financial strength in the union. In all-Negro or Mexican operations the FTA was able to hold its membership after the war, but in racially mixed operations like tobacco plants the union's inability to gain white support and its Communist leadership virtually destroyed it.

ANTILABOR LEGISLATION AND ORGANIZATIONS

The growth of unions during the war motivated several southern states to enact laws restricting them. The laws were promoted throughout the south by business and farmers' organizations, and Christian American (CA), an organization chartered in Texas in November 1936. At first, the movement was primarily directed against the efforts of what a CA memorandum termed "a bunch of cunning radicals . . . to subvert peace-loving Christian ministers and laymen by getting close enough to them by subterfuge to jab the hypodermic of radicalism into them."[43] But during the war, it turned its attention to the passage of antilabor legislation. The basic labor objectives of Christian American included the passage of "right-to-work" laws and constitutional amendments outlawing union security, limiting strikes and pickets by "antiviolence" statutes, regulating internal union affairs, requiring union organizers and officers to be registered, and amending the Wagner Act. Christian American professed to "believe in the right of the laboring man and woman to organize and bargain collectively and we acknowledge their privilege to strike and picket; but we . . . read the Holy Bible [and] fail to find a provision that tribute must be first paid for this God-given right and duty to John L. Lewis, Bill Green or Phil Murray." In addition, "The CIO is committed to a Marxian Tax Program that will TOTALLY communize America. Christian American stands for limiting the taxing powers of Congress with a new amendment to the Federal Constitution." In 1943, Christian American concentrated on having laws passed in Arkansas, Alabama, Florida, Texas, and Louisiana.

The antiunion movement was not restricted to Christian American, however, because it was also supported by the American Farm Bureau

Federation, the Chamber of Commerce of the United States, the Southern States Industrial Council and many southern politicians who considered this a good issue. In Florida, for example, Attorney General J. Tom Watson instituted legal action to outlaw the closed shop on the grounds that it violated public policy. The Florida attorney general brought suit to have the Tampa Shipbuilding Corporation's charter revoked because its closed-shop agreements with AFL unions violated public policy.[44] However, the Florida Supreme Court upheld the AFL's contention that the union shop was not contrary to public policy; that there had been no abuses under the closed-shop agreement because "it enabled the company to secure the services of thousands of skilled union members who would not have been available for hiring were they required to work with non-union employees"; that Florida had no jurisdiction in the question of whether the closed shop impaired war production because this was a federal responsibility; and that Florida could not prohibit union security agreements because this would violate freedom of contract. Florida and Arkansas then passed right-to-work amendments to their constitutions, and Alabama passed a law outlawing union security provisions. The Florida amendment provided that "the right of persons to work shall not be denied or abridged on account of membership or non-membership in any labor union." The AFL's general counsel advised member unions to ignore these laws and, if the employer refused to grant a closed shop, to appeal to the conciliation department of the Department of Labor if the employer had war production. The unions not involved in war production were advised to settle their disputes "by the ordinary rules of collective bargaining." These laws proved unenforceable but set precedent for the state right-to-work laws when they were permitted by the Taft-Hartley Act in 1947. Florida, Texas, Arkansas, Mississippi, and Alabama passed "antiviolence in strikes" laws. Louisiana was called "The Red Spot on the Gulf Coast" by Christian American because it had consistently refused to enact antilabor legislation. Christian American launched an unsuccessful campaign to defeat members of the Louisiana House who voted against the bill and members of the senate who indefinitely postponed consideration of a union registration bill.

In 1941, Governor W. Lee O'Daniel of Texas called a special session of the legislature and in a highly emotional speech about "labor-leader racketeers" asked the legislature to pass his "antiviolence" bill. The bill provided for imprisonment of those who engaged in violent activity while participating in a strike. Governor O'Daniel also is reported to have campaigned in other states for the passage of anti-union laws.

The Arkansas antiviolence law was similar to the Texas law and made unlawful the use of force or violence, or threat of force or violence.

Antiunion forces also succeeded in passing several laws requiring the registration of unions. In 1943, after a vigorous antiunion campaign by Governor O'Daniel and others, the Texas legislature passed the Manford Act, which: required all union organizers to register and obtain identification cards from the secretary of state; required unions to file annually an itemized financial statement; prohibited unreasonable initiation fees; and prohibited the collection of outstanding indebtedness from returning veterans. In an obvious blow at CIO unions, the Texas law exempted unions that had been in existence over 15 years or charged less than a $15 initiation fee. Texas made it unlawful for an alien or any person convicted of a felony to serve as a union officer and prohibited financial contributions by unions to any political party or person running for political office. Agreements providing for the check-off also had to be filed with the secretary of state within 20 days of their execution. Texas provided that unions could not create funds in excess of "the reasonable requirements of such union in carrying out its lawful purposes if it will impose an undue hardship on applicants or members." One of the biggest complaints against unions in the south during the war was the sale of work permits granted to workers who were not admitted to the union. Texas required that permit fees be held until the person became a regular union member and returned if he was not accepted; the law also provided that state courts could order members reinstated if they were expelled without good cause. The Texas law provided for civil actions of not over $1000 in each violation by a labor union. Violations by union officers were criminal offenses punishable by a fine of not over $500 and imprisonment not to exceed 60 days. The Texas attorney general ruled invalid the sections of this act prohibiting the collection of indebtedness from veterans and excessive initiation fees.

Union leaders were afraid that these registration laws would make information about their activities available to employers, undermining the position of financially weak unions during collective bargaining. At the same time, the law could make it impossible for the unions to build up strike funds if state officials thought them unnecessary.

R. J. Thomas, a UAW official, was cited for contempt in 1943 for violating the Manford Act. The Texas Supreme Court upheld the law because state officials had no discretion in granting union organizers identification cards when the necessary information was filed. This decision did not deal with the provisions regulating internal union affairs, but the AFL filed a complaint challenging the entire act. In January 1944, the District Court of Travis County, Texas, invalidated the provisions prohibiting the accumulation of "unreasonable" funds, providing for annual elections and prohibiting back payments by members of the armed forces in order to become members of the union in good standing. The AFL was not satisfied with this decision, but was reluctant to appeal to the Texas Supreme Court which had "shown an antipathy towards organized labor." However, R. J. Thomas and the CIO appealed the act to the U.S. Supreme Court which held its licensing provisions to be unconstitutional.[45] In March 1944, an Alabama court invalidated a state law of June 1943, limiting secondary and primary boycotts and requiring unions to conduct strike votes, but held that financial statements and other reports could be required from unions; the court refused to pass on the portion of the Alabama act which made it unlawful to charge money for work permits and prohibited supervisors from joining unions. In 1944, the United States Supreme Court, in *Hill* v. *State of Florida,* held that the state law requiring business agents to be licensed and requiring unions to be registered in order to operate in Florida conflicted with the National Labor Relations Act and therefore was unconstitutional.[46] The AFL's general counsel reported in August 1945 that union court challenges and lobbying activities had stemmed the tide of state antilabor legislation and that there remained at that time only minimal interference with normal trade union activity.

Although most of the antilabor organizations formed in the south toward the end of the war were opposed to all unions, some were especially aimed at the CIO. One such group formed in Texas was known as the Fight for Free Enterprise (FFE). The FFE's approach was to carry on a public relations campaign against the CIO. A "Confidential Memorandum" issued to businessmen and others in the Rio Grande Valley of Texas in order to raise money, declared that "We have determined by means of field tests of public opinion and reaction that the tying-in of the CIO with Communism and Communistic doctrine is a weapon of the greatest importance, for we can couple it with the fact that Communism is atheistic."[47] A part of the organization's publicity campaign called for court action to cripple the CIO. "It should be noted that, quite regardless of the chances for success in this suit, it affords an opportunity to make allegations of a sensational nature without regard to libel, and allows the newspapers of the State to Print these allegations with complete immunity from any action by C. I. O. or its leadership." In addition to publicity, FFE proposed to conduct radio broadcasts and inject the CIO as an issue in political campaigns. Moreover, "in order to split labor in general away from any possible moral support of the CIO the broadcasts will laud the general purposes of the old line America unionism." FFE also proposed to exert intense pressure, including the withdrawal of advertising "against those newspapers in the area which are running with the CIO wolf pack."

CONCLUSIONS

Our discussion of the War Labor Board and the experiences of various unions during the war make it clear that World War II greatly stimulated union growth in the south. While it obviously is not possible to determine the exact effects of the favorable attitude of the federal government and the tight labor market, it is clear that both stimulated union growth in the region. This was countered, however, by increasing antiunion legislation which was partially offset by federal pre-emption and the refusal of the War Labor Board to permit the antiunion laws to supersede its directives. The war did not, however, have equal effects on all unions. Organizations of skilled workers were directly stimulated by the war, but other organizations, particularly the low-paid textile and garment workers, received less incentive. The textile and garment industries were aided by the War Labor Board in gaining contracts they could never have otherwise secured— because the board had the power to order a contract after a dispute over contract terms—but these industries were also troubled by the exodus of workers to better jobs in other industries; moreover, the WLB's rules permitted employers to raise wages voluntarily to 50 cents an hour, which some of them reportedly did to counteract unions during organizing campaigns. On balance, however, the WLB encouraged union growth in the south in low- as well as high-wage industries. The task for trade unions after the war was to maintain these gains; this was one of the objectives of the organizing drives launched by both the AFL and the CIO in the postwar period. As we have seen, however, antiunion forces were gaining momentum in the south by the end of the war.

CHAPTER XV

Operation Dixie

THE AFL CAMPAIGN

Despite great wartime gains, there were many unorganized workers in the south when the war ended. The textile industry, for example, was considered the key to unionism in the region, and was only about 20 per cent organized in 1946 as compared with about 70 per cent in the north.[1] Unionism was even weaker in the important food, food-processing, service, and furniture industries, all of which were expanding in the region.

In order to unionize these industries, stem the tide of antiunion legislation, maintain their wartime gains and perhaps preserve or enhance their hegemony in the American Labor Movement, both the AFL and the CIO launched organizing campaigns after the war. The AFL campaign, which had been deferred since the 1940 Southern Labor Conference, was terminated after one year, but the CIO drive continued until 1953.

Although the AFL campaign, like that of the CIO, stressed both political and economic objectives, the AFL placed more emphasis on its traditional approach of "cooperation" with southern employers and community leaders. It emphasized its objectives and those of the south: "Our plans we know must be segments of larger plans to develop Southern industries and trade, to diversify Southern agriculture."[2] The AFL also stressed its sympathy with the historic struggle of the south to overcome the destitution imposed by the Civil War and Reconstruction.

246

The AFL opened its drive in May 1946, with the Southern Labor Conference at Asheville, North Carolina.[3] William Green, George Meany and other AFL notables addressed the conference, which was attended by 3286 delegates from 12 southern states. It was decided that the campaign would be "an operation primarily by Southerners for Southerners."[4]

It also became clear at the conference that the AFL intended to stress the Communist domination of the CIO. AFL President Green brought the delegates to their feet cheering when he declared: "Neither reactionary employers nor Communists in the CIO can stop the campaign of the American Federation of Labor to enroll 1,000,000 unorganized Southern workers in the next twelve months." Green advised southern industrialists: "Grow and cooperate with us or fight for your life against Communist forces."

In an attempt to counter this attack, Van Bittner, director of the CIO drive, had announced that no Communists would participate in his campaign, but Meany said that the CIO's National Executive Board would control the campaign:

> He then proceeded to call out the names of "the devoted followers of Moscow who control that Board." Those listed by Mr. Meany were Joseph Curran, Harry Bridges, Julius Emspak, Lewis Merrill, Abram Flaxer, Joseph Selly, Ben Gold, Michael Quill, Lee Pressman and Sidney Hillman.
> "The workers of the South have their choice," Mr. Meany said, "between an organization of trade unions and trade unionists who have never swerved for a single minute from the principle laid down long ago by Sam Gompers—the principle that you cannot be a good union man unless you are first a good American—and an organization that has openly followed the Communist line and is following that line today."

Structure and strategy. To carry out the southern campaign, the AFL established a policy board made up of 45 leading AFL representatives in the south. The board met in Atlanta June 3-5, 1946, and decided that the basic structure of the campaign would be the "already strong and well established system of State Federations and local central bodies combining organization experience and community knowledge."[5] The state federations became the center for all southern organizing activity. They were to appoint organizers and field representatives and could call on the AFL organizer-pool for assistance as the circumstances warranted. It was planned that the local central bodies would furnish information on the extent of organization and other economic factors in each local area. Efforts were also made to stimulate affiliation with the state federations in the south; the average affiliation of local unions with the state federations was only 33 per cent.

The policy board urged each organizer to work for affiliation of the locals; while it was recognized that "the first duty of representatives was to their own internationals," it was hoped that they would work as integrated units during the campaign and "report their activities and help others when in a locality."[6] The representatives were told that their own organizing programs would in turn benefit from this unified and mutual approach.

The policy board meeting was told that the executive council would match funds raised by the state federations and the central bodies and that the national unions would not be asked to contribute to the campaign at that time. George Googe told the meeting that future financial grants from the executive council would depend on the drive's initial accomplishments.

On the important question of jurisdiction, the policy board decided that conflicts would be resolved by AFL unions at the local level. In representation elections, AFL unions would stand as a unit through the appropriate council, and the predominant numerical group in a plant would be given the initiative, and other groups would be asked to yield where there were few involved in a craft. "In no degree does this involve any surrender of organization autonomy in any essential sense but merely the necessary expedient in order to handle successfully the problems of organization in mass production industries."

All representatives of AFL unions were to consider themselves attached to the southern campaign. It was planned that the AFL would furnish 70 organizers, and the state federations an average of five each in addition to the general AFL organizers; there were also 300 international organizers, with "strong indications" that the internationals would put a total of 500 men in the field in coming months. It was estimated that the local trade union officers, business agents, and others would bring the number of organizers to 1500.

The race problem. The policy board felt that special efforts should be taken to counteract the CIO's appeal to Negro workers:

> The opinion of the Policy Board on the need and importance of special attention to negro workers was emphatic and unanimous. The Policy Board called for the elimination of what few remaining handicaps and discriminations still exist against negro workers in [AFL] unions in the South . . . International Unions having a large negro present or potential membership have supplied themselves with qualified negro organizers and reported harmonious and just relations between white and negro workers within their ranks. A. F. of L. organizers of both races will be

available for special work among negroes. Equal employment opportunity for the negro worker and full participation in A. F. of L. unionism was a keynote of the Policy Board meeting.

By the time of the 1946 organizing campaign, the CIO had gained a much more favorable image in the Negro community than the AFL, which cost the AFL some members in the early days of the organizing campaign. Of particular importance was the loss of the strategic Masonite Corporation at Laurel, Mississippi. The CIO woodworkers won Masonite in 1946 with the aid of the Negro vote, which proved decisive in this case. This caused the AFL to redouble its efforts to attract Negro workers, because Negroes were important in all of the unorganized industries in the south.

The AFL made a survey of its Negro membership, and got statements from its many Negro leaders which it issued in a widely circulated pamphlet called "Pie in the Sky." The AFL claimed 650,000 dues-paying Negro members, which it claimed was "the largest and best paid Negro membership of any labor organization in the world." Moreover, according to the pamphlet, "The cheap peddling of propaganda that the AFL discriminates against Negro workers is a false and lying campaign to deceive the unorganized Negro worker, and is an injury and set-back to that worker." The pamphlet also claimed that "there are only a half dozen small AFL unions with no Negro members. But a check of these unions shows that employer employment practice—not union discrimination—is the reason. If the Air Line Pilots Association has no colored members it is no more the union's fault than it is the fault of the Brotherhood of Sleeping Car Porters that they have no white members." In addition, the AFL pointed to the many strikes by CIO members against working with Negroes during the war as evidence that members of all organizations practiced discrimination. Of the 650,000 Negro AFL members, 450,000 were in the south, according to the AFL, which was more than the CIO's total southern membership.

Emphasizing the theme of the AFL's campaign, the pamphlet claimed that 21 of 36 CIO international unions were dominated by leaders who followed the Communist Party line. The AFL admitted having many segregated locals in the south, but argued that they were frequently required by law or were desired by the Negro workers themselves. The AFL also emphasized that it had many more Negroes in official positions than the CIO. The AFL pamphlet concluded: "The AFL offers you results now—not hot-air promises of pie in the sky by and by." This pamphlet proved so effective in some areas that the AFL used it among Negroes on the West Coast.

Financial problems. While the AFL's financial difficulties were not as acute as those of the CIO, the problem had to be faced by the executive council before the campaign could be launched. The AFL was fortunate in having a defense fund that had been established to finance strike benefits for federal labor unions attached directly to the federation. Although George Meany and William Green discussed the possibility of using the fund to finance the campaign, Meany had reservations.[7] President Green, on the other hand, felt that the executive council had to raise the money immediately in order to "accept the challenge of the CIO to campaign in the South." He argued that the defense fund had been established for the federal locals while they were attached to the AFL, but that many of them had been transferred to other international unions.

The council decided to transfer $200,000 from the defense fund for the campaign and to appoint a committee—consisting of Meany, Dan Tobin of the teamsters, and David Dubinsky of the ladies' garment workers—to study finances for the campaign and to report to the next executive council meeting.

The AFL's director of organization, Frank Fenton, transferred 12 additional AFL organizers into the south, bringing the AFL's total in that region to 47, not counting ten assigned to the campaign being conducted by both the AFL and the CIO at the atomic installation at Oak Ridge, Tennessee. There were, in addition, 30 organizers from the state federations and ten from the various city central bodies, making a total of 117 AFL organizers in the south. Of these, 12 were Negroes, and two were white women. The AFL's international unions had at least 380 full-time representatives in the southern states. This was therefore less than one third of the 1500 organizers the policy board had expected. The full-time representatives spent about half their time organizing and the rest servicing their locals, negotiating contracts and attending to other union business. It was plain, therefore, that the main organizing force in the south would be the international representatives, and that the AFL organizers would be used around this core.[8]

George Googe prepared a comparison of the AFL and CIO organizing staffs for the October 1946 AFL Executive Council meeting. He told the council that the CIO "put all they have into big fights and [this] has caused them to grab off some big industries, whereas we have in the past tended to lone wolf our way along—everyone for himself, and while our progress has been great, we need not ignore the advantage of better centralization and unity, and that is what we are trying to accomplish as quickly as possible." The AFL was covering 14 states (including West Virginia), and the CIO only 13, but the CIO had a headquarters staff of 11 plus 17 secretaries and assistants. The AFL had a headquarters staff of two with three secretaries and assistants. However, the AFL had a larger organizing force; 469 as compared with the CIO's 353. A major difference was that CIO international unions had only 50 representatives in the south, while AFL affiliates had 380; most of the CIO organizers were thus hired directly by the director of the southern campaign—Googe had 50 organizers under his direction, while Bittner had 243.

Googe reported some significant progress by August 1, 1946. The AFL had gained 100,000 new members and won over 200 NLRB elections. Googe emphasized, however, that the AFL did not rely on the NLRB very much in its southern organizing activities because only about 20 per cent of the plants organized by the SOC were by elections; in 80 per cent of the cases, "employers recognize our unions and sign contracts when we organize their employees due to threat of strikes or otherwise."[9] The Southern Conference of Teamsters, for example, had organized 99 new companies but had gone through only 20 NLRB elections; the teamsters had installed 300 new charters in the south. Other major victories during 1946 included a 10 per cent increase in the bricklayers' membership; 6000 new members in the cement, lime and gypsum workers; 3000 new members in hotel and restaurant employees; 1000 new International Brotherhood of Electrical Workers members in the Arkansas Power and Light Company and 2000 fishermen in the newly formed south Atlantic fishermen organization.

Late in the 1946-1947 season, the AFL started an extensive drive to organize citrus workers. During the next year it filed 25 petitions for elections with the NLRB, and won 23 of them. The federation reported 31 locals in the area by the spring of 1948. The National Farm Labor Union, which had played a large part in the effort, reported 17 unions in the citrus groves by that date. The farm labor union "was not handicapped by the Taft-Hartley law."[10]

Organizing problems. These gains were not made without difficulties, however. Many southerners would not believe that only the CIO was undesirable, and fought all unions with equal vigor. Throughout the region, civic and veterans' groups had been formed. The groups led by veterans were particularly effective in casting unions in an unpatriotic role. They also worked among farmers to convince them that unionism was particularly inimical to their interests, trying to secure farmers' votes for the antiunion legislation that was being introduced.

One organization was the Louisiana Citizens' Committee, which ran antilabor advertisements in the newspapers and over the radio.[11] The

252   WAR AND POSTWAR DEVELOPMENT

situation which was largely responsible for its formation drew wide-spread reaction and publicity. This occurred at Shreveport where the W. F. Aldrich Company was constructing a highway. AFL construction workers entered into an oral contract with the company. Management later repudiated the agreement and imported nonunion labor.

"Leader" of this army of scabs was one James T. Karam, who made a disgusting parade of publicity of the fact that he was a veteran and former football star. Karam, who had led a strike-breaking organization in Arkansas, arrived on the scene with apparently unlimited funds and promptly inserted advertisements in the Shreveport papers offering jobs to veterans at "high wages." Many were duped by these advertisements.

Karam and the strikebreakers, organized into a Veteran's Industrial Association, armed themselves with "pick handles and other weapons," but before they could attack the union pickets, 1000 union men intercepted them.[12] Then the company sought an injunction from Judge J. U. Gallow of the Caddo Parish District Court, who refused it on the grounds that the company's negotiations with the union had been "feeble" and the mediation and conciliation machinery had not been exhausted. The Aldrich case became the "cause célèbre" of the anti-union press throughout Louisiana.

The AFL also complained of opposition from the CIO. In fact, both unions claimed that the other spent more time raiding than organizing. For example, they spent large sums fighting each other in a contest for bargaining rights at the atomic installation in Oak Ridge, where 80,000 construction and operational employees were hired during the war. By agreement with the War Department, the major unions refrained from organizing during the war. Unions did conduct aggressive postwar campaigns, however, and the AFL won two Oak Ridge plants of Union Carbide, and the CIO won one Oak Ridge plant and one at Paducah. But the bitterness generated by these contests was still evident in 1965.

After the winter of 1947, unions encountered even greater obstacles, particularly in the legislative field. This difficulty caused Googe to declare in the spring of 1948: "The handicaps imposed by the Taft-Hartley Act, pyramided upon the state anti-union statutes have caused the organization of new local unions and unorganized plants to decline approximately 75 per cent."[13]

Discontinuation of the campaign. The opposition encountered by the AFL in the south forced George Googe and other AFL leaders to decide in the spring of 1947 that the drive should be terminated. Googe made a confidential financial report to the April 1947 executive council meeting in which he disclosed that the AFL had spent $355,451.84

since the campaign started, not including the expenses of the "normal, regularly employed organizers and facilities that have been for many years expended in the South as regular work and expense of the Organization Department of the AFL."[14] Several weeks before the meeting, Googe told George Meany that because of antilabor sentiment and legislation, "they had practically reached the point where . . . they are not making any progress insofar as securing new members is concerned; but Representative Googe feels that the activity must be kept up on a reduced scale and gradually taper it off with the idea of winding it up around September."[15] President Green told the executive council that Googe had made a similar report to him, and had pointed out that in Georgia, Oklahoma, Arkansas, the Carolinas, and Texas, antilabor legislation had been passed which had "upset the morale, caused confusion and uncertainty, and for that reason a wide opportunity to carry on a continued successful drive in the South does not present itself." Meany told the executive council that he personally felt that this was "not the place to spend our money at the present time." By October 1947, the AFL reported that a check with central bodies, organizers' reports, and international representatives throughout the south revealed 425,000 members in new groups organized and an increase of 65,000 to 70,000 new members in old locals in the south, bringing the total gain to almost 500,000 during the campaign. Although the AFL campaign achieved more results in a shorter period than the CIO drive, the results were disappointing to most federation leaders, especially the United Textile Workers whose president told his 1948 convention:

> Frankly, however, the results of the Southern drive did not meet our expectations. Our records show that since the last convention [1946] the paid membership of the United Textile Workers in the South has increased by approximately 5,000 members.
>
> We estimate that the total cost of our Southern drive for the period from July 1946 to January 1947, when the drive was in full swing, was approximately $85,000. When we compare this expenditure with the ultimate results gained, we find that the Southern campaign cost us approximately $20 for each new worker organized. This cost was too prohibitive to continue our Southern campaign on such a large scale, so we were forced to retrench.[16]

Again, the definitions of the south used by the AFL and for this study are different, and figures are not available for the exact period of the drive. The AFL claimed 1,800,000 when the campaign started and a gain of 500,000, for a total of 2,300,000.[17] However, the UMW's withdrawal from the AFL in 1947 probably cost the federation 200,000 members in these states. Including West Virginia, Leo Troy in his study of union membership credited the AFL with 1,218,000 members in the south in 1953 as compared with 453,900 for independents.[18]

THE CIO CAMPAIGN

The motives of the CIO campaign, like those of the AFL, were more than economic, though the CIO emphasized social and political objectives more than the AFL.

Philip Murray told the CIO Executive Board in 1946 that the southern organizing drive was "the most important drive of its kind ever undertaken by any labor organization in the history of this country."[19] Murray's estimate of the importance of the campaign was shared by most other CIO leaders.

Structure and strategy. Van Bittner of the steelworkers was made director of the drive and was aided by six assistant directors: Jack Kroll (ACWA), George Baldanzi (TWUA), Phil Clowes (USA), George Craig (USA), and Tom Starling (UAW). Each assistant director was assigned two or more states. A Southern Organizing Committee (SOC) was established to advise Bittner and other active participants. The chairman of the SOC was Allan Haywood, the secretary was David McDonald of the steelworkers, and Lee Pressman became general counsel; other members were George Addes, Julius Emspak, George Baldanzi, J. B. Carey, Charles Lanning, William Pollock, Jacob Potofsky and Joe Curran.

The SOC established 12 state directors in the south with regional and area directors under them.[20] In order to counter the charge that the CIO was made up of "foreigners" and "Communists," Bittner drew 85 per cent of his staff from the south. Alan Swim, former reporter for the Memphis *Press-Scimitar,* and a militant anti-Communist member of the American Newspaper Guild, became public relations director. Lucy Randolph Mason, from one of the foremost families of Virginia, was hired to contact local authorities and prominent citizens in communities where the union was active or expected to become active. John Ramsey, director of church and community relations for the United Steelworkers, acted as a liaison between churches and the SOC.

Some members of the CIO Executive Board were wary about the south. George Baldanzi, executive vice-president of the textile workers warned that more money would be needed because there would not be as many agents to help the organizers; he predicted that the SOC would be "confronted with every vicious move which is at all possible."[21]

The SOC had to establish a policy to handle racial problems. Bittner said, "we made up our minds that . . . we are organizing men and women regardless of creed, color, or national origin, because they are God's human beings and are workers, and we are organizing all workers."[22]

To finance the drive, the initial plan presented by David J. McDonald of the steelworkers to the March 1946 executive board meeting called for a contribution of one million dollars to be paid to the CIO's secretary-treasurer within six months of the campaign or before the campaign started. The planning committee felt that a million dollars would make it possible to hire 200 representatives for ten months, including overhead. The planning report emphasized that 200 was the minimum number of organizers required, though it realized that this number could not begin to organize the south. It was felt, however, that the organizers could concentrate on key states. The report warned against spreading them too thin and suggested that they not stay and negotiate after union recognition was secured from employers.

The report suggested that initiation fees be set at $1.00 and dues at $1.50 per month, though it also implied that dues could probably not be collected in the south before the employer recognized the union. Later, however, the CIO adopted the policy of waiving initiation fees because many AFL and CIO internationals were organizing without collecting them.

The planning report also emphasized that practically every CIO union stood to gain from the campaign, although organizing was not to be done on an industrial basis.

The CIO was encouraged by enthusiasm for the CIO during the 1946 strikes.[23] Allan Haywood, in discussing the momentum generated by the wage increases following these strikes, quoted the following letter from one of his southern organizers: "One of the most remarkable things to me during the recent steel strike was the way workers of hitherto completely unorganized plants came into the union office in Atlanta and elsewhere asking help in organizing. The strikes did not scare them off but rather seemed to prove that the unions were in earnest about their wages and working conditions."[24] Haywood told the CIO Executive Board that a real base for organization had been established in Georgia and North Carolina. Atlanta, he said, was "like a beehive of activity," and Birmingham, Montgomery, Mobile, New Orleans and Memphis "are definitely CIO today." Haywood was optimistic and thought the CIO could "bring it back to the period of 1937."[25]

By July 1946, the CIO's strategy for the southern campaign had become fixed. It was decided that all state directors for the SOC would resign their Political Action Committee jobs in order to concentrate on organizing; Bittner told the executive board that the CIO was "not going to make any political gains in the South until we organize the workers."[26] The plan to organize on a state-by-state basis was abandoned in favor of concentrating on "everything as in the steel campaign, concentrating on large companies that have chains of plants, because we can't get much improvement until the big fellows are organized." The SOC's main objectives were the workers at the Oak Ridge, Tennessee atomic installation, the Bibb and Cannon textile chains in North Carolina and Georgia, lumber workers in Georgia, Alabama, and Louisiana, oil workers in Texas, and textile workers everywhere.[27]

Bittner had developed no special procedures for the campaign other than to contact as many workers as possible and to use techniques tailored to each situation. "I have generally found that where the employer is most vicious that is generally the easiest place to organize." For example, Gadsden, Alabama, had had a reputation of being absolutely nonunion a few years earlier, but by 1946 it was possible to get public statements from preachers, businessmen, the postmaster, a judge and others saying "what a great change for the good the CIO has brought to Gadsden."[28]

CIO leaders in the south were particularly sensitive to the AFL's widely publicized charge that the CIO was Communist-led. This caused Bittner to reject the offers of outside organizations. He told the internationals early in the drive not "to try to put organizers on our staff you wouldn't have on your own."

The CIO had some jurisdictional problems during the early stages of the campaign. The rule had been established that the SOC would do the organizing and iron out jurisdictional problems after the workers were signed up. However, Walter Reuther, president of the UAW, complained that this rule was not being followed and that "some people are putting their unions ahead of the CIO." Bittner replied that the only jurisdictional case he knew of during the campaign involved the furniture workers at Louisville. When some officers of the union told southern workers that they were resigning because "the Communists had gained control of the Unions," Bittner responded by saying that if the furniture workers' officers took this attitude, the SOC would put furniture workers into local industrial unions attached directly to the CIO.

Financial problems. By November 1946, it was obvious that the CIO campaign was going to encounter stiff opposition and that the SOC's greatest problem would be financial. By the end of September 1946, the

CIO had raised only $768,806.14 of the more than one million dollars needed before the campaign was to get underway. The SOC was therefore in some trouble when the executive board met in October 1964; it owed a balance of some $438,000 in October and had only $87,000 in the bank. Moreover, Murray informed the board at that time that the costs of the campaign would be $1,800,000 a year instead of the $1,000,000 planned. The CIO thus spent considerably more the first year than the $355,452 spent by the AFL the year its campaign lasted.

Murray and Bittner were distressed that the CIO unions had not met their commitments to the drive. Murray told the executive board that the SOC was going to have trouble meeting its payroll and added: "That would be fatal, absolutely and positively fatal, if anything of that description should occur. It would constitute a black mark, and there would trail in its wake very devastating repercussions all over the country if it should become known that the National CIO did not care to put the necessary finances into that drive to keep it in motion."[29] Bittner told the board that ten months was not long enough to organize the south, but that "it would not only be disastrous but it would be disgraceful, absolutely disgraceful for the CIO to give up this campaign now because they couldn't get the money."

Despite their efforts, Murray and the SOC were unable to get affiliated unions to give the desired two million dollars for 1947, so they tried to get each union to give 2.5 cents per member per month. David McDonald read the SOC budget and announced that "This means cutbacks, severe cutbacks in operations; this means layoffs of personnel." The CIO leaders agreed at this session to put up $192,498.32 of the amount pledged for 1946. This meant that the SOC would have only $365,000 for its operations during the remainder of 1946. The commitments of $97,500 a month for 1947 were never met, and, after reducing his staff by 50 per cent, Bittner told the executive board in March 1947, that if there were any further reductions in funds, "I will leave the South." The blow to the southern organizing drive was softened somewhat when other unions, particularly the textile workers, the steelworkers and the woodworkers agreed to employ some of the people discharged from the SOC. By March 1947, contributions from CIO unions were running 30 per cent behind pledges, and Jacob Potofsky said the situation looked much worse than he had ever expected; he termed the 30 per cent deficit "outrageous." In January 1948, the SOC had a budget of $90,007.76, but unions paid in only $54,375 of their commitments. Bittner told the executive board that he had gone south with the idea of organizing, not collecting money. In 1947, he said that the appropriation for the campaign had been reduced 50 per cent to $97,500 a month and that he had discharged about 120 men, but "at no time did the Board send $97,500 a month."

In spite of these difficulties, Bittner announced that 400,000 new members and 794 local unions had been organized by January 1948, and that the SOC still had 120 men scattered in 12 southern states. He denied ever having said that the SOC sought to organize a million workers in ten months. "Those statements," he said, "were given out by people who have never done any organizing and who knew nothing about the problems that confronted us." Bittner said, "Things look better than they ever have, but you can't get men to work an average of 16 hours a day organizing with no security."

The campaign was also being impeded by the growing split between the CIO and the left-wing unions. Several of these unions were delinquent in their payments. Harry Bridges of the Longshoremen said that his union had voted down the appropriation for the southern drive. Moreover, some left-wing leaders criticized Bittner for recommending that CIO unions use the NLRB at a time when many leaders refused to sign the non-Communist oaths and were thus denied the use of the board's facilities. Other unions threatened to pull out of the southern drive because it was not "going fast enough" to suit them.

The showdown on financing the drive did not come until September 1948, when Philip Murray delivered a long talk to the executive board in which he said that the object of the southern drive had been to "organize the unorganized in the South regardless of how long it takes." In spite of numerous difficulties, the CIO had made some membership gains and had accomplished important political results by defeating reactionary politicians in Florida, North and South Carolina, Alabama, Tennessee and other southern states. The CIO had also incurred much good will, and, while "violence and mob action against labor" continues "in many communities throughout the South," largely through CIO legal tests, organizers could then operate without legal hindrances and restraints. At first, according to Murray, "dozens of organizers were arrested and union meetings were prohibited under restrictive ordinances and statutes designed to impose servitude upon the working people of the South." In addition, Murray told the CIO officers that the drive had accomplished important social results because the CIO was conducting unsegregated meetings, often presided over by Negroes elected by jurisdictions in which whites predominated. Murray emphasized that the southern organizing drive "was a civil rights program . . . which not only encompassed the organization of workers into unions

. . . but the freedom of Southern workers from economic and political bondage, . . . to exclude from . . . the South all types of racial and other forms of discrimination."

Other problems. The SOC's financial problems were overcome in 1948 when the convention voted a 3 cents per capita increase per month, 2 cents of which went to the SOC.[30] But other problems replaced finances to plague the drive after the 1948 convention, the most serious of which was the Communist question. Moreover, the drive suffered a severe setback in 1949 when Van Bittner died. Bittner was replaced by George Baldanzi in August 1949, but he was soon supplanted by John V. Riffe. Internal strife between George Baldanzi and Emil Rieve of the textile workers also hurt the drive as the CIO was forced to use part of its organizing staff to keep southern textile workers from going over to the AFL with Baldanzi.

The conflict between Baldanzi and Rieve affected the organizing campaign in other ways. Baldanzi accused Rieve of having removed TWUA organizers from the SOC when Baldanzi became director[31] and Rieve accused Baldanzi of ineffectiveness in organizing the south. Baldanzi's followers also accused Rieve of having weakened the union by unwise activities in the south for purely political reasons.[32] They referred to the situation in 1951, when the TWUA called a strike of 40,000 southern textile workers at the five largest plants organized by the union. The strike was ill-timed because of a decline in both civilian and military demand for textile products.[33] Union officials believe that employers in the industry concentrated on breaking the union at Dan River because the mill had been the pattern-setter; the Marshall Field mills some 20 miles from Dan River remained closed during the strike and, according to a Dan River union leader, "spent their time rounding up all the scabs they could possibly find in their organization, sending them over to get jobs in Dan River mills in order to break the Union at Dan River."[34] As the strike went on, the expense to the TWUA (the international spent $1,260,000, not including contributions from other local unions), worsening economic conditions, an abundance of strike-breakers, and the union's weakness made it obvious that the strike could not be successful. On May 5, TWUA accepted an offer by the Federal Mediation and Conciliation Service to appoint a tripartite mediation panel. The committee's decision was ratified by the strikers, and the general strike ended.[35] The TWUA's defeat in this strike—and the conviction that it was politically inspired—turned many southerners away from Rieve and caused them to support Baldanzi at the 1952 TWUA convention.

At the convention a whole slate of officers was run against the Rieve forces, with George Baldanzi opposing Rieve for the presidency. The Baldanzi forces were all defeated. Within two weeks after the convention, Baldanzi had shifted to the UTWA-AFL as director of organization, and a total of sixty local presidents were reported ready to join him.

It is difficult to determine the total impact of the Rieve-Baldanzi fight, because it was already apparent by the time of the 1952 convention that textile unionism in the south was finding it increasingly difficult to maintain its wartime gains. George Baldanzi contends that the TWUA lost 400 local officers and 50,000 members because of this fight.[36] Several important bargaining units went over to the AFL, and others became unorganized.[37] The TWUA paper reported that in 72 elections encompassing 54,380 workers by February 28, 1954, the AFL won 45 covering 27,019 and the CIO won 24 covering 26,926.[38] The UTW reported that it had gained only about 15,000 members as a result of this conflict.[39] The AFL's most important victory was at Dan River, where there were some 11,000 eligible voters, 7700 of whom voted for the UTW, 1624 for "no union," and 278 for the TWUA. However, the AFL gained less than 2000 dues-paying members at Danville because many workers would not join the union and the company refused to grant a check-off. The CIO would undoubtedly have lost more members if it had not moved its southern organizing staff into the textile areas to help ward off raids by the AFL.[40]

The CIO's losses might also have been greater if the UTW had been in better shape to take advantage of the unrest within the TWUA. It turned out, however, that the UTW's principal officers had apparently misused the union's funds and were without sufficient resources to engage in an extended conflict with the TWUA.[41] Meany told the AFL Executive Council that he was suspicious and concerned about the UTW's financial manipulations because the AFL "had spent many thousands in textiles." Meany's suspicions were later confirmed by the AFL-CIO Ethical Practices Committee which felt that the UTW's officers had converted union funds to their own uses and threatened to expel the union unless it "cleaned up" by November 15, 1957.[42] In December 1957, the executive council agreed to changes that had been worked out by the UTW.

The effect of the Rieve-Baldanzi fight is indicated by comparing NLRB election results in the textile states of Virginia, the Carolinas and Georgia between 1952 and 1953. In 1952, the AFL got 5653 NLRB votes in these states to the CIO's 9443. In 1953, 29,106 workers voted for the AFL, and 11,566 voted for the CIO; since most of the transfers from the CIO to the AFL went through the NLRB, it is obvious that the CIO was the net loser.

The organizing drive also produced conflicts between the directors of the CIO organizing committees, officials of the state industrial union councils, and the CIO regional directors, whose respective functions were not clearly defined.

As the CIO's campaign entered its third year, membership gains became increasingly difficult, particularly in the key textile industry. Of 111 bargaining elections in the period from 1949 to 1951, TWUA-CIO lost 63 and won 48. In Georgia the union had fewer contracts in 1954 than in 1948. The CIO claimed 120,000 textile workers in the south in 1952, but only 90,000 were under contract. Before "Operation Dixie," TWUA had about 20 per cent of the southern textile workers, but in 1952 it had only 14 per cent. UTWA-AFL had about 1 per cent, which gives a total of 15 per cent of the industry in the region under union contract.[43] Van Bittner said: "When you organize the textile industry of the South, you have not only the textile industry of America organized, but you have practically all industries in the South under the banner of the CIO. So, our main drive . . . has been in the textile industry."[44]

A senate subcommittee held investigations on the activities of various employers and citizens' groups to counteract the unionization of textile workers, and found many cases of armed violence against unions and blacklisting of members in Georgia, Tennessee, and South Carolina. In all these cases a pattern of company resistance with the aid of local law enforcement officials, conflict with the union if organized, strike, violence, use of the national guard, slow response from the NLRB, and, finally, defeat for the union, can be observed.[45]

Activity in Mississippi. The CIO probably had its greatest success in Mississippi at the Masonite Corporation at Laurel, which was already unionized. The contest at Masonite was less with the company than with the AFL carpenters, and pulp, sulphite and paper mill workers. There is some evidence that the company preferred the AFL to the CIO, because it is reported to have given raises and defeated the union just before elections on the CIO's two previous attempts at unionization before victory was achieved.[46] Mississippi CIO director R. W. Starnes wrote Bittner: "The people in the plant have not had a general raise in over four years. During the War, only one raise was secured, that applying to only a small percentage of the total workers—skilled."[47]

The CIO's attempts to organize the Grenada Industries Company, makers of ladies stockings, illustrate the difficulty with a new industry which has been brought in under one of the south's many promotional schemes. Grenada Industries was established in 1938 under Mississippi's Balance Agriculture with Industry program. This program provided that municipalities, counties or groups of municipalities could issue bonds for the construction of new buildings. The value of the bonds could not exceed 20 per cent of the value of property in the issuing agent, and could be sold only after an election by the political subdivision. Incoming plants were also exempt from taxation for five years.[48]

The NLRB scheduled an election for December 3, 1946, after the company rejected the American Federation of Hosiery Workers' demand for recognition. About a week after the NLRB set the election date, the Grenada *Daily Sentinel-Star* (November 19, 1946) declared: "The CIO organizers have circulated among the hitherto well-satisfied employees of Grenada Industries for approximately 90 days . . . Should the majority favor surrendering their rights to the CIO it is believed by many that the Industry will cease operations as has been the case in several other places."

In the same issue of the *Sentinel-Star*, the editor reasoned:

> Communist-influenced national laws set up the machinery under which such elections are called, providing that a majority vote of workers in an industry may transgress the individual rights of all employees, and make the individual who prefers to keep his rights as such, subservient to the CIO . . . and support it with their finances . . .
>
> Left out in the hearing and in the voting, will be the citizens and taxpayers of Grenada—who in their desire to provide jobs for the workers from surrounding sections, agreed to tax themselves and mortgage their homes and other real estate to launch an Industry. Since those who are mortgaged, or possibly taxed, cannot vote to protect their interests can this not be called "taxation without representation" as representation in this election is denied to those so gravely involved and concerned?

Other editors entered the attack on the CIO. The editor of the *Grenada County Weekly* declared on November 21, 1946, that he had nothing personally against the CIO, but "It is generally assumed that the CIO is shot through with Communism, and I do not like Communism. I do not like to get orders from Washington, much less Moscow." This editor said he feared "none of the prospective industries dickering with Grenada will come here at all if Grenada is dominated by the CIO."

The same issue of the *Grenada County Weekly* carried a full page advertisement signed by John Rundle, chairman of the "Grenada Citizens' Committee" entitled "Think Some Yourself," suggesting that all the CIO wanted was the workers' dues.

Ministers also joined the attack against the union. Fourteen of them from the nearby town of New Albany, which had an ACWA local, announced in a letter to the *Sentinel-Star*, November 27, 1946: "We, and our respective denominations, are in sympathy with the principle of organizing labor for the betterment of the working man. But neither we, nor our denominations, endorse the particular labor organization known as the CIO, which we deem communistic and un-American in spirit."

Throughout the campaign against the CIO, much was made of its political activities. It was pointed out that the CIO supported FEPC, repeal of poll taxes, elimination of segregation, international organization, "all of which are against American and Southern principles."

The CIO lost the election 297 to 122.

Termination of the SOC. The CIO southern organizing campaign was terminated officially in 1953. Philip Murray died in 1952, and Walter Reuther was elected president of the CIO. Reuther thought it unwise to have special committees like the SOC, contending that efforts should be made to build within the international unions.[49] Reuther and John Riffe, who became CIO executive vice-president, thought separate organizing campaigns caused inefficiency and duplication of staff.[50] In the reorganization that started in April 1953, the SOC was abolished. It was decided that the CIO organizing apparatus would be placed under the direction of the international unions because, according to Riffe, the CIO was "not going to have people organizing haphazardly"; he complained that during the southern drive workers had frequently been organized who could not be serviced by the internationals.[51] By June 1953, the number of regional and subregional directors in the CIO had been reduced from 60 to 16, and by August the CIO had assigned 160 field organizers to various international unions in numbers from one to 21 each; for example, the TWUA was assigned 18 CIO organizers who were to work directly under the international's supervision in the south.[52] Moreover, since Riffe considered textiles "the political and economic key to those states," he went to Charlotte, North Carolina to assist Emil Rieve. The TWUA, like the CIO, started a reorganization program because it had staff duplication and a disproportionate number of representatives in staff positions and too few in the field organizing; the TWUA therefore assigned 30 representatives who had been doing administrative work to organizing duties.

The two years following the abolition of the SOC were devoted largely to the continuing fights with the Communist unions and preparations for merger with the AFL. Both federations realized that raiding was costing a great deal of money and yielding very little results. It was estimated that the CIO and the AFL had been involved in NLRB elections covering 385,000 people claimed by both unions, and that "In these tugs of war AFL unions won 40,000 members from the CIO and the CIO won 44,000 from the AFL. In other words, the two federations spent millions of dollars for the net exchange of approximately 4,000 members."[53]

In so far as organizing is concerned, it is apparent that the CIO drive fell far short of its objective, in spite of the enormous expenditures. The TWUA alone spent $4,000,000 in the south between 1946 and 1948 and gained only 15,000 members. The TWUA probably had many fewer members in 1953 than in 1946 partly because of the Baldanzi-Rieve affair. The SOC reported organizing gains of 280,000 new members at the end of one year,[54] 400,000 at the end of one year and a half,[55] and 450,000 by November 1948.[56]

The largest membership increases the first year were reported in North Carolina, Texas and Tennessee, though the greatest relative gains were in Arkansas and Mississippi; the CIO had doubled its Arkansas membership at the end of the first year of the campaign, and Bittner said that, despite the opposition of Senator Bilbo, the CIO "probably made more real progress in Mississippi than in any other southern state" because of the organization of the Masonite Corporation at Laurel, the state's largest employer.

One of the CIO's greatest gains during the southern drive did not come from the unionization of new members but from the affiliation of the Communications Workers of America (CWA), with 32,000 members in nine southern states and another 20,000 in Texas. The Southern Federation of Telephone Workers (SFTW) was formed after the NLRB ordered the Southern Bell Telephone Company to disestablish its company unions in 1941. The loosely organized National Federation of Telephone Workers helped the SFTW win an NLRB election over the International Brotherhood of Electrical Workers, and the union was certified as exclusive bargaining agent at Southern Bell in 1944. The Communications Workers of America was formed in 1947 and affiliated with the CIO in 1949. The old SFTW became the southern division of the CWA and was one of the largest CIO affiliates in the south.[57]

Membership gains for the CIO campaign for the ten months ending in February 1947 were:[58] between 70,000 and 85,000 in Tennessee;

14,500 in Texas; 22,000 in North Carolina; 7000 in Virginia; and 15,000 in Alabama.

NLRB elections. Between 1946 and 1952, the total votes cast in NLRB representation elections in the south were:

AFL	215,927
CIO	276,969
Unaffiliated	77,484
No union	260,685

These results are more indicative of membership gains in the CIO than the AFL, however, because affiliates of the latter organization frequently gained recognition without the NLRB election procedures.

The evidence from both NLRB elections and membership statistics indicate that the CIO and the AFL gained considerably in southern membership during the most active first two years of the organizing campaign. During 1947, statistics show that 65,614 workers in the south voted for the CIO and 53,234 voted for the AFL. The CIO won about 30 per cent of its elections in the region in 1947, slightly less than the proportion it won outside the south (31 per cent); the AFL won a slightly higher proportion of elections in the south than it did in the nonsouth, but was defeated in 29 per cent of southern elections and 23 per cent of those outside the south. The effect of the organizing drives is suggested by the fact that there was little change in the CIO's activity outside the south between 1946 and 1947, but participation in representation elections dropped considerably in 1948. There was a great increase in CIO participation in the south relative to its non-southern activity in 1950—although the number of workers voting for the AFL and the proportion of elections won declined significantly in that year—which probably reflects the stabilization of the CIO drive and its raids against unions expelled from the CIO for Communist domination. The Korean War also probably benefited the CIO more than the AFL. The CIO gained considerably during 1950 in the per cent of the total vote it got in the nonsouth as well as the south. The CIO's concentration on the south in 1948 and 1949 is reflected in the fact that it got a much higher proportion of the NLRB vote during these years (26 per cent and 20 per cent) relative to the proportion it won in the nonsouth (15 per cent both years). It will be noted, however, that the number of NLRB elections won by the AFL and the CIO in the south declined in 1950 and increased in the nonsouth, which means that the average election in the south involved a larger number of workers. The great increase in number of votes cast for, and the proportion of representation elections won by, the AFL in 1953 undoubtedly reflects the switch of unions from the TWUA-CIO to the UTWA-AFL as a result of the Rieve-Baldanzi conflict.

The results of NLRB elections also indicate that the trend has been for unions to lose higher proportions of NLRB elections since 1946. In 1946 "no union" won in only 24 per cent of the elections in the south and 20 per cent in the nonsouth. In 1950 "no union" won 35 per cent of the southern and 24 per cent of the nonsouthern elections. As we shall see, this trend has continued. In 1960 "no union" won 47 per cent of the elections in the south and 40 per cent in the nonsouth; in 1962 the comparable figures were 49 per cent and 40 per cent.

In spite of the opposition encountered and the disappointing organizing results of "Operation Dixie," participants do not agree that the CIO drive was a failure. Tom Starling, former UAW executive board member from the south and a member of the SOC, felt that the campaign "had to take place" and disagrees with the charge that there were fewer members in the south when the drive ended than when it started.[59] Many other workers in the campaign expressed the same feeling.[60] The union leaders also emphasize the number of current labor leaders in the south who were brought into the union because of the organizing campaign.

Participants in the drive disagree as to whether or not it should have been launched with fanfare or undertaken quietly, though most of those interviewed agree that the publicity given the campaign invited opposition from the community and alerted employers to the unions' objectives. There can be little question that much of the anti-union legislation gained support from fears that the organizing drives would upset power relations in the south and interfere with the region's industrial progress.

The CIO also made other planning and strategic mistakes during the early phase. The attempt to charge initiation fees, while the AFL and some international unions granted exemptions, was probably a mistake, and this policy was finally abandoned by Bittner. Bittner was also obviously mistaken in his belief that it would be no more difficult to organize the south than other regions, since the history of southern unionism clearly demonstrated that there were important institutional impediments in the south which were much less important in other areas.

The CIO apparently underestimated the strength of the AFL and the importance of the employers' attitude as a factor influencing organization. Since many employers preferred to deal with the AFL, they took measures to insure that AFL unions represented their employees.

Table 4. Southern membership in some selected international unions, 1939 and 1953.

Unions	1939	1953
Building trades		
Asbestos workers	800	2,800
Bricklayers, masons and plasterers	10,800	15,600
Carpenters and joiners	36,500	119,200
Electrical workers	16,100	74,000
Operating engineers	2,100	12,700
Hod carriers and common laborers	16,100	54,800
Bridge, structural and ornamental iron workers	5,900	23,500
Painters, decorators and paperhangers	8,900	31,100
Journeymen and apprentices of the plumbing		
and pipefitting industry	5,600	42,400
Sheet metal workers	1,200	11,100
Total	104,000	387,200
Railroad and related		
Boilermakers and iron ship builders	3,200	22,300
Firemen and oilers	1,300	17,000
International Association of Machinists	16,300	85,500
Maintenance-of-way employees	17,600	41,600
Railroad telegraphers	9,600	12,100
Railway carmen	13,200	29,600
Railway and steamship clerks	27,900	68,900
Railway trainmen	25,300	39,200
Railway conductors	7,400	8,700
Locomotive engineers	11,000	13,800
Locomotive firemen and enginemen	13,300	15,800
Total	146,100	354,500
Government employees and public utilities		
Fire fighters	4,800	14,100
American Federation of Government Employees	2,900	10,800
National Association of Letter Carriers	6,700	15,500
National Federation of Post Office Clerks	7,300	18,200
Communication workers		83,200
Total	21,700	141,800
Transportation		
International Association of Longshoremen	16,600	15,800
Street, electric railway and motor coach		
employees	6,900	16,300
Teamsters, chauffeurs, and warehousemen	16,700	33,400
Total	40,200	65,500

Table 4. (*Continued*)

Unions	1939	1953
Entertainment		
American Federation of Musicians	7,500	20,400
Theatrical stage employees and motion		
picture operators	6,800	7,500
Total	14,300	27,900
Printing trades		
Printing pressmen	6,200	12,100
Typographical	5,200	6,700
Newspaper guild	1,200	900
Total	12,600	19,700
Food and tobacco workers		
Meat cutters and butcher workmen	6,700	21,900
Bakery and confectionery workers	2,100	9,700
Tobacco workers	14,900	27,600
Packinghouse workers		10,900
Total	23,700	70,100
Industrial		
United Garment Workers	3,300	5,100
International Ladies' Garment Workers	2,100	7,700
Amalgamated Clothing Workers	3,200	18,300
International Brotherhood of Paper Makers	3,700	13,500
Pulp, sulphite and paper mill workers	1,700	22,600
United Textile Workers		17,700
Textile Workers' Union	9,900	36,400
United Mine Workers	89,200	62,100
Rubber workers	200	12,800
Steelworkers	9,800	83,200
Automobile workers	500	44,600
Total	123,600	320,000
Totals		
Total southern membership	627,000	1,788,000
Total AFL membership	388,700	1,148,100
Total CIO membership	143,600	362,200

Source: Calculated from unpublished estimates derived mainly from union materials supplied to the writer by Professor Leo Troy. See Professor Troy's *Distribution of Union Membership Among the States, 1939 and 1953* (New York: National Bureau of Economic Research, occasional paper 56, 1957).

268

The CIO's racial and political programs made the AFL clearly a more acceptable alternative to the southern white community. Although the CIO was able to dislodge some plants, like Masonite, with the aid of Negro votes, most Negro union members remained with the AFL. In addition the AFL had fewer financial problems than the CIO, and organized more workers at less cost.

The figures in Table 4 reveal that in spite of impressive gains by industrial unions in the auto, steel, textile, packinghouse, rubber and communication industries, the bulk of the south's membership remained in the older AFL and railroad unions. Indeed, the AFL increased its share of the south's total membership from 62 per cent in 1939 to 64 per cent in 1953; the CIO's share of the south's total membership declined from 23 per cent to 20 per cent during this period.

CHAPTER XVI

Organizing Experiences after Operation Dixie

Both the AFL and the CIO encountered increasing opposition in the south—and in the nation—during the 1950's and 1960's. The obstacles to union growth were many, including: state, federal, and municipal antilabor legislation; strike defeats and declining membership, especially in the textile industry; and the resistance to repeated organizing efforts by unorganized firms in the relatively well-organized petroleum refining, tobacco, pulp and paper, building construction, boat building, and coal-mining industries.

THE AFL-CIO MERGER

The difficulties faced by unions, especially the organizing problems, played a large part in the 1956 AFL-CIO merger, and it was generally expected that a southern organizing drive would be one of the first tasks of the organization. In anticipation of the merger, Professor Leo Wolman declared: "It is a fair guess that, once the merger has been effected, the combined resources of a powerful collection of labor unions will be used to make the South the next battleground for the expansion of union membership and power."[1]

The importance of organizing the south occupied a prominent place in the discussions at the AFL-CIO Executive Council's first meeting in February 1956. A report to the council showed a potential membership of 42,000,000 in jurisdictions normally organized by unions, but only 15,800,000 members. It was estimated that of the 26 million organizable workers in the United States, approximately half were white-collar workers, and ten million of the organizable were in the south; there were an estimated four million white-collar workers in the south, and a potential of six million workers in other categories.[2]

President Meany warned the council that the proportion of organized to unorganized workers was steadily declining especially in the south and that unions had lost in other areas because of the relocation of firms in the southeast. Meany expressed the hope that when unions saw the need to help the unorganized and protect their standards they would work out their jurisdictional problems and launch a drive. Walter Reuther said that strong unions should help weak unions and that organizing was the key problem facing the federation, because it could not fulfill its economic or political missions, "unless this picture is reversed." Indeed the members of the executive council seemed to agree on the necessity of an organizing campaign, but felt that the jurisdictional problems would have to be settled and money would have to be raised before it could get underway. Jurisdictional conflicts proved especially frustrating to organizers attached directly to the AFL-CIO regional offices, because they were frequently forced to abandon the drives when some international union raised jurisdictional questions.

Perhaps the most important problem for the federation was the continued conflict between the UTW and the TWUA, because it had long been recognized that the psychological key to organizing the south was the textile industry. At the time of the merger, there were over one million textile workers in the United States, only 300,000 of whom were organized; 575,000 of the unorganized were in the south. Moreover, 100,000 of them were in the giant Burlington, Stevens and Cannon chains, which the AFL-CIO organizing staff felt had to be organized first. But the executive council concluded, that, "any campaign by the organizing department and the TWUA would be endangered by the UTW," so that the "UTW's position . . . in effect [constitutes] a veto over the organizational plans of the AFL-CIO."

The AFL-CIO sought to overcome these difficulties by obtaining voluntary agreements between unions and by rendering direct assistance to the internationals when they had initiated campaigns. It was apparently on this basis that the AFL-CIO announced in the summer of 1956 that it was helping the TWUA with a drive (which failed) among the Burlington, Cannon and Pepperell chains in the south. The AFL-CIO had also committed a large part of the staff

to an unsuccessful effort to organize the large R. J. Reynolds Tobacco Company, which was the main nonunion firm in that industry. At R. J. Reynolds, racial divisions played a part in the union's
defeat because Negro workers generally refused to support the TWIU.

Since the TWUA considered the campaign in the south a "matter
of life and death," the AFL-CIO had assigned organizers to help, but
the union's general president, William Pollock, told George Meany
that "manpower alone is not enough."

> The South today is in the grip of a widespread and powerful conspiracy
> aimed at preventing union organization by any and all means. It is our
> belief that traditional organizing techniques, no matter how diligently
> applied, cannot in themselves prevail against this conspiracy, but must
> be supplemented by a program designed to change the thinking, the
> atmosphere in the southern community.[3]

Pollock told Meany that unions usually relied upon organizing to
change the climate of opinion, but that in the south this procedure
would have to be reversed and suggested a program to: (1) show
that unions would help the entire south; (2) bring before the whole
United States the problems faced by the unions; (3) promote union
sentiment among unorganized textile workers; (4) reassure the members that they are part of "a powerful and growing movement"; and
(5) increase wages and fringe benefits in southern textiles.

The TWUA suggested that labor leaders spend $30,000 to $50,000
in eight southern newspapers and in one in Washington and "cultivate
special sources of influence on public opinion—radio and TV men
with whom we've had contacts; educators and do-gooders known to
the education department; any community leaders known to our local
administrators or other AFL-CIO people." Pollock pointed out that if
the AFL-CIO spent $50,000 on an organizing campaign, it might have
nothing to show for it, so at least this publicity campaign would do
a little good.

When the AFL-CIO discussed the proposal at its January-February
1957 meeting, AFL-CIO Vice-President George Harrison, president of
the railway clerks, thought the unions' inability to organize textiles in
the south was their own fault. "It would seem," he said, "if the unions
themselves would apply themselves to organizing rather than coming
to the Federation and asking the other unions to relieve them of their
jobs, help might be given when the opportunity presents itself."[4] Jacob
Potofsky supported the textile workers' proposal and pointed out that
the south was not just the textile workers' problem. David McDonald,
president of the steelworkers, proposed a levy of 2 cents a month on

AFL-CIO members to raise 1.8 million dollars in six months for a campaign; he also suggested that the levy be continued for six months after the campaign, at which time the program would be renewed to see if it should be continued. Walter Reuther told the council that organizing, education, and publicity were inseparable, and that once an objective had been decided upon, the amount of money needed could be determined. Potofsky wanted immediate action in the region, and Harrison suggested that the AFL-CIO find out how many internationals wanted to organize in the south, how much money they would contribute, and how much support would be needed from the AFL-CIO. It was finally decided that the publicity committee would study the proposal.

The committee warned the executive council that there was no guarantee that any publicity campaign would succeed, but that an effective program would have to be long-range—three to five years—and should thoroughly cover a chosen geographic area. The committee reported that the southeast was growing rapidly and must be organized because it was a threat to American standards of living, but that: "Traditional organizing methods, even when applied with imagination and skill, have not proved adequate to surmount the almost universal hostility to unions, particularly in such industries as wood, furniture, textiles, apparel, service trades, etc." The committee report felt that "the southern community has been sold on the idea that anti-unionism has spurred the growth of industry, created vast numbers of new jobs to raise the standard of living throughout the area."[5]

The study committee felt that an organizing campaign in the south would be speculative, but if it failed the labor movement would be no worse off, and if it succeeded the unions would gain "great benefits." There were several alternatives, according to this report: (1) To promote an immediate full-dress campaign which would cost approximately 7.5 million dollars at least, "and we lack experience with a campaign of this sort." (2) to launch a campaign in one state for $750,000 to $1,000,000 a year; Florida or North Carolina were suggested as possible choices. (3) To undertake limited community programs of short duration for $50,000 to $100,000 a year.

The executive council decided unanimously against an all-out campaign in favor of a survey by a national research organization at a cost of $40,000 to $50,000. This was to be a "preliminary confidential study of Southern opinion and methods by which it may be changed."[6] Specifically, the study was designed to determine (1) whether an educational and public relations campaign was desirable, from the view of probable effectiveness, at that time; (2) whether insight could be gained into the *real* reasons for resistance to unionism as contrasted with stated reasons; (3) which population groups offered the greatest opportunity for success.

The national research organization studied ten communities in Mississippi, Louisiana, Alabama, Georgia, South Carolina, North Carolina, and Virginia and, in a confidential report, concluded that southern workers "lacked many of the psychological and sociological assets that union organizers in other parts of the country take for granted."[7] Many organizers with experience in the south vigorously disagreed.[8] The report also suggested that there was "optimism for the long-term future of the unionism in the South," but that unionism faced "formidable difficulties." There was a strong implication in the report that unions would be better off to consolidate and strengthen their current positions than to start a new campaign.

The AFL-CIO's southern organizing plans also were influenced by its preoccupation with other problems, especially the conflict over corruption and internal racial problems. The corruption issue led to the expulsion of the important teamsters' union. And although their fears proved to be exaggerated, union leaders were afraid that their equalitarian racial position would lead to the defection of union members in the south. The labor movement also suffered several serious strike defeats after the merger.

The Henderson strike. The November 1958 strike by 1038 textile workers against the Harriet-Henderson Mills in Henderson, North Carolina, was one of the most important events in the south for the textile workers during these years. Indeed, this was the largest strike in the TWUA's 24-year history and was considered crucial in its efforts to organize the south. Although union leaders considered the strike a plot by employers to rid the area of an important union base, Harriet-Henderson management denied the charge. North Carolina officials were concerned with the Henderson strike because they considered the absence of unions and strikes to be an important inducement for plants to locate in North Carolina.[9]

The immediate cause of the strike was management's insistence that the arbitration clause be amended to permit the company to veto demands. Management claimed that arbitration decisions were interfering with its prerogatives and taking too much time from other functions. The union pointed out, however, that of 198 grievances at the mill in the previous thirteen years, only 25 had been decided by arbitrators. Other observers claimed that the company was really upset by the skill with which the union's area representative prosecuted grievances. Since management knew less about industrial relations than the union's expert, the company was at a disadvantage in grievance and arbitration cases.

There is general agreement that the strikers exhibited remarkable solidarity, causing the plants to remain closed for three months. However, a wave of violence started in February 1959, after the company obtained sufficient strikebreakers to reopen the mills. Of 1038 strikers, only 56 responded to the back-to-work call for February 16, but the employer had little difficulty recruiting strikebreakers from the surrounding countryside for beginning wages of $1.135 an hour. On November 30, 1959, the company told the unemployment compensation office that it had hired its complement of workers and therefore had no objection to the payment of unemployment insurance to the strikers.

Despite the widely publicized acts of violence against strikebreakers and company property, there were no deaths during the two and one-half-year strike. Some of the plants' windows were shot out, strikebreakers' automobile windows were broken, automobiles were stoned, and acid was thrown on some of the company's carding machines. The union and the employer offered rewards for information leading to the conviction of persons involved.

In February 1959, Boyd Payton, TWUA regional director, was hospitalized with a mild concussion which he said occurred when someone assaulted him outside his motel. A month later, he was injured after his car was forced off the road and rocks thrown through his windshield. However, North Carolina's attorney-general claimed that these events were "hoaxes" perpetrated by Payton to gain sympathy for the strikers. Payton offered $10,000 to anyone who could prove a hoax and sued the attorney-general for slander and defamation of character.

Before Payton could prosecute charges, however, he along with seven other TWUA representatives was convicted of conspiring to damage the company's property. The union men were convicted on testimony from an undercover agent of the state bureau of investigation. The union and some leading North Carolina citizens—Jonathan Daniels and Harry Golden, among others—felt that these convictions were based on questionable evidence because the state's only witness had been paid $1100, had furnished the union men with whiskey, and had initiated the discussions of destroying company property. Moreover, there was no evidence that Boyd Payton knew anything of the alleged plot to destroy the company's property. Payton and two other TWUA officials nevertheless were sentenced to prison for between six to ten years; four of the defendants received five to seven year terms; and one man was sentenced to from two to three years. They were later paroled, and Governor Terry Sanford reduced their sentences by three years after the character of the state's key witness was impugned.[10]

The TWUA officially terminated the strike June 1, 1961, because it could not continue the heavy financial drain and because it felt that an official termination would help obtain clemency for the convicted union members. The TWUA spent and estimated $1,500,000 during the Henderson strike, $250,000 of which was contributed by other unions. There was some criticism of the union by the 300 strikers who could not find other employment by the summer of 1961; many felt that the union had deserted the workers. However, most of the strikers felt that the TWUA had given as much support as could be expected but that the situation had become hopeless.

The TWUA's defeat at Henderson joined a long list of defeats for textile unions in the south which symbolizes a fundamental weakness that will make it difficult for unions even to regain their former strength. In 1965, probably less than 8 per cent of the workers in the southern textile industry were union members.

Employer opposition: The Deering, Milliken case. The Deering, Milliken case attracted much interest because of the importance of the issue of whether or not a plant can close to avoid collective bargaining. This is important to union organizing because organizers agree that the workers' fear of plant closings is a great obstacle to union growth in the south. Organizers usually tell workers that employer and community threats of plants being closed if unionized are merely "bluffs" to keep unions out, but there have been enough publicized cases in each area to make workers wary.

Few employers have offered stiffer opposition to unions than Deering, Milliken & Company, a New York textile merchandising concern that owns or controls some 30 mills as exclusive selling agent. In 1945, for example, the company's Gaffney, S.C., mill was seized by the army after it defied a War Labor Board directive that it bargain with the TWUA.[11] When the plant was returned to private hands, the company again refused to deal with the union, which was broken after a 22-month strike. Concerning the defeat of the union at Gaffney, the *American Wool and Cotton Reporter* said that Milliken had "licked the everlasting daylights out of the union." The *Wool and Cotton Reporter* also admired the way Deering, Milliken had handled other union problems:

> More recently, Dallas Manufacturing Co. of Huntsville, Alabama, controlled by Milliken has been liquidated altogether. We were a small stockholder; he paid us off at $190 a share. We were sure that Milliken

liquidated Dallas to get rid of the g—d union, to give them a hell of a licking, to show them that he would do the same in all of his mills—if he has to—and he controls something like 22 mills. The fact that he liquidated Dallas doesn't mean that he isn't going to make Dallas constructions in other mills.[12]

On September 6, 1956, the employees at the Darlington Manufacturing Company, Darlington, South Carolina, voted for the TWUA by a narrow margin. On September 12, the company's board of directors called a stockholders' meeting to liquidate the company. By the end of 1956, machinery had been moved out and the remaining equipment sold at public auction. Darlington's mayor went to New York in a fruitless effort to persuade Roger Milliken not to close the town's major source of employment; Milliken also ignored a petition signed by 400 Darlington Manufacturing Company employees retracting their support of the union in an effort to keep the plant from closing.

The TWUA filed unfair labor practice charges in an effort to get back pay and job rights in other plants of the Deering, Milliken chain for Darlington's 500 employees.[13] The NLRB found the Darlington Manufacturing Company guilty of coercing its employees and closing to avoid collective bargaining, and ordered Deering, Milliken to rehire the workers at another of its plants or to put them on a rehiring list and give them back pay from the time of their discharge until they found "substantially equivalent employment." Deering, Milliken appealed the decision, arguing that the company had an absolute right to go out of business. The company also argued that the decision to close the plant was based on economic grounds and denied the company's liability for back wages ordered by the NLRB, which it said amounted to $8 million in 1964. The Court of Appeals, in a three to two decision, upheld the company, arguing that Darlington had an absolute right to terminate the business and that the board exceeded its authority when it imposed a penalty on the company.[14] In 1964, the solicitor general petitioned the U.S. Supreme Court for a review of the case, arguing, with the union, the NLRB, and the Justice Department, that the basic issue was not whether or not the company had the right to go out of business but whether a penalty could be imposed upon it for terminating its business in order to avoid bargaining with the union in violation of the National Labor Relations Act. The NLRB argued that the company did not go out of business but merely transferred work to other plants. According to TWUA's general counsel: "The suggestion that Darlington closed its plant to avoid further economic losses has no support whatever in the record of the case. The Labor Board found that Darlington closed its plant not for economic reasons but to avoid dealing with the union . . . Neither the dissenter on the Labor Board nor any member of the Circuit Court which reversed the decision disputed this finding."[15] Also at issue was whether or not Deering, Milliken was a "sales agent for Darlington," as the company contended, or whether the connection was closer, making Deering, Milliken liable for Darlington's actions. The union's general counsel argued: "Actually there is abundant evidence, and the board so found that Darlington and Deering Milliken are commonly owned corporations constituting part of a tightly integrated giant textile complex, and . . . when the Darlington plant was shut down its orders and products were shifted to other Deering Milliken affiliates."

The United States Supreme Court decided in 1965 that a company had the absolute right to go out of business but that it could not close one of its plants "if innovated by a purpose to chill unionism in any of the remaining plants of a single employer and if the employer may reasonably have foreseen that such closing will likely have that effect."

Since the NLRB's original decision did not deal with this aspect of the closing, the court sent the case back to the board. In August, 1966, an NLRB trial examiner ruled that the shutdown was not designed to discourage unionization in Deering, Milliken's other plants. The TWUA appealed the decision and the trial examiner was reversed by the NLRB in June 1967.

The TWUA's organizing strategy was influenced by Darlington's closing. In 1958, for example, after an organizing campaign in the Cannon chain, the union felt that it had enough support to conduct NLRB representation elections in five branches, but withdrew because it could not organize the entire chain and was afraid that election victories in these plants would cause them to be closed and their production transferred to others operated by the company.

In addition to their failure to organize the giants in the industry and their difficulties at Henderson and Darlington, the textile unions suffered a general demoralization as a result of these and past failures. This resulted in a decline in membership in locals representing companies like Dan River Mills and the Irwin and Cone chains, even though workers in these companies refused to decertify their locals. Of course, the textile unions' difficulties in the south were not of recent origin. They suffered serious psychological handicaps because of a history of failures, stretching in recent memory to the 1929 strikes, the defeat of the 1930 organizing campaign, and the 1934 general strike. Although the textile unions made some progress during the

Second World War with the aid of the War Labor Board, and during the early stages of "Operation Dixie," they suffered serious setbacks because of their defeats during the 1950's and because of internal conflict.

Although it is difficult to determine what effect past failures and changed conditions had on textile organizing difficulties following the Second World War, the experience of the latter period raises a question of whether a well-financed campaign during 1929-1934 might not have organized the southern textile industry, as the AFL's critics allege. Perhaps the federation's critics are right in the sense that sufficient resources might have made it possible for unions to maintain a base in the south during the 1930's and might have avoided the image of failure which pervades southern textile unionism. However, the obstacles presented by the depression of the 1930's, the surplus labor supplies in the textile areas, and the absence of a well-organized non-southern base from which to operate all suggest that the costs of a campaign during the 1929-1934 period probably would have been prohibitive. The experiences of postwar campaigns suggest that a well-financed campaign would probably not succeed even in the more prosperous 1960's.

The building trades. Labor organizations even had difficulties in unionized strongholds like the building trades, where such important firms as the Daniel Construction Company in the southeast and Brown and Root and H. B. Zackery in the southwest successfully fought organization. Indeed, Brown and Root countered a campaign which started in 1950 with legal action and an injunction against the Texas AFL and 93 building trades unions. Brown and Root alleged that the unions were engaged in a conspiracy to damage its business, to require the signing of unlawful closed shop agreements, and were using unlawful boycotts and other means to damage the company's business.

The unions replied that they had been engaged in a running dispute with Brown and Root for 16 years, that the company misclassified workers, had been found by federal agencies to have paid substandard wages ranging from 50 to 75 cents per hour below "fair" rates, had been found guilty of violating the National Labor Relations Act[16] by interfering with, restraining, and coercing employees, and refusing to bargain, and had flouted the decisions of the War Labor Board. In spite of the unions' position, Texas courts issued a temporary restraining order against secondary boycotts, picketing and other efforts to advertise Brown and Root's substandard conditions. Although this case was still unsettled 15 years later, the restraining orders had successfully stymied the organizing campaign against Brown and Root and had cost the unions large sums of money in court costs and attorneys' fees. The Texas AFL alone spent almost $50,000.[17]

Various construction unions also attempted unsuccessfully to organize the Daniel Construction Company of Greenville, South Carolina, which is one of the most antiunion towns in the south. Greenville is near Spartanburg, which, as we shall see later, also was vigorously antiunion before the 1961 IUD drive. Daniel was the second largest general construction company in the United States in 1963 and operated in eight southeastern states. The plumbers lost a 1961 election to represent 1500 Daniel employees at 50 sites in four southern states, but the NLRB set the election aside because the company encouraged reports on union sentiment and interrogating employees concerning the union.[18]

Another problem of increasing importance to building trades unions was the growing amount of nonunion highway and heavy construction work in the south.

Despite these difficulties, the building trades unions remain relatively strong in the south. An important factor favoring the growth of the unions has been the amount of federal construction work in the region, most of which is unionized. Project Apollo is particularly important to Florida, Louisiana, Mississippi and Texas. Indeed, this program will have an economic impact on the region greater than the construction of the TVA during the 1930's; total expenditures for TVA were $1.2 billion, whereas it was reported in 1962 that $2 billion a year would be spent on Apollo for 20 years.[19] Employment at Cape Kennedy was approximately 25,000 in 1962 and was scheduled to increase to 50,000 by 1967. In New Orleans, the Michaud plant to construct Saturn boosters created many new jobs at its peak in 1963. Construction of the Mississippi test site required an expenditure of $93 million dollars and gave employment to 6000 construction workers. The Mission Control Center at Houston was scheduled to have 2500 construction workers at its peak. Since these projects were being undertaken on both no-discriminatory and unionized bases, they had significant implications for race relations as well as collective bargaining.

The IUD campaign. In 1961 the AFL-CIO Industrial Union Department (IUD) launched a pilot organizing drive in Spartanburg-Greenville, S. C. The campaign was based on the idea that the IUD would coordinate the organizing efforts of various unions, and it grew out of a meeting of needle trades unions at the 1959 AFL-CIO convention. The Spartanburg area was selected because it had 15,000 unorganized workers and because the International Ladies' Garment Workers (ILG) had established a base there.

Following its usual strategy of concentrating on southern branches of plants it had already organized in the north, the ILG organized a firm in Spartanburg with which it had contracts in New York.[20] Even with this leverage, the ILG was forced to spend two years, undergo an eight-month strike, and spend $600,000 in direct strike costs before organizing this relatively small firm with about 150 people. The ILG paid benefits of $20.00 a week to the strikers and transported them to New Jersey where they picketed in an effort to gain a sympathetic walkout at the firm's northern plant which had 700 employees. This failed, however, because the New Jersey workers, two thirds of whom were Negroes, refused to honor the picket lines put up by the Spartanburg workers. Northern workers ordinarily support southern strikes in order to equalize labor costs and lessen the flow of work to the southern plants. In this case, however, the New Jersey local's business agent had been promised by the company that work would not be transferred from New Jersey to Spartanburg.

As has frequently been the case in southern garment industry strikes, the Spartanburg walkout was settled with the aid of the teamsters' union, who honored the ILG's roving pickets at terminals and warehouses. Teamster members also "lost" the struck goods and shipped them to the wrong addresses.

Under the terms of the settlement, the employer agreed to build a new plant outside Spartanburg, rehire the strikers, and bargain with the union while the Spartanburg shop continued on a nonunion basis. The reason for this rather unusual agreement, as well as the reason for the employer's resistance to the union, was according to his attorney a fear that he would "wind up on the chain gang" if he dealt with the union. The company had agreed, as a condition for its subsidy from Spartanburg, never to deal with the union.

The next stage in this drama occurred after the ILG had established a beachhead in the plant outside Spartanburg when a large New York dress company informed ILG representatives that it was looking for a southern shipping center and knit dress factory, and would deal with the union if the New York Joint Dress Board would not resist the establishment of the southern center. An ILG representative suggested Spartanburg as the logical place. It was also pointed out to the New York manufacturer that the company against which the ILG had conducted the eight-month strike would be willing to sell out. This transaction was therefore carried out in time for the plant, with its 700 employees, to be the first victory in the IUD's pilot organizing campaign in 1961. The firm organized by the ILG in Spartanburg had 600 employees in 1965 and, together with 400 other ILG members in that area, formed one of the union's most important concentrations in the south. Its other main center was Miami, where the ILG had about 2000 members in 1965. However, the potential in Spartanburg was 12,000 to 15,000 additional members and only 5000 to 6000 in Miami.

The ILG victory gave an important boost to the IUD's organizing drive. In winning 11 of 16 NLRB elections by February 1963, unions acquired bargaining rights for 2600 employees.[21] The union's victories, and the realization that many important New York firms wanted to deal with the union in their southern branch plants, also changed the attitude of Spartanburg's leaders toward unions. New firms locating in the city no longer are required not to deal with unions.

The relative success of the Spartanburg pilot project caused the IUD and 18 of its affiliates to agree in January 1963 to expand and extend the drive to five areas including North and South Carolina and the Dallas–Houston–Fort Worth sections of Texas. The IUD considered that the main factors accounting for the success of the Spartanburg project were its concentration on specific targets and the prior settlement of jurisdictional problems so that only one union appeared on NLRB election ballots.

Although statistics are not available for the number of elections won and lost during the IUD drive, in 28 elections during 1963, 5900 workers voted for IUD unions in South Carolina, and 2700 against. In North Carolina 100 elections were held, and 12,000 workers voted against the IUD, and 5800 for.[22] In Texas, between March 13, 1963 and January 31, 1965, unions had won elections covering 6581 employees, had lost 48 elections covering 5411 employees, and the IUD was protesting seven elections covering 1710 employees.

Unions encountered strong opposition during this expanded drive. In Hartwell, Georgia, for example, UAW and IUD representatives were assaulted and chased out of town, and their automobile tires were slashed while they tried unsuccessfully to organize 600 employees of the Monroe Shock Absorber Company.

Although it is too early to evaluate the 1963 IUD campaign, it obviously is not going to be as successful as the 1961 pilot project in Spartanburg. An important disadvantage of the 1963 drive was that the wider area involved dissipated much of the organizers' time. In addition, there has been nothing like the ILG victory at Spartanburg to provide the psychological lift to the campaign.

CHAPTER XVII

Paper, Coal, and Agricultural Workers

THE PULP AND PAPER INDUSTRY

The production of wood pulp continued to grow after World War II, until by 1959 the south produced 59 per cent of the nation's output.[1] Of the ten states producing over a million tons in 1959, seven (Florida, Georgia, Louisiana, Mississippi, North Carolina, South Carolina, and Virginia) were in the south.

As noted in Chapter XIII, the pulp, sulphite and papermill workers (IBPSW) and the International Brotherhood of Paper Makers (the IBPM, which merged with the paperworkers' union in 1957 to become the United Papermakers and Paperworkers' Union [UPP]) had a relatively high degree of organization in the southern paper industry by the end of World War II and continued to unionize plants as they were established in that region. Not only is the southern paper industry well organized, but, in 1961, hourly wage rates in the south were $2.51 as compared with $2.21 in the north and $2.48 in the west.[2] In 1958, the highest minimum labor rate of any paper mill was set at $2.12 at the Gulf States Paper Corporation in Demopolis, Alabama.[3]

The UPP and the IBPSW had about 63,000 members in the south in 1961. Of these, the IBPSW had 35,000, and the UPP had 28,000.[4] The IBPSW had a total membership of 105,000 in 1961, including 30,000 Canadian members; the UPP had about 140,000 members. United Mine

Workers' District 50 represented the workers of the Continental Can Company in Hopewell, Virginia, and there were three major unorganized mills in the south: two Champion Fibre Company mills at Houston, Texas and Canton, North Carolina, and the Calcasieu Paper Company at Elizabeth, Louisiana. In 1964, however, another small mill in Dallas with about 300 employees was under contract with the UPP, but the local there had no members. The UPP ceased servicing the local after its members refused to strike or accept a contract.

Since the industry is generally so well organized, it is instructive to examine the reasons for the failure at Elizabeth, Louisiana. The Calcasieu Paper Company was established in 1926, and an organizing campaign was launched by the paper makers during the NRA period in 1933. The campaign ended, however, after the company discharged a group of union members and when the union was unable to obtain their reinstatement. The Industrial Lumber Company sold the Calcasieu Paper Company to a Jacksonville, Florida paper jobber around 1945, and both the CIO Paperworkers and the IBPSW sent organizers into Elizabeth in 1946.[5] The CIO was given an opportunity to establish its only deep south local in the pulp and paper industry when it won the election at Calcasieu in 1947; the CIO's only southern contract in the industry was at a plant of the West Virginia Paper Company. However, the CIO soon withdrew from Elizabeth after its efforts to negotiate a contract failed.

The grievances which caused the workers to call in the unions in 1947 persisted thereafter and included: lower wages than in other paper mills; complete control over promotion and discharge by the company; and poor working conditions. According to union organizers, workers were particularly concerned about safety conditions at Calcasieu; three workers were killed between 1950 and 1952. The employer denied that his mill had inadequate safeguards and attributed the deaths to the natural risks involved in the industry.[6]

In 1950, the IBPSW and the IBPM launched another organizing campaign at Elizabeth. As before, there was much feeling for union organization, but some workers were disillusioned because of the CIO's inability to negotiate a contract in 1947. Organizers also faced the natural resistance of workers who were afraid to lose jobs that offered them better living conditions than the farms from which most of them came. Moreover, Elizabeth was a company town, almost completely controlled by the Calcasieu Paper Company. The single organizer sent in by the unions also faced an unusual racial problem because the workers were divided among Negroes, whites, "Acadian" French, and a racial mixture known locally as "Redbones."

In spite of the difficulties, the union got enough support in 1951 to petition for an election, which the IBPSW lost by 296 to 298. Another was held in May 1952, and this time some of the hostility to the union was overcome by dividing the workers into separate locals according to occupations. This time the union won 459 to 207.

It proved easier, however, to win a representation election than to negotiate a contract. The union's request for seniority and fringe benefits common in other Louisiana paper mills and a 25-cent hourly wage increase was rejected. The employer declared, "The union wanted me to put up my money and they would run the mill."

The parties' inability to compromise their positions caused a bitter strike which started on September 13, 1952, and which was supported by about 500 of the company's 700 employees. The strike was relatively peaceful the first two months, but thereafter violence was committed by strikers and nonstrikers. On one occasion, a nonstriker who was arrested for shooting into a picket's truck, claimed that a plant official had "encouraged him to attack the picket line." In November, the company got an injunction against mass picketing, and, thereafter, gas lines, homes, automobiles, bridges and business property were dynamited; shots were fired into houses and automobiles; picket shacks and houses were burned; and pastures were even poisoned.[7] In October 1953, 57 families were evicted from company houses, and many others were given notice to vacate. The union spent much time and money in unsuccessful court action to prevent these evictions. The company had had little difficulty getting strikebreakers, especially since many skilled workers refused to support the strike. When another NLRB election was held in 1954, there were only 18 votes for the union, and 672 for "no union." The strikers could not vote in this election under the terms of the Taft-Hartley Act. However, the union continued its efforts to organize the Calcasieu plant and lost another election in 1961. The IBPSW and the papermakers spent over $500,000 on strike benefits alone.

Thus the Calcasieu Paper Company is one of the very few paper companies in the United States to win out against union organizers. Some of the reasons were: the abundance of strikebreakers on the farms in the surrounding area; the company's control of the town, including the strikers' houses; the racial division of the work force; and the fact that the employer had no non-southern operations and sold his products through his own jobbing outlets, making it difficult to conduct a successful boycott. This case again demonstrates that it takes more than victory in a union representation election to organize a plant.

THE COAL MINERS

As noted in Chapter IX, most southern miners were well organized by the time of World War II, with the exception of the De Bardeleben interests in Alabama and a few truck miners who offered no serious challenge to the organized mines at that time. With the increased demand for coal during the war and increasing labor costs in unionized mines, however, the number of small truck operations increased considerably. The existence of many of the operations depended on being exempt from union conditions, particularly the royalty of 40 cents a ton all union mines were required to pay to the UMW's health and welfare fund. The UMW's problems were also aggravated by increasing unemployment in the coal mining regions. The number of bituminous and lignite miners declined from 441,000 in 1940 to 147,000 in 1962.[8]

In an effort to overcome the competition from the truck mines, the UMW inaugurated a campaign in 1959 to organize the ramp owners to whom the truckers sold their coal. The contract proposed by the UMW would have prohibited the ramp operators from buying coal from nonunion mines, which would have put nonunion operations out of business because the ramps provided the only economical marketing outlets. Many truck operations would not agree to the UMW's demands, however, because the $24.25 daily wage required by the union and the welfare payment would have put them out of business. The truck miners paid their workers between $12.25 and $14.25 a day on the average, and no welfare payment.

The strike that started in eastern Kentucky in March 1959, when the truck and ramp operators rejected the UMW's demands, was reminiscent of the bloody organizing activities of the 1930's. About 7000 miners were involved in seven Kentucky counties. Pickets were stationed at the ramps serving the 750 truck mine and ramp operations in southeastern Kentucky. Three men were killed, and five ramps were destroyed by dynamite and fire. The ramp operators armed themselves to resist the strikers' activities, and gunfights were frequent. The union miners used mass picketing, an organizing tactic employed to advantage during the 1930's. In March, for example, 1200 pickets threatened to tear down and burn a coal tipple near Colson in Letcher County, but were stopped by 15 state troopers.[9] Governor A. B. Chandler sent 2000 guardsmen into the strike zone in April because he considered the lives of state troopers on duty there to be in danger. Since the national guard patrolled only in the daytime, violence continued at night.

Picketing ended after the national guard was sent in, and the NLRB got a restraining order against the UMW. According to the NLRB, the UMW's demand that the ramp operators cease buying nonunion coal was a secondary boycott and thus violated the Taft-Hartley Act.

Not only did growing economic adversity make nonunion employers resist the union, but it also caused marginal union operators to renounce their contracts in an effort to survive. In southeastern Kentucky, for example, violence flared in 1963 after many employers either ceased paying the 40 cents a ton royalty or ignored their contracts and paid less.[10] These employers were picketed by the miners, even though the UMW ordered its members to stop harassing the small operators. Picketing continued, however, because of the intensity of feeling when the UMW was forced to withdraw hospital care from the miners whose employers no longer paid the royalties and sell four of its six Kentucky hospitals.

A strike in southeastern Tennessee in December 1962 also led to violence when union miners attempted to prevent the Grundy Coal Company of Tracy City from opening eight new mines with nonunion labor. Workers at the small mines formed a Southern Labor Union and agreed to work at the Grundy mines at the minimum permitted by the federal government, which was 30 per cent less than the UMW scale.

The UMW also faced prosecution under the Sherman Antitrust Act for its activities in the south. The Supreme Court dealt with this issue in the 1965 Pennington case, which began as a suit by the UMW Welfare and Retirement Fund trustees to recover some $55,000 in royalty payments from the Phillips Brothers Coal Company. The UMW trustees alleged that this sum was due and payable under the provisions of the National Bituminous Coal Wage Agreement of 1950, as subsequently amended (which produced relative peace in the industry until 1966). Phillips, joined by some small coal mine operators, claimed that the Sherman Act was violated by an industrywide agreement between the UMW and the large employers which imposed wage scales that the smaller employers could not pay. Phillips also charged that the large companies and the UMW had agreed upon other measures to exclude small employers including: an agreement by the large companies not to lease coal lands to or buy coal from nonunion operators; the companies and the union jointly prevailed upon the secretary of labor to establish minimum wages under the Walsh-Healy Act for contractors selling coal to the Tennessee Valley Authority, which the smaller contractors could not pay; and that four large companies, two of which were controlled by the UMW, engaged in a "destructive and collusive price-cutting campaign in the TVA spot market for coal" (which was exempt from the Walsh-Healy minimum wage) in order to drive the smaller companies out of that market. The federal district court for eastern Tennessee awarded damages against the United Mine Workers of $90,000, which was automatically trippled because of the provision of the Sherman Act, and the Court of Appeals for Sixth Circuit confirmed the decision of the lower court. The UMW then appealed to the U. S. Supreme Court which reversed the lower court and remanded the case for further proceedings.

The Supreme Court ruled that unions were subject to the antitrust laws if they attempted to set product prices or entered into collusive agreements with employers to impose contract terms on others, or entered into agreements intended to drive the other employers out of business. The court ruled, however, that the union could enter into an agreement with several employers fixing wages higher than other employers could pay, as long as the contract was not designed to drive small employers out of the product market. A union could also "unilaterally, and without agreement with any employer . . . adopt a uniform wage policy and seek vigorously to implement it even though it may suspect that some employers cannot effectively compete if they are required to pay the wage scale demanded by the union . . . . There must be additional direct or indirect evidence of conspiracy." Moreover, the court ruled that concerted efforts by unions and employers to influence the secretary of labor or other public officials were exempt from the Sherman Act "regardless of intent or purpose." One of the reasons for remanding this case for further proceedings in the lower courts was the Supreme Court's finding "that Phillips could not collect any damages under the Sherman Act for any injury which it suffered from the action of the Secretary of Labor."

In 1965, nine coal companies in Harlan and Bell counties, Kentucky, sued the UMW for $4 million damages, which the companies claim to have suffered because the union ignored restraining orders and sought to prevent them from operating without contracts. Following the Pennington decision,[11] these suits were combined with that one, and although the court fights were far from over, the UMW won an important victory in July 1966, when a federal district court ruled that the 1950 national contract did not violate the Sherman Act. At the same time, however, the court awarded damages of $311,787 to two companies for losses growing out of violence accompanying organizing activities.

AGRICULTURAL UNIONS: THE LOUISIANA EXPERIENCE

Except for the unionization of Florida citrus workers by the AFL during the southern organizing drive, the main activity among agricultural workers was in Louisiana where the teamsters attempted to organize dairy farmers, strawberry farmers and sugar cane workers. Other field workers organized locals of the National Agricultural Workers Union (NAWU).[12]

Dairy farmers. Unionism among Louisiana dairy farmers in 1947 was precipitated by conflicts with New Orleans health authorities growing out of a 1942 ordinance requiring the farmers to install coolers and remodel their milking rooms.[13] This led, in 1945, to the formation of an organization known as the United Milk Producers. The farmers, feeling the need for affiliation with the regular labor movement, were granted a charter by the International Brotherhood of Teamsters (IBT) in 1947. Locals of the IBT organization, which was named the United Milk Producers of America, were established at Franklinton, Amite, Lake Charles, Baton Rouge, and New Orleans; but the most active organizations were at Franklinton and Amite.

A New Orleans dairy began a conflict with the dairy farmers in March 1947, when it announced plans to raise milk prices to consumers and lower prices paid to producers. The dairymen's union countered this announcement by demanding union recognition and a restoration of prices.

The 1947 strike started March 24, after the milk distributors adamantly refused to deal with the union.[14] On March 25, at Amite, Louisiana, armed dairymen stopped an Illinois Central train, removed cans of milk from the mail car and poured the milk in ditches.[15] At Amite, eight tank trucks, each containing from 1800 to 2200 gallons of milk, were stopped and their tires deflated. At the St. Charles Dairy's pasteurization plant at Independence, 700 gallons of milk were seized and emptied into the Tangipahoa River.

The strike came to an end, however, eight days after it started, when United States marshals arrested 25 strikers for retarding the passage of mail and for the theft of milk from mail trains. Most of the arrested strikers were fined and imprisoned, including the teamster representative who was fined $5000 and sentenced to one year in prison.

These events disenchanted dairy farmers in the Florida parishes with unions because they blamed the teamsters for much of their trouble. Some of the farmers were illiterate and unaccustomed to union activities; they believed that the labor movement could protect them in their activities because they had heard that unions elsewhere engaged in picket line activity with impunity. Union leaders, on the other hand, argued that the farmers were unruly and quick to resort to violence. Wherever the blame for the violence lies, dairy farmers in the Florida parishes are not likely to call on unions for help in the near future.

Strawberry farmers. Hammond, Louisiana is known as the "straw-berry capital of the world." Weather and soil conditions in this area are conducive to an early harvest, and there are excellent rail connec-tions to important marketing centers.

However, the strawberry producers of the Hammond area were only marginal farmers in 1951 when they formed Fruit and Vegetable Pro-ducers' Union, Local 312, NAWU.

The union maintained affiliated chapters at Independence, Spring-field, Albany, Amite, Tickfaw, Maurepas, Ponchatoula, Doyle, and Gonzales; by April 1952, Local 312 had a membership of 3168 which was about 90 per cent of the strawberry farmers in the area.

The farmers sought to sell their 1952 crop through an agency under contract with the union "as its sole and exclusive agency for the pur-pose of handling, marketing, and disposing of the strawberry crop."[16] In keeping with the pre-1952 practice, berries were still sold at public auction in Hammond. In 1952, however, the union attempted to im-pose uniform conditions on handlers; those who refused to deal with the union were picketed and sometimes threatened with violence. The 1952 selling agency and especially reduced acreage brought the grow-ers one of the highest prices on record.

The union's success was short-lived, however. In 1953, the antitrust division of the Justice Department had the strawberry farmers con-victed as "a combination and conspiracy in unreasonable restraint of commerce in strawberries and other perishable produce" in violation of the Sherman Act.[17] The Capper-Volstead Act of 1922 and the Louisi-ana Cooperative Act of the same year supposedly exempted agricul-tural unions from the antitrust provisions of the Sherman Act. But the documents registering Local 312 as a cooperative were never properly filed with the Louisiana secretary of state, so the union could not legally qualify for exemption.

The union members were sentenced on April 28, 1954. Four of the officials were fined $500 and given suspended prison sentences of six months; three others, including a vice-president of the NAWU, were fined the $4000 remaining in its treasury.[18]

The convictions brought protests from throughout the United States. Several prominent senators, including Paul Douglas and Hubert Hum-phrey, wrote Attorney-General Brownell asking for information on the suit and protesting what they regarded as an unwarranted action by the Department of Justice.

The activity among Louisiana dairy and strawberry farmers failed to produce lasting organizations affiliated with the regular trade union movement. Cooperatives are probably more advantageous for farmers because they are exempt from the antitrust laws. Unions, of course, are also exempt from the antitrust laws for most purposes, but not when they are involved in fixing prices.

Sugar cane workers. In 1953, the National Agricultural Workers' Union attempted to unionize the workers in the sugar cane fields of south Louisiana. There were some 45,000 workers employed there in 1953 during the peak of the crop year; this compared with 3000 in Florida, 10,600 in Hawaii, and 148,000 in Puerto Rico.[19] Wages in Louisiana were higher than in Puerto Rico, but much lower than in Hawaii and Florida. In 1953, for example, Louisiana workers made $4.71 for a nine-hour day in addition to noncash benefits of 20 to 30 cents per day, while Florida wages averaged $7.99 on the same basis.

Minimum wages for sugar cane field workers were established by the United States Secretary of Agriculture under the terms of the Jones-Costigan Act of 1934. But they did not preclude the union from bargaining for higher rates and the elimination of what union leaders considered inequities and substandard conditions. It was estimated, for example, that in 1953 the average Louisiana family of a sugar cane fieldhand earned from $700 to $1200.[20] There was also some dissatisfaction with the Department of Agriculture's definition of the workday as starting in the field, because much work was done before the workers got there. Union leaders and their supporters also complained of irregular wages, poor housing, and paternalism.

These conditions caused local Catholic priests to invite the NAWU to launch the 1953 drive to organize the workers.[21] The union had made enough progress by the end of July to ask 23 sugar planters to meet with union representatives. The Louisiana commissioner of labor determined that the union had adequate worker representation, but was unable to get the employers to agree to a meeting.[22]

When all efforts to bargain failed, the NAWU representatives held a strike vote among the union's 2000 members, almost all of whom were Negroes; 1808 of the 1816 ballots cast in the secret election held in September 1953 favored the strike if employers refused to bargain after one more offer.[23] The union wrote the employers on October 2 and asked them to reconsider.[24]

The American Sugar Cane League of the U.S.A., Inc., a growers' association, answered the union by declaring:[25]

> The "union" has demanded that sugar cane farmers recognize it as collective bargaining agent of the agricultural labor employed on the farms. The sugar cane farmers at all times welcome discussion with their employees. However, the farmers have refused to deal with the "union" because: considering the Federal Sugar Act there is no need or room for

collective bargaining in sugar cane farming; complete organization of the sugar cane farms and collective bargaining through any union would place in the hands of one man or a few men power to destroy, and would destroy, all sugar cane farmers and the entire Louisiana sugar industry; and the farmers will not deal with this particular "union" *IN ANY EVENT*.

The League added that it was not required by law to bargain and:[26]

Collective bargaining in agriculture would give a few the power to control the food supply of the nation, and thus control the nation itself. A widespread strike in agriculture would so adversely affect the public that the welfare of organized labor as a whole would be jeopardized by public reaction.

The League called union leaders outsiders and criminals who were supported by a group labeled as a "Communist front organization," and said that small growers could not even meet the minimum wages established by the Department of Agriculture, citing statistics to show that the number of sugar cane growers had declined by 2000 between 1948 and 1952. The league's general manager argued:

It is my firm conviction that no sugar cane grower will deal with the union under any circumstances. If he did, he would have a strike or threatened strike every year at harvest time. That is the reason our Congress and State Legislature have never given the same encouragement for farm labor unions as given to industrial unions. Every fair minded person must certainly understand the reasons for the distinction.[27]

The NAWU called a strike against the plantations of four of the largest sugar companies in Louisiana when efforts to gain recognition failed. The strike began on October 12, 1953, at the height of the sugar cane harvest, and was later extended to other plantations when the struck employers attempted to borrow workers from plantations not on strike. Within 24 hours, between 40 and 75 per cent of the field hands on 50 sugar plantations failed to report to work; by the end of the second day, 1600 union members were off the job.[28]

The employers retaliated immediately by importing strikebreakers, serving eviction notices to workers in company-owned housing, threatening to cut off utilities in the houses, having company stores call in outstanding bills, and starting a back-to-work movement.[29]

The strikers received support from the labor movement and the Catholic church. Prominent labor officials, including George Meany, issued statements attacking the corporation officials; many unions, especially the teamsters' local unions in New Orleans and the United Automobile Workers, contributed money and supplies. The priests in rural areas helped the strikers by permitting them to use church buildings for meetings; they also actively aided the strikers by making speeches, planning strategy, and writing for contributions.

Workers in the sugar refineries were members of the CIO packing-house workers, but they cooperated to a degree with the NAWU—which was affiliated with the AFL—by refusing to cross picket lines. Indeed, on one occasion workers who lived inside refinery gates went outside the gates before working hours in order to refuse to cross NAWU's picket lines. The packinghouse workers cooperated with the strikers despite the no-strike clause in their contract with the refineries.

If the NAWU had not been enjoined from picketing, it might have brought sufficient economic pressure to bear on the employers to gain recognition. But the employers succeeded in getting injunctions which, according to H. L. Mitchell, "were the worst ever. They prohibited meetings of the Union; prohibited distributions of relief—actually prohibited our attorney from advising us on how to fight the injunction."[30]

The immediate cause for the cessation of this strike was the scope of the injunction issued by the courts, but it is obvious that the basic reasons for the failure of the walk-out are more complex. The union's interpretation of the legal theory behind the injunction was:

> that farm workers do not have the human and constitutional right to or-ganize and bargain collectively . . . Our constitutional rights to help our-selves to obtain the help of others has been paralyzed. The rights of property have been held to transcend the rights of people during the harvest. And not one single injunction has been issued against those who have done irreparable harm to human beings during the strike on the theory that during the certain seasons of the year property is more valu-able than persons.

The union's interpretation was based upon the reasoning of the Louisiana courts which issued these injunctions. The state court judge at Houma enjoined the strikers from picketing. "So vital does the ele-ment of time appear to us to be in the joint harvesting and processing operations," this judge said, "that we are disposed to regard any affirma-tive act intended to disrupt, deter, or prevent such operations as wrongful."[31] The avoidance of delay or interruption was, according to the judge, more important for the moment than any right the union might have to impress demands upon Southdown Sugars, Inc.

Other Louisiana courts issued injunctions against the strikers, and the union failed in having the decisions reversed.[32] In 1955, two years after the end of the strike, the United States Supreme Court refused to hear the case on its merits because it was declared to be moot; Jus-tice Black and Chief Justice Warren dissented in this opinion. The Louisiana Supreme Court then refused to reopen hearings in the case.[33]

The failure to improve the economic conditions of Louisiana sugar cane workers raises some rather fundamental questions about unionism among agricultural workers. The basic reason was the inability of the workers to halt the employers' operations. Although the NAWU received some support from the labor movement, its efforts were generally hampered by internal differences between Louisiana union leaders and the officers of the NAWU.

These differences came to a head in 1956 when Louisiana unions succeeded in repealing the state's "right-to-work" laws for all workers except those in agriculture. For about two years prior to the passage of the 1954 Louisiana "right-to-work" law, the state experienced several bitter strikes, including the 1953 sugar cane dispute. Immediately after the 1953 cane harvesting season, rumors of proposed "right-to-work" legislation began to appear. A council to promote "right-to-work" laws was formed primarily at the behest of agricultural pressure groups, especially the Louisiana Farm Bureau and the American Sugar Cane League, affiliates of the American Farm Bureau Federation.[34]

Immediately after the "right-to-work" law was passed, organized labor launched a campaign to have the act repealed. Of the seven senators who introduced the bill in 1954, only two were reelected in 1956, and the five new members who defeated them all opposed the laws. In spite of its successful election campaign, the Louisiana Federation of Labor (LFL) could not overcome the strength of the rural interests in the 1956 legislature, and decided to make a deal with the "agricultural bloc" through a plan to substitute a law pertaining to agricultural workers only. NAWU President, H. L. Mitchell, severely criticized Louisiana labor leaders for this "double cross." When called before the AFL-CIO Executive Council in August 1956 to explain the betrayal, Louisiana union leaders explained that the "right-to-work" bill could not have been repealed without the support of the "agricultural bloc," and were exonerated by the executive council. George Meany described the Louisiana leaders' action as "economic expediency."[35]

Union Growth in the South: Status, Causes, and Prospects

Part V

Limited Growth in Size, Number,
Space, Time, and Resources

CHAPTER XVIII

Quantitative Aspects of Union Membership in the South

UNION MEMBERSHIP IN THE SOUTH has increased relative to the nonsouth since 1939—the first year for which reasonably comprehensive and accurate statistics are available. As indicated in Table 5, between 1939 and 1953, southern membership increased by 185 per cent as compared with 148 per cent for the nonsouth, and it increased by 9.7 per cent between 1953 and 1964, and by 6.1 per cent in the nonsouth. Although the south gained absolute membership relative to the United States, it gained membership slightly relative to the extent of nonagricultural employment between 1939 and 1953 but lost between 1953 and 1964.

The proportions of nonagricultural employees organized in the southern states were not significantly correlated with nonagricultural or manufacturing employment in either 1953 or 1964, since the coefficients or correlation between these variables ($-.13$ and $-.35$ and $-.32$ and $-.47$ respectively) were not significant at the 95 per cent confidence level. (The coefficient of correlation for 13 observations must be about .55 to be significant.) The correlation coefficients between union membership in 1964 and the following factors were:

nonagricultural employment, 1964	.85
nonagricultural employment, 1953	.85
average hourly wages in manufacturing, 1964	.58

union membership, 1953   .96
average weekly wages in manufacturing, 1964   .57
change in nonagricultural employment, 1953-1964   .66

A comparison of membership changes in the 1939, 1953, and 1953-1964 periods reveals several important differences. The high correlation between the increase in union membership between 1939 and 1953 and union membership in 1953 (.98) was not repeated for the increase between 1953 and 1964; the correlations between the 1953-1964 increase in union membership and union membership in 1953 (−.21) and 1964 (.05) are not significant. The correlation coefficients indicate that membership did not increase between 1939 and 1953 where unions were strong in 1939 and did not increase between 1953 and 1964 where they were strong in 1953. Indeed, the correlation between the proportion of nonagricultural employees organized in 1953 and the percentage increase in membership between 1939 and 1953 was −.68; this means that the states with the highest degree of unionization in 1953 had the lowest percentage increase between 1939 and 1953. However, the .96 correlation between 1963 and 1953 indicates that relative absolute membership levels did not change very much between the states. Indeed the relative positions of the states in terms of percentage of nonagricultural employment unionized did not change significantly except for Arkansas, which moved from fourth to first place; no other state moved more than one place. There were, however, some important shifts between 1939 and 1953: Virginia declined from fourth to sixth place; Florida declined from sixth to eighth; Georgia declined from ninth to eleventh; and Louisiana advanced from eighth to fifth. The relative positions of Texas, Tennessee, Alabama, Kentucky, North Carolina, Mississippi, Oklahoma and South Carolina remained relatively constant between 1939 and 1953.

There was a very high correlation between the 1939-1953 increase in nonagricultural employment and the increase in union membership (.94), but no telling correlation between the increase in nonagricultural employment between 1953 and 1964 and the increase in membership for that period (.36). There was, however, a significant correlation for 1953-1964 between the increase in union membership and the percentage changes in nonagricultural employment (.70) and manufacturing employment, (.73). This suggests that the increase in membership between 1939 and 1953 was associated with increases in nonagricultural employment between 1939 and 1953, but that the increase since 1953 has been associated with relative and not absolute growths in employment. Moreover, the absolute and relative changes in manufacturing employment were associated with changes in mem-

Table 5. *Union membership and per cent of nonagricultural employment organized, southern states and United States, 1939–1964.*

States	Union members (thousands)			Per cent of change		Per cent of nonagricultural employment organized		
	1939	1953	1964	1939–1953	1953–1964	1939	1953	1964
Texas	111	375	370	237.8	− 1.3	10.3	16.8	13.3
Tennessee	71	187	184	163.4	− 3.3	15.3	22.5	17.6
Alabama	64	168	151	162.5	−17.3	16.1	24.7	18.0
Virginia	68	156	179	129.4	14.7	12.8	17.3	15.5
Kentucky	85	155	187	82.4	20.6	22.5	25.0	25.7
Florida	44	136	201	209.1	47.9	11.3	16.3	13.1
Georgia	36	136	150	277.8	10.5	7.0	14.3	12.7
Louisiana	38	136	147	257.9	8.2	9.6	19.5	17.1
North Carolina	26	84	89	223.1	6.2	4.2	8.3	6.7
Arkansas	25	68	112	172.0	64.9	12.7	21.5	26.2
Mississippi	13	50	53	284.6	6.0	6.5	14.7	11.6
Oklahoma	34	87	86	155.9	− 8.0	10.4	16.1	13.7
South Carolina	12	50	52	316.7	4.6	4.0	9.4	7.9
Total South	627	1,788	1,961	185.2	9.7	10.7	17.2	14.4
Total Nonsouth	5,891	14,616	15,227	148.1	6.1	21.5	34.1	29.5

Source: Nonagricultural employment figures from U.S. Bureau of Labor Statistics, *Employment and Earnings*, July 1958 and U.S. Bureau of the Census, *Statistical Abstract of the United States*; Union membership figures: Leo Troy, *Distribution of Union Membership Among the States, 1939 and 1953* (National Bureau of Economic Research, occasional Paper 56, 1957); 1964 figures, Bureau of Labor Statistics.

bership much more in the 1953-1964 period than they were in 1939-1953. This is undoubtedly due to the relatively greater growth in 1939-1953 of membership in the construction, mining, and other nonagricultural industries than in manufacturing. That changes in union membership are more likely to be associated with relative than absolute changes in employment is probably because membership is growing more rapidly in the newer manufacturing industries in states like Arkansas, Florida, and Kentucky than in the older textile manufacturing states of the Piedmont.

The correlation coefficients also suggest that the newer industries arising in the south between 1939 and 1953 were much more likely to be unionized than those established before 1939; the correlation coefficients between the 1939-1953 increase in union membership and employment changes were:

Manufacturing employment, 1939	.18
Manufacturing employment, 1953	.56
Nonagricultural employment, 1953	.93
Increase in nonagricultural employment, 1939-1953	.94
Value added by manufacturing, 1953	.82
Value added by manufacturing, 1939	.52
Increase in manufacturing employment, 1939-1953	.83
Value added by manufacturing, 1953	.82
Value added by manufacturing, 1939	.52
Percentage increase in nonagricultural employment, 1939-1953	.65

The percentage changes in nonagricultural employment for various categories between 1940 and 1962 are shown in Table 6.

These data suggest that one of the reasons for the south's increasing union membership after 1953, relative to the United States, was the continued growth in the traditionally well-organized construction and manufacturing sectors in the south, while they were declining elsewhere. The mining sector declined less relatively between 1957 and 1962.

Membership changes in the various southern states also can be explained in large measure by the shifts in industry composition. The two states with the greatest relative changes in membership between 1953 and 1964 were Arkansas and Florida, and they were also the states with the greatest relative variance in manufacturing employment; manufacturing employment increased by 85.4 per cent in Florida and 50.9 per cent in Arkansas; 49.3 per cent in Mississippi; 22.2 per cent in North Carolina; 22.1 per cent in South Carolina; 19.4 per cent in Texas; 19.2 per cent in Kentucky; 18.7 per cent in Virginia; 17.4 per

Table 6. Change in nonagricultural employment by industries, 1940–1962 (in per cent).

Category	1940–1947		1947–1957		1957–1962	
	South	Non-south	South	Non-south	South	Non-south
Mining	8.4	1.7	—11.6	—14.8	—14.0	—26.8
Contract construction	41.0	56.0	56.1	36.6	6.3	—9.2
Manufacturing	40.5	42.0	15.8	8.8	7.8	—4.6
Transport and public utilities	37.3	36.7	8.4	—0.6	—10.0	—6.7
Trade	43.4	30.8	47.1	18.8	5.5	5.7
Finance, insurance, and real estate	44.2	13.0	87.3	37.9	21.6	13.6
Service and miscellaneous	38.9	38.2	42.2	30.2	19.7	19.4
Government	34.4	29.3	45.6	38.6	18.6	20.6

Source: Calculated from data from U.S. Bureau of the Census, *Statistical Abstract of the United States,* 1950, 1960, 1964.

cent in Georgia; 13.6 per cent in Oklahoma; and 9.7 per cent in Alabama. It declined in Louisiana by 7.3 per cent.

The relatively large growth in membership in Arkansas can be explained in part by the changing composition of the work force. For one thing many of its new manufacturing industries are branches of large national concerns, and, as we shall see later, such branches are more easily organized than single plant firms. With respect to industry composition, the comparatively well-organized contract construction industry increased from 5.5 per cent to 6.5 per cent of nonagricultural employment between 1960 and 1963; manufacturing employment grew from 26.3 per cent of the total in 1957 to 28.6 per cent in 1963. Arkansas also experienced a relatively rapid growth in expenditures for new plant and equipment between 1954 and 1952; Arkansas' rate of increase was 74 per cent, as compared with 28 per cent for the United States, 12 per cent for the west south central, and 33 per cent for the east south central.

The membership gains in Florida probably reflect the rapid growth of manufacturing, construction and government employment in that state as indicated by the following increases between 1950 and 1963: contract construction from 67,000 to 115,000; manufacturing, 98,000 to 260,000; and government, 117,000 to 260,000.

The membership losses in Alabama and Tennessee undoubtedly reflect declining employment in coal mining. Mine employment lessened as follows in the south's main coal mining states between 1950 and 1963: Tennessee, from 13,000 to 7000; Virginia, 22,000 to 16,000; Kentucky 59,000 to 30,000; Alabama, 24,000 to 9000.

Textiles accounted for the following proportions of manufacturing employment in 1962: South Carolina, 51.5 per cent; North Carolina, 42.9 per cent; Georgia, 27.8 per cent; Alabama, 15.8 per cent; Virginia, 12.7 per cent; Tennessee, 9.6 per cent; Mississippi, 4.1 per cent; Arkansas, 1.8 per cent; Kentucky, 1.6 per cent; Texas, 1.3 per cent; the United States, 5.3 per cent; and the south, 20.0 per cent. Since the southern textile industry is probably only about 7 per cent organized (as compared with perhaps 20 per cent in 1948 and 10 per cent in 1958), the concentration of employment produces relatively low union membership in North Carolina and South Carolina, and makes membership comparatively low in those states. The rank coefficient of correlation between the proportion of nonagricultural employees organized and the proportion of textile employment to total employment was —.55, and would have been higher except for the fact that Alabama, with a high percentage of nonagricultural employment organized, also had a high degree of textile employment, and Mississippi, Louisiana, and Texas, with relatively low percentages of nonagricultural employment unionized also have low ratios of textile to total employment. We may conclude, therefore, that although textile employment is a significant explanation for low degrees of union organization, other factors are also at work. These factors will be discussed at greater length.

INDIVIDUAL UNION MEMBERSHIP

Although we do not have adequate membership figures for all international unions in the south, we have some information on the number of locals of various internationals registered with the Bureau of Labor Management Reports. The unions with the most locals were in the building and railroad crafts. Except for unusual industry patterns, the carpenters (UBCJ) usually have more locals than any other union. In 1964, for example, they had 532 locals in the south as compared with 447 for the railway clerks and 356 for the machinists (the unions with next highest numbers).

The number of locals does not, of course, represent the relative membership strength of each local, because of the differences in the sizes in various unions. The membership figures for several unions in the spring of 1964 for the southern states are shown in Table 7.

It is, of course, very difficult for international unions to determine their southern membership figures precisely because their structures

Table 7.   Southern membership of selected international unions, 1964.

Unions	Southern membership Number	Per cent of U.S.
United Mine Workers	120,000	33
Glass and ceramic workers	7,000	18
Chemical workers	17,776	22
Electrical workers (IBEW)	100,000	12
Steelworkers	85,000	8
Printing pressmen	11,000	10
Communications workers	7,589	24
Boilermakers and blacksmiths	21,319	14
Machinists	90,000	10
Letter carriers	32,404	20
Teamsters[a]	104,092	7
United papermakers	30,000	20
Textile Workers Union of America	13,000	11
Hod carriers and common laborers	41,495	10
Pulp and sulphite workers	37,000	33
United Federation of Postal Clerks	27,840	23
State, county and municipal workers[a]	17,844	8
International Longshoremen's Association	19,000	33
Sheet metal workers	12,000	10
Oil, chemical and atomic workers	30,000	30
Amalgamated clothing workers	20,000	4
Ladies' Garment Workers	18,900	5
American Federation of Teachers[b]	6,000–7,000	3–4
United Auto Workers	50,000	4

Source: Various international unions.

[a] Average 1963 membership.

[b] Estimate from New York Times, March 13, 1966.

do not coincide with our definition of the south. But the statistics in Table 7. are in many cases the best approximations that the various internationals could make. It should also be noted that these figures do not represent the number of workers covered by union contracts. The textile workers, for example, had only about 13,000 southern members in December 1965, but had 32,000 workers under contract.

With respect to the extent of organization of the unions mentioned, the following reported that their jurisdictions were about as well organized in the south as elsewhere: mine workers, steelworkers, communications, craft locals of the machinists, letter carriers, papermakers, pulp and sulphite workers, postal clerks, and the International Longshoremen's Association. The oil, chemical and atomic workers was the only union to report that a higher proportion of its southern jurisdiction was organized.

Texas state federation leaders report that membership was down from about 400,000 in 1952 to about 350,000 in 1962 and 365,000 in 1964. The main losses in Texas were in the OCAW, which had 31,000 members in Texas in 1955 and about 20,000 in 1964; the UAW, whose membership had declined from 16,057 in 1955 to about 14,000 in 1964; the carpenters, who had 27,321 members in Texas in 1957 and about 15,000 in 1964; the packinghouse workers, who had 2035 members in 1955 and 1200 in 1964; and the textile workers who had 720 members in 1955 and only 185 in 1964.

The main unions to gain membership in Texas between 1960 and 1964 were the American Federation of Government Employees, the National Association of Letter Carriers, the state county and municipal employees; the International Brotherhood of Electrical Workers; the International Union of Electrical Workers and the Amalgamated Meat Cutters. Technological change has benefited these unions, just as it has been responsible for most of the losses suffered by Texas unions. In addition, most of the organizations which have gained membership, especially the machinists, electrical workers, and meat cutters, have been organizing actively.

Alabama AFL-CIO leaders report that the main unions to lose membership were the steelworkers, because of automation; the textile workers, because of obsolete plants, foreign competition and new synthetics; and the auto workers, because of declining employment in the airplane industry and the shift to missiles. The main unions gaining membership in Alabama were the Retail, Wholesale and Department Store Union, because of increasing demand for services, and the machinists, because of increasing employment in the missile industry in Alabama.

The principal unions losing membership in Kentucky were the mine workers, because of technological change; textile workers, because of loss of markets, and the brick and clay workers because of technological change. The main organizations gaining membership in Kentucky were the Amalgamated Clothing Workers, the teamsters, and the auto workers, all because of increasing employment in their jurisdictions and aggressive organizing.

The chief unions gaining membership in Louisiana were the state, county, and municipal employees; the oil, chemical and atomic workers; and the machinists. The building trades unions were losing membership because of a decline in new construction during this period following several years of expansion.

North Carolina union leaders reported the textile workers to be the main losers of union membership between 1960 and 1964. The building trades' gains offset these losses. In South Carolina, the machinists, woodworkers, and garment workers gained membership between 1960 and 1964 because of growing employment and intensive organizing. The main losers in South Carolina were the textile workers and the communications workers. In Tennessee, the machinists, rubber workers, and electricians were the principal gainers between 1960 and 1964, and the mine workers, railroad unions, steelworkers, and the communications workers were the basic losers. The losses were attributed mainly to technological changes and the closing of coal mines.

Thus the available evidence suggests that the south's general trend in union membership is not unlike that of the United States; some unions, like the auto, steel, mine, and textile workers have lost membership, while others like the government employees' unions, the electrical workers, Amalgamated Meat Cutters and the machinists seem to be gaining. The chief reasons for increasing membership are associated with growing employment and intensive organizing, except for the government employees' unions which also have benefited from President Kennedy's 1962 Executive Order encouraging their collective bargaining.

Collective bargaining coverage by industry. While there are no figures available for union membership in industries by regions, a 1958 BLS study compares manufacturing establishments with labor-management agreements covering a majority of workers by regions; however, the definition of "south" used by the BLS includes Delaware, the District of Columbia, Maryland and West Virginia, in addition to the states included in our definition.[1] The BLS definition, therefore, probably gives a higher proportion of workers organized in each industry than would be given if our definition were used, because West Virginia had 44 per cent of its nonagricultural employees organized in 1953, as compared with 17.1 per cent for the south, and the other states had higher degrees of unionization than the south: Maryland, 25.2 per cent; District of Columbia, 21.2 per cent; and Delaware, 18.4 per cent.[2]

Arnold Strasser's figures[3] show the proportion of production and related workers in various manufacturing establishments by regions where there was a majority of workers under collective bargaining contracts for 1958 and 1962 respectively: northeast, 67.9 per cent and 65 per cent; south 46.1 per cent and 41 per cent; north central, 76.5 per cent and 71 per cent; and west, 76.6 per cent and 65 per cent. These statistics show that contract coverage declined in all regions during this period, but that the greatest relative change was in the west.

We unfortunately do not have information on contract coverage by industries for several years, but the available evidence indicates that unions in broad industry categories are weaker in the south than elsewhere. Kenneth Thompson's figures[4] indicate that the construction industry was relatively well organized in Louisiana, but that no industry was as well organized in that state as it was in the United States. While each industry is likely to be better organized in the northeast than in the south, there were the following important exceptions in the 1958 BLS study (the south's percentage is given first in each case): primary metals 95 per cent and 88 per cent; products of petroleum and coal, 88 per cent and 85 per cent; paper and allied products, 79 per cent and 73 per cent; tobacco manufactures, 72 per cent and 27 per cent; lumber and wood products 27 per cent and 23 per cent. However, in most industries collective bargaining coverage is lower in the south as compared with the United States. These figures were (in each case the south's percentage is first): stone, clay and glass, 65 per cent and 78 per cent; machinery (except electrical), 63 per cent and 67 per cent; chemical and allied products, 62 per cent and 66 per cent; printing, publishing and allied industries, 61 per cent and 66 per cent; fabricated metal products, 54 per cent and 71 per cent; food and kindred products, 41 per cent and 67 per cent; instruments and related products, 35 per cent and 52 per cent; leather and leather products, 32 per cent and 50 per cent; apparel, 30 per cent and 60 per cent; furniture and fixtures, 28 per cent and 50 per cent; and textile mill products, 14 per cent and 28 per cent.

As the figures indicate, the south had a smaller proportion of workers covered in the industries in which employment is concentrated. For example, 55 per cent of the south's manufacturing workers were in the food, instruments, leather, apparel, furniture, lumber and textile industries in 1957, all of which had less than 50 per cent coverage; only 29 per cent of the nation's employment was concentrated in these industries, all of which, except textiles and lumber, had over 50 per cent coverages in other regions. It is therefore clear that one of the reasons for the south's low proportion of unionization is the concentration of that region's employment in industries which are not well organized.

The importance of the low degree of textile unionization is suggested by the fact that if we deduct this industry from the BLS figures, the south's manufacturing coverage increases from 46 per cent of workers, in plants a majority of whose workers are organized, to 54 per cent; the nonsouth's coverage is increased from 73 per cent to 74 per cent by this adjustment.

UNIONIZATION BY GEOGRAPHIC AREA AND COMPANY SIZE

In an absolute sense, unionism in the south and in the United States is mainly an urban phenomenon. It is not true, however, that the proportion of organized nonagricultural workers is higher in the larger cities, because there is no statistically significant correlation between extent of membership and size of cities. The area in each southern state with the greatest degree of unionization is not likely to be the largest metropolitan area, which usually contains large numbers of unorganized commercial workers, who are even likely to be covered by collective bargaining contracts in the south than elsewhere.[5]

Thompson's 1956 study revealed that 19.6 per cent of nonagricultural employees in Louisiana were organized as compared with 20 per cent for New Orleans, 23 per cent for Shreveport, and 19 per cent for Baton Rouge; these three metropolitan areas had 59 per cent of the state's total union membership.[6] The next three largest Louisiana cities were Lake Charles, with 33 per cent of nonagricultural workers organized, Alexandria, 20 per cent, and Monroe, 25 per cent, but these three areas contained only 15.5 per cent of the state's total union membership. In Louisiana, Bogalusa was relatively small town (its population was 17,798 in 1950) but had the highest proportion of unionization— over 50 per cent of nonagricultural workers—in the state. In Texas, Frederic Meyers found that the comparatively well-organized oil complex in Beaumont-Port Arthur had between 65 and 70 per cent of organized nonagricultural workers as compared with 45-50 per cent for Houston and Dallas.[7]

The size of companies would appear to be an important determinant of union strength everywhere. A 1955 Bureau of Labor Statistics (BLS) study found the extent of collective bargaining coverage related to plant size,[8] and Meyers found that 59 per cent of the Texas firms investigated, employing over 250 employees, were unionized as compared with only 10 per cent of those with less than 250 employees; he also found that, while large plants were no more likely to be organized in urban than rural areas, small plants were more likely to be organized in urban areas.[9] In a study of plants in Alabama, Georgia, North Carolina, Tennessee and Virginia, H. Ellsworth Steele and Sherwood C. McIntyre found plant size to be an important determinant of degree of unionization in almost every industry; the average size of the nonunion plants in their 1952 survey was 487 as compared with an average size of 1187 for unionized plants.[10] Though there were a number of industries in the south with large unorganized firms, there was a significant difference between unionization in large and small plants.

Unions are generally weaker in the south than in the nonsouth, but some areas of the south are more highly unionized than some places in the nonsouth. A 1951-1952 study of various labor markets by the BLS reveals that while southern cities dominate the list of areas with low (20-49 per cent) proportions of plant workers covered by collective bargaining contracts, Louisville and Richmond ranked ahead of Scranton and Denver and were in the same class with Boston, Cincinnati and Hartford in the proportions of manufacturing workers covered by union agreements, while Memphis and Norfork-Portsmouth ranked ahead of the latter areas.[11] Nonsouthern states with lower percentages of unionized nonagricultural workers than the average for the south in 1953 were North and South Dakota and New Mexico. Kentucky, Alabama, Tennessee and Arkansas all had greater proportions of unionization than North Dakota, South Dakota, Idaho, New Mexico, Utah, District of Columbia, and Oklahoma.[12]

In conclusion then:

1. Unions in the south generally have a lower proportion of their jurisdiction organized than in the nonsouth, though in some places and in some industries unions are as strong or stronger in the south than in other areas of the country.

2. The south's employment is concentrated in industries with comparatively low degrees of union organization; in these areas, the south's industries are usually markedly less well organized than elsewhere.

3. Union membership is generally greater in large firms than small firms and is concentrated in the larger metropolitan areas, though smaller towns might have higher proportions of union membership.

4. Newer firms with high value added were more likely to be unionized than older firms between 1939 and 1953, but employment increases were less likely to be unionized in 1953-1964 than in 1939-1953. For the latter period increases in union membership were significantly related to percentage growth in manufacturing and nonagricultural employment. There was no correlation between any single variable and the proportion of nonagricultural workers organized in 1964.

CHAPTER XIX

Factors Influencing Union
Growth in the South

Unions, we have seen, have generally been weaker in the south than in the nonsouth, but some southern unions have been relatively strong. As John T. Dunlop has emphasized, "the facts do not speak for themselves,"[1] and require a theoretical or analytical framework in order to be properly understood.

Although we must simplify and generalize in order to elucidate the main factors influencing the status of unions in the south, union growth is very complex and cannot be explained in any concrete situation by a single proposition, because the constellation of factors is such that in any given situation other factors might counteract the one that ordinarily strengthens or weakens unions. We have seen, for example, that plant size is an important determinant of union growth, and, other things being equal, large plants are more likely to be organized than small ones. But other things are not always equal, and factors such as geographic location or peculiar prounion or antiunion histories might offset the influence of plant size.

The reader is asked to keep in mind the fact that union growth is dynamic, so that causal factors that are important at one time lose their intensity under different circumstances. We have observed, for example, that company towns have impeded union growth in the textile, lumber, coal mining, and other industries. With the development

309

of better roads, improved communication and transportation facilities, and the general use of the automobile, however, the company town has become a much less formidable obstacle.

Similarly, although we have argued that racial factors were important in the south before World War II, we shall contend that they were relatively unimportant determinants during the racial turmoil following the U.S. Supreme Court's 1954 school desegregation decision. When the AFL launched its southern organizing campaign during the 1890's, racial segregation was becoming institutionalized; the AFL was fairly weak and wanted to gain the affiliation of many locals which had already been organized on a discriminatory basis and which often were strong enough to continue without the support of either the AFL or national unions; there was considerable hostility between Negro leaders and union leaders; there were many Negroes in strategic positions on the railroads, in the building trades, and on the docks and levees; and the federal government was not too concerned about the race problem (which was considered mainly southern) and had no policies to deal with racial discrimination in employment. Similarly, we noted that the CIO was forced to overcome opposition from the Negro community in order to accomplish its political and economic objectives because Negroes had entered strategic positions in many of the large industrial firms it sought to organize. The Negroes were important to the CIO because the Railway Labor Act and the National Labor Relations Act gave them a voice in the selection of bargaining representatives, and the AFL and the CIO were competing for bargaining rights.

When employers and segregationists attempted to capitalize on the racial unrest of the 1950's and 1960's, on the other hand, unions were much stronger; the south was much more industrialized, and its economy was therefore more integrated into that of the nation, destroying some of the isolation that had localized the problem of racial discrimination; the courts and the executive branch of the federal government had become very involved in racial problems (which were no longer restricted to the south) and had taken measures to eliminate discrimination in employment; a much larger proportion of the south's industry was controlled by nonsoutherners; there was little opposition to Negroes from southern white workers on strictly trade union grounds; most of the large firms where Negroes were concentrated had been organized, and there was much more integration in the unions and in the larger community; national unions were much stronger relative to the southern locals so that southerners had no effective alternatives to remaining affiliated with nonsouthern unions; and the

AFL-CIO merger had reduced union rivalry, making it more difficult for unions to use racial discrimination as a means of attracting southern whites. Indeed, the basic nature of the "race problem" had changed from a question of whether or not to organize Negroes—which is still a problem in a few unions—and the use of Negro strikebreakers, to opposition to the equalitarian racial policies of the entire labor movement and equal treatment of Negroes already in the unions. In 1910, therefore, the race issue had a much more direct bearing on organizing than it does today.

UNITY AND DIVERSITY OF UNION GROWTH

We also have frequently observed that, although unions in the south have certain unique features, they also have characteristics in common with unions in the rest of the country, or, indeed, anywhere.[2] Northern and southern unions are subject to the same general factors which influence union growth. Since southern unions are also mainly collective bargaining organizations, their growth patterns will be influenced by the employer's willingness to deal with them or their ability to force him to bargain. This means that unions have been stronger among highly skilled workers or those—like transportation workers or the jack screwmen—whose strategic location in the work process made it possible for them to organize and bargain collectively. We also noted that unions in the south have been stimulated by the same general short-run factors—wars and upheavals and the social ferment of the New Deal period—which caused great spurts in union membership elsewhere. And southern unions have generally experienced the same fluctuations of membership over the business cycle as other unions. With some exceptions, like the fewness of shoemakers in the south, the order of appearance of southern unions and their early growth in the major cities and along major transportation arteries seem to have been about the same as in the rest of the nation. Nor should these unifying features be surprising because, as Dunlop has pointed out, a number of general conceptions can be used to explain any industrial relations system. The first is that of the actors and, the second, the context of the system which comprises "(1) technological characteristics of the work place and the work community, (2) the market or budgetary constraints which impinge on the actors, and (3) the locus and distribution of power in the larger community."[3] The final concept is that of "an ideology or a set of ideas and beliefs commonly held by the actors that helps to bind or to integrate the system together as an entity."

While the foregoing factors have tended to create unity between unions in the south and nonsouth, the region's unique characteristics discussed in Chapter I have produced diversity. For instance, the south had slavery and the plantation system and established a separate set of political, social and economic institutions after the Civil War. These institutions unified the region and produced a political and economic system hostile to the growth of unions. The leaders obviously were afraid that unions would upset traditional political and social arrangements and would interfere with industrialization. Of course, other areas also have adopted industrialization programs, but because of the nature of the agriculture and the political, economic, and cultural history, of the south, the industrialization urge became a more pervasive objective than it did in any other region. However, this same history caused southern workers to be less receptive to unions than workers in other areas.

Unions in the south not only have been united by geography and membership in a common national labor movement but also have had mutual problems which caused them to differentiate themselves from the labor movement in the rest of the country. The AFL recognized the south as a distinct area in 1928 when it appointed George Googe as the federation's representative, and southern unionists have long met together to discuss their problems. In 1952, the southern state federations formally organized a Southern Labor School which provides an educational vehicle and a means to share information and ideas.

Conceptual framework. It is our basic proposition that union growth is not caused by any single factor but is the result of the relationships between: (1) workers, who have varying motives for supporting or refusing to support unions; (2) unions with varying motives, structures, and resources which influence their ability and will to expand; (3) employers or managers, who either resist unions or voluntarily or involuntarily deal with them; and (4) government officials, who also have varying pressures to promote or retard union growth. These actors, as Dunlop calls them, operate within economic, political, social, and ideological contexts which influence union growth.

Of all the factors influencing the structure of union organization in the south, the most decisive are the economic, or, what Dunlop calls, technological-budgetary constraints, market forces, and the degree of competition. These economic factors influence the ideological, political and social contexts which in turn affect union membership, but, as we shall see, the influence of noneconomic forces usually is more indirect.

Company structure is important because it influences the attitudes of employees and managers as well as the union's motives and ability to organize. The high correlation between union membership and company size undoubtedly comes from the fact that relations between managers and workers cannot be close and personal in large plants, making it necessary for workers to have an organized means of making their attitudes and grievances known. In addition, unions serve valuable personnel functions for large employers by translating the workers' attitudes into contracts, helping enforce the contracts, and providing a grievance adjustment mechanism. It is significant that large employers whose employees are not formally organized have themselves formed company or independent unions to perform these functions.

The high correlation between branch plants and union organization can probably be explained by the fact that many branches are extensions to the south of companywide collective bargaining agreements. This helps explain the high degree of unionization in the steel, auto, farm equipment, pulp and paper, telephone, trucking and other industries. In these cases, organization is fairly easy, and the southern employees usually have a high attachment to the union because the national agreement gives them wages and benefits likely to be much higher than those prevailing in the local communities. Where employers feel that unionization is inevitable or desirable, they are likely to favor companywide bargaining for its convenience and because this arrangement is more conducive to stable industrial relations. The master agreement makes it possible for employers to protect themselves from "whipsawing," a process whereby unions raise wages or other benefits by playing one plant against another.

Unions also favor companywide bargaining for its convenience, and they are stronger in branch than in single-plant firms because they can use the leverage of an organized base elsewhere to organize plants in the south. Unions can, for example, strike plants in the north to get the same company to deal with that union in its southern branches. Also, unions can sign agreements in New York and other states requiring employers to deal with unions in the south, which might be illegal if enforced in the south because of local and antiunion laws.

Of course, if all of the plants of one firm are in the south and unorganized, employers can close one branch and expand production elsewhere, as they have done on several occasions in the textile industry. The unionization of branch plants thus depends upon the unions' strength to organize all the branches and the employers' attitudes concerning collective bargaining.

In addition, unions have a strong motivation to organize to prevent the companies from defeating the union or lowering conditions in unionized branches.

Finally, unions in many cases have an advantage as they expand into the south if skilled union members from older plants are used in the newer branches. For example, members from northern mills formed the nucleus for unionization in the relatively well-organized pulp and paper industry, probably with the employers' blessings because they wanted to avoid dealing with the CIO paperworkers.

Although other factors are at work, the comparative ease with which branches may be organized also helps explain the high correlation between union growth and the establishment of new firms in the south, because many of the market-and-raw-material-oriented firms which have located in the south since 1939 are branches of nonsouthern firms. Branch managers also are more willing to deal with unions because they are not influenced or controlled by the old antiunion economic power structure. Because unions are likely to upset this structure, there have been strong family, political and social pressures on the older employers not to deal with unions. It is significant that many areas which can be identified as strong union towns (Bogalusa, Laurel, Birmingham, Beaumont-Port Arthur) were relatively new industrial areas or were places whose nonagricultural work forces were dominated by large branches of national or international companies.

In the past, company towns have deterred union growth. During the early stages of industrialization, employers in many rapidly growing areas had to furnish living accommodations in order to attract workers. These towns easily controlled the workers. The company-controlled police could deny union organizers the use of public buildings, and joining a union meant that workers would lose their jobs and be evicted from their homes. Company towns contribute to the explanation for the success textile, agricultural and lumber employers have had in defeating strikes and organizing campaigns.

Industrial structure and location. Another important determinant of the south's degree of unionization is the highly competitive structure of the region's industry. There is, for example, a significant correlation between concentration ratios, extent of union membership and wages.[4] Before the period of the New Deal the large oligopolistic firms had sufficient strength to resist unions. But, because of the events of the 1930's, most of them became well organized by the end of the Second World War. The most significant reason for their capitulation was the generally prounion attitude of the public and the federal government. In addition, the large firm is strong enough to protect itself in collective bargaining, and, because of its size and conspicuousness, refusing to deal with a union when collective bargaining has become accepted public policy might cause unnecessary loss of prestige, particularly after the process has become established in other industries. Also, collective bargaining presents positive benefits to the large company and to the private enterprise society, a realization which seems more prevalent now than in the 1920's. These industries have also had higher concentration ratios because of the technical or capital requirements for entry, not because of labor considerations. Labor costs have consequently been a lower proportion of total costs than in industries with high labor requirements. Oligopolistic industries also have some control over prices, making it possible to pass wage increases on to consumers, and labor costs can be more easily absorbed because they form smaller parts of total costs. These market limitations provide more room for bargaining over wages than would be possible in more highly competitive industries, making it possible for unions to demonstrate their ability to gain benefits for their members. Such a demonstration usually is a necessary condition for the survival and growth of collective bargaining. The tendency for newer industries to be organized is explained in part by the fact that many of them have been less competitive. A high precentage of the older industries were attracted by lower labor costs, while newer ones are attracted by markets and raw materials.

Because of the concentration of employment in competitive industries, employers often fight unions in order to maintain their positions. Each employer also might be powerless to accede to union demands, though a concerted attack on the whole industry might prove successful. We noted that such an attack, with the tacit approval of a segment of the industry, was necessary for the unionization of the coal industry. At the same time, however, the fact that there were many producers meant that the mine workers had a much more difficult problem organizing and staying organized than the auto or steel workers. In order to organize individual firms in a competitive industry, the union must ordinarily have some other advantage to offset its competitive disadvantage, or be content with a weak position.

The regional concentration of industry is also important because it determines both the intensity of the union's motivation to organize the south and its power to do so. If most of the industry is concentrated outside the region, like the automobile, steel, and garment industries, unions can form a strong base from which to support their activities. Indeed, with the exception of the organizations in building construction, printing, coal mining, and local-market-oriented industries, most of the well-organized unions have strong bases outside the region in cities like Detroit (automobiles), Akron (rubber), Pittsburgh (steel), or New York (garments). Concentrations are likely to be well organized because the costs of organizing are low, the unions have a strong motive to organize, and because unionism is contagious.

Although they are not well organized in the south, the garment workers' unions would certainly be unable to finance their activities without their strong outside concentrations. In the case of the Ladies' Garment Workers, for example, expenditures in the southeast in the 1950's and 1960's averaged between $600,000 and $700,000 a year, and collections averaged about $40,000 a year. These expenditures are much higher during strikes or extended litigation. One strike involving 200 people costs the ILGWU some $8000 a week. In a strike in Tennessee, an attorney was paid $35,000 by the ILGWU, and an additional $27,000 was paid in fines.[5] Obviously costs of this kind can not be borne unless the union is in good financial condition. Of course the ILGWU and the ACWA incur large deficits in the south in order to protect their nonsouthern bases. In textiles, on the other hand, the unions were not strong enough to take advantage of the organizing opportunities of the 1930's and, unlike the mine workers, were not considered by employers to be an important stabilizing influence. Moreover, two thirds of the industry is located in the south, and the major firms in the industry are unorganized. The textile unions are not only weak and divided but find themselves in the very difficult situation of having inadequate and declining resources with which to organize an important sector of the industry. As a consequence, the northern textile workers have been unable to improve their wages and working conditions, or, indeed, to gain even some of the fringe benefits given by such southern nonunion giants as Burlington, Cannon, and J. P. Stevens.[6] The southern nonunion firms also set the wage patterns in the textile industry during the 1950's and 1960's.

The only industries with sizeable southern concentrations outside of building construction, printing, and the railroads, which can be considered fairly well organized, are pulp and paper, tobacco, and petroleum refining. They all differ from textiles and garment manufacturing in having few large firms and high concentration ratios. These industries, with the exception of pulp and paper, are also more concentrated geographically than textiles. The petroleum refining industry is mainly in the southwest and is highly organized partly because independent unions exist in the firms which are not organized by national unions. The relationship between the extent of collective bargaining coverage, concentration ratios (proportion of the industries in each industry

Table 8. Collective bargaining coverage, proportion of industry in the south, and concentration ratios by industry group.

Industry group	Per cent collective bargaining coverage in the south[a]		Per cent south of United States[b] 1962		Concentration ratio[c]	
	Per cent	Rank	Per cent	Rank	Rates[e]	Per cent
Food and kindred products	41	(13)	22.7	(8)	10/42	(23)
Tobacco products	72	(7)	73.0	(1)	0/4	(0)
Textile mill products	14	(19)	66.2	(2)	7/32	(22)
Apparel and related products	30	(16)	29.8	(5)	28/41	(68)
Lumber wood products	27	(18)	39.4	(3)	6/17	(35)
Furniture and fixtures	28	(17)	35.4	(4)	4/15	(27)
Paper and allied products	79	(5)	21.3	(10)	1/9	(11)
Printing, publishing and allied products	61	(11)	13.9	(12)	7/16	(44)
Chemicals and allied products	62	(10)	26.7	(7)	3/41	(07)
Petroleum and coal products	88	(2)	29.6	(6)	1/5	(20)
Rubber products	81[d]	(4)	4.6	(18)	0/4	(0)
Leather and leather products	32	(15)	10.8	(13)	5/12	(42)
Stone, clay and glass products	65	(8)	21.7	(9)	4/28	(14)
Primary metal	95	(1)	10.2	(15)	3/15	(20)
Fabricated metal	54	(12)	17.2	(11)	12/28	(43)
Machinery except electrical	63	(9)	8.8	(17)	8/40	(20)
Electrical machinery, equipment and supplies	73[d]	(6)	9.6	(16)	0/21	(0)
Transportation equipment	86	(3)	10.8	(14)	2/13	(15)
Instruments and related products	35	(14)	2.5	(19)	0/9	(0)

[a] Per cent of workers in establishments a majority of whose employees were covered by collective bargaining agreements from H. M. Douty, "Collective Bargaining Coverage in Factory Employment, 1958," *Monthly Labor Review,* April 1962.

[b] Computed from U.S. Bureau of Labor Statistics, *Earnings and Employment Statistics,* BLS Bulletin 1370, 1963.

[c] Computed from U.S. Bureau of the Census, *Concentration Ratios in Manufacturing Industry,* 1958.

[d] U.S. figures.

[e] Proportion of industries in the industry group where the four largest firms had less than 20 per cent of employment in 1958.

3185

group in which the four largest firms had less than 20 per cent of the
employees in the industry) and the proportion of total employment in
the industry group in the south in 1962 is shown in Table 8.

The rank correlation coefficient between the proportion of the industry concentrated in the south and the extent of collective bargaining coverage (—.96) is significant at the 95 per cent confidence level,
and shows an inverse relationship between the proportion of the industry located in the south and the extent of collective bargaining
coverage. The main exception is the tobacco industry, where the
south's high proportion is offset by the high concentration of this industry in relatively few firms, as indicated by the concentration ratios,
which show that in none of the four tobacco products industries was
less than 20 per cent of employment concentrated in the four largest
firms.

Another organizing difficulty faced by unions in the south is the
tendency for industry to locate in rural areas. Table 9 indicates that a
relatively small proportion of the south's employment is located in
metropolitan areas.

*Table 9. Production workers and manufacturing employment in metropolitan
areas, 1954, 1958, and 1962 (in per cent).*

Area	Production workers in large metropolitan areas[a]			Manufacturing employment in all metropolitan areas[b]		
	1954	1958	1962	1954	1958	1962
United States	58.7	61.4	58.8	85.9	82.6	80.4
Nonsouth	65.4	70.1	68.3	90.2	88.5	87.0
South[c]	29.3	25.3	23.3	51.3	50.6	53.8
South Atlantic[d]	11.0	10.5	10.2	40.7	41.1	41.5
East south central	48.1	43.5	39.7	74.5	68.6	68.5
West south central	35.0	34.8	32.8	62.9	63.2	61.9

Source: U.S. Bureau of the Census, *U.S. Census of Manufacturers, 1958,* vol. III,
Area Statistics, Tables 5 and 6, U.S. Government Printing Office: Washington,
1961; *Annual Survey of Manufacturers, 1962,* U.S. Government Printing Office:
Washington, 1964.

[a] Metropolitan areas with over 40,000 industrial employees.

[b] A standard metropolitan area is a county or group of continuous counties
which contains at least one central city of 50,000 inhabitants or more.

[c] Southern figures include upward bias due to cities on state line. For example,
all Cincinnati production workers are included in east south central manufacturing
employment in large metropolitan areas, while only Kentucky production workers
are included in east south central total of production workers.

[d] South Atlantic: Virginia, North Carolina, South Carolina, Georgia, Florida.

CHAPTER XX

Industrial Development
and the Law

INDUSTRIAL DEVELOPMENT

Leaders in every area of the United States are eager to attract and retain industry, but nowhere has it been so important as in the south. This is true, of course, because tradition has made the south more homogeneous and less developed economically. Since the 1880's, moreover, the concept of the "new south" has been based on the idea that the region's salvation lay in industrialization.

It is not surprising, therefore, that the leaders who have invested state and local funds in plant and equipment to attract industry should promote antiunion legislation. Indeed, many of the older industrial leaders were intimately involved in the region's political structure.[1] The south's experience is similar to that of most under-developed countries. These countries have felt that unions and free collective bargaining impede industrialization by interfering with capital formation. In the United States and Great Britain there also was considerable official opposition to unions during the initial periods of industrialization.

There can be little question that the desire to attract industry has been one of the main reasons for the antiunion legislation in the south. The so-called "right-to-work" laws, for instance, have been passed principally for this purpose. In seeking passage of the Oklahoma

319

right-to-work law (defeated in a 1964 election by a Negro-labor-farmer coalition) the measure's backers "confirm [ed] that their drive . . . [was] prompted primarily by the suspicion that the Sooner State [was] losing prospective industry because of the lack of such a law."[2]

After voting a $150,000 bond issue for a new plant, Star City, Arkansas, passed an ordinance requiring a $1000 daily fee from union organizers, because, according to the town's mayor, the subsidized garment manufacturer "told us that if the union ever got into the plant here, they might have to close up. We've got too big a stake in this to let anything like that happen." The town of Whitesburg, Kentucky, repealed its right-to-work law in 1964 after the unions in that city undertook various activities to help children in the area, and after the garment manufacturer who said he would locate there if the city outlawed the union shop failed to carry out his promise.[3]

One publicity release from the National Right to Work Committee (NRTWC) quotes southern officials:

> Arkansas: "We of the Arkansas Industrial Development Commission feel that this (the state "right-to-work" law) has been a useful tool in the development of our program and has in no way been used to exploit labor." William P. Rock, Executive Director Arkansas Industrial Development Commission.
>
> Florida: "I am pleased to note . . . that Florida's population growth, its industrial development, its personal income, and its job opportunities have been expanding faster than those of any other state in the nation, and this has occurred while the State Right To Work Law was in effect." Governor Farris Bryant.
>
> Mississippi: "since the Right To Work law became part of our Constitution, capital investment in Mississippi has amounted to three and a half times more than the average in any one of the last ten years." Governor Ross R. Barnett.
>
> Texas: "The Texas Right To Work Law has been important to the industrial development of this state." Governor Price Daniel.[4]

Similar statements are given by the NRTWC from the governors of Tennessee and North Carolina. Quotations from officials of only two of the southern states, Alabama and Georgia, stressed personal freedom as a benefit of these laws. Moreover, in listing the benefits, it is significant that the NRTWC places "greater industrialization and more well-paying jobs" first, "greater measure of individual freedom for all workers" fourth, and "better management-labor relations" sixth and last.

As a matter of fact, the right-to-work laws probably have had little effect on industrialization, and, as we shall argue later, relatively little effect on union growth. There is an obvious assumption that the laws, by demonstrating a state's antiunion position, will attract antiunion employers. This assumption fails to consider, however, that most of the major employers in the more desirable high-wage industries are already organized. Even the employers who wish to avoid unions realize that an antiunion environment might breed more labor unrest in the long run than places where collective bargaining is freely permitted. An NLRB survey of southern businessmen found many of them opposed to the right-to-work laws, which restricted their collective bargaining rights and interfered with their efforts to recruit skilled workers, who are in short supply in the south.[5]

If it were not for the fact that few of the laws are enforced, there is a possibility that they would actually deter industrialization because employers who already deal with unions in most of their branches might have considerable difficulty if they refused to deal with the union in the south. There have been a number of cases—Spartanburg, South Carolina, for example—where employers with many employees and sound businesses wanted to deal with a union but were opposed by local officials. In 1964, the Revere Copper and Brass Company at Oneonta, Alabama, refused to cooperate with an antiunion effort, "apparently . . . fomented by garment plants and other, older plants in town." The company even refused to permit the chief of police to arrest a machinist organizer on company property and helped him escape.

Of course, small employers who intend to halt their operations entirely in the north and accept subsidies from local communities in the south might be motivated to locate in an area because of its antiunion climate.[6]

In an Indiana study of 100 plants, only one firm with 60 employees felt that the right-to-work law was a primary attraction; 86 of the 100 firms listed markets as a first consideration; only seven listed right to work as even a secondary factor. The poor results of the right-to-work law contributed to its repeal in 1965.[7]

Unions. Although antiunion laws clearly have little influence on industrial location, the influence of unions on the south's economic development is less clear. Generally, however, southern unions probably have little ability or inclination to impede the development of industry. Indeed, it will not be possible for unions of less-skilled workers to develop sufficient strength to hinder industrialization until labor surpluses have been sufficiently reduced to render this action of little consequence, because labor surpluses are primary impediments to union growth.

Unions in oligopolistic industries, which are well organized, can, of course, raise wages, and seem especially able to narrow regional wage differentials in multiplant firms and national market industries.[8] It is doubtful, however, that wages play much of a role as attractions to these industries, because they usually are either market- or resource-oriented, and labor forms a small part of total costs. By increasing wages and purchasing power, on the other hand, unions can promote the industrialization of the south as well as protect workers from arbitrary management decisions.

Moreover, by working to improve the south's educational system, opposing the region's backward-looking, undemocratic power structure, and promoting federal legislation to help underdeveloped areas, unions contribute to economic development.

The influence of national unions on southern industrial growth depends partly on the wage policy of the union involved. Equalizing southern wages with those of other areas will impede industrialization unless the region has some other economic advantage. In the coal industry, for example, the UMW would have destroyed much of the Alabama coal industry if it had succeeded in equalizing wages with those of more productive mines elsewhere. We saw, however, that this condition forced the UMW to accept wage differentials. In fact, economic conditions throughout the coal industry made it necessary for the UMW to accept piece rate differentials everywhere. Other industries—autos, steel, pulp and paper, and petroleum—have sufficient advantages (proximity to resources and markets or more modern equipment) so that wage equalization did not impede their development.

National unions also can block industrialization by bringing pressure on firms to prevent them from moving south. For example, the Amalgamated Clothing Workers succeeded in including provisions in contracts in the north which prohibit plants from moving without union approval. In 1960, Hickory Clothers, Inc., moved from New York to Coffeeville, Mississippi, where a factory was built with a $360,000 community bond issue. The ACWA protested the move, and the case went to arbitration. The arbitrator awarded the union $204,681 damages and ordered the company to open a plant in New York similar in size to the one it previously maintained there.[9] In another case, a U.S. District Court in Philadelphia awarded the shoe workers $78,000 in damages after the Brooke Shoe Manufacturing Company closed its Philadelphia plant and expanded its operations in a non-union plant elsewhere. The court ruled that the shoe workers' reputation was "gravely undermined in the working community by the shutdown in violation of the union contract." Not only did the company's action violate the contract, according to this decision, but it also violated "the national labor policy fashioned by Congress."[10]

A 1961 NLRB decision on this matter could have far-reaching effects.[11] In 1960, Sidele Fashions, Inc., which bargained with the ILGWU in Philadelphia, closed its operations in Philadelphia and expanded in Ware Shoals, South Carolina, where the same employers operated the Personality Sportswear, Inc. The union filed a complaint with the NLRB, and the board found that even though the company had established its South Carolina operation for "legitimate economic considerations and not . . . to avoid collective bargaining," its 1960 action was an unfair "device for attempting to wrest bargaining concessions from the workers' union."[12] The board ordered the company either to offer all of its previous employees substantially the same jobs at a reopened Philadelphia plant or to offer them similar jobs at Ware Shoals with full seniority and other rights, "dismissing, if necessary, all employees at the Ware Shoals plant." Moreover, the board ordered the company to pay the family moving costs of the workers who elected to go to South Carolina.

Since unions try to protect jobs in the nonsouth, they tend to halt the shift of industry into the south.[13] However, the extent to which contract provisions and NLRB cases have deterred the industry shift does not appear to have been significant.

LEGISLATION

The Wagner Act undoubtedly was one of the basic causes of the growth of unions in the United States, but its influence can easily be exaggerated because union expansion in the south's basic industries occurred either before the act was passed, as in the case of the crafts and the coal industry, or during the war. It is true that the Wagner Act made it easier for unions to gain recognition, changed some of the employers' antiunion tactics, and protected unions from each other, but it did little to procure concessions from recalcitrant employers. The Wagner Act's greatest influence was probably psychological. Since unions and workers thought the act gave them the right to organize and secure contracts, unions were encouraged to organize and workers were emboldened to join. The law also gradually focused great psychological—as well as material—pressures on the country's major employers. However, because it came at a time when other things—like the spirit of the time and the AFL-CIO rivalry—were stimulating union growth, we cannot assess its impact accurately.

The War Labor Board procedures unlike those of the Wagner Act made it possible for unions to translate representation elections into contracts, because the War Labor Board had the power to fix contract terms, including maintenance of membership and the check-off,[14] which the parties could not and would not have negotiated in the absence of this process.

Several features of the Taft-Hartley Act are cited by unions as obstacles to their growth in the south.[15] By making it possible for employers to file charges of unfair labor practices against unions and imposing other procedural changes, the law lengthened the time required to hear the cases (a 1960 study found that a contested unfair labor practices cases took an average of two years, four months and 20 days from the filing of the complaint until effective judicial decree was issued compelling compliance with the act),[16] so that by the time a decision has been reached the discharged worker will have been unemployed for a long time or forced to find another job. The legal maxim that "justice delayed is justice denied" is particularly true in unfair labor practices cases where employers are willing to risk the modest penalties of the NLRB in order to defeat unions. As a result of criticism of the time involved, the 1959 Landrum-Griffin Act permitted certain procedures to speed up cases which reduced the median age of cases pending from 52.5 days in 1958 to 22.5 days in 1960;[17] the median days from the filing of a charge to the issuance of a complaint were reduced from 116 to 52 for the same dates.

Under Taft-Hartley, the time required for representation elections was lengthened by the repeal of the prehearing election procedure. Time is important in these cases because delays cause workers to lose interest in the union. However, by delegating authority to the regional directors, the NLRB appointed by President Kennedy reduced the median time from 89 days in 1961 to 42 days in 1962 and 39 days in 1963.

The Taft-Hartley Act changed the definition of "employer" in such a way as to remove antiunion citizens' committees from the NLRB's jurisdiction. By outlawing the secondary boycott, Taft-Hartley made it difficult, but not impossible, for strong unions to help weaker ones. Perhaps even more important than the provisions of the act are its philosophy and administration. The Wagner Act probably aided unions in the south because workers really believed that the President of the United States wanted them to join unions, and because there are many subtle ways in which the NLRB can encourage or discourage union growth while remaining within the letter of the law. Taft-Hartley and the publicity accompanying its passage leaves the impression that unions are undesirable and do not represent the true interests of the workers. Union leaders also point out that the "free speech" or "captive audience" provision of Taft-Hartley gives the employer an advantage because he only has to imply that the plant will move if organized to induce many southern workers to vote "no union."

Union representatives are prepared to cite an endless number of cases to illustrate the detrimental effects of Taft-Hartley. For example, the workers at the O'Sullivan Rubber Corporation in Winchester, Virginia, voted 343 to 2 for affiliation with the United Rubber workers in April 1956, but went on strike the following month because they were unable to get a contract. In October of the following year the union was voted out 288 to 5 by strikebreakers. (In 1966, the United Auto Workers won an NLRB election at O'Sullivan, 325 to 37.) We noted many cases throughout this study where unions won NLRB election victories but were defeated because of the inability to obtain contracts. Indeed, there are a number of labor lawyers in the south who specialize in not bargaining while appearing to bargain within the law. When strikes took place, employers could start back-to-work movements, and, under the Taft-Hartley Act, the strikers were denied the right to vote in subsequent representation elections. Unions were thus frequently voted out (O'Sullivan, the Calcasieu Paper Company, and many other cases). Taft-Hartley has been blamed because strikers were not permitted to vote in the elections. Actually, the law only permitted formal recognition of underlying realities; the real reason the strikes were lost was the employers' ability to recruit strikebreakers. The 1959 Landrum-Griffin Act permits strikers to vote in representation elections after a year, but it is doubtful that this will have much effect in the south because most of the elections have taken place more than a year after the strikes started. It is commonly assumed that representation elections and union organization are the same. O'Sullivan and many other examples in the south demonstrate that effective unionization takes place only when a contract is signed.

Union representatives contend that the so-called "Kennedy NLRB" which has been in operation since 1961, has taken a more prounion position and has therefore encouraged union growth. In addition to speeding up unfair labor practices and representation-election procedures, the board has helped union organizing by: determining appropriate bargaining units to make it more likely that unions will win elections; set elections aside where employers have made antiunion statements that would have been allowed by the previous board; liberalized the "Eisenhower board's" restrictions on recognitional and organizational picketing.[18] The Kennedy board also took measures to curtail the use of inflammatory racial arguments by employers during representation elections,[19] though employers presumably remain free to advise employees in a "temperate" tone of the unions' racial practices.[20]

"Right-to-work" laws. Union representatives have vigorously opposed the right-to-work laws, arguing that, by denying the union shop, the laws have impeded union growth. According to Solomon Barkin, former research director of the TWUA, and a close observer of union growth in the south for many years:

> [The laws] have tended to give legal confirmation to anti-union attitudes. Equally important, they have tended to weaken union positions in presently organized plants, particularly those employing high proportions of semiskilled workers and having a locally controlled industrial relations policy. In some of these plants, unions necessarily become more preoccupied with promoting and processing grievances and cajoling dissident groups in order to maintain their following. The others, where management is willing to continue an informal understanding on maintaining membership, the union leadership has become less militant.[21]

Frederic Meyers, on the other hand, concluded from his Texas study:

> The Right-to-Work statute, taken by itself and apart from the whole body of state labor legislation, has had a minimal direct effect. In the traditional areas of the closed shop the law has been generally disregarded, and the practices that have continued are illegal under federal as well as state legislation. In the industries in which initial hiring is in the hands of the employer, the forms of the law have been observed, and union membership has not been a formal condition for continued employment; yet, organization of the unorganized has proceeded at a remarkably rapid rate since 1947 even though the statute may have changed the general attitude toward unionism in some marginal cases and thus impeded the maximum growth of the labor movement.
> Indeed . . . the real meaning of the statute seems to be symbolic.[22]

Meyers' study found that in many situations where the closed shop was the normal procedure, nonunion employers countered the unions' demands for recognition by filing charges under the state's secondary boycott law as well as the right-to-work statute. Indeed, while major litigation under the Texas law had been rare, most of the cases reaching the appellate courts involved union practices of the building trades that would probably have been illegal under federal law even if there had been no right-to-work law. Meyers concedes:

> It may have been that some judges, acting under the color of the statute, may have restrained lawful activities or issued broader injunctions than the law, properly construed, warranted. Since, in labor disputes, particularly those involving new unions, timing is of first importance, such decisions might have had great influence in deterring or destroying labor organization.

Meyers' observation that judges tend to follow the political strength of the unions is confirmed by union leaders in every part of the south. Indeed, the main impact of the law is probably to demonstrate the extent of the unions' political power. The subtle way in which judges can interpret labor laws frequently is more important than the laws themselves. Labor leaders note that Louisiana judges and other government officials took a more favorable attitude toward unions when the unions proved their political power by repealing the right-to-work law in 1956. Similarly, Oklahoma labor leaders detect a much more receptive attitude from public officials after the right-to-work forces were defeated in that state in 1964. By the same token, unions in Texas and other states find officials more hostile to them because of their inability to repeal the laws. Moreover, regardless of the laws, practices—such as union or closed-shop provisions—which have been accepted by unions and employers, continue in every part of the south.

With respect to organizing new employees, Meyers concluded: "In general, the 'Right-to-Work' statute carries some weight in developing a social atmosphere, a general attitude against unions in rural areas as well as in the less well-organized cities. But in the industrial centers the union climate is more than adequate to offset any great impact which the law might otherwise have on the new worker." With respect to nonmembership in organized plants: "It is hard to see how 'Right-to-Work' has been a major factor in protecting the rights of substantial numbers of workers who did not want membership but who might have been 'coerced' under a union shop agreement." Finally, Meyers concluded that the Texas right-to-work law inspired unions to prosecute every grievance to the fullest because "every grievance is a crisis." Although this means that the law might have pushed union leaders into action, it did not necessarily improve industrial relations because grievances of little merit were prosecuted in order to convince the membership that the union was worth-while.

NLRB elections. It is also instructive to take a look at the possible effects of the right-to-work laws on representation elections conducted by the NLRB in the south.[23] In the first place, it should be noted that the laws cannot be the only reason for the union's difficulty in winning representation elections because they had problems long before the acts were passed. "No union" won a constantly increasing percentage of elections in the south and the nonsouth in the years after World War II. In 1946, for example, "no union" won 24 per cent of elections in the south and 20 per cent in the nonsouth; other comparable figures were: 1950, 24 per cent and 35 per cent; 1955, 41 per cent and 31 per cent; 1961, 48 per cent and 43 per cent; and 1965, 41 per cent and 40 per cent. Although only three of the eleven effective right-to-work laws in 1947 were in the nonsouth (Arizona, Nebraska, and South Dakota), the ratio of "no union" victories in the nonsouth to those in the south did not change significantly until 1950, when the nonsouth's proportion declined to 69 per cent of the south from 85 per cent the previous two years; this decline can probably be attributed mainly to the slowing down of Operation Dixie. After Operation Dixie's greatest impact (1946-1949), the proportion of no-union victories in the nonsouth relative to the south declined markedly, but increased again in the early 1960's.

Since the differences between the south and the nonsouth with respect to the forces influencing union growth probably are greater than the forces within the south, it is more meaningful to compare "no-union" victories in southern states with and without right-to-work laws than to compare all right-to-work states in the United States with all states without these laws. There were six southern states without right-to-work laws between 1947 and 1953. (Kentucky, Oklahoma, Alabama, Louisiana, Mississippi, and South Carolina). If we compare the percentage of "no union" victories in NLRB elections in states with and without right-to-work laws, we find "no union" winning a higher proportion in the right-to-work states than the average for the south in 1948, 1951, and 1952. "No union" won a higher proportion in the states without these laws in 1947, 1949, 1950 and 1953. These figures fail to reveal any evidence that the right-to-work laws made it more difficult for unions to win representation elections. However, the laws appear to have made it more difficult for unions the year following their passage. For example, in 1948 "no union" won a higher proportion of elections in five of the six states that passed the laws in 1947, but in only two of the six states that did not have the laws. Similarly, three southern states passed right-to-work laws in 1954, and "no union" won a higher proportion than the average for the south in all these states the following year but in only two of the seven states that had right-to-work laws since 1947. In each case, however, the disadvantage caused by the passage of the laws seems to have been only temporary, which suggests that the impact is largely psychological.

In conclusion, the writer's observations in the south and the analysis of NLRB election results fail to produce evidence that the right-to-work laws have had a significant effect on union growth. The laws are probably most important as symbols registering union political strength, which does have important implications for union operations. Employers who have traditionally dealt with unions were not disturbed very much by these laws. Finally, the antiunion laws weaken unions to the extent that they are forced to use resources to fight these bills that might otherwise be used for organization.

Other laws. In addition to the right-to-work laws, the southern states have passed other legislation to curb union activities. We noted some of the laws passed by Alabama, Texas, Florida, and Arkansas during the war. Much of this legislation coincided with and was designed to counter the expansion of unionism during and immediately after World War II.[24] Texas has been the leader in the passage of such legislation. The 1943 Texas Union Regulation Act declared it to be the public policy of the state "in the exercise of its sovereign constitutional police powers" to regulate the activities and affairs of labor unions, their officers, agents, organizers and other representatives. Texas has also passed laws to prohibit closed and union shops, to ban bargaining and strikes by public workers, to ban picketing of public utilities, to make unions sueable, to ban the compulsory check-off, to prohibit secondary boycotts, strikes and picketing, and to regulate picketing.[25]

The Texas act was tested in 1944 by R. J. Thomas, president of the United Automobile Workers who was organizing for the oil workers at the Baytown refinery of the Humble Oil & Refining Company. In a speech at Baytown, Thomas deliberately solicited membership from a worker without first obtaining a license required by the Texas law. Moreover, at the time he made the speech, Thomas was under a state court injunction restraining him from violating the act. In its decision in this case,[26] the U.S. Supreme Court ruled that a state could require the licensing of occupations, but, unless justified by some clear and present danger, it could not require a license for making a speech because freedom of speech was a liberty guaranteed by the First Amendment.[27]

The Florida licensing law required that union business agents be citizens of the United States for ten years, with no convictions for felony, that they be of good moral character, and that they pay a fee

of one dollar for the license. A Florida state court enjoined an organizer and his union from operating in that state until they complied
with the statute, but the U.S. Supreme Court ruled that the Florida
law was invalid because it conflicted with the Wagner Act.[28] The
Supreme Court ruled in this case that states could regulate such union
activity as mass picketing, threats, violence and related actions unless
the regulations "affected the status of employees, or . . . caused a
forfeiture of collective bargaining rights." But, according to the court:
"It is apparent that the Florida statute has been so construed and
applied that the union and its selected representatives are prohibited
from functioning as collective bargaining agents, or in any other
capacity, except on conditions fixed by Florida." In 1961, union
organizers reported that Florida was attempting to revive this statute
by applying it to business agents who were not involved in collective
bargaining.

A number of cities and counties in the south have adopted regulations requiring union organizers to register and pay license fees before
they can operate. And a number of localities in Kentucky, which has no
right-to-work law, have adopted ordinances outlawing the union
shop.

Most of the local ordinances have been in relatively rural areas,
which also have plans to attract industry. Moreover, there is some
tendency for these ordinances to be clustered as indicated by the eight
South Carolina measures passed within four months of each other in
1957; three Mississippi ordinances were passed in 1956, the same year
in which at least nine other local ordinances were passed in the south.
Many of the measures also have almost identical provisions.

While the local laws usually require prohibitive license fees, some
make relatively low levies. Also, the measures require the filing of certain information with respect to the union and the organizer and frequently contain minimum residence requirements and various oaths of
allegiance. For example, the Dublin and Newnan, Georgia, measures
required, among other things, foreswearing of beliefs in communism
and "in the overthrowing of the municipal or state laws in regard to
segregation." Moreover, the issuance of a license customarily is at
the discretion of local officials.

There have been a number of tests of specific provisions of these
laws. As early as 1938, the U.S. Supreme Court ruled that the Griffin,
Georgia, ordinance requiring organizers to obtain licenses before
handing out circulars violated freedom of the press.[29]

Perhaps the most celebrated case involved the Baxley, Georgia,
ordinance which required a $2000 license fee and $500 for each

member obtained, as well as information concerning the union's assets and liabilities, compensation of organizers and their age and residence for the past ten years and so forth. The Baxley mayor and city council were permitted to grant the license after considering "the character of the applicant and the nature of the business of the organization for which members are desired to be solicited, and its effects upon the general welfare of the City of Baxley."

In February 1954, two ILGWU organizers, Rose Staub and Mamie Merritt, were arrested in Baxley for organizing without a license. Various Georgia courts refused to reverse the organizers' convictions, but in 1958 the U.S. Supreme Court ruled that the Baxley ordinance was unconstitutional on the grounds that it violated freedom of speech.[30] In this case, the unusually high fee was not an issue because, according to the opinion of the court, "One of the most vulnerable provisions of this ordinance, the drastically high license fee, was taken out of the controversy by the respondent's admission of its invalidity." The court noted that Baxley had the right to require the licensing of occupations (presumably at a reasonable fee) where the licenses were granted as a matter of course and not at the discretion of the city officials, but could not require a permit for the exercise of a right guaranteed in the constitution.

Thus, while these ordinances are unconstitutional if they permit licensing at the discretion of city officials, many localities keep them on their books for their intimidation value. Even ordinances which permit licensing as a matter of course might give local antiunion elements information with which to fight unions. Moreover, the ordinances, whether valid or not, place a stigma on union organizers which might make workers reluctant to join. That these ordinances, like state right-to-work laws, are designed to advertise the communities' opposition to unions, is suggested by the fact that on several occasions organizers have tried unsuccessfully to be arrested in order to test an ordinance. The mayor of DeWitt, Arkansas said "we didn't pass the ordinance to keep them out—just to expose them. Once they've registered we can get the publicity rolling."[31]

CHAPTER XXI

The Unions and the Workers

THE UNIONS

Perhaps the most important internal factors influencing a union's ability to grow are its motives, financial strength, structure, and the public image that it projects. A union's financial strength is particularly important in the south where the dispersion of workers in small towns and rural areas, the absence of volunteer organizers, court and police action, are all likely to make organizing very expensive. Indeed, few unions in most of the south's poorly organized industries can expect to collect as much in dues and fees as they must pay out in organizing expenses.

The financial power of the union to launch a campaign in the south also is related to the structure of the American labor movement. Its narrowness has created jurisdictional rivalries which have sapped the strength of the region's unions. Strong unions have, with some few exceptions, given only token support to the weaker ones. A general workers' union would be a much better structure for organizing many of the south's scattered workers.

A union's financial strength also influences its ability to win strikes and stay organized. The history of organized labor in the south is full of examples of workers seeking out unions in times of trouble and being abandoned by them after strikes, despite great sacrifices on the part of the workers. A disastrous strike defeat, like the 1934 textile general strike—and countless others in that industry—or the 1938 Mid-Continent petroleum strike at Tulsa, can alienate workers and cause tremendous psychological problems for unions for many years.

Sometimes locals in the south have atrophied because the national union did not have sufficient resources to service them after they were organized. During "Operation Dixie" for example, a common complaint was that the unions were more interested in organizing than servicing, and in some cases contracts were never negotiated.

The union's motivation to organize determines the zeal with which it will attempt to push its growth. Although its impact is difficult to measure, union growth in the south obviously was stimulated by the rivalry between the AFL and the CIO and the desire by such unions as the mine workers, clothing workers, garment workers, and railroad brotherhoods to protect themselves from nonunion competition.

Another factor is the degree of internal cohesion or the stability of internal union power relations. Internal power struggles have sometimes neutralized the unions' organizing efforts and disillusioned southern workers. The success of the United Mine Workers illustrates the importance of internal cohesion and control. The UMW's economic power was enhanced by financial integrity and centralized control over the union's affairs. It is doubtful if it could have carried off its organizational coup in the south if the districts had not been placed firmly under the control of the national union.

AGRICULTURAL WORKERS

The abundance of low-income agricultural workers in the south has been a great obstacle to union growth. Not only have the workers frequently been willing to break strikes in order to escape their poor conditions, but they were also likely to be satisfied with their manufacturing jobs, removing the element of discontent which is usually a prerequisite to union organization. In addition, they generally have the values of rural people which precludes interest in or sympathy for unions.[1]

Although it has hurt unions in the past, the steady decline in the agricultural work force and a shift from labor to capital-intensive agricultural production is a favorable factor for future union growth. Agricultural employment declined from 48.5 per cent of the south's civilian employment in 1940 to 18.0 per cent in 1962.[2] Many of the workers found jobs in the expanding nonagricultural industries, but there has also been a heavy out-migration from the region, particularly of nonwhites. Farm employment declined from 5.5 million in 1940 to

2.8 million in 1963; hired farm laborers declined from 1.3 to .9 million during the same years. The south had 48 per cent of the nation's hired farm employment in 1940 and 50 per cent in 1963.

Average hourly earnings of farm workers in the south were much lower than those of farm workers elsewhere or by workers with comparable skills in other industries. In 1963, for example, average hourly farm earnings were $1.05 in the United States, $.70 in the east south central, $.81 in the south Atlantic and $.85 in the west south central. An indication of the extent of the wage differential between agricultural and manufacturing workers may be had by comparing these rates with the $1.27 average hourly earnings of nonsupervisory workers in the apparel, lumber, and wood products industries, which was the lowest rate found in a 1962 U.S. Department of Labor survey of non-metropolitan areas in the southeast.[3]

WAGES

Since wages are a basic objective of collective bargaining, it is not surprising that the level and structure of wage rates should have significant influences on union growth. As noted in Chapter I, the general level of wages in the south has been considerably lower than in the rest of the country, and the occupational differentials between the south and the nonsouth tend to narrow in the higher-paying occupations. Moreover, the differential in the level of wage rates is greater in the southeast than in the southwest, and the differential between the southwest and the United States is disappearing more rapidly than that between the southeast and the United States. Gross average weekly earnings in manufacturing in the southern states relative to the United States ranged from 68.0 per cent in Mississippi to 97.9 per cent in Texas and Oklahoma in 1950, and 67.6 per cent in Mississippi and 99.5 per cent in Texas in 1962.[4]

These wage patterns have both positive and negative effects on union growth. We have already noted the negative effects of low agricultural wages. The positive effects include the motivation for national unions to organize the south, as well as the motivation for northern employers to help unions organize the south. In addition, the workers in the very low-wage jobs often joined unions because they "had nothing to lose." Lower wages also have made it possible for organizers to use wage differentials as inducements for workers to join unions, especially where the southern workers were in branches of firms which were organized and had higher wages elsewhere. Where southern workers are organized as part of master agreements, for example, their wages are likely to be higher than those prevailing in their communities, and workers are likely to give unions most of the credit for these high wages as well as increases after the plants are organized.

We noted in wartime experience that minimum wage laws have differential effects on union organizing. Of course the laws affect the south more than the rest of the country. To the extent that minimum wages reduce wage competition and eliminate the incentive for low-income workers to act as strikebreakers, unions obviously gain. But unions are damaged to the extent that higher wages create unemployment and increase the labor supply in industries not covered by the laws. Moreover, higher legal minimum wages take away one of the unions' main selling points. On the other hand, union officials in the garment industry argue that minimum-wage laws have helped them because they get credit for helping enforce the laws.

The net direct effect of these laws would thus seem to depend on whether they cause workers to feel that unions continue to be necessary after the laws are passed, as well as the extent to which the laws reduce employment in unionized industries. The main indirect effects depend upon how much unemployment is created, how much these unemployed workers compete with the union members, and the net effect of higher wages on purchasing power and employment.

Of course, higher minimum wages in the south help unions in the low-wage industries elsewhere by reducing the employers' motives for moving south. Since the workers in these industries are more likely to be organized in the nonsouth, minimum wages probably help union organization in the United States.

Low and rising wages in the south's unorganized industries also have some clearly negative effects. Low wages, by causing low savings, make it difficult for workers to hold out during strikes, make them more fearful of joining unions and losing their jobs, and make them more reluctant to pay dues. At the same time, rising wages in unorganized plants in the south have hurt unions because they do not get credit for the wage increases. This is especially true of the southern textile industry, which has comparatively good wages and where the nonunion firms set the patterns for wage changes. A 1962 study by the Bureau of Labor Statistics of nonsupervisory personnel in nonmetropolitan areas found the following average hourly earnings of manufacturing workers in the southeast:[5]

Food and kindred workers	$1.36
Textile mill products	1.46
Apparel and related products	1.27
Lumber and wood	1.27

Furniture and fixtures	1.30
Paper and allied products	2.24

Even though unions are indirectly responsible for wage increases in unorganized plants, they do not gain membership because the workers get higher wages without the problems of union organization. Indeed, if they joined the union the workers would lose the value that this threat gives them and, if the union is weak, can see little benefit in joining.

Rising wages in the south also have hurt union organizing in many cases where workers have based their current expenditures and debt structures on their higher wages and are therefore afraid to join unions for fear that strikes or loss of jobs might reduce their living standards. Moreover, the positive effects of low wages on union organization are reduced in the southern textile industry by the tendency for the whole family to work in the mills, making the family income more significant than individual earnings.

THE RACE PROBLEM

As noted earlier, the changed social context within which unions, Negroes, white workers, and employers operated after the Second World War changed the importance of the race question for union organization.[6] Although it is agreed that the race problem created some difficulties for unions during the 1950's and 1960's, union organizers are in accord that their equalitarian racial positions have not hurt them significantly in organizing the south. Indeed, on balance it can probably be demonstrated that a forthright equalitarian racial position will cause the unions to gain more than they lose. For example, a Georgia teamsters' official whose local grew from 1500 to 9000 members between 1952 and 1964, listed the three main reasons: "First, we have plenty of free advertising . . . Secondly, . . . our union does not equivocate or pussyfoot on the race question. On the job and at the hall all members are union brothers. . . . Thirdly, we work harder than most unions."[7]

If the election is otherwise close, the race issue might be important, but workers who have become convinced that it is to their advantage to join unions will probably pay little attention to the issue. We noted that Negroes frequently constituted the balance of power throwing elections to unions.

A few unions—the United Packinghouse Workers, the American Federation of Teachers, the National Association of Letter Carriers, and the United Automobile Workers, for example—have lost locals, and others have lost members and had locals threaten to secede over the racial equalitarian view of the national unions. In the UPWA case, however, the issue became so confused with internal union politics and the Communist question, that it is not possible to prove that the locals left because of the race issue. The UAW expelled a large local at Dallas for refusing to admit nonwhites to membership. Not many UAW leaders are convinced that expulsion is the way to handle this problem, and it probably will not be used in the future. In Memphis, for example, the UAW placed the large International Harvester local under receivership, instead of expelling it, for its refusal to desegregate facilities within its new headquarters. TWUA also placed its Front Royal, Virginia, local under trusteeship to prevent it from giving financial support to a private segregated school. The Harvester and other locals representing branches of companies with nationwide contracts are not eager to withdraw from national unions, because their wages and other conditions have been equalized with those of the nonsouth; the national's power over its local affiliate is also strengthened when the national, not the local, is certified by the NLRB as bargaining agent.

The teachers expelled locals at Chattanooga, Atlanta, and New Orleans for refusing to integrate, but these unions could not be considered bargaining agents in the usual sense, and they apparently gained no real power from national affiliation. Several attempts have also been made to form segregationist labor organizations, but none of these generated much support or leadership. The evidence suggests, therefore, that racial factors have not been important impediments to union organization in the south, though they have created some serious operational problems, especially with respect to union political activities.

The results with respect to the impact of racial factors on union organizing confirm our conclusion that the basic factors influencing collective bargaining are economic. The main organizations which have lost membership for racial reasons were non-collective bargaining organizations like the teachers and the state federations of labor.

Although the influence of racial conflict probably has been exaggerated, it would be a mistake to imply that the issue is not important to unions in the south. For one thing, many of the building trades and railroad unions have not organized their jurisdictions as fully as they should have because of their refusal to accept Negro members. Surprisingly, however, although there has been considerable criticism of unions in the Negro community for their continued racial discrimination in the south, few unions apparently have lost Negro members for this reason and report that Negroes usually remain much more organizable than whites.

There has also been considerable friction within the labor movement in the south because of pressures by the federal government, through the government contract committees, the NLRB, and the Civil Rights Act of 1964, to eliminate discrimination and segregation. A number of firms in the petroleum refining, pulp and paper, rubber, automobile, aircraft, tobacco and other industries desegregated jobs during the 1950's and 1960's. Because job integration violates prevailing racial views of southern workers and threatens their seniority, there have been vigorous protests, but apparently few cases where white workers have been sufficiently dissatisfied to quit good jobs.

There have also been many cases where previously segregated local unions have been integrated. Here, however, the main resistance apparently has come from the Negro union members and leaders who do not wish to become minorities within integrated locals. Such a minority position would, Negroes fear, cause them to lose delegates to union conventions and control over their own affairs. However, whether or not Negroes favor the continuation of segregation depends upon how segregation has influenced their job opportunities. In some cases, as in locals of the longshoremen, musicians, and bricklayers, Negroes apparently have had adequate job opportunities on segregated bases, but, in other cases, like the carpenters, painters, railway clerks, and tobacco workers, Negroes have felt that segregation helped perpetuate inadequate job opportunities. The tobacco workers, for example, had trouble integrating their last remaining segregated union in Durham, North Carolina, because the Negroes insisted that they be given better seniority and job rights. The particular seniority arrangement adopted as a part of the integration plan obviously has an important impact on the extent to which Negroes will get jobs from which they were formerly barred.

In addition to the formation of the unsuccessful segregationist unions, one of the main manifestations of racial unrest in the labor movement has been public protests by southern locals and financial support by those locals for segregationist causes. These protests and segregationist activities, as well as the pervasive use of racial arguments in representation elections, undoubtedly acccount for the fears by national union leaders that integrationist policies would cost them membership in the south. It will be noted, however, that few of these threats have been carried out and that they frequently involve protests against such activities as union support of the NAACP, school integration, or civil rights demonstrations. These protests come, of course, from the desire of a minority of southern unionists to associate themselves with dominant racial views of their communities. Nor should this be surprising. Southern workers frequently violate community mores when they join unions and do not wish to risk social ostracism for being identified as integrationists.

Negro-labor political alliances. There seems to be fairly general agreement among southern labor leaders that one of the most significant aspects of the civil rights movement for unions will be its effect on southern politics. This is true because the south's political future could well depend upon what happens to Negro-labor political relations as the political power of both groups continues to increase. Although labor's political influence appears to have grown somewhat during the years immediately after the Second World War, it declined around 1950 as a result of the antiunion counterattack of those years. At that time, open support of political candidates was considered to be the "kiss of death" in most southern states. Today, on the other hand, labor's support is openly solicited by candidates in every southern state except Mississippi. The main reason for these changes, of course, is that labor's political power has increased and probably will continue to increase as urban areas get more political power, Negroes and unions continue to have similar political interests, and unions maintain their political power nationally.

Similarly, as Negroes leave the rural south their political power increases. Especially significant has been the ability of Negroes in pivotal states outside the south to use their political power to influence conditions in the south. At the same time, however, there has been a great increase in political power of Negroes within the south. It is significant that in the 1964 presidential election, Senator Goldwater failed to carry a single southern state where over 45 per cent of eligible Negroes were registered. Of course the value of the Negro vote will become more decisive as the Republican vote grows and splits the white vote along economic lines. Since the overwhelming proportion of Negroes now live in urban areas in the south, and since all of the trends indicate that the racial barriers to voting are falling, the Negro vote obviously is going to be an important factor in the south's political future.

Statistics indicate the power and the potential of Negro-labor coalitions. In 1965, informal Negro-labor alliances existed in every southern state, and were important political forces in Tennessee, Kentucky, Oklahoma, and Virginia. Negroes, unions and Mexican-Americans in Texas have organized a formal political coalition which promises to be an important political power in that state. In Oklahoma, where there were about 50,000 members in unions affiliated with the AFL-CIO and "a few thousand" in unaffiliated unions,[8] a coalition of Negroes, unions, and farmers (in the areas where the Populist tradition was strong) defeated a right-to-work referendum by 376,555 to 352,267 in 1964. Surveys of the Negro areas reveal that Negroes voted 20 to 1 against the measure and the farm vote split about half and half.[9]

Of course, segregationists are not unmindful of the potential political power of Negro-labor coalitions and have attempted to split these alliances or change some of the factors making them effective. The Mississippi legislature even went so far as to contemplate measures to curb the power of the Republican Party in that state by requiring it to go to considerable expense to put up candidates for state, federal, and local office. Although the bill passed the Mississippi Senate, it failed in the House, partly because of the realization that many of the people the state's industrial developers were trying so desperately to attract were Republicans.[10] In addition, segregationists have attempted to split Negro-labor coalitions at the local level by inciting racial opposition from white union members and by supporting pro-labor segregationists in areas where unions are strong.

Although the trend toward increased power of Negro-labor coalitions is unmistakable, it would be false to conclude that these coalitions are inevitable. Relations between Negroes and union leaders are far from close in most of the deep south, and there are many differences in Texas, Tennessee, Virginia, and North Carolina. In Arkansas, for example, Negroes and unions supported Faubus when he ran for governor in 1956, but unions continued to support him after 1957 when Negroes obviously were unable to do so. The potential power of these coalitions is also limited because of the apathy of Negro voters, many of whom fail to register and vote. In 1962, for example, a Chicago survey revealed that 68 per cent of Negroes were registered as compared with 78 per cent of whites, but that only 47 per cent of eligible Negroes, as compared with 64 per cent of eligible whites, actually voted.[11]

WOMEN WORKERS

Not only are more firms locating in rural areas of the south, but many of these firms have lower wages and higher ratios of women to men than workers in the United States as a whole or in metropolitan areas. Since much of the south's increasing manufacturing employment is in firms with large proportions of women employees,[12] the organizability of females has an important bearing on the present and future strength of unions in the region. Although it is true that women are concentrated in the textile, garment, food, service, and other industries which have low degrees of unionization, it is not at all clear that women make unions weak. It is assumed by some that women make poor union members because they are reluctant to get involved in strike activity and are only temporarily attached to the labor market. But the experience of the comparatively well-organized telephone industry in the south, half of whose 260,000 members in 1960 were women, and the experiences of union organizers in the garment industry cast some doubt in this theory. Organizers for the ILGWU (three fourths of whose 447,000 1960 members were women) and the ACWA (which had 266,000 women members out of a total of 377,000 in 1960) seem to agree that, although different organizing tactics must be used, women are no more difficult to organize in the south than men. The southern director of the ILGWU from 1955 to 1965 also felt that women made very militant union members once they became organized.[13] It therefore seems safe to conclude that industry size, structure, and location are more important determinants of union growth than the sex of workers.

RELIGION

Religion and religious institutions have been important influences in the south. It is, however, impossible to say whether the net effect of religion on the labor movement has been detrimental. It is true that many preachers have fought unions. But there are other examples in which ministers and churches have organized unions and fought for the right of workers to organize. Many southerners have been induced to promote unionism because of religious convictions. For example, Lucy Randolph Mason performed much valuable work for the CIO after she joined it in 1937. She helped CIO organizers by talking the clergy out of fighting unions and by persuading them to promote the union. She was even successful in convincing the strongest religious body in the south, the Southern Baptist Convention, to adopt a resolution favoring collective bargaining.[14] We have frequently noted, moreover, that religious procedures often have been included in union meetings. This is probably because the only organizational experience many southern workers had before unions was the church.

But employers also have used religion and religious leaders in their antiunion campaigns. The following statement from a mill preacher in Liston Pope's study indicates the conception that many of them had of their functions in the mill villages.

> Mill churches serve the mill as much as they serve the folks; let the
> mill pay for the service. Churches help the mills to have a steadier and

more intelligent supply of labor. . . . Why Mr. —— (one of the largest textile manufacturers in North Carolina), a Jew, helps the preachers, and the first thing he does when a strike threatens is to call them up—and the strikers can't win with the preachers against them.[15]

Pope concluded: "For the most part, the churches and ministers . . . serve as an arm of the employers in control of the mill villages. Ministers rationalize their position by equating paternalism (though they avoid the word) with Christian principles."

Lucy Mason encountered many antiunion mill preachers in her work with the CIO after World War II. She described one such incident:

> Early in 1946, I was asked to go to a small mill village in South Carolina, where . . . a preacher was being used by the textile companies to intimidate union people. . . . One morning after a Sunday service, the preacher said he had a special message for union members and requested them to stay after the service. He first made a vicious attack on the CIO, calling it all the bad names he could think of, and finished with a declaration that no CIO members could be "saved" and that the people would have to decide between the church and the union. Union members were not welcome and would not be accepted in the church, he declared. As a result there was a large withdrawal from the union.[16]

A second aspect of the religious problem is the effect that religion has upon workers' attitudes concerning unions. Many of the minor sects denounce "worldly things," and teach that social action is of no avail since evil is inherent in human affairs. Indeed, in this view suffering is a virtue, and the main purpose of this life is not to combat evil but to prepare for the hereafter. These attitudes obviously are incompatible with unionism.

In a detailed study of the attitudes of workers in South Carolina toward unions, Bernard Cannon concluded that all of the minor sects, to which most of the southern textile workers belonged, were conservative and suspicious of change. They invariably insisted upon unanimity of thought and action, and deviation was the signal for the formation of a new church or sect. The workers in Cannon's study felt that work was the sure way to avoid sin. He also found a correlation between the small sect and antiunionism, but expressed the belief that this religion was not conducive to any social action. "The worker hears about the union, he is asked to join, yet he tends to react indifferently to such endeavor to have him join an organized labor movement. Unionization is 'worldly' and does not appear to the sectarian to be the means to salvation. Hard work at low wages is the more virtuous of the two courses."[17]

Mention should also be made of several semireligious publications and organizations which have been formed to fight unions. Two of them are the *Militant Truth* and *Trumpet*. They have appeared in workers' mail boxes just before NLRB elections. One observer reported, after an interview with Sherman Patterson, editor of *Militant Truth*:

> *Militant Truth's* anti-union line is peculiar. First it takes as its text the Biblical admonition, "Be ye not unequally yoked together." Then the non-Rev. Patterson interprets this as meaning that Christians should not join any organization which includes people of other creeds. And the final step is a vicious attempt to demonstrate that unions are not Christian.[18]

OTHER SOCIAL FACTORS

A survey conducted by a national research organization for the AFL-CIO concluded that one of the main impediments to unionization in the south was the lack of social cohesion among southern whites. Union leaders with experience in the south discount this. It is perhaps more applicable to the textile community than elsewhere, but is probably exaggerated even here.[19]

Organizers from every union are quick to point to strong locals in various areas of the south. The evidence suggests that, once organized, southerners make loyal and militant members of strong unions. For example, UAW representatives maintain that when that union was operating without a contract in 1958, and had to collect union dues on a voluntary basis, southerners paid up in higher proportions than members from other areas of the country. In the Henderson, North Carolina textile strike, fewer union members went back to work, despite the ease with which the company secured nonunion strikebreakers, than in the Kohler strike in Wisconsin. Moreover, the present study has documented many examples of tremendous sacrifices and unity by workers in every section of the south. When the national research organization concluded that southerners lacked the social cohesion to form unions, a national union president with experience in that region declared: "The idea that one southerner doesn't co-mingle with the other just doesn't square with the facts as I know them. . . . We have had strikes in the South . . . where we walked picket lines . . . for as high as 18 months; and I have never seen a more cohesive, more determined, more brave people in all my life than in the South." The director of organization for an international union declared: "I found in 11 years of organizing that the best people to work with were in the South. I found the greatest trouble in the South was not that the people were against unionization, but it was the tactics that the companies were able to use against organizing."

CHAPTER XXII

The Future of Unions
in the South

Since we have argued that union growth in the south will primarily be determined by the changing patterns of industry, it is necessary to note some of the expected changes in employment in order to be able to say much about the future.

These trends are, on balance, favorable for the continued growth of unions in the south, particularly the southwest. Civilian employment has shifted and is expected to continue to shift out of the southern states with the lowest proportions of organized nonagricultural workers into those with higher proportions. The main exception is Alabama, which has been fairly well organized and which is expected to continue to lose employment relative to other areas. With the exception of Virginia and Georgia, all the textile states are expected to lose their relative shares of employment.

Perhaps more important as an indication of union growth is the changing composition of manufacturing employment shown in Table 10, which illustrates that the industrial composition of the south's employment is becoming increasingly diversified as the region industrializes. A smaller percentage of southern employment is concentrated in the older textile, tobacco, lumber and wood products, and petroleum refining industries, and a larger percentage in all the other industries listed, most of which are better organized. The main exceptions to the

344

favorable trends for organizing are the apparel and other finished textile products, which, are increasing rapidly and are not very well organized, and petroleum refining and tobacco, which are older comparatively well-organized industries.

The NPA's projections of the occupational composition of the civilian labor force in 1972 are shown in Table 11 and suggest that the absolute changes in employment in the south between 1962 and 1972 will be:

farmers	— 500,000
blue-collar workers	+ 700,000
craftsmen, foremen and operatives	+ 800,000
nonfarm laborers	— 100,000
service workers	+ 700,000
white-collar workers	+3,100,000
professional, technical and operatives	+1,900,000
clerical and sales	+1,200,000

The expected decline in farm employment will help unions, as will the increase in blue-collar and some service categories. Of the white-collar groups, the most likely to be organized are clerical and sales groups which constitute 1,200,000 of the expected increase. White-collar workers among government employees also are likely to continue to organize gradually. The increasing political power of unions in the south should be particularly beneficial to unions among state, county and municipal workers. Employment is increasing among these government workers, but most southern states discourage collective bargaining among their employees.

The percentage distribution of civilian employment between agricultural and various nonagricultural occupations, in 1940-1962 is shown in Table 12.

Thus, although some of the industry trends tend to encourage union growth, others tend to make it more difficult. On balance, the industry trends favor the continued growth of unions, but at a slower rate than the increase in nonagricultural employment unless unions are able to break through into formerly less well-organized groups like the white-collar workers.

In summary, then, the trends which favor union growth in the south include:

(1) The migration of workers out of agriculture and out of the south will help by reducing the supply of labor. Mechanization and improvement in agricultural income will reduce the tendency for farm workers to cross picket lines. The increasing size of hired work forces may make organization possible.

Table 10. Production workers in manufacturing in the south and in the nonsouth by major industry group, 1939, 1947, and 1962 (in thousands).

Major industry group	South 1939 Number	South 1939 Per cent of total	South 1947 Number	South 1947 Per cent of total	South 1962 Number	South 1962 Per cent of total	Nonsouth 1939 Number	Nonsouth 1947 Number	Nonsouth 1962 Number	Nonsouth 1962 Per cent of total	Per cent south of nonsouth 1939	Per cent south of nonsouth 1962
Food and kindred products	126	9.3	202	10.0	402	12.0	676	896	1,370	10.5	18.6	29.3
Tobacco manufacturing	41	3.0	62	3.1	65	2.0	47	42	24	0.2	87.2	270.8
Textile mill products	476	35.3	554	27.4	583	18.0	605	593	298	2.3	78.7	195.6
Apparel and other finished textile products	82	6.1	130	6.4	356	11.0	671	844	879	6.8	12.2	40.5
Lumber and wood products	203	15.0	299	14.8	239	7.0	220	300	368	2.8	92.3	63.6
Furniture and fixtures	49	3.6	75	3.7	135	4.0	140	208	246	1.9	35.0	54.9
Paper and allied products	37	2.7	66	3.3	132	4.0	233	323	469	3.6	15.9	28.1
Printing, publishing and allied industries	31	2.3	46	2.3	130	4.0	293	392	803	6.2	10.6	16.2
Chemical and allied products	72	5.3	120	5.9	227	7.0	204	347	623	4.8	35.3	36.4
Petroleum refining and related products	30	2.2	51	2.5	58	2.0	78	119	138	1.1	38.5	42.0
Rubber and miscellaneous plastic products	—	—	—	—	18	0.5	—	—	371	2.9	—	4.0
Leather and leather products	—	—	—	—	39	1.0	—	—	322	2.5	—	12.1

Table 10. (Continued)

Major industry group	South 1939 Number	South 1939 Per cent of total	South 1947 Number	South 1947 Per cent of total	South 1962 Number	South 1962 Per cent of total	Nonsouth 1939 Number	Nonsouth 1947 Number	Nonsouth 1962 Number	Nonsouth 1962 Per cent of total	Per cent south of nonsouth 1939	Per cent south of nonsouth 1962
Stone, clay, and glass products	35	2.6	58	2.9	124	3.0	232	348	448	3.4	15.1	27.7
Primary metal industries	—	—	—	—	119	3.0	—	—	1,047	8.0	—	11.4
Fabricated metal products	28	2.1	59	2.9	136	4.0	423	763	983	7.6	6.6	13.4
Machinery (except electrical)	21	1.6	56	2.8	129	4.0	515	1,188	1,330	10.2	4.1	9.7
Electrical machinery	—	—	—	—	146	5.0	—	—	1,382	10.6	—	10.6
Transportation equipment	22	1.6	68	3.4	178	6.0	523	917	1,467	11.3	4.2	12.1
Instruments and related products	—	—	—	—	9	0.3	—	—	349	2.7	—	2.6
Miscellaneous manufacturing industries	—	—	—	—	26	0.8	—	—	367	2.8	—	7.0
All other	96	7.1	177	8.7	—	1.4	1,599	—	—	—	—	—
Total	1,349	100.0	2,023	100.0	3,251	100.0	6,459	9,895	13,016	100.0	—	—

Source: C. B. Hoover and B. U. Ratchford, Economic Resources and Policies of the South (New York: Macmillan, 1951) for 1939–1947; 1962 from U.S. Bureau of Labor Statistics, Earnings and Employment Statistics, BLS Bulletin 1370, 1963, and U.S. Department of Commerce, Bureau of the Census, Statistical Abstract of the United States, 1963.

Table 11. *Distribution of civilian employment by major industry group, south and nonsouth, 1940–1962, and 1972 projections.*

	South						United States			
	Number (millions)			Per cent of total			Number (millions)		Per cent of total	
Major industry group	1957	1962	1972	1957	1962	1972	1962	1972	1962	1972
Professional, technical	1.3	1.6	2.8	8.1	9.8	13.6	8.0	13.3	11.9	16.0
Managers, proprietors	1.5	1.7	2.4	10.0	10.7	11.6	7.4	9.2	10.9	11.1
Clerical	1.7	2.0	2.8	10.9	11.9	13.8	10.1	13.3	14.9	16.1
Salesworkers	0.9	1.0	1.4	5.8	6.0	6.7	4.3	5.7	6.4	6.9
Craftsmen, foremen	1.8	1.9	2.3	11.7	11.4	11.1	8.7	10.2	12.8	12.4
Operatives	2.8	2.9	3.3	18.3	17.9	16.4	12.0	12.5	16.5	15.4
Service workers	1.8	2.3	3.0	11.9	14.3	15.0	8.8	11.1	13.1	13.3
Nonfarm laborers	1.0	0.9	0.8	6.4	5.7	4.2	3.6	3.2	4.5	3.8
Farmers	2.6	2.0	1.5	16.7	12.3	7.6	4.9	4.0	5.9	4.9
All occupations	15.5	16.4	20.3	23.8	24.2	24.5	67.8	82.7	10.0	10.0

Source: National Planning Associate projections as reported in *Nation's Manpower Revolution*, U.S. Senate Committee on Labor and Public Welfare, Subcommittee on Employment and Manpower, 1963, part 5, pp. 1402–1403.

Table 12. Distribution of employment by occupations, south and nonsouth, 1940–1964 (in per cent).

Occupation	1940 South	1940 Non-south	1947 South	1947 Non-south	1957 South	1957 Non-south	1960 South	1960 Non-south	1962 South	1962 Non-south	1964 South	1964 Non-south
Agriculture	48.5	15.9	36.7	11.0	25.6	7.1	19.5	9.1	18.0	8.6	16.6	7.3
Nonagricultural	51.5	84.1	63.3	89.0	74.4	92.9	80.5	90.9	82.0	91.4	83.4	92.7
Mining	1.9	2.3	1.8	1.8	1.4	1.4	2.1	0.9	2.0	0.8	1.8	0.7
Construction	2.7	3.2	3.4	3.9	4.7	4.8	5.0	4.6	5.1	4.1	5.2	4.6
Manufacturing	17.1	28.4	21.4	31.5	21.9	30.4	21.4	29.4	21.7	28.9	22.3	28.3
Transportation and public utilities	4.9	7.9	6.0	8.5	5.8	7.4	6.1	6.7	5.5	6.6	5.6	6.3
Trade	10.5	18.4	13.4	18.9	17.4	19.8	18.0	18.9	18.0	18.9	18.2	19.1
Finance, insurance and real estate	1.3	4.0	1.7	3.5	2.9	4.3	3.6	4.6	3.8	4.8	3.9	4.8
Service and miscellaneous	5.3	9.2	6.5	10.0	8.2	11.5	10.1	12.7	10.7	13.2	11.7	13.9
Government	7.8	10.7	9.4	10.9	12.1	13.3	14.1	13.9	14.9	14.9	15.0	14.9

Source: 1940, 1947, and 1957 data from S. L. McDonald, "The Significance of the South's Changing Occupational Structure," a paper read at the Annual Meeting of the Southern Economic Association, Atlanta, Georgia, November 21, 1958; 1960 and 1962 figures are the writer's calculations from U.S. Department of Agriculture and Bureau of Labor Statistics data; 1964 agricultural statistics from U.S. Department of Agriculture Agricultural Statistics 1965, nonagricultural statistics from U.S. Department of Labor, Bureau of Labor Statistics, 1964–1965, Statistical Supplement—Monthly Labor Review.

(2) The prevailing southern ideology is being changed by industrialization and will become increasingly compatible with collective bargaining. The main reason for the changing attitudes will undoubtedly be: the growing economic and political power of unions; the declining agricultural population, which has been the most antiunion segment of the southern population; as the region industrializes the role that the urge to industrialize plays in causing antiunion attitudes will be reduced; growing experience with unions and collective bargaining will demonstrate its advantages as a means of handling the workers' problems in an industrial society; and industrialization brings more employers into the south who favor collective bargaining.

(3) We have noted that governments have the power to influence union growth in many ways, particularly by influencing the prevailing attitudes of public officials, and also by encouraging (or discontinuing their opposition to) unions among government employees and government contractors. In this connection, the trend is toward both an increase in the number of government employees and the political power of unions. The political power probably will grow because of mounting cooperation between Negroes (whose political power can be expected to expand greatly in the future) and unions, reapportionment in favor of urban areas (where most Negroes and union members are located), and the growth of the Republican Party in the south. Indeed, it can be expected that the unions' political power will grow faster than their economic power, if such a comparison is possible.

(4) In all probability the attitudes of southern workers toward unions will also change as the region industrializes and their agricultural backgrounds recede into history. The prospects are that workers will turn more to unions to represent their political and economic interests. Especially significant will be a decline in the tendency to make a favorable comparison of nonagricultural with agricultural conditions.

(5) The motive to organize will be the growing industrialization of the south relative to the nonsouth and the consequent necessity to protect union conditions elsewhere. And, in spite of talk about the decline of collective bargaining, the American labor movement is a financially strong and a generally accepted part of the American economy. Moreover, the labor movement has been strengthened by the solution of the important problems of communism and corruption which dissipated its energies in the 1947-1960 period. At the same time, unions have come a long way in solving the race problem, particularly at the policy level. This will continue to cause difficulty but it will not be an important factor in union growth. Perhaps unions have also learned something about organizing in the south and realize that general campaigns are

not likely to succeed as well as smaller campaigns concentrated on particular targets. Although unions have done some important things to overcome jurisdictional disputes, this will continue to be one of their most serious internal weaknesses.

(6) Although the trend is very slow, there is increasing unionization of important white-collar workers, particularly among government employees. It could well be that they will supply the leadership and techniques to produce the breakthrough in unionization at the right time.

The trends which will make it more difficult for unions to organize include: the tendency for plants to locate in smaller communities; the scattering of workers from the plant gates, making it more difficult for union organizers to contact them; rising living standards and changed patterns of living which make the worker "more responsive to family, community, and neighborhood influences";[1] the workers' rising educational levels which make them "more questioning of both managements and unions," requiring the latter to change their organizing techniques; technological changes which increase employment in nonunion areas and increase management's ability to operate during strikes; management's growing sophistication in fighting unions where it wishes to avoid them; the growing disenchantment with unions by intellectuals and union staff people—who contributed greatly to the growth of the labor movement in the 1930's, and, although there is growing concentration of employment within particular firms, there is a trend toward smaller plants within those firms.

What are the prospects? No one knows of course, and it is very hazardous to guess because the most important determinants of union membership are likely to be dramatic and unpredictable events that could cause general increases in union membership throughout the region. Projecting the membership trends relative to industries, however, indicates that, although union membership in the south probably will continue to increase absolutely and relative to the nonsouth, unions will have great difficulty bringing their membership up to the nonsouth's 1962 proportion (30 per cent) of nonagricultural employment. To do this would require an increase of 3,000,000 between 1962 and 1972. The south will have to increase its membership by 1,455,000 between 1962 and 1972 just to hold its 1964 proportion of 14 per cent of the nonagricultural work force. To hold the 1964 proportion would therefore obviously require unions to organize considerably more workers each year than the 16,000 average net increase between 1953 and 1964.

Nevertheless, there is obviously considerable slack for union growth in the south, and, although the region is not likely to become as well organized as the nonsouth in a short period of time, the gap between the south and the nonsouth will continue to narrow. And since membership growth in the south is far from saturated,[2] unions will continue gradually to increase their membership and thus will have strong bases from which to grow rapidly during times which are psychologically and economically conducive. Until such times, however, the south's union membership probably will continue to increase faster than that of the nonsouth but not as fast relatively as the change in nonagricultural and manufacturing employment.

Notes

CHAPTER I

The Institutional Setting

1. John T. Dunlop, *Industrial Relations Systems* (New York: Henry Holt and Co., 1958), pp. 24-25.

2. This includes the following states: North Carolina, South Carolina, Georgia, Florida, Kentucky, Tennessee, Alabama, Mississippi, Arkansas, Louisiana, Oklahoma, and Texas.

3. Quoted by Howard W. Odum and Harry Estill Moore, *American Regionalism* (New York: Henry Holt and Co., 1938), p. 2.

4. Odum and Moore, *American Regionalism*, which also contains 28 different definitions of region.

5. W. W. Rostow, *The Stages of Economic Growth* (Cambridge: Cambridge University Press, 1960), p. 18.

6. "Growth of Manufactures in the South," *Annals* of the American Academy of Political and Social Science, January 1931, p. 24.

7. Richard A. Easterlin, "Interregional Differences in Per Capita Income, Population and Total Income, 1840-1850," *Trends in the American Economy in the Nineteenth Century* (Washington: National Bureau of Economic Research Studies in Income and Wealth, 1960), pp. 138-140.

8. Jeffrey G. Williamson, "National Economic Development and Interregional Inequality," paper presented at symposium on Approaches to Regional Analysis, University of Texas, April 27-28, 1964.

9. Easterlin, "Interregional Differences in Per Capita Income," p. 13, Table B-12, p. 128.

10. Odum and Moore, *American Regionalism*, pp. 454, 526, 530, 546, and 586.

11. Quoted by Howard Odum, *Southern Regions of the United States* (Chapel Hill: University of North Carolina Press, 1936), p. 159.

12. For a discussion of the profitability of slavery, see: Robert Evans, Jr., "The Economics of American Negro Slavery, 1830-1860," *Aspects of Labor Economics* (New York: National Bureau of Economic Research, 1962).

13. James McBride Dabbs, *The Southern Heritage* (New York: Alfred A. Knopf, 1958), p. 172.

14. Richard Hofstadter, *The American Political Tradition* (New York: Alfred A. Knopf, 1948), pp. 81-82.

15. W. J. Cash, *The Mind of the South* (New York: Alfred A. Knopf, 1941), p. 70.

16. Broadus Mitchell, *The Rise of Cotton Mills in the South* (Baltimore: Johns Hopkins University, 1921), Studies in Historical and Political Science, pp. 25-27.

17. C. Vann Woodward, *The Burden of Southern History* (New York: Vintage Books, 1961), ch. 5; John H. Franklin, *Reconstruction After the Civil War* (Chicago: The University of Chicago Press, 1962).

18. C. Vann Woodward, *Strange Career of Jim Crow* (New York: Oxford University Press, 1955), p. 40.

19. Vernon L. Wharton, *The Negro in Mississippi, 1877-1880* (Chapel Hill: The University of North Carolina Press, 1947).

20. George B. Tendall, *South Carolina Negroes, 1877-1900* (Chapel Hill: University of North Carolina Press, 1952).

21. For a more detailed summary of these decisions and the current status of discrimination in various areas based on the Report of The United States Commission on Civil Rights, see Wallace Mendelson, *Discrimination* (Englewood Cliffs, New Jersey: Prentice-Hall, Inc., 1962).

22. Bureau of Labor Statistics, U. S. Department of Labor, *Labor in the South*, Bulletin No. 898, 1946, p. 5.

23. William H. Nicholls, *Southern Tradition and Regional Progress* (Chapel Hill: University of North Carolina Press, 1960), p. 24.

24. C. Vann Woodward, *Origins of the New South* (Baton Rouge: Louisiana State University Press, 1951), p. 140.

25. George S. and Broadus Mitchell, *Industrial Revolution in the South* (Baltimore: Johns Hopkins University Press, 1930), p. 294.

26. Woodward, *Origins of the New South*, pp. 139-140.

27. Twelve Southerners, *I'll Take My Stand* (New York: Harper and Bros., 1930).

28. Woodward, *Origins of the New South*, p. 148.

29. Broadus Mitchell, *The Rise of Cotton Mills in the South* (Baltimore: Johns Hopkins University Press, 1921), Johns Hopkins University Studies in Historical and Political Science, p. 133.

30. Albert B. Moore, *History of Alabama and Her People* (Chicago and New York: American Historical Society, 1927), p. 636.

31. Moore, *History of Alabama and Her People*, pp. 150, 180-181; Victor S. Clark, *History of Manufactures in the United States* (New York: McGraw-Hill Co., Inc., 1929), vol. III, p. 173: Woodward, *Origins of the New South*, p. 307: U. S. Department of Labor, Bureau of Labor Statistics, *Labor in the South*, Bulletin 898, 1946, ch. IX.

32. Woodward, *Origins of the New South*, ch. V (tends to discount the importance of this motive).

33. BLS, *Labor in the South*, p. 9.

34. Paul W. Gates, "Federal Land Policy in the South, 1866-1888," *Journal of Southern History*, 1940, pp. 303-330.

35. J. F. Duggar, "Areas of Cultivation in the South," *South in the Building of the Nation*, ch. VI, p. 17, quoted by Woodward, *Origins of the New South*, p. 118.

36. Harold U. Faulkner, *American Economic History* (New York: Harper and Bros., 1949), p. 418.

37. Edwin C. Eckel, "The Iron and Steel Industry of the South," *Annals of the American Academy of Political and Social Science*, January 1931, p. 54.

38. Clark, *History of Manufactures in the United States*, vol II, p. 213.

39. Ethel Armes, *The Story of Coal and Iron in Alabama* (Birmingham: Birmingham Chamber of Commerce, 1910), p. 260.

40. J. Allen Tower, "The Industrial Development of the Birmingham Region," *Bulletin of Birmingham—Southern College*, XLVI, no. 4, 1953, p. 12.

41. Armes, *Coal and Iron in Alabama*, ch. XIII.

42. Woodward, *Origins of the New South*, p. 126.

43. H. H. Chapman *et al.*, *The Iron and Steel Industries of the South* (Tuscaloosa, Alabama: University of Alabama Press, 1953), p. 104.

44. Clark, *History of Manufactures in the United States*, vol. II, p. 217.

45. Chapman *et al.*, *The Iron and Steel Industries of the South*, p. 104.

46. Calvin B. Hoover and B. U. Ratchford, *Economic Resources and Policies of the South* (Chapel Hill: University of North Carolina Press, 1951), pp. 65-88, minimize this factor as an impediment to the economic development of the south.

47. Woodward, *Origins of the New South*, pp. 315, 316.

48. Clark, *History of Manufacturers in the United States*, ch. III.

49. Woodward, *Origins of the New South*, pp. 120-121, 125-126, 302.

50. George W. Stocking, *Basing Point Pricing and Regional Development; A Case Study of the Iron and Steel Industry* (Chapel Hill: University of North Carolina Press, 1952), p. 155.

51. Odum, *Southern Regions of the United States*, p. 353.

52. *Report to the President on the Economic Conditions of the South* (Washington: U. S. Government Printing Office, 1938).

53. Clarence H. Danhof, "Four Decades of Thought on the South's Economic Problems," in Melvin L. Greenhut and W. Tate Whitman, eds., *Essays in Southern Economic Development* (Chapel Hill: University of North Carolina Press, 1964), pp. 1-68.

54. Hoover and Ratchford, *Economic Resources and Policies of the South*, p. 78.

55. Clarence Danhof, "Four Decades of Thought on the South's Economic Problems," p. 47 and Chapman *et al.*, *The Iron and Steel Industries of the South*, p. 389.

56. John B. McFerrin, "Resources for Financing Industry in the South," *Southern Economic Journal,* 1947, p. 61.

57. Danhof, "Four Decades of Thought on the South's Economic Problems," p. 50.

58. Joseph J. Spengler, "Southern Economic Trends and Prospects," in John C. McKinney and Edgar T. Thompson, eds., *The South in Continuity and Change* (Durham, N. C.: Duke University Press, 1965), p. 101.

CHAPTER II

General Developments and Problems of Unions Before 1928

1. R. B. Morris, "Labor Militancy in the Old South," *Labor and Nation,* May-June 1948, p. 35.

2. *New York Times,* August 22, 1869.

3. John R. Commons and Associates, *History of Labour in the United States* (New York: Macmillan Co., 1918), vol. I, p. 66.

4. *Atlanta Constitution,* March 10, 1869; April 9, 1869; Nov. 2, 1869.

5. See, for example, account of the convention in *New York Times,* August 22, 1869.

6. John R. Commons and Associates, *A Documentary History of American Industrial Society* (Cleveland: Arthur H. Clark Co., 1910), vol. IX, pp. 159, 185.

7. Sterling D. Spero and Abram L. Harris, *The Black Worker* (New York: Columbia University Press, 1931), p. 24.

8. Frederic Meyers, "The Knights of Labor in the South," *Southern Economic Journal,* April 1940.

9. Holman Head, "Development of the Labor Movement in Alabama Prior to 1900," unpub. diss., University of Alabama, 1954.

10. Meyers, "The Knights of Labor in the South," and Ruth A. Allen, *Chapters in the History of Organized Labor in Texas* (Austin: University of Texas Press, 1941), pp. 20-21.

11. Ruth A. Allen, *The Great Southwest Strike* (Austin: University of Texas Press, 1942), p. 25.

12. Knights of Labor, General Assembly, *Proceedings,* 1884, p. 580.

13. H. M. Douty, "Early Labor Organization in North Carolina," *South Atlantic Quarterly,* July 1935, p. 262; George S. Mitchell, *Textile Unionism and the South* (Chapel Hill: University of North Carolina Press, 1931), pp. 23-24.

14. Mercer G. Evans, "History of the Organized Labor Movement in Georgia," unpub. diss., University of Chicago, 1929, p. 27.

15. Allen, *Chapters in the History of Organized Labor in Texas;* R. W. Shugg, "The New Orleans General Strike of 1892," *The Louisiana Historical*

Quarterly, April 1938, p. 550; F. Ray Marshall and Lamar B. Jones, "Agricultural Unions in Louisiana," *Labor History,* Fall 1962, p. 287.

16. Charles H. Wesley, *Negro Labor in the United States* (New York: Vanguard Press, 1927), p. 245.

17. Wesley, *Negro Labor in the United States;* Knights of Labor, General Assembly, *Proceedings,* 1886, p. 44.

18. Head, "Development of the Labor Movement in Alabama Prior to 1900," Table 3, p. 202.

19. *Atlanta Constitution,* March 14, 1886.

20. Douty, "Early Labor Organizations in North Carolina," p. 262.

21. Allen, *Chapters in the History of Organized Labor in Texas,* p. 174.

22. Spero and Harris, *The Black Worker,* p. 174.

23. Knights of Labor, General Assembly, *Proceedings,* 1886, p. 254.

24. Allen, *The Great Southwest Strike;* Frank W. Taussig, "The South-Western Strike of 1886," *Quarterly Journal of Economics,* 1886-1889, vol. I, pp. 184-222.

25. Meyers, "The Knights of Labor in the South."

26. Federation of Trades and Labor Unions, *Report of Proceedings,* 1881, p. 14.

27. Unless otherwise stated, information on the AFL for the early years came from the official *Convention Proceedings* of that organization.

28. Head, "Development of the Labor Movement in Alabama Prior to 1900," pp. 137 and 138; Birmingham *Labor Advocate,* January 18, 1890 and April 7, 1894.

29. Roger W. Shugg, "The New Orleans General Strike of 1892," *Louisiana Historical Quarterly,* April 1938, p. 563.

30. AFL *Convention Proceedings,* 1891, p. 9.

31. Samuel Gompers, *Seventy Years of Life and Labor* (New York: E. P. Dutton and Co., 1925).

32. AFL *Convention Proceedings,* 1893, pp. 31, 38, 40, 67-69.

33. Grady L. Mullenix, "A History of the Texas State Federation of Labor," unpub. diss., University of Texas, 1954.

34. For a discussion of these see *American Federationist,* November 1928. This entire issue is devoted to organizing in the south.

35. AFL *Convention Proceedings,* 1890, p. 31.

36. For further discussion of AFL racial practices see Ray Marshall, *The Negro and Organized Labor* (New York: John Wiley and Sons, 1965).

37. Gompers, *Seventy Years of Life and Labor.*

38. Booker T. Washington, "The Negro and the Labor Unions," *Atlantic Monthly,* June 1913, p. 756.

39. Statement by Will Winn, *American Federationist,* February 1898.

40. Editorial in *American Federationist,* April 1901.

41. AFL *Executive Council Minutes,* February 12, 1918, pp. 21-23.

42. Louisiana State Federation of Labor, *Official Proceedings,* 1912.

43. Joint Legislative Board of Texas, *Report,* 1905, p. 7; 1913, p. 5.

44. James A. Tinsley, "Labor in Politics: The Case of Texas, 1903-1914," unpublished paper read at the 1960 annual meeting of the Southern Historical Association.

45. AFL, *Convention Proceedings*, 1915, pp. 30, 251, 472.

CHAPTER III

Printing and Building Trades

1. John R. Commons and Associates, *History of Labour in the United States* (New York: Macmillan Co., 1918), vol. I, p. 109.

2. Ethelbert Stewart, *Documentary History of Early Organizations of Printers* (Indianapolis: International Typographical Union, 1907), pp. 112, 902-904.

3. R. B. Morris, "Labor Militancy in the Old South," *Labor and Nation*, May-June 1948, p. 35.

4. George A. Tracy, *History of the Typographical Union* (Indianapolis: International Typographical Union, 1913), pp. 229-230, *passim*.

5. Houston *Telegraph and Texas Register*, May 2 and 5, 1838.

6. Quoted by Tracy, *History of the Typographical Union*, pp. 97-98, 185, 215-218, 239, 248, 229.

7. Mercer G. Evans, "History of the Organized Labor Movement in Georgia," unpub. diss., University of Chicago, 1929, pp. 52-53.

8. *Typographical Journal*, May 1903, p. 46; United Typothetae of America, *Proceedings*, 1903, pp. 35-40; *Atlanta Constitution*, January 16, 1901; *American Pressman*, May 1903, p. 193.

9. *Typographical Journal*, May 1903, p. 461.

10. Elizabeth Faulkner Baker, *Printers and Technology* (New York: Columbia University Press, 1957), p. 129.

11. Evans, "History of the Organized Labor Movement in Georgia," p. 60.

12. Morris, "Labor Militancy in the Old South," p. 35; George Googe, AFL southern representative from 1928 to 1948, told the author that a mechanics' society had been formed in Savannah in 1742.

13. James V. Reese, "The Worker in Texas, 1821-1876," unpub. diss., University of Texas, 1964.

14. Harold Shapiro, "The Labor Movement in San Antonio, Texas," *Southwest Social Science Quarterly*, September 1955, p. 160.

15. Ruth Allen, *Chapters in the History of Organized Labor in Texas*, (Austin: University of Texas Press, 1941), p. 136.

16. Information on the IBEW from the national office.

17. *American Federationist*, March 1901.

18. Carpenters' and Joiners' International Union, *Convention Proceedings,* 1888 p. 12; 1898, p. 38.

19. Evans, "History of the Organized Labor Movement in Georgia," *passim.*

20. *New Orleans Tribune,* April 23, 1865.

21. Roger Shugg, "The New Orleans General Strike of 1892," *Louisiana Historical Quarterly,* April 1938.

22. *America Federationist,* August, September, and October 1901; December 1908; November 1928, p. 1347.

23. United Brotherhood of Carpenters and Joiners, *Convention Proceedings,* 1940, p. 87.

24. Sterling D. Spero and Abram L. Harris, *The Black Worker* (New York: Columbia University Press, 1931), pp. 66; Wesley, *Negro Labor in the United States,* p. 235.

25. Charles H. Wesley, *Negro Labor in the United States* (New York: Vanguard Press, 1927), p. 112.

CHAPTER IV

Railroad Workers and Longshoremen

1. "Transportation by Land," *Eleventh Census of the United States,* pt. 1, pp. 4-6.

2. C. Vann Woodward, *Origins of the New South* (Baton Rouge: Louisiana State University Press, 1951), pp. 120-22.

3. J. J. Thomas, *Fifty Years on the Rail* (New York: Knickerbocker Press, 1912).

4. *The Machinist* (special section), May 1, 1958.

5. See the original circular issued by the IAM's founders September 10, 1888, in Mark Perlman, *The Machinists* (Cambridge, Mass.: Harvard University Press, 1961).

6. *The Machinist,* May 1, 1958.

7. The writer is indebted to Professor Mark Perlman of the University of Pittsburgh for material on the early history of the machinists.

8. The Boilermakers' Union, *Proceedings of the Eighth Convention,* 1901, *passim; Proceedings of the Ninth Convention,* 1903, *passim.*

9. John R. Commons and Associates, *History of Labour in the United States* (New York: Macmillan Co., 1918), vol. 2, p. 66.

10. Mercer G. Evans, "History of the Organized Labor Movement in Georgia," unpub. diss., University of Chicago, 1929, p. 118.

11. Commission on Industrial Relations, *Reports and Testimony,* vol. 10, "Harriman Railroad System Strike," pp. 9699-10042, 64th Cong., 1st sess.

The material on the Illinois Central strike came from this source unless otherwise indicated.

12. Leo Wolman, *The Ebb and Flow in Trade Unionism* (New York: National Bureau of Economic Research, 1936), pp. 116, 118.

13. Evans, "History of the Organized Labor Movement in Georgia," p. 121.

14. AFL *Executive Council Minutes,* August 27-September 1, 1923, pp. 27, 31.

15. Samuel Gompers, *Report to the AFL Executive Council on Mob Violence in North Arkansas,* February 17, 1923.

16. Circular reproduced in *International Steam Engineer,* March 1923, p. 171.

17. Gompers, *Report to AFL Executive Council on Mob Violence in North Arkansas.*

18. Statement in *International Steam Engineer,* March 1923, p. 171.

19. Evans, "History of the Organized Labor Movement in Georgia," p. 31.

20. *Locomotive Firemen's Magazine,* August 1899, p. 203.

21. Sterling D. Spero and Abram L. Harris, *The Black Worker* (New York: Columbia University Press, 1931), p. 286.

22. *Locomotive Firemen's Magazine,* April 1901, p. 440; September 1902, pp. 426-432

23. L. J. Greene and C. G. Woodson, *The Negro Wage Earner* (Washington: Association for the Study of Negro Life and History, 1930), pp. 104-105.

24. Evans, "History of the Organized Labor Movement in Georgia," pp. 145, 146.

25. *Locomotive Firemen's Magazine,* April 1911, p. 519; May 1911, p. 15; Spero and Harris, *The Black Worker,* pp. 292, 293.

26. See Ray Marshall, *The Negro and Organized Labor* (New York: John Wiley & Sons, 1965), part III, for further discussion of this argument.

27. *Crisis,* June 1913, p. 63.

28. Spero and Harris, *The Black Worker,* p. 313.

29. The main groups engaged in storing and transporting cotton in New Orleans were: longshoremen who unloaded cotton from various conveyances onto the docks and loaded it aboard ship; draymen or teamsters; yardmen, who unloaded the cotton in the yards and moved it to cotton presses and warehouses; cotton classers who classified cotton according to various grades; scalehands who loaded and unloaded cotton at the scales; weighers, who weighed the cotton; pressmen, who operated the cotton presses; and the screwmen who stored the cotton aboard ship after it was brought to them by others. There were also workers who specialized in other jobs or commodities, such as banana handlers, freightcar unloaders, clerks and checkers or wharf clerks, sacksewers, and water boys. These groups were ultimately organized into separate unions.

30. Arthur R. Pearce, "The Rise and Decline of Labor in New Orleans," unpub. diss., Tulane University, 1938, p. 12.

31. Richard B. Morris, "Labor Militancy in the Old South," *Labor and Nation*, May-June 1948, pp. 33-34.

32. Pearce, "The Rise and Decline of Labor in New Orleans," pp. 13-17.

33. Roger W. Shugg, *Origins of the Class Struggle in Louisiana* (Baton Rouge: Louisiana State University Press, 1931) pp. 115, 301.

34. International Longshoremen's Association Local 1419, *Souvenir Program: New Building Dedication*, (New Orleans: Nathan J. King, 1959), p. 22.

35. Spero and Harris, *The Black Worker*, p. 183.

36. Herbert Northrup, "New Orleans Longshoremen," *Political Science Quarterly*, vol. LVII, 1942, p. 528.

37. Pearce, "The Rise and Decline of Labor in New Orleans," pp. 17-18.

38. All the other southern states combined acquired only 15 new locals during this period, and the only other states to acquire more locals than Louisiana were Ohio (38) Indiana (33) and Illinois (33). (AFL *Convention Proceedings*, 1892, "Secretary's Report," p. 18.)

39. Roger Wallace Shugg, "The New Orleans General Strike of 1892," *Louisiana Historical Quarterly*, vol. XXI (1938), p. 547.

40. U.S. Commissioner of Labor, *Tenth Annual Report*, 1894.

41. New Orleans *Times Democrat*, November 5-11, 1892.

42. Shugg, "The New Orleans General Strike of 1892," p. 559.

43. United Labor Council of New Orleans, *Directory*, 1894.

44. New Orleans *Picayune*, March 13, 1895.

45. Pearce, "The Rise and Decline of Labor in New Orleans," pp. 31-36, 43, 45.

46. *American Federationist*, November 1901, p. 489.

47. Northrup, "The New Orleans Longshoremen," p. 529.

48. Pearce, "The Rise and Decline of Labor in New Orleans," pp. 61-69.

49. Carrol George Miller, "A Study of the New Orleans Longshoremen's Unions from 1850 to 1862," unpub. diss., Louisiana State University, 1962, p. 23.

50. Screwmen's Benevolent Association, Galveston, Records, Manuscript Archives, University of Texas Library. The material on the GSBA is from these materials unless otherwise indicated.

51. Screwmen's Benevolent Association, *Minutes of the Meetings*, August 13, 1918.

52. *Galveston Daily News*, July 31, August 1, and August 2, 1877.

53. Maud Cuney Hare, *Norris Wright Cuney*, (New York: Crisis Publishing Co., 1913) pp. 42, 44.

54. Allen, *Chapters in the History of Organized Labor in Texas*, p. 173.

55. *Nation*, May 17, 1914, p. 515.

56. Spero and Harris, *The Black Worker*, pp. 183, 195, 196.

57. Pearce, "The Rise and Decline of Labor in New Orleans," p. 74.

58. Spero and Harris, *The Black Worker*, pp. 186, 190.

59. Northrup, "New Orleans Longshoremen," p. 533.

60. Northrup, "New Orleans Longshoremen," p. 532.

CHAPTER V

Coal Miners and Textile Workers

1. H. H. Chapman *et al.*, *The Iron and Steel Industries of the South* (University, Alabama: University of Alabama Press, 1953), map 3.

2. Nashville *Daily American*, August 23, 1892, cited by C. Vann Woodward, *Origins of the New South* (Baton Rouge: Louisiana State University Press, 1951), p. 233.

3. For information on these strikes, see: U. S. Commissioner of Labor, "Strikes and Lockouts," *Tenth Annual Report*, 1894; John R. Commons and Associates, *History of Labour in the United States*, vol. II, pp. 486, 499; American Federation of Labor, *Convention Proceedings*, 1892, pp. 11, 12; Woodward, *Origins of the New South*, pp. 231-234; A. C. Hutson, Jr., "The Coal Miners' Insurrection of 1891 in Anderson County, Tennessee," in East Tennessee Historical Society's *Publications*, no. 7 (1935), pp. 105-115 and "The Overthrow of the Convict Lease System in Tennessee," no. 8 (1936), pp. 82-103.

4. Birmingham *Iron Age*, June 1, 1882; Birmingham *Age-Herald*, April 15, May 8, 22 and 29, 1894, cited by Holman Head, "The Development of the Labor Movement in Alabama before 1900," unpub. diss., University of Alabama, 1954, p. 104.

5. Chris Evans, *History of the United Mine Workers* (Indianapolis: United Mine Workers, 1919), vol. II, pp. 586-592.

6. Head, "The Development of the Labor Movement in Alabama before 1900," pp. 170, 230.

7. United Mine Workers, *Proceedings of the Twentieth Annual Convention*, 1909, pp. 65-67, 863-864, 873.

8. Sterling D. Spero and Abram L. Harris, *The Black Worker* (New York: Columbia University Press, 1931), p. 208.

9. Herbert Northrup, "The Negro and the United Mine Workers of America," *Southern Economic Journal*, April 1943, p. 314.

10. Milton A. Fies, "Industrial Alabama and the Negro," speech before the Alabama Mining Institute, October 1922, cited by Spero and Harris, *The Black Worker*, pp. 363-366.

11. United Mine Workers, *Proceedings of the Thirty-Second Constitutional Convention*, 1932.

12. United Mine Workers, *John L. Lewis and the International Union*

of United Mine Workers (Washington: The United Mine Workers, October 1952), p. 22.

13. E. E. Hunt, F. G. Tyron and J. H. Willits, *What the Coal Commission Found* (Baltimore: The Williams and Wilkins Co., 1925), pp. 233-34.

14. West Virginia is not in our definition of the south for other purposes, but we include it here because it is impossible to separate it from other southern fields, and it is generally regarded as southern in the industry.

15. Ruth A. Allen, *Chapters in the History of Organized Labor in Texas* (Austin: University of Texas Press, 1941), pp. 96, 99.

16. See: U. S. Senate, 63rd Cong., 2nd sess., Report on Investigations of Conditions in Paint Creek Coal Fields of West Virginia in Pursuance of S. Res. 37.

17. United Mine Workers, *Proceedings of the Thirty-seventh Constitutional Convention*, 1942, p. 419.

18. United Mine Workers, *Proceedings of the Thirty-second Constitutional Convention*, 1937, p. 108.

19. Appeal to AFL International Unions from West Virginia Federation of Labor, Charleston, West Virginia, Jan. 5, 1922.

20. United Mine Workers, *Proceedings of the Thirty-second Constitutional Convention*, 1932, p. 237.

21. United Mine Workers, *John L. Lewis and the United Mine Workers*, pp. 29-30.

22. Winthrop D. Lane, *Civil War in West Virginia* (New York: B. W. Huebsch, Inc., 1921); McAllester Coleman, *Men and Coal* (New York: Farrar and Rinehart, Inc., 1921), pp. 94-104.

23. Washington, D. C. *Post*, March 22, 1922.

24. Washington, D. C. *Star*, March 21, 1922.

25. United Mine Workers, *Proceedings of the Thirty-second Constitutional Convention*, 1932, p. 237.

26. AFL *Executive Council Minutes*, July 29-August 4, 1925.

27. United Mine Workers, *Proceedings of the Thirty-second Constitutional Convention*, 1932, Officers' Report, p. 41.

28. National War Labor Board, "Report on Wages and Related Problems in the Bituminous Coal Industry," (mimeographed), April 28, 1943, prepared by Waldo E. Fisher.

29. See especially the 1932 Convention debate.

30. United Mine Workers, *Proceedings of the Thirty-second Constitutional Convention*, 1932, pp. 126-127, 237; 1936, p. 126; 1942, p. 237; 1936, p. 131.

31. Bureau of Labor Statistics, Bulletin 898, pp. 8-9.

32. See Commons and Associates, *History of Labour*, vol. I, p. 544.

33. Ben F. Lemert, *The Cotton Textile Industry of the Southern Appalachian Piedmont* (Chapel Hill: University of North Carolina Press, 1933), p. 113.

34. Seymour L. Wolfbein, *The Decline of a Cotton Textile City* (New York: Columbia University Press, 1944), p. 75.

35. Marjorie A. Potwin, *Cotton Mill People of the Piedmont* (New York: Columbia University Press, 1927), pp. 30, 48.

36. *American Federationist,* February 1898, pp. 275-278.

37. AFL *Convention Proceedings,* 1898, p. 10.

38. Evans, "History of the Organized Labor Movement in Georgia," pp. 88-89.

39. Atlanta *Constitution,* July 17, 1896.

40. Evans, "History of the Organized Labor Movement in Georgia," pp. 39, 83-84, 86.

41. AFL *Convention Proceedings,* 1899, pp. 9, 50, 56, 65, and 147.

42. Robert Sidney Smith, *Mill on the Dan* (Durham, N. C.: Duke University Press, 1960), p. 51.

43. See *American Federationist,* May 1901, p. 167; July 1901, p. 244.

44. Smith, *Mill on the Dan,* p. 53.

45. Atlanta *Constitution,* March 29, April 8 and 9, May 21, 27 and August 7, and 28, 1902.

46. Evans, "History of the Organized Labor Movement in Georgia," pp. 87-88, 90.

47. Mitchell, *Textile Unionism and the South,* pp. 39-40: AFL *Executive Council Minutes,* June 7-24, 1919, p. 6; and Evans, "History of the Organized Labor Movement in Georgia," p. 90.

48. AFL *Executive Council Minutes,* August 22-30, 1920, pp. 2-4, 37, 54-56 and 57.

49. Mitchell, *Textile Unionism and the South,* p. 52.

50. Report of Edgar Wallace to Samuel Gompers and AFL Secretary-Treasurer Morrison, August 20, 1921.

51. *Southern Textile Bulletin,* August 25, 1921.

52. AFL *Executive Council Minutes,* November 14-19, 1921, pp. 42, 48; February 21-25, 1922, p. 20; June 10-25, 1922, p. 6.

53. *American Federationist,* March 1901, p. 86.

54. J. D. De Haan, *The Full-Fashioned Hosiery Industry in the U. S. A.* (The Hague: Mouton and Co., n.d.), p. 18.

CHAPTER VI

Agricultural and Lumber Workers

1. Broadus Mitchell, *The Rise of Cotton Mills in the South* (Baltimore: Johns Hopkins University Press, 1921), pp. 161, 171.

2. Rudolf Heberle, "The Mainsprings of Southern Urbanization," *The Urban South,* Rupert B. Vance and Nicholas Demerath, eds. (Chapel Hill: University of North Carolina Press, 1954), p. 10.

3. For a comparison of a Georgia mill with conditions in the north during the early industrialization of the south, see: Clare de Graffenried, "The Georgia Cracker in the Cotton Mill," *Century Magazine*, vol. XIX (1891), pp. 487-488; C. Vann Woodward, *Origins of the New South* (Baton Rouge: Louisiana State University Press, 1951), pp. 222-225.

4. Thomas D. Clark, "Imperfect Competition in the Southern Retail Trade After 1865," *Journal of Economic History*, December 1943, p. 40.

5. Woodward, *Origins of the New South*, ch. VII; Benjamin H. Hibbard, "Tenancy in the Southern States," *Quarterly Journal of Economics*, vol. XXVII (1913).

6. R. L. Hunt, *History of Farmer Movements in the Southwest, 1873-1925* (n. p., n.d.), p. 153.

7. "The Progress of Southern Education," *Annals* of the American Academy of Political and Social Science, September 1903, p. 310.

8. Solon J. Buck, *The Granger Movement* (Cambridge, Mass.: Harvard University Press, 1913); Hunt, *A History of Farmers Movements in the Southwest, 1873-1925;* C. W. Macune, "The Farmers' Alliance," essay written in 1920, University of Texas Library, Austin; Woodward, *Origins of the New South*, ch. VII.

9. Quoted by John R. Commons and Associates, *History of Labour in the United States* (New York: MacMillan Co., 1918), vol. II, pp. 491-492, 463.

10. Woodward, *Origins of the New South*, p. 203.

11. *Southern Mercury*, official organ of the Texas Alliance, May 5, 1892; May 11, 1893.

12. Woodward, *Origins of the New South*, p. 198.

13. Hunt, *A History of Farmer Movements in the Southwest*, p. 69.

14. Texas Federation of Labor, *Proceedings*, 1908, p. 24.

15. Fort Worth, Texas *Record*, February 17, 1905.

16. Report of the Joint Labor Legislative Board of Texas, 1905, p. 7; 1907, pp. 4, 6.

17. *Dallas Morning News*, August 9, 1906.

18. Texas Federation of Labor *Proceedings*, 1906, p. 13; 1913, p. 45; 1915, p. 4; 1917, pp. 3-4.

19. C. W. Woodman, Fort Worth, to T. C. Jennings January 21, 1911, in C. W. Woodman Letter Press, Labor Movement in Texas Mss., University of Texas Archives; *Fort Worth Union Banner*, April 25, 1914.

20. *Southern Mercury*, November 29, 1906.

21. Report of the Commissioner of Corporations on Cotton Exchanges, vol. III, pt. V, p. 321, cited by Woodward in *Origins of the New South*, p. 414.

22. See *The International Socialist Review*, 1910, pp. 622, 637; *The Rebel*, March, 23, 1911: a file of *The Rebel* is in the University of Texas library.

23. Oscar Ameringer, *If You Don't Weaken* (New York: Henry Holt, 1940), pp. 267, 269.

24. Grady McWhiney, "Louisiana Socialists in the Early Twentieth Century: A Study of Rustic Radicalism," *Journal of Southern History,* August 1954, pp. 262-267, 315.

25. Thomas A. Hickey, "The Land, Legally, Morally, Philosophically and Biblically Considered," pamphlet, n.d., Hallettsville, Texas.

26. U. S. Department of Labor, Bureau of Labor Statistics *Labor in the South,* Bulletin 898, p. 12.

27. A. Berglund, G. T. Starnes, and F. T. de Vyver, *Labor in the Industrial South* (Charlottesville: The University of Virginia, 1930; The Institute for Research in the Social Sciences), p. 54.

28. Vernon H. Jensen, *Lumber and Labor* (New York: Farrar and Rinehart, 1945), pp. 86-87.

29. Arthur Lee Emerson, "I Am Here for Labor," *International Socialist Review,* vol. XIII (1912-1913), p. 223: Covington Hall, "Labor Struggles in the Deep South" (MS), Howard Tilton Library, Tulane University.

30. *Saint Louis Lumberman,* September 15, 1911, p. 54.

31. New Orleans *Daily Picayune,* June 20, 1911.

32. *The Lumberjack* (official paper of the Brotherhood of Timber Workers), January 9, 1913, cited by Jack C. Wimberly, "Labor and Collective Bargaining in the Louisiana Lumber Industry," unpub. diss., Louisiana State University, 1960. The *Lumberjack* was edited by Covington Hall; the paper later became *The Voice of the People* after the BTW affiliated with the IWW, and was moved to Portland, Oregon in 1914.

33. Reproduced in *Saint Louis Lumberman,* August 15, 1911, p. 58; September 10, 1911, p. 54; September 1, 1911, p. 83; October 1, 1911.

34. Covington Hall, "Revolt of the Southern Timber Workers," *The International Socialist Review,* July 1912, pp. 51-52.

35. W. D. Haywood, *Bill Haywood's Book* (New York: International Publishers, 1929), pp. 241-242.

36. Hall, "Labor Struggles in the Deep South," pp. 136-138.

37. Phineas Eastman, "The Southern Negro and One Big Union," p. 891 and Covington Hall, "Negroes Against Whites," p. 349, in *International Socialist Review,* vol. XIII (1912-1913).

38. *Southern Lumberman,* February 22, 1913.

39. Covington Hall, "The Victory of the Lumberjacks," *International Socialist Review,* December 1912, p. 470.

40. *Southern Lumberman,* October 12, 1912; October 26, 1912, p. 27; November 9, 1912.

41. *The Voice of the People,* January 1, 1914; November 23, 1912, p. 29.

42. *Southern Lumberman,* February 22, 1913; March 15, 1913, p. 28.

43. Letter reproduced in *Southern Lumberman,* March 1, 1913.

44. Letter from Covington Hall to New Orleans *Daily News,* February 1913, p. 36.

45. *Southern Lumberman,* March 15, 1913.

46. Bogalusa, Louisiana, *Enterprise and American,* May 9 and 16, 1918; September 9, 1919; November 27, 1919.

CHAPTER VII

Revolt of the Textile Workers

1. U. S. Department of Labor, Bureau of Labor Statistics, Bulletin 898, *Labor in the South*, pp. 5-9.

2. Oliver Carlson, "Southern Labor Awakes," *Current History*, November 1934, p. 155.

3. Broadus and George S. Mitchell, *The Industrial Revolution in the South* (Baltimore: Johns Hopkins University Press, 1930), p. 168.

4. U. S. Senate, *Working Conditions in the Textile Industry in North Carolina, South Carolina and Tennessee*, Report of Committee on Manufactures, 71st Cong., 1st Sess., S. Rep. 28 (Washington: U. S. Government Printing Office, 1930), vol. A, part 2, pp. 4-5.

5. Carlson, "Southern Labor Awakes," p. 155.

6. Leo Wolman, *Ebb and Flow of Trade Unionism* (New York: National Bureau of Economic Research, 1936), p. 34.

7. *American Federationist*, November 1928, pp. 1326, 1378.

8. U. S. Department of Labor, Bureau of Labor Statistics, "Strikes in the U. S., 1880-1936," (Washington: U. S. Government Printing Office, 1937); Bulletin 651.

9. AFL *Executive Council Minutes*, October 1925, p. 20; April 24-May 2, 1928, pp. 20-22; July 31-August 7, 1928, pp. 62-63; April 24-May 2, 1928, p. 87.

10. AFL *Convention Proceedings*, 1928, Resolution 18.

11. AFL *Executive Council Minutes*, February 18-25, 1929, pp. 45, 46.

12. Cleveland Cloth Mills, *Minutes of Stockholders Meeting*, June 1, 1930-January 16, 1934, cited by William Geer in unpublished paper presented to the Annual Meeting of the Southern Historical Association, Tulsa, Oklahoma, 1960.

13. Broadus Mitchell, "The Present Situation in the Southern Textile Industry," *Harvard Business Review*, April 1930, p. 302.

14. Letter from UTW to William Green reproduced in AFL *Executive Council Minutes*, February 18-25, 1929, pp. 65-66.

15. *American Federationist*, May 1929, p. 546.

16. Tom Tippett, *When Southern Labor Stirs* (New York: Jonathan Cape and Harrison Smith, 1931), p. 63.

17. *American Federationist*, June 1929, p. 662.

18. George Fort Milton, "The South Fights the Unions," *New Republic*, July 10, 1929.

19. *Labor*, June 8, 1929.

20. *American Federationist*, June 1929.

21. AFL *Executive Council Minutes*, August 8-20, 1929, p. 73.

22. Tippett, *When Southern Labor Stirs*, p. 71.

23. Kenneth Meiklejohn and Peter Nehemkis, *Southern Labor in Revolt* (New York and Philadelphia: The Intercollegiate Student Council for Industrial Democracy, 1930), p. 18.

24. *Labor,* March 15, 1930.

25. William Z. Foster, *American Trade Unionism* (New York: International Publishers, 1947), pp. 177-178.

26. B. U. Ratchford, "Economic Aspects of the Gastonia Situation," *Social Forces,* March 1930, p. 359.

27. William F. Dunne, *Gastonia, Citadel of the Class Struggle in the New South* (New York: Workers Library, for the National Textile Workers Union, 1929), p. 19.

28. Albert Weisbord, "Passaic—New Bedford—North Carolina," *Communist,* June 1929, p. 319.

29. Fred E. Beal, *Proletarian Journey* (New York: Hillman-Curl, Inc., 1937), pp. 156, 159-160.

30. Reproduced by Tippett, *When Southern Labor Stirs,* p. 81-88, 89.

31. *Gastonia Gazette,* April 4, 1929; April 10, 1929.

32. Letter to Governor Max Gardner from the strike committee, May 16, 1929, reproduced by Dunne, *Gastonia,* p. 40.

33. Reproduced by Tippett, *When Southern Labor Stirs,* pp. 92-93.

34. Quoted by Paul Blanshard, "Communism in Southern Cotton Mills," *Nation,* April 24, 1929.

35. Beal, *Proletarian Journey,* p. 120.

36. Blanshard, "Communism in Southern Cotton Mills."

37. Dunn, *Gastonia,* p. 27.

38. Beal, *Proletarian Journey,* p. 140.

39. Cyril Briggs, "The Negro Question in the Southern Textile Strikes," *Communist,* June 1929, pp. 324, 327.

40. Briggs, "Our Negro Work," *Communist,* September 1929, p. 494.

41. "Draft Resolution on the Negro Question," *Communist,* February 1931, pp. 156-158.

42. *New York Times,* April 7, 1929.

43. *Gastonia Gazette,* June 10, 1929.

44. *New York Times,* August 3, 1929; "Justice in North Carolina," *Nation,* August 14, 1929.

45. "Justice in North Carolina."

46. American Civil Liberties Union, *Justice—North Carolina Style* (New York: American Civil Liberties Union, May 1930).

47. Tippett, *When Southern Labor Stirs,* p. 104.

48. American Civil Liberties Union, *Justice—North Carolina Style,* p. 6.

49. Nell Battle Lewis, "Anarchy vs. Communism in Gastonia," *Nation,* September 24, 1929, p. 595; Margaret Larkin, "Ella May's Songs," *Nation,* October 9, 1929.

50. Weimar Jones, "Southern Labor and the Law," *Nation,* July 2, 1930.

51. "The Gastonia Strikers Case," *Harvard Law Review,* May 1931, p. 1124.

52. Samuel Yellen, *American Labor Struggles* (New York: Harcourt Brace and Co., 1936), pp. 314-315.

53. *Time*, October 30, 1939, p. 11.

54. "Communism in the Southern Cotton Mills," *Nation*, April 24, 1929.

55. Charles A. Gulick, Jr., "Industrial Relations in Southern Textile Mills," *Quarterly Journal of Economics*, August 1932, p. 236.

56. Tippett, *When Southern Labor Stirs*, p. 171.

57. *Advance*, October 25, 1929.

58. Harriet S. Herring, "The Southern Mill System Faces a New Issue," *Social Forces*, March 1930, p. 350.

59. Benjamin Stolberg, "Madness in Marion," *Nation*, October 23, 1929, p. 462.

60. Letter to William Green from Thomas F. McMahon, August 15, 1929; reproduced in AFL *Executive Council Minutes*, August 8-20, 1929, pp. 120-121.

61. Tippett, *When Southern Labor Stirs*, pp. 119-120.

62. American Civil Liberties Union, *Justice—North Carolina Style*, pp. 12-13.

63. Louis Stark, "The Trial at Marion, North Carolina," *American Federationist*, January 1930, p. 42.

64. Stolberg, "Madness in Marion," p. 464.

65. Tippett, *When Southern Labor Stirs*, pp. 136-138.

66. For summaries of the legal aspects of these cases, see Weimer Jones, "Southern Labor and the Law," *Nation*, July 2, 1930, and American Civil Liberties Union, *Justice—North Carolina Style*.

67. Yellen, *American Labor Struggles*, p. 320.

68. *Labor*, May 27, 1930.

69. Tippett, *When Southern Labor Stirs*, pp. 163-165

70. BLS Bulletin 651, "Strikes in the U. S. 1880-1936."

71. Louis Stark, "The Meaning of the Textile Strike," *New Republic*, May 8, 1929, p. 323.

72. *American Federationist*, June 1929, p. 797; *Labor*, July 20, 1929.

73. Paul Blanshard, "One Hundred Per Cent Americans on Strike," *Nation*, May 8, 1929.

74. Powell Patterson, "Organizational Possibilities in South Carolina," *American Federationist*, June 1929, pp. 673-674.

CHAPTER VIII

The 1930 AFL Organizing Campaign

1. Letter to William Green from Norman Thomas, August 14, 1929.

2. A. J. Muste, "AFL's Biggest Task," *Labor Age*, October 1929.

3. AFL *Executive Council Minutes*, August 8-20, 1929, p. 73; October 6, 12, 18, 1929.

4. AFL *Convention Proceedings*, 1929, pp. 265-283.

5. AFL *Executive Minutes*, October 6, 12, 18, 1929.

6. *American Federationist*, Editorial, p. 145, February 1930: see also *New York Times*, January 7, 1930.

7. AFL, *Southern Workers Handbook*, 1930.

8. *Jackson Daily News*, April 4, 1930.

9. Geoffery Brown, "The New Trade-Unionism," *American Federationist*, May 1930, p. 542; and "What the Union Offers the South," p. 1068.

10. "Labor's Message to the South," pamphlet, p. 16, cited by Jean Carol Trepp, "Union-Management Cooperation in the Southern Organizing Campaign," *Journal of Political Economy*, October 1933, pp. 617-619.

11. Louis Lorwin, *The American Federation of Labor* (Washington: Brookings Institution, 1933), note 22, p. 256 reports 10,340 members in May, while F. J. Gorman, in a letter to G. T. Schwenning, dated May 8, 1931, reported about 30 locals and approximately 25,000 members during the campaign, but pointed out that not all of them paid dues. (G. T. Schwenning, "Prospects of Southern Textile Unionism," *Journal of Political Economy*, December, 1931, p. 875).

12. Letter from Thomas F. McMahon to William Green, January 15, 1931.

13. Cited by Lorwin, *The American Federation of Labor*, note 22, p. 256.

14. Tom Tippett, *When Southern Labor Stirs* (New York: Jonathan Cape & Harrison Smith, 1931) ch. IX, presents a complete account of the activities at these places, especially at the Cone Mills.

15. George S., and Broadus Mitchell, *The Industrial Revolution in the South* (Baltimore: Johns Hopkins University Press, 1930), pp. 150-151.

16. Robert S. Smith, *Mill on the Dan* (Durham, Duke University Press, 1960) ch. 5, for a description of this welfare system; pp. 266, 295.

17. *American Federationist*, May 1930, p. 411.

18. Duane McCracken, *Strike Injunctions in the New South* (Chapel Hill: University of North Carolina Press, 1931) pp. 248-253.

19. Tippett, *When Southern Labor Stirs*, p. 225.

20. AFL *Convention Proceedings*, 1930, pp. 334-335.

21. Louis Adamic, "Virginians on Strike," *New Republic*, December 24, 1930, p. 164.

22. Smith, *Mill on the Dan*, p. 318.

23. Tippett, *When Southern Labor Stirs*, p. 232.

24. Letter to William Green from Thomas F. McMahon, January 15, 1931.

25. AFL *Executive Council Minutes*, January 13-23, 1931, p. 21.

26. Letter to William Green from Thomas F. McMahon, October 1, 1930.

27. Tippett, *When Southern Labor Stirs*, pp. 250-251.

28. These reports are in the Industrial Relations Library at Harvard University.

29. Letter to William Green from Matilda Lindsey, January 16, 1931.

30. Letter to Green from O. E. Woodbury, January 17, 1931.

31. AFL *Executive Council Minutes,* January 13-23, 1931.

32. Report by E. F. McGrady on Southern Organizing Campaign, to AFL Executive Council, January, 1931, in *Executive Council Minutes,* January 13-23, 1931.

33. Danville *Bee,* January 29, February 1, 1930; Smith, *Mill on the Dan,* p. 223; and Tippett, *When Southern Labor Stirs,* pp. 267-269.

34. Quoted by Smith, *River on the Dan,* p. 223.

35. In 1931-1932 the AFL was forced to lay off part of its staff and put those remaining on a four-day week; William Green and Secretary-Treasurer Frank Morrison took a one-third reduction in salary. In 1932 every AFL employee was furloughed except George Googe, who was busy organizing government employees in the south after the Federation of Federal Employees withdrew from the AFL in order to save per capita payments and because they felt they were white-collar workers and not laborers. The federal employees affiliated with the AFL later were organized into the American Federation of Government Employees. (AFL *Executive Council Minutes,* February 2-12, 1932, p. 58-70, 71; July 12-22, 1932, pp. 50-54, 70, 71; October 18-27, 1932, pp. 26, 47; and personal interview George Googe, April 11, 1959). In the 13 months and 20 days before October 20, 1932, the AFL lost 454,615 members. (AFL *Executive Council Minutes,* October 18-27, 1932). Between August, 1931 and August, 1932, AFL receipts fell from $569,105.82 to $466,350.18 and expenditures went from $561,985.13 to $468,747.28. (AFL *Executive Council Minutes,* October 18-27, 1932.)

36. Cited by Oliver Carlson, "Why Textiles Vote to Strike," *New Republic,* September 5, 1934, p. 159.

37. Lorwin, *The American Federation of Labor,* p. 258.

38. Quoted from *Twenty-second Annual Report of the Riverside and Dan River Cotton Mills, Inc.,* 1931, by Smith, *Mill on the Dan,* p. 238.

39. H. M. Douty, "Labor Unrest in North Carolina, 1932," *Social Forces,* May 1933, pp. 579, 585-586.

CHAPTER IX

Coal Mining

1. U.S. Senate, 76th Cong., 1st sess., *Violations of Free Speech and Rights of Labor,* Rept. 6, part 2, "Private Police Systems, Harlan County, Kentucky," 1939, p. 11. This report and others based on hearings and reports by a subcommittee of the U. S. Senate Committee on Education and Labor headed by Senator Robert M. La Follette will be referred to hereafter as the La Follette Committee Hearings.

2. UMW *Convention Proceedings,* 1930, *passim.*

3. American Civil Liberties Union, *The Kentucky Miners Struggle* (New York: American Civil Liberties Union, May 1932), pp. 3, 17.

4. Cited by La Follette Committee Report, p. 13.

5. Oakley Johnson, "Starvation of the 'Reds' in Kentucky," *Nation,* February 8, 1932, p. 141.

6. Jack Stachel, "Lessons of Two Recent Strikes," *The Communist,* June 1932.

7. *Nation,* March 2, 1932.

8. McAllister Coleman, *Men and Coal* (New York: Farrar and Rhinehart, 1943), p. 139.

9. UMW *Convention Proceedings,* 1932, p. 173; 1936, pp. 114, 423.

10. *Birmingham News,* July 23, 1933.

11. UMW *Convention Proceedings,* 1940, p. 62.

12. Republic Steel Corporation, Southern District, Birmingham, Alabama, Sayreton Coal Mines, *Plan of Employees Representation,* June 1933, p. 7.

13. Letter to TCI Employees from H. C. Ryding June 15, 1933.

14. UMW *Convention Proceedings,* 1936, p. 136; 1942, p. 237.

15. Copy in Roosevelt Papers, quoted by Arthur M. Schlesinger, Jr., *The Coming of the New Deal* (Boston: Houghton Mifflin Co., 1959), p. 139.

16. The Secret Diary of Harold L. Ickes, *The First Thousand Days* (New York: Simon and Schuster, 1953), pp. 24, 30, 35.

17. UMW *Convention Proceedings,* 1930, pp. 448-449.

18. Morton S. Baratz, *The Union and the Coal Industry* (New Haven: Yale University Press, 1955), p. 9.

19. UMW *Convention Proceedings,* 1936, p. 20; 1934, p. 32.

20. *Birmingham News,* June 5, 1933 and personal interview with William Mitch, January 20, 1960.

21. *Birmingham News,* July 23, 1933.

22. UMW *Convention Proceedings,* 1942, p. 469.

23. *Birmingham Age-Herald,* February 26, 1934; *Birmingham Post,* February 27, 1934.

24. *Birmingham News,* March 13, 1934; March 19, 1934.

25. *United Mine Workers Journal,* April 1934, carries the story of the settlement.

26. *Birmingham Age-Herald,* April 9, 1934.

27. *United Mine Workers Journal,* October 1, 1938.

28. La Follette Committee Report, "Armed Guards—West Point Mfg. Co., 1934," p. 43.

29. *Birmingham News,* April 2, 1934; November 22, 1934.

30. *Birmingham Post,* December 20, 1934; October 28, 1935.

31. Letter, *Birmingham Post,* October 28, 1935.

32. *Union News,* Jasper, Walker County, Alabama, December 6, 1934; 1938, p. 279.

33. Walter Galenson, *The CIO Challenge to the AFL* (Cambridge, Mass.: Harvard University Press, 1960), p. 203.

34. An account of this trial can be found in the Knoxville, Tenn. *News-Sentinal,* October 1937-May 1938.

35. UMW *Convention Proceedings,* 1940, p. 345.

36. *Birmingham News,* April 8, 1934.

37. Statement by the Alabama Coal Operators, April 6, 1934.

38. *Birmingham News, Birmingham Age-Herald,* April 18, 1934.

39. *Birmingham Age-Herald,* April 13, 1934.

40. UMW, *John L. Lewis and the International Union of United Mine Workers of America* (Washington: The United Mine Workers, October 1952), pp. 56-57.

41. UMW, *John L. Lewis and the International Union United Mine Workers of America,* p. 134.

42. Baratz, *The Union and the Coal Industry,* pp. 159-160.

43. UMW *Convention Proceedings,* 1934, p. 372.

44. George S. Mitchell and Horace R. Cayton, *Black Workers and the New Unions* (Chapel Hill: University of North Carolina Press, 1939) p. 323.

45. George S. Mitchell, "The Negro in Southern Trade Unionism," *Southern Economic Journal,* 1936, p. 26.

46. *Birmingham Age-Herald,* May 2, 1934.

47. Pamphlet issued during 1936 by John Altman.

48. *The Union News* (Jasper, Alabama), May 21, 1936.

49. UMW *Convention Proceedings,* 1936, p. 126.

50. *United Mine Workers Journal,* January 15, 1938.

51. UMW *Convention Proceedings,* 1940, p. 62.

CHAPTER X

Communists, Socialists, and Sharecroppers

1. The technical difference between a tenant and a sharecropper is that the tenant rents the use of land, furnishes his own capital and manages his own affairs, while the sharecropper pays part of the crop to the landlord, who furnishes capital (including food and clothing for him and his family) and assumes control of the work routine; the cropper, in short, furnishes little other than his own labor and that of his family.

2. Calvin B. Hoover and B. U. Ratchford, *Economic Resources and Policies of the South* (New York: Macmillan Co., 1951), pp. 107, 108.

3. Louis J. Ducoff, *Wages of Agricultural Labor in the United States* (Washington: U.S. Bureau of Labor Statistics, 1945, p. 77).

4. Oren Stephens, "Revolt on the Delta," *Harpers Magazine,* November 1941, p. 664.

5. Gunner Myrdal, *An American Dilemma* (New York: Harpers, 1944, p. 257.

6. National Emergency Council, *Report on Economic Conditions of the South* (Washington: U.S. Govt. Printing Office, 1938), pp. 1, 46.

7. Wilson Record, *The Negro and the Communist Party* (Chapel Hill: University of North Carolina Press, 1951).

8. John Beecher, "The Share Croppers' Union in Alabama," *Social Forces*, October 1934, p. 64.

9. See, also: John Pittman, "A Perspective for Furthering Negro-White Unity," *Communist*, January 1944; Harry Haywood, "The Struggle for the Leninist Position on the Negro Question in the U.S.A.," *Communist*, September 1933, p. 888; "The Scottsboro Struggle and the Next Steps; Resolution of the Political Bureau," *Communist*, June 1933.

10. J. S. Allen, *The American Negro* (New York: International Publishers, 1932), p. 5.

11. Beecher, "The Share Croppers' Union in Alabama," p. 124.

12. "Resolution on the Negro Question," *Communist*, February 1931, p. 153.

13. Record, *The Negro and the Communist Party*, p. 89.

14. *Southern Farm Leader*, February 1937.

15. Stuart Jamieson, *Labor Unionism in American Agriculture* (Washington: U.S. Dept. of Labor, Bureau of Labor Statistics, 1945), p. 29.

16. *Communist*, May 1933, p. 448.

17. Albert Jackson, "On the Alabama Front," *Nation*, September 18, 1935; Thomas Burke, "We Told Washington," *Nation*, December 4, 1934.

18. Jamieson, *Labor Unionism in American Agriculture*, pp. 297, 298, 300.

19. Personal interview, June 26, 1959.

20. Mimeographed form letter from William Backmann, Editor of the *Southern Farm Leader*, January 28, 1957.

21. The author is indebted to H. L. Mitchell for much of the following material on the STFU. Mr. Mitchell was kind enough to discuss the STFU at great length and to make material available on its activities. There are some general sources of information on the STFU including Jamieson, *Labor Unionism in American Agriculture;* Southern Tenant Farmers' Union, "History of S.T.F.U., S.T.F.U. Study Course" (Memphis, Tennessee: S.T.F.U., mimeographed, no date); STFU *Convention Proceedings;* Howard Kester, *Revolt Among the Sharecroppers* (New York: Covici-Friede, 1935); and a mimeographed oral history by H. L. Mitchell for the Columbia University Oral History Project, 1956 and 1957.

22. Arthur M. Schlesinger, Jr., *The Coming of the New Deal* (Boston: Houghton Mifflin Co., 1959), p. 77.

23. Gordon W. Blackwell, "The Displaced Tenant Family in North Carolina," *Social Forces*, October 1934, p. 69; David L. Cohn, "Sharecroppers in the Delta," *Atlantic Monthly*, June 1937, p. 579; Paul S. Taylor, "Power

Farming and Labor Displacement in the Cotton Belt," *Monthly Labor Review*, March-April 1938.

24. Field reports on STFU locals, September 23, 1936, in the author's possession.

25. Quoted by Schlesinger, *The Coming of the New Deal*, pp. 79, 80-83, 374-376.

26. STFU, *Proceedings of the Fifth Annual Convention*, 1939 (mimeographed), p. 4.

27. *Time*, March 20, 1939.

28. H. L. Mitchell, "The Cropper Learns his Fate," *Nation*, September 14, 1935.

29. AFL *Executive Council Minutes*, January 1936, p. 61.

30. See H. L. Mitchell's description of the strike in the STFU, *Proceedings of the Third Annual Convention*, 1937, pp. 57-60.

31. STFU, *Proceedings of the Sixth Annual Convention*, January 5-7, 1940, p. 4.

32. AFL *Executive Council Minutes*, September 30 to October 10, 1940.

CHAPTER XI

Textile and Clothing Workers

1. Mathew Josephson, *Sidney Hillman* (Garden City: Doubleday & Co., Inc., 1952), pp. 372-373.

2. A. Kendrick, "Alabama Goes on Strike," *Nation*, August 29, 1934, p. 233.

3. Herbert J. Lahne, *The Cotton Mill Worker* (New York: Farrar and Rinehart, 1944), p. 226.

4. H. M. Douty, "Development of Trade-Unionism in the South," in *Labor in the South*, Bureau of Labor Statistics Bulletin No. 898, 1946, p. 168.

5. *Time*, September 17, 1934, p. 13.

6. Personal interviews with George Googe, April 1959; Benjamin Stolberg, "Buzz Windrip—Governor of Georgia," *Nation*, March 4, 1936, p. 270; March 11, 1936; and Edward Levinson, *I Break Strikes* (New York: Harper & Bros., 1935).

7. AFL, *Executive Council Minutes*, September 28-October 14, 1934, pp. 71-72.

8. Douty, "The Development of Trade-Unionism," p. 169.

9. Lucy Randolph Mason, *To Win These Rights* (New York: Harper & Bros., 1952) p. 19; See also Joseph J. King, "The Durham Central Labor Union," *Southern Economic Journal*, July 1938.

10. Edward Levinson, *Labor on the March* (New York: Harper & Bros., 1938), p. 240.

11. *Gulf Coast Oil Worker,* April 17, 1937.

12. Textile Workers Union of America, *Proceedings of the First Constitutional Convention,* 1939, p. 29.

13. ACWA, *Documentary History,* 1936-1938, p. 58.

14. *Advance,* April 1937, p. 4.

15. ACWA, *Documentary History,* 1936-1938, pp. 57-60.

16. *Advance,* August 1937.

17. ACWA, *Documentary History,* 1936-1938, p. 59.

18. Walter Galenson, *The CIO Challenge to the AFL: A History of the American Labor Movement, 1935-1941* (Cambridge, Mass.: Harvard University Press, 1960), pp. 339, 341.

19. *Textile World,* April 1939, p. 64, cited by Galenson, *The CIO Challenge to the AFL,* p. 341.

20. Lahne, *The Cotton Mill Worker,* p. 273.

21. UTW, *Special Convention Proceedings,* May 8-10, 1939.

22. Statement by George Googe in the UTW *Special Convention Proceedings,* May 8-10, 1939, pp. 33-34; pp. 22, 25.

23. Lahne, *The Cotton Mill Worker,* p. 275.

24. UTW, *Special Convention Proceedings,* 1941, pp. 28, 43, 44.

25. TWUA, *Convention Proceedings,* 1941, pp. 25, 37, 42-43, 45.

26. ACWA, *Proceedings of the Tenth Biennial Convention,* 1934, p. 59.

27. Galenson, *The CIO Challenge to the AFL,* p. 284.

28. ACWA, *Proceedings of the Tenth Biennial Convention,* 1934, pp. 96, 97.

29. ACWA, *Documentary History,* 1934-1936, pp. 44, 45.

30. *Advance,* December 1935.

31. ACWA, *Documentary History,* 1934-1936, pp. 45, 46.

32. Bertha Daniel, "The Epic of La Follette, Tennessee," *Advance,* March 1937, p. 13.

33. *Advance,* March 1937; ACWA, *Documentary History,* 1936-1938, p. 125.

34. *Advance,* April 1937; May 1937; April 1938; May 1937; June 1937, p. 4.

35. ACWA, *Documentary History,* 1936-1938, p. 21.

36. *Advance,* July 1937.

37. ACWA, *Documentary History,* 1936-1938, p. 129.

38. *Advance,* May 1940, p. 26, and ACWA, *Documentary History,* 1938-1940, pp. 41-42.

39. *Advance,* July 1937.

40. ACWA, *Documentary History,* 1938-1940, p. 152.

41. *Advance,* March 1941, p. 11; April 1941, p. 4; January 1, 1942, p. 5.

42. ACWA, *Documentary History,* 1938-1940, p. 76.

43. *Gulf Coast Oil Worker,* April 17, 1937.

44. UGW, *Proceedings of the Twenty-first Convention,* 1927, pp. 9-13.

45. UGW, *Proceedings of the Twenty-second Convention,* 1937, p. 176.

CHAPTER XII

Growth of CIO Unions

1. "Employment in Manufactures," *Labor in the South,* BLS Bulletin 898, pp, 29-31.

2. Horace Cayton and George S. Mitchell, *Black Workers and the New Unions* (Chapel Hill: University of North Carolina Press, 1939), pp. 308, 338-339.

3. George S. Mitchell, "The Negro in Southern Trade Unionism," *Southern Economic Journal,* January 1936, p. 26.

4. Quoted by Lucy R. Mason, *To Win These Rights* (New York: Harper & Bros., 1952), p. 133.

5. *Black Workers and the New Unions,* p. 328.

6. Walter Galenson, *The CIO Challenge to the AFL: A History of the American Labor Movement, 1935-1941* (Cambridge, Mass.: Harvard University Press, 1960).

7. Birmingham *Age-Herald,* July 3, 1936; July 26, 1936.

8. Birmingham *Post,* October 26, 1936.

9. Birmingham *News,* November 6, 1936; July 29, 1936; August 20, 1936; March 18, 1937.

10. Galenson, *The CIO Challenge to the AFL,* p. 116.

11. SWOC, *First Wage and Policy Convention Proceedings,* December 1937.

12. Galenson, *The CIO Challenge to the AFL,* pp. 100-101.

13. SWOC, First Wage and Policy Convention, 1937, "Report of the Regional Director, Southern Region."

14. Glen W. Gilman and James W. Sweeney, *Atlantic Steel Company and United Steelworkers of America* (Washington: National Planning Association. The NPA Committee on the Causes of Industrial Peace Under Collective Bargaining, 1953), Case Study Number 12, p. 17.

15. SWOC, *Proceedings of the Second International Wage and Policy Convention,* May 14, 15, 16, 17, 1940, Chicago, p. 43.

16. Mason, *To Win These Rights,* p. 21.

17. Personal interview, R. E. Farr, Birmingham director (District 36), United Steelworkers of America, January 22, 1960.

18. *Fortune,* June 1942, pp. 157-158.

19. Harold S. Roberts, *The Rubber Workers* (New York: Harper and Brothers, 1944), pp. 356-357.

20. U. S. Senate, Subcommittee of the Committee on Labor and Education (La Follette Committee), 74th Cong., 2nd sess., Hearings, part 8, pp. 2939, 2954.

21. John Newton Thurber, *Rubber Workers' History* (Akron: United Rubber Workers, Public Relations Department, 1955), p. 16; the *United Rubber Worker*, July 1936, p. 2.

22. Birmingham *Post*, May 27, 1937.

23. Quoted by Hilton Butler, "Charley's Story Paints Labor Picture at Gadsden's Great Industries," Birmingham *Post*, May 26, 1937.

24. Butler, "Charley's Story."

25. Birmingham *News*, July 28, 1936.

26. Steel Workers Organizing Committee, *Reports of Officers to the Wage and Policy Convention*, Pittsburgh, December 14, 15, 16, 1937, p. 185.

27. Thurber, *Rubber Workers' History*, p. 22; Gadsden *Times*, February 18, 1941; *United Rubber Worker*, August 1941.

28. Roberts, *The Rubber Workers*, pp. 341; 385-386.

29. Mason, *To Win These Rights*, pp. 106-107.

30. Memphis *Press-Scimetar*, September 30, 1940; August 30, 1941.

31. Memphis *Commercial Appeal*, December 24, 1940.

32. Thurber, *Rubber Workers' History*, p. 25.

33. NLRB Release R-4469, May 9, 1941.

34. Roberts, *The Rubber Workers*, p. 401.

35. In the Matter of Ford Motor Company, Cases Nos. C-1554 to C-1558, inclusive, August 8, 1940.

36. R. J. Thomas, "Report to the Special UAW Convention," 1939, p. 33.

37. Personal interview, April 10 and 11, 1959.

38. Mason, *To Win These Rights*, p. 36.

39. UAW, *Proceedings of the 1941 Convention*, pp. 11-23.

40. Heywood Broun's original article reproduced in American Newspaper Guild's *Guild Reporter*, December 26, 1958.

41. Abraham Weiss, "Collective Bargaining by the American Newspaper Guild," *Monthly Labor Review*, April, 1940.

42. *Guild Reporter*, November 23, 1933; December 8, 1933; January 12, 1934; May 1934.

43. Letter to the author from Robert W. Christofferson, Associate Director, Research and Information, ANG, December 29, 1964.

44. *Guild Reporter*, June 1, 1939; June 13, 1939.

45. Flyer, issued by the Monroe Newspaper Guild, December 17, 1940.

46. *Guild Reporter*, June 1, 1941; September 15, 1941; January 1, 1942.

47. All estimates of oil workers' membership were calculated from OWIU *Convention Proceedings* for various years.

48. OWIU *Convention Proceedings* for various years.

49. Harvey O'Conner, *History of Oil Workers International Union-CIO* (Denver: Oil Workers International Union, 1950), p. 306.

50. Information from field interviews, Beaumont and Port Arthur, Texas, 1959-1960.

51. *Gulf Coast Oil Worker,* March 20, 1937; April 16, 1937; April 17, 1937.

52. Ruth A. Allen, *Chapters in the History of Organized Labor in Texas* (Austin: University of Texas Press, 1941), p. 237.

53. Galenson, *The CIO Challenge to the AFL,* p. 421.

54. From OWIU Auditor's Reports to various conventions.

55. O'Conner, *History of the Oil Workers,* p. 377.

56. Annual Report of the Executive Council, 1939, p. 4.

57. OWIU, *Proceedings of the Tenth National Convention,* 1939, pp. 69, 83, 90.

58. OWIU, *Proceedings of the Eleventh National Convention,* 1940, pp. 4, 17.

59. Henrietta Larsen and Kenneth Wiggens Porter, *History of Humble Oil and Refining Company* (New York: Harper and Bros., 1959).

60. OWIU, Report of O. A. Knight, *Proceedings of the Eleventh National Convention,* 1941, pp. 1-6, 605.

61. Clarence J. Hicks, *My Life in Industrial Relations* (New York: Harper and Bros., 1941).

62. Esso Standard Oil Company, Employee Relations Research, *Patterns of the Past,* pp. 16, 17, 18, 33.

63. James Hubert Dumesnil, "Labor-Management Relations at the Esso Standard Oil Company (Louisiana Division) 1919-1953," unpub. diss., Louisiana State University, 1954, pp. 61, 81.

CHAPTER XIII

Growth of AFL Unions

1. U.S. Department of Labor, Bureau of Labor Statistics, *Cargo Handling and Longshore Labor Conditions,* Bulletin 550, 1932, p. 88.

2. Robert C. Francis, "Longshoremen in New Orleans," *Opportunity,* March 1936, pp. 83-85.

3. See testimony of George Googe, AFL southern representative before the Senate Committee on Education and Labor, 76th Cong., 1st sess., "Hearings on the National Labor Relations Act and Proposed Amendments," part 7, May 22-24, 1939. Hereinafter referred to as "Hearings on the NLRA, 1939."

4. International Longshoremen's Association, *Proceedings of the Thirty-*

First Convention, 1935, Report of M. J. Dwyer, Vice-President, on South Atlantic and Gulf Coast District.

5. *In the Matter of the Aluminum Line,* 8 NLRB 1336 (1938).

6. For statistics on the relative importance of various southern ports, see *Report of the Maritime Labor Board* to the President and Congress, 1940, pp. 107-112.

7. Herbert R. Northrup, "The New Orleans Longshoremen," *Political Science Quarterly,* December 1942, p. 535.

8. Personal interview with George Googe, April 11, 1959.

9. Statement by President Joseph Ryan in the *Proceedings of the Thirty-first Convention,* 1935, p. 13.

10. ILA, *Proceedings of the Thirty-First Convention,* 1935, p. 13.

11. "Strike of Longshoremen on the Gulf Coast," *Monthly Labor Review,* February 1936, pp. 391-395.

12. New Orleans *Times Picayune,* October 23, 1935; La Follette Committee, "Armed Guards—Lake Charles, Louisiana, 1939," *Violations of Free Speech and Rights of Labor,* p. 108.

13. *International Oil Worker,* December 13, 1935.

14. Francis, "Longshoremen in New Orleans," p. 85.

15. *American Federationist,* March 1941, p. 20.

16. Personal interview, George Googe, April 11, 1959.

17. Birmingham (Alabama) *News,* October 14, 1938.

18. New Orleans *Times Picayune,* July 2, 1938.

19. NLRB "Proceedings," Cases Nos. XV-R-168, *et al.*; Northrup "The New Orleans Longshoremen," p. 539.

20. *Birmingham News,* October 14, 1938.

21. New Orleans *Times Picayune,* October 12, 1938.

22. Hearings on the NLRA, p. 1356.

23. U. S. Congress, House, 76th Cong., 3rd sess., *Report* of the Special Committee to investigate the National Labor Relations Board, H. R. 3109, part 1, 1939, p. 149; Northrup, "New Orleans Longshoremen," p. 540.

24. Personal interview with George Googe, April 11, 1959.

25. New Orleans *Times Picayune,* October 16, 1938; 9 NLRB 72; *The Progress* (New Orleans) October 21, 1938.

26. ILWU, *Proceedings of the 1939 Convention,* "Officers Report," p. 93.

27. Senate Waterfront Investigation.

28. See the testimony of George Googe in Report of the Special House Committee to Investigate the NLRB, cited in note 23.

29. U.S. Senate, 83rd Cong., 1st sess., Committee on Interstate and Foreign Commerce, Subcommittee on *Waterfront Investigation,* part 2, "New Orleans Waterfront," June 24, 25, and 26, 1953, p. 793.

30. See C. G. Miller, "The New Orleans Longshoremen."

31. Personal interview with Father Jerome A. Drolet, April 1964.

32. Leaflet from *The Labor Leader,* n.d., distributed by the RWDSU.

33. Leaflet, distributed during 1943 to Negro members of ILWU Local 207.

34. Letter to Philip Murray from Harry Bridges, June 17, 1943.

35. Letter to Father Jerome A. Drolet from Philip Murray, October 8, 1943.

36. New Orleans *Sentinel Informer*, January 22, 1944.

37. *Saturday Evening Post*, January 13, 1945.

38. *Report of the Maritime Labor Board*, p. 113.

39. ILA *Proceedings of the Thirty-second Convention*, 1939, p. 103.

40. *Report of the Maritime Labor Board*, p. 113.

41. Statement by George Googe in the 1939 ILA *Convention Proceedings*, p. 221.

42. IBPSW, President's Report to the Fourteenth Convention, 1931, pp. 12, 15.

43. *United Paper*, January 30, 1958, pp. 5, 6.

44. International Brotherhood of Paper Makers, *Proceedings of the Fifteenth Convention*, 1939, *passim*.

45. Personal interview, George Googe, April 12, 1959.

46. "Employment in Manufactures," *Labor in the South*, BLS Bulletin 898, pp. 30-31.

47. AFL *Executive Council Minutes*, July 31-August 7, 1928, pp. 32-33; February 18-25, 1929, pp. 13, 14, 62-65.

48. Personal interviews with George Googe, April 11, 1959 and R. J. Petree, Secretary-Treasurer, TWIU, June 25, 1959.

49. Herbert Northrup, "The Tobacco Workers International Union," *Quarterly Journal of Economics*, August 1942, pp. 615, 619.

50. Kentucky State Federation of Labor, *Convention Proceedings*, 1939, Secretary's Report, p. 13; 1940.

51. AFL *Executive Council Minutes*, May 13-21, 1940, p. 185.

52. "The Tobacco Workers International Union," p. 624.

53. *Union Agreements in the Tobacco Industry*, (Washington: 1945), BLS Bull. 847, pp. 1-2, 13-14.

54. George L. Googe, "A Report from Atlanta," *American Federationist*, January 1943. There is voluminous literature on the industrial relations experiences at TVA: D. E. Lilienthal, *TVA: Democracy on the March* (New York: Harper and Bros., 1944); M. M. Kampleman, "TVA Labor Relations: A Laboratory in Democratic Human Relations," *Minnesota Law Review*, April 1946, pp. 332-372; Judson King, TVA Labor Relations Policy at Work, Bulletin No. 192-A of the National Popular Government League: "Labor and the TVA Experiment," *Monthly Labor Review*, June 1934, p. 1277; U. S. Congress, Senate, *Report of the Joint Committee on Labor-Management Relations in TVA*, Report No. 372, 81st Cong., 1st sess. (Washington: U.S. Government Printing Office, 1949); Stanley Rounds, "Labor Relations with TVA," *American Federationist*, November 1936.

55. Personal interview, Vincent Morreale, General Counsel, Hod Carriers and Common Laborers, June 25, 1959.

56. Gordon Clapp, "Tennessee Valley Authority," *American Federationist,* March 1938.

57. Personal interview, George Googe, April 11, 1959.

58. *Teamwork* (official publication of the Tennessee Valley Trades and Labor Council) April 1952.

59. "TVA Goes to War," *American Federationist,* February 1943, p. 27.

60. Personal interview wtih George Googe, April 11, 1959.

61. *Teamwork,* January 1949.

62. Personal interview, Vincent Morreale, June 25, 1959.

63. *Teamwork,* January 1951.

64. AFL *Executive Council Minutes,* April, 1937; May, 1937.

65. AFL News Release, March 2, 1940.

66. Atlanta *Journal of Labor,* March 1, 1940.

67. *American Federationist,* April 1940.

68. Speech by William Green at Atlanta, Georgia, March 2, 1940, mimeographed.

CHAPTER XIV

World War II

1. U.S. Department of Labor, Bureau of Labor Statistics *Labor in the South* (Washington: U.S. Government Printing Office, 1946), pp. 27-29.

2. Broadus Mitchell, "The Broad Meaning of the CIO Organizing Drive in the South," *Labor and Nation,* April-May 1946, pp. 42-43. In addition, for effects of the war on the south's economy see: Julien Boyd, "The South and the Fight," *Atlantic Monthly,* February 1944, pp. 53-59; Elmer C. Bratt, and D. Stevens Wilson, "Regional Distortions Resulting from the War," *Survey of Current Business,* October 1943, p. 3; "Effect of Federal Policy in the South," *Monthly Labor Review,* September 1949, pp. 146-150; February 1951, pp. 106-123; Thomas A. Kelly, "World War II and the Southeastern Economy," Social Science Research Center, Mississippi State College, published in *Social Science Bulletin,* January-February 1951; H. C. Nixon, "The South After the War," *Virginia Quarterly Review,* Summer 1944, pp. 321-334; and U.S. Congress, Report of the Joint Committee on the Economic Report on the *Impact of Federal Policies on the Economy of the South,* 81st Cong., 1st Sess. (Washington: Supt. of Docs., 1949.)

3. Frederic Meyers, "Organization and Collective Bargaining in the Local Mass Tranportation Industry in the Southeast," *Southern Economic Journal,* April 1949, pp. 426-429.

4. George Googe, "Dixie Reporting," *American Federationist,* August 1943, pp. 25, 26.

5. George Googe, "Rolling Forward in Dixie," *American Federationist,* April 1946.

6. David Botter, "Labor Looks at Texas," *Southwest Review,* Spring 1946, p. 111.

7. *Dallas-Fort Worth CIO Progress,* Labor Day, 1943.

8. Letter, J. E. Crossland to Ruth A. Allen, March 28, 1944.

9. Allan L. Swimm, *One Out of Six* (pamphlet), July 1946.

10. United Rubber Workers, *Officers Report, Ninth Annual Convention,* 1944, pp. 29-31, 40-43.

11. H. M. Douty, "Development of Trade-Unionism in the South," in BLS, *Labor in the South,* p. 173.

12. R. J. Thomas, "Automobile Unionism," Report submitted to the 1944 United Automobile Workers Convention, pp. 26c, 30c.

13. Washington *Post,* April 20, 1942.

14. Letter to Texas employers from Porter A. Whaley, Executive Vice-President, TSMA, December 6, 1944.

15. *In the matter of Southport Petroleum Company of Delaware and Oil Workers' International Union Local 499,* Case No. 2898-CS-D, June 5, 1943.

16. NWLB, *Terminal Report,* vol. 1, ch. 12.

17. Quoted in CIO *Oil Facts,* June 7, 1943; News Release, April 21, 1945; May 5, 1945, June 16, 1945; May 5, 1945; June 9, 1945; June 16, 1945, pp. 5, 6; April 1, 1944.

18. Atlanta *Journal,* October 10, 1945.

19. NWLB, Fourth Region, Press Release, February 10, 1945.

20. NWLB, *Terminal Report,* p. 663; "Report on Region IV," p. 649 and "Report on Region VIII," p. 708.

21. *Advance,* May 15, 1944, p. 4.

22. OWIU, *Proceedings of the Twelfth National Convention,* 1941, p. 6.

23. Unless otherwise indicated, information on the oil workers is from the OWIU's *Convention Proceedings* and officers reports.

24. Harvey O'Conner, *History of the Oil Workers' International Union* (Denver: Oil Workers International Union, 1950), pp. 47, 309.

25. OWIU, *Proceedings of the Thirteenth National Convention,* 1942, pp. 6-7; 38; 12. 31; 34; 36.

26. OWIU, Report of O. A. Knight to the Fifteenth National Convention, 1944, p. 3.

27. CIO *Oil Facts,* August 26, 1943; December 20, 1943 and March 16, 1944; March 16, 1944.

28. TWUA, *Executive Council Report,* 1943, p. 53.

29. *Decisions and Orders of the National Labor Relations Board,* vol. 42, 1942; p. 41.

30. Robert Sidney Smith, *Mill on the Dan* (Durham, N.C.: Duke University Press, 1960), pp. 491-502.

31. UTW, *Proceedings of the Eighth Biennial Convention,* 1944, p. 20.

32. UTW, *Proceedings of the Ninth Biennial Convention*, 1946, pp. 21, 22.

33. UTW, *Proceedings of the Eighth Biennial Convention*, pp. 21, 52.

34. International Ladies' Garment Workers' Union *Report of Proceedings of the Twenty-sixth Convention*, 1947, p. 152.

35. Membership figures taken from proceedings of the IBPSW and the UPP for various years.

36. Letters to P. F. Kennedy from Donald Henderson, January 24, 1939; January 28, 1939.

37. Report by Donald Kobler to Donald Henderson, no date.

38. Report by Donald Kobler, March 14, 1942, written for *UCAPAWA News*.

39. Letter from Malcolm Caldwell to W. M. Aiken, June 5, 1945, and February 8, 1946.

40. Letter to Donald Kobler from Donald Henderson, March 8, 1942.

41. "The 'Food for Victory' Program and the Peaceable Settlement of Agricultural Labor Disputes," Statement of the National Executive Board of the United Cannery, Agricultural, Packing and Allied Workers of America, CIO, June 17, 1942.

42. Confidential memorandum to all international representatives, UCAPAWA, from Harold J. Lane, General Secretary-Treasurer, July 6, 1942.

43. Copy of the circular in the author's possession.

44. AFL *Executive Council Minutes*, January 18-27, 1943, pp. 47, 104-105, and May 17-32, 1943, pp. 47-66; January 17-27, 1944, pp. 42-44, 64-81.

45. CIO *Oil Facts*, April 16, 1945.

46. AFL, "Legal Report to the Executive Council Meeting" AFL *Executive Council Minutes*, August 6-14, 1945, pp. 48-61.

47. Copy of memorandum in the author's possession, reproduced by the Texas CIO.

CHAPTER XV

Operation Dixie

1. Rose Theodore, *Union Agreements in the Cotton-Textile Industry* (Washington: U.S. Department of Labor, Bureau of Labor Statistics, 1946) Bulletin 885, p. 1.

2. Report of the Policy Committee, Southern Labor Conference, Asheville, N. C., May 11-12, 1946; p. 2.

3. George Googe, Chairman, Southern Organizing Campaign Committee, "Report to the AFL Executive Council," August 10, 1946.

4. *American Federationist*, May 1946, p. 7; June 1946, p. 7.

5. Googe, "Report to the AFL Executive Council," August 10, 1946.

6. Southern Organizing Committee, AFL, Policy Board Meeting, *Minutes,* June 3-6, 1946, Atlanta, Georgia.

7. AFL *Executive Council Minutes,* May 15-22, 1946, p. 51, 52.

8. Googe, "Report to the AFL Executive Council," October 1946, AFL *Executive Council Minutes,* October 6-18, 1946, p. 44.

9. Googe, "Report to AFL Executive Council," October 1946.

10. George Googe, "Southern Labor Fights Back," *American Federationist,* April 1948.

11. E. H. Williams, "Down Louisiana Way," *American Federationist,* August 1, 1946, pp. 23, 32.

12. Personal interview with E. H. Williams, October 28, 1958.

13. Googe, "Southern Labor Fights Back."

14. Googe, "Report to the AFL Executive Council," April 21-25, 1947.

15. AFL *Executive Council Minutes,* April 21-25, 1947, pp. 34, 36.

16. UTWA, *Tenth Biennial Convention Proceedings,* May 15-19, 1948, p. 3.

17. "Organization Gains in the Southern Campaign," mimeographed report to the Sixty-sixth Convention of the American Federation of Labor, San Francisco, California, October 6 to 16, 1947, inclusive.

18. Leo Troy, *Distribution of Union Membership Among the States* (New York: National Bureau of Economic Research, 1957) Occasional Paper 56, pp. 4-5.

19. CIO *Executive Board Minutes,* November 13, 15, 16, 17, 23, 1946, p. 27, 46; August 30-September 1, 1948, p. 15; March 15 and 16, 1946, p. 198.

20. CIO *News,* January 14, 1946, p. 9.

21. *The Sunday Star* (Washington, D.C.), May 19, 1946.

22. "Report of the Southern Organizing Director," CIO *Executive Board Minutes,* July 18, 1936, p. 42.

23. CIO *Economic Outlook,* May 1946.

24. Allan S. Haywood, "We Propose to Unionize Labor in the South," *Labor and Nation,* April-May 1946, p. 35.

25. CIO *Executive Board Minutes,* March 15 and 16, 1946, p. 198.

26. CIO *Executive Board Minutes,* July 18, 1946, p. 43.

27. CIO *News,* July 22, 1946, p. 5.

28. CIO *Executive Board Minutes,* July 18, 1946, pp. 4, 59.

29. CIO *Executive Board Minutes,* November 13, 15, 16, 17, 23, 1946, pp. 27, 39, 52, 154; March 13, 14, and 15, 1947, p. 481; January 22, 23, 1948, pp. 355, 357, 369; August 30, 31, September 1, 1948, pp. 19-23, 51.

30. CIO *News,* January 17, 1949, p. 4.

31. TWUA, *Proceedings of the Sixth Biennial Convention,* 1950, pp. 61-62, 81.

32. UTWA, *Proceedings of the Thirteenth Biennial Convention,* 1954, pp. 46-47.

33. TWUA, *Proceedings of the Seventh Biennial Convention,* 1952, p. 54.

34. Statement by Emanuel Boggs in UTWA, *Proceedings of the Thirteenth Biennial Convention,* 1954, pp. 46-47.

35. TWUA, *Proceedings of the Seventh Biennial Convention,* 1952, pp. 54-55, 120.

36. Personal interview, July 14, 1959.

37. For additional discussion of this conflict see: *New York Times,* April 17, May 1, 16-18, and June 20, 1952; *Textile Challenger,* June 1953; *Textile Labor,* June 6, 1953.

38. TWUA, *Proceedings of the Eighth Biennial Convention,* 1954, p. 21.

39. UTWA, *Proceedings of the Thirteenth Biennial Convention,* 1954, p. 10.

40. CIO *Executive Board Minutes,* February 5 and 6, 1953, pp. 50-64, 219.

41. AFL *Executive Council Minutes,* September 14, 22, 24, 1952, pp. 8-17.

42. AFL-CIO *Executive Council Minutes,* September 24-25, 1957, pp. 1, 2, 9.

43. W. S. Fairfield, "The Southern Textile Industry; Union Man's Nightmare," *Reporter,* July 22, 1952, pp. 33-36.

44. TWUA, *Proceedings of the Fifth Biennial Convention,* 1948, pp. 64-65.

45. U.S. Senate, 82nd Cong., 2nd Sess., Committee on Labor and Public Welfare, *Report of the Subcommittee on Labor and Management Relations in the Southern Textile Industry* (Washington: U.S. Government Printing Office, 1952), p. 49; Willard Shelton, "Why Operation Dixie Failed," *New Republic,* Sept. 15, 1947, p. 34; "Setbacks for Unions," *U. S. News,* Feb. 22, 1952, p. 60; "'Operation Dixie' A Union Setback," *U. S. News,* May 25, 1951, pp. 44-47: "Operation Dixie Slows Up: CIO's Enthusiasm Fails," *Business Week,* October 25, 1947; N.M. Gould, "Union Resistance Southern Style," *Labor and Nation,* May-June 1948; and "Southern Organizers Take Stock," *Labor and Nation,* May-June 1948.

46. For a detailed account of the CIO organizing activities at Masonite, based on an examination of the CIO files, see Eugene Roper, "CIO Organizing Committee in Mississippi," unpub. diss., University of Mississippi, 1949.

47. Letter from Starnes to Bittner, June 9, 1946, cited in Roper, "CIO Organizing Committee in Mississippi," p. 20.

48. Report of the Mississippi Agricultural and Industrial Board, no date.

49. CIO *Executive Board Minutes,* June 4, 1953, p. 55.

50. See William Grogan, *John Riffe* (New York: Coward-McCann, Inc., 1959), p. 101; and CIO, *Convention Proceedings,* 1953, p. 535 ff.

51. CIO *Executive Board Minutes,* June 4, 1953, pp. 54-55.

52. TWUA, *Proceedings of the Eighth Biennial Convention,* 1954, p. 52.

53. Grogan, *John Riffe,* p. 103.

54. CIO *News*, June 23, 1947, p. 6.

55. CIO *Executive Board Minutes*, January 22-23, 1948, p. 357.

56. CIO *News*, November 15, 1948, pp. 6-7; October 13, 1947; June 23, 1947, p. 6.

57. Jack Barbash, *Unions and Telephones* (New York: Harper and Bros., 1952); and Lucy R. Mason, *To Win These Rights* (New York: Harper and Bros., 1952), pp. 87-92.

58. CIO *News*, January 27, 1947, p. 16; February 3, 1947, p. 6; February 10, 1947; February 24, 1943; March 3, 1947, p. 6; March 24, 1947, p. 11.

59. Personal interview, April 11, 1959.

60. Personal interview, June 24, 1959.

CHAPTER XVI

Organizing Experiences after "Operation Dixie"

1. Quoted by *Nation's Business*, June 1955.

2. AFL-CIO *Executive Council Minutes*, June 5-7, 1956, pp. 5, 7; February 6-14, 1956, pp. 24-35; June 5-7, 1956, pp. 5, 7; pp. 16, 17, 53-58.

3. Letter to George Meany from William Pollock, General President, TWUA, August 9, 1956.

4. AFL-CIO *Executive Council Minutes*, January 28-February 6, 1957, pp. 7, 11, 48.

5. AFL-CIO Publicity Committee, "Southern Publicity Campaign Report," 1957.

6. AFL-CIO *Executive Council Minutes*, May 20-May 23, 1957, pp. 16, 101.

7. Copy of the report in the author's possession.

8. See AFL-CIO, "Number one objective . . . A Report of the First AFL-CIO National Organizing Conference," January 6-7, 1959.

9. *New York Times*, April 12, 1959, p. 84.

10. Douglas Cater, "Labor's Long Trail in Henderson, N.C.", *The Reporter*, September 14, 1936, p. 36.

11. *New York Times*, June 25, 1961, pp. 1, 58.

12. *American Wool and Cotton Reporter*, March 23, 1950.

13. For a discussion, see Robert M. Segal, and John E. Teagan, "Some Comments on the Right of An Employer to go out of business 'the Darlington Case,'" *Boston College Industrial and Commercial Law Review*, Spring 1963, pp. 581-600.

14. *New York Times*, December 10, 1964.

15. Letter to the Editor of the *New York Times* from Irving Abramson, October 24, 1964; March 30, 1965.

16. *In re Brown and Root, Inc.* 86 NLRB 72.

17. Material from the Texas AFL's files in this case in the author's possession.

18. *AFL-CIO News,* July 27, 1963 and February 8, 1964.

19. *New York Times,* August 4, 1962.

20. Unless otherwise indicated, material on the IUD campaign came from personal interviews.

21. Letter to the author from Oscar Jager, IUD Director of Publications and Public Relations, February 6, 1963.

22. *IUD Bulletin,* January 1964.

CHAPTER XVII

Paper, Coal, and Agricultural Workers

1. U.S. Department of Commerce, Bureau of the Census, "Pulp and Paper Board," *Current Industrial Reports, 1950 and 1959* (Washington: U.S. Government Printing Office, 1960), pp. 1-13.

2. Official figures from the IBPSW, cited by Huey Latham, Jr., "A Comparison of Union Organization in Two Southern Paper Mills," unpub. diss., Louisiana State University, 1961, p. 27.

3. *United Paper,* January 30, 1958, p. 1.

4. Latham, "A Comparison of Union Organization in Two Southern Paper Mills," pp. 19-20.

5. IBPSW, *Proceedings of the Twenty-third Convention,* October 1953, pp. 60, 62-63.

6. New Orleans *Item,* December 1, 1953; November 29, 1953; November 26, 1953.

7. International Brotherhood of Paper Makers and the International Brotherhood of Pulp, Sulphite and Paper Mill Workers, "Little Korea . . . USA," pamphlet issued in December 1954, based on a series of articles by Thomas Sancton in the New Orleans *Item,* November 22, 1953-December 3, 1953.

8. U.S. Dept. of Commerce, *Statistical Abstract of the United States,* 1964, p. 714.

9. Associated Press News Release, March 25, 1959; April 26, 1959.

10. *New York Times,* December 6, 1963; January 8, 1964.

11. *United Mine Workers of America* v. *Pennington et al.,* 85 S. Ct. 1585 (1965).

12. This section is based on F. Ray Marshall and Lamar B. Jones, "Agricultural Unions in Louisiana," *Labor History,* Spring 1962. The author is also indebted to H. L. Mitchell for information concerning these episodes.

13. New Orleans (Louisiana) *Times-Picayune*, March 26, 1942; March 25, 1947.

14. Field interview, Franklinton, Louisiana, September 1, 1960.

15. *Times-Picayune*, March 26, 1947; December 6, 1947.

16. Olin B. Quinn and Charles K. Baker, "Marketing Strawberries Through the Louisiana Fruit and Vegetable Producers' Union, Local 312, in 1952," *Mimeographed Circular No. 141*, Department of Agricultural Economics, Louisiana State University, August 1952.

17. *United States of America v. Louisiana Fruit and Vegetable Producers' Union, Local 312; L. C. Felder; R. M. Singletary; H. M. Howes; C. H. Jones; L. M. Edwards; G. Forstall; H. E. Hasiwar; and the Louisiana Fruit and Vegetable Producers Co-operative Marketing Union, Local 312*, Criminal Indictment No. 24,906, issued by the New Orleans Federal Grand Jury, 1953.

18. National Agricultural Workers' Union AFL, *News Service*, April 30, 1954.

19. *Sugar Reports* No. 29 (Washington: United States Department of Agriculture, September 1954), pp. 39-42; September, 1958, p. 41.

20. Stephen P. Ryan, "Labor in the Sugar-cane Fields," *America*, LXXXIX (August 15, 1953).

21. National Agricultural Workers' Union, *Workers in Our Fields*, 25th Anniversary publication, 1959, p. 22.

22. Sugar Workers Union 317 News Release, Reserve, Louisiana, October 12, 1953.

23. *Times-Picayune*, September 27, 1953.

24. Letter from Henry E. Hasiwar, Vice-President, National Agricultural Workers' Union, to Southdown Sugars Inc., Houma, Louisiana, October 2, 1953. Similar letters were sent to Godchaux Sugars, Milliken and Farwell, Inc., and South Coast Inc.

25. The American Sugar Cane League of the U.S.A., Inc., In Behalf of its 7,000 Members, "The Sugar Cane Strike, A Statement to the Public," adv. in the *Times-Picayune New Orleans States*, Sunday, Oct. 25, 1953, p. 22.

26. *Ibid*.

27. *Times-Picayune New Orleans States*, October 4, 1953.

28. National Agricultural Workers' Union AFL, Report on the strike of Sugar Workers Union Local 317, October 15, 1953.

29. *Times-Picayune*, October 20, 1953.

30. *Workers in Our Fields*.

31. Houma (Louisiana) *Courier*, November 3, 1953.

32. *Paul Chaisson et al. v. South Coast Corporation*, 350 U.S. 899 (1955).

33. *Godchaux Sugars, Inc. v. Chaisson et al.*, 78 So. 2d 673 (1955).

34. Senate Industrial Relations Committee Hearings, *The Right To Work Law*, Louisiana Legislature, May 1954.

35. AFL-CIO *Executive Council Minutes*, August 27-30, 1956, pp. 12, 17.

CHAPTER XVIII

Quantitative Aspects of Union Membership in the South

1. H. M. Douty, "Collective Bargaining Coverage in Factory Employment, 1958," *Monthly Labor Review*, April 1960, pp. 345-349.

2. Leo Troy, *Distribution of Union Membership Among the States, 1939, and 1953* (New York: National Bureau of Economic Research, 1957), pp. 18-19.

3. Arnold Strasser, "Factory Workers Under Bargaining Agreements," *Monthly Labor Review*, February 1965, p. 166.

4. Kenneth M. Thompson, *Labor Unions in Louisiana* (Baton Rouge, Louisiana: Louisiana College of Business Administration, 1959).

5. "Extent of Collective Agreements," *Monthly Labor Review*, January 1955, p. 67.

6. Thompson, *Labor Unions in Louisiana*, p. 88.

7. Frederic Meyers, "The Growth of Collective Bargaining in Texas— a Newly Industrialized Area," IRRA, *Annual Proceedings*, December 28-29, 1956, p. 286, and "Factors Influencing the Patterns of Growth and Change of Collective Bargaining of Newly Industrialized Areas," unpublished paper presented at the 1954 annual meeting of the Southern Economic Association.

8. "Extent of Collective Agreements," *Monthly Labor Review*, January 1955, p. 67.

9. Meyers, "Factors Influencing the Pattern of Growth and Change of Collective Bargaining of Newly Industrialized Areas."

10. H. Ellsworth Steele and Sherwood C. McIntyre, "Company Structure and Unionization," *The Journal of the Alabama Academy of Science*, January 1959, p. 38.

11. United States Department of Labor, Bureau of Labor Statistics, *Wage Differentials and Rate Structures Among 40 Labor Markets, 1951-1952*, Bulletin No. 1135, p. 17.

12. Troy, *Distribution of Union Membership Among the States, 1939 and 1953*, pp. 18-19.

CHAPTER XIX

Factors Influencing Union Growth in the South

1. John T. Dunlop, "The Development of Labor Organization: A Theoretical Framework," in Richard A. Lester and Joseph Shister, *Insights into Labor Issues* (New York: Macmillan Co., 1948).

2. See Joseph Shister, "The Logic of Union Growth," *Journal of Political Economy*, October 1953; Irving Bernstein, "The Growth of American

Unions, 1945-1960," *Labor History*, Spring 1961; Horace B. Davis, "The Theory of Union Growth," *Quarterly Journal of Economics*, August 1941.

3. John T. Dunlop, *Industrial Relations Systems* (New York: Henry Holt and Company, 1958), p. 9.

4. See Martin Segal, "Unionism and Wage Movements," *Southern Economic Journal*, October 1961, pp. 174-181.

5. Information from personal interviews February 7, 1965.

6. See *AFL-CIO News*, January 16, 1965.

CHAPTER XX

Industrial Development and the Law

1. C. Vann Woodward, *Origins of the New South* (Baton Rouge: Louisiana State University Press, 1951).

2. *Wall Street Journal*, July 17, 1962; July 12, 1962.

3. *AFL-CIO News*, December 26, 1964.

4. National Right To Work Committee, "The Proof of Right-To-Work Benefits," leaflet, no date.

5. *The Machinist*, January 3, 1963; July 23, 1964.

6. See Benson Soffer and Michael Korenich, " 'Right to Work' Laws as a Location Factor: The Industrialization Experience of Agricultural States," *Journal of Regional Science*, vol. 3, no. 2, 1961, and a release of the National Council for Industrial Peace summarizing a *Forbes* survey of 100 Indiana manufacturing plants, October 14, 1963.

7. *New York Times*, January 31, 1965.

8. Martin Segal, "Regional Wage Differences in Manufacturing in the Postwar Period," *The Review of Economics and Statistics*, May 1961, p. 153.

9. Baton Rouge (Louisiana) *State-Times*, July 14, 1960.

10. *AFL-CIO News*, October 8, 1960, p. 9.

11. "The Fight for Industry," *IUD Digest*, Fall 1961, p. 43.

12. Quoted by Baton Rouge, Louisiana, *Morning Advocate*, October 4, 1961.

13. For other cases see *AFL-CIO News*, August 20, 1960; November 9, 1963; February 8, 1962; January 19, 1963; December 28, 1963.

14. NWLB, Eighth Region, Releases, August 9, 1944, November, 1944; *Terminal Reports*, vol. 1, Chap. 12.

15. United States Senate, 82nd Cong., 2nd Sess., *Report on Labor Management Relations in the Southern Textile Industry* (Washington: U.S. Government Printing Office, 1952).

16. United States Senate, 86th Cong., 2nd Sess., S. Doc. 81, *Organiza-*

tion and Procedure of the National Labor Relations Board (Washington: Government Printing Office, 1960), pp. 1-2.

17. NLRB *Annual Report*, 28th, 1963, pp. 10, 13, 17.

18. See the symposium "Labor Relations and the Kennedy Administration" in *Industrial Relations*, February 1964.

19. *Sewel Mfg. Co.* 138 NLRB 66 (1963).

20. *Allen-Morrison Sign Co., Inc.* 138 NLRB 73 (1963).

21. Solomon Barkin, *The Decline of the Labor Movement,* (New York: Fund for the Republic, 1962), p. 24.

22. Frederic Meyers, *The "Right to Work" in Practice* (New York: The Fund For the Republic, 1959), pp. 4-5, 11, 27-28.

23. The following statistics were calculated from the *Annual Reports* of the National Labor Relations Board for various years.

24. Charles C. Killingsworth, *State Labor Relations Acts* (Chicago: University of Chicago Press, 1948); and Sanford Cohen, *State Labor Legislation* (Columbus, Ohio: Bureau of Business Research, Ohio State University, 1948).

25. See Sam Houston Clinton, Jr., *Labor Law Manual for Texas Workers* (Austin: Texas AFL-CIO, 1964).

26. *Thomas* v. *Collins,* 323 U.S. 516 (1944).

27. *Thomas* v. *Collins,* 65 S.Ct. 315 (1945).

28. *Hill* v. *Florida,* 325 U.S. 538 (1945).

29. *Lowell* v. *Griffin,* 303 U.S. 444 (1938); see also *Pittman* v. *City of Madison,* 38 LRRM 2567; *Denton* v. *City of Carrollton,* 235 F.2d 481; *Starnes* v. *City of Milledgeville,* 15 LRRM 526; and *United Steelworkers* v. *Fuqua,* 40 LRRM 2241.

30. *Staub* v. *City of Baxley,* 355 U.S. 313.

31. Quoted in *Wall Street Journal,* July 12, 1962.

CHAPTER XXI

The Unions and the Workers

1. See John T. Dunlop, "The Development of Labor Organization: A Theoretical Framework" in Richard A. Lester and Joseph Shister, *Insights into Labor Issues* (New York: Macmillan Co., 1948).

2. Calculated from Bureau of Labor Statistics and U. S. Department of Agriculture data.

3. *Monthly Labor Review*, September 1963.

4. U. S. Bureau of Labor Statistics, *Earnings and Employment Statistics,* Bulletin 1370, 1963.

5. *Monthly Labor Review*, September 1963.

6. For further discussion of this point see Ray Marshall, *The Negro and Organized Labor* (New York, London, and Sydney: John Wiley and Sons, 1965).

7. Tony Zivalich, "The Process of Unionization in the South," Industrial Relations Research Association, *Proceedings of the Spring Meeting,* 1964, p. 472.

8. *AFL-CIO News,* May 30, 1964.

9. *The Machinist,* May 21, 1964; *Labor,* May 16, 1964.

10. *New York Times,* April 12, 1961.

11. *New York Times,* April 5, 1964.

12. See Edgar S. Dunn, Jr., *Recent Southern Economic Development* (Gainesville, Florida: University of Florida Press, 1962).

13. Personal interview, February, 1965.

14. Lucy Randolph Mason, *To Win These Rights* (New York: Harper & Bros., 1952), pp. 180-181.

15. Liston Pope, *Mill Hands and Preachers* (New Haven: Yale University Press, 1942), pp. 149-150.

16. Mason, *To Win These Rights,* p. 183.

17. Bernard M. Cannon, "Social Deterrents to the Unionization of Southern Cotton Textile Mill Workers," unpub. diss., Harvard University, 1951, p. 527.

18. Stetson Kennedy, *Southern Exposure* (Garden City: Doubleday and Co., 1946), p. 234.

19. AFL-CIO, *Number One Objective . . . A Report of the First AFL-CIO National Organizing Conference,* January 6-7, 1949, pp. 38-47.

CHAPTER XXII

The Future of Unions in the South

1. John T. Dunlop, "The American Industrial Relations System in 1975," in Jack Stieber, ed., *U. S. Industrial Relations: The Next Twenty Years* (East Lansing: Michigan State University Press, 1958), p. 27.

2. For a discussion of this point, see Irving Bernstein, "The Growth of American Unions, 1945-1960," *American Economic Review,* June 1954, p. 301; "Union Growth and Structural Cycles," *Proceedings* of the Industrial Relations Research Association, 1954; and "Discussion," by Daniel Bell, in *Proceedings,* pp. 231-236.

Index

Advance, quoted, 170
Advance Bag and Paper Co., 212
Agricultural Adjustment Administration, 154, 159, 160
Agricultural Extension Service, 165
Agricultural organizations, 86-93; industrialization and, 86-90; Farmers' Union, 90-92; agrarian Socialists, 92, 93
Agricultural workers' unions, 157, 288-94, 333-34; and dairy farmers, 289; and strawberry farmers, 290-91; and sugar cane farmers, 291-94
Air Line Pilots Association, 249
Alabama: slave percentage in (1840), 6; iron industry, 14-16; bauxite, 18; unionizing of coal miners in, 72-75, 143-46, 150-52; union renewal in 1920's, 102; Communists in, 182-84; union membership in 1960's, 304
Alabama Agricultural Workers' Union, 157
Alabama Blackshirts, 183
Alabama Fuel and Iron Co., 140, 144, 145-46
Alabama Mining Institute, 74
Alabama State Federation of Labor, 151, 152, 220
Alliance Paper Co., 212
Altman, John W., quoted, 152
Aluminum Company of America, 226
Amalgamated Association of Iron, Steel, and Tin Workers, 182, 185
Amalgamated Clothing Workers of America, 166, 169, 220, 226, 304, 316, 322, 314; growth during New Deal, 175-81; and World War II, 230
Amalgamated Meat Cutters, 304, 305
American Alliance for Labor and Democracy, 26
American Bemberg Corp., 172
American Civil Liberties Union, 110, 114, 118, 138-39, 156, 161

American Enka Corp., 229
American Farm Bureau Federation, 241-42, 294
American Federation of Full-Fashioned Hosiery Workers, 85
American Federation of Government Employees, 304
American Federation of Hosiery Workers, 169, 262
American Federation of Labor, 52, 82, 83, 85, 89, 99, 102, 115, 119, 157, 242; growth, 1881-1928, 24-36; racial practices, 29-36, 310-11; and Southern Labor Congress, 37-38, 221-22; southern organizing campaign (1890's), 62; helps organize textile workers (1920's), 103-05; *1930* organizing campaign, 121-33; *Southern Workers Handbook,* 123; and Danville strike, 124-31; supports Southern Tenant Farmers' Union, 163, 165; reorganizes United Textile Workers, 171-73; and federal labor unions, 183; Metal Trades Council, 196; growth during New Deal, 202-22; and reorganization of longshoremen, 202-11; and paper workers, 211-14; and tobacco workers, 214-18; influenced by CIO, 220-21; merger with CIO, 220 (*see* next entry); in 1940, 220-22; and World War II, 225-26; postwar organizing campaign, 246-54, structure and strategy, 247-48, and race problem, 248-50, and financial problems, 250-51, organizing problems, 251-52, terminated, 252-54
American Federation of Labor–Congress of Industrial Organizations, 260, 311; organizing experiences in 1950's and 1960's, 270-82; and Henderson strike, 274-76; and Deering, Milliken case, 276-79; and building trades, 279-80; Industrial Union Department campaign, 280-82

American Federation of Teachers, 336, 337
American Federationist, quoted, 221
American Guardian, 159
American Legion, 183, 187
American Lumber Co., 98
American Newspaper Guild, 192-94
American Railway Union, 58
American Society of Mechanical Engineers, 101
American Sugar Cane League, 292, 294
American Tobacco Co., 14, 215, 217, 238, 240
American Wool and Cotton Reporter, quoted, 276-77
Ameringer, Oscar, 92, 159; quoted, 93
Anderson Clayton Co., 239
Anzeiger, Der, 92
Apollo project, 280
Appalachian Joint Conference, 142, 147
Arkansas: slave percentage (1840), 6; bauxite, 18; antiunion violence (1922), 55-56; Socialist organizing in 1930's, 158-65; Antiviolence Law, 241; "right-to-work" law, 320
Arkansas Fertilizer Co., 239
Arkansas Power and Light Co., 251
Armour Co., 226, 227
Asheville Citizen, quoted, 118
Association of Colored Railway Trainmen, 59
Association of Train Porters, Brakemen and Switchmen, 59
Atlanta, Ga.: early labor movement in, 21; and printers' unions, 44-45; importance as railroad center, 51
Atlanta, Birmingham and Atlantic Railroad, 55
Atlanta Employing Printers' Club, 44
Atlantic Coast Line, 55
Atlantic Steel Corp., 187
Atlas Shirt Co., 177
Augusta, Ga., textile strikes, 81, 82-83
Augusta Cotton Manufacturers' Association, 82
Augusta Federation of Trades, 81
Austin *American-Statesman,* 193
Axton-Fisher Co., 215
Ayman, Paul J., 106, 127

B. F. Goodrich Co., 191, 233
Baldanzi, George, 254, 259, 260, 264, 266
Baldwin-Felts, detectives, 153
Barkin, Solomon, quoted, 326

Baxley, Ga., antiunion ordinance, 330-31
Beal, Fred, 108; quoted, 112; *Proletarian Journey,* 114
Beddow, Noel R., quoted, 186, 207
Bemberg-Glanztoff Co., 105
Benjamin, George, 216
Berry, George, 38
Bibb textile chains, 256
Birmingham *Age-Herald,* quoted, 151
Birmingham *News,* 189
Birmingham Post, 194
Bittner, Van, 247, 251, 254, 259, 266; quoted, 256, 257, 261
Black Mountain Coal Co., 138
Blackton-Cahaba Coal Co., 143
Blanshard, Paul, quoted, 112
Bogalusa, La., antiunion violence, 99-100
Boilermakers' Union, 52
Branstetter, Otto, 92
Bricklayers, Masons and Plasterers' Union, 29
Bridge, Structural Steel and Ornamental Iron Workers, 188
Bridges, Harry, 161, 247, 258; and New Orleans campaign, 207-08, 210, 211
Brooke Shoe Manufacturing Co., 322-23
Brookwood Labor College, 118, 122
Brotherhood of Locomotive Engineers, 50, 52, 77, 91
Brotherhood of Locomotive Firemen and Enginemen, 50, 58, 91
Brotherhood of Maintenance of Way Employees, 51
Brotherhood of Railway Clerks, 51, 53
Brotherhood of Railroad Trainmen, 50, 91
Brotherhood of Sleeping Car Porters, 59, 249
Brotherhood of Timber Workers, 94-99
Broun, Heywood, quoted, 192
Brown, Geoffery, 124
Brown Foundry Co., 187
Brown and Root, 279, 280
Brown and Williamson, 215
Building trades unions, 45-49; growth, 45-47; race problems, 48-49; in 1950's, 1960's, 279-80
Bulwinkle, A. L., 113
Bureau of Conciliation, 240
Burke, John P., 212
Burlington Mills, 236, 271, 316
Burns, Thomas F., 169
Burns Detective Agency, 97, 204-05
Butler, J. R., 161, 162

Calcasieu Paper Co., 237, 284-85, 325
Calhoun, John C., quoted, 8
Cannon, Bernard, quoted, 342
Cannon Mills, 236, 256, 211, 278, 316
Capper-Volstead Act, 290
Carlisle, Floyd, 212
Carnegie-Illinois Steel Corp., 186
Cash, W. J., quoted, 8
Cayton, Horace, 184
Chamber of Commerce of the United States, 242
Champion Fibre Co., 284
Champion Mills, 237
Charleston *Daily News,* 67
Chastain, Gordon L., 172
Chattanooga *Evening News,* 193
Chattanooga Iron Co., 14
Cherry, R. G., 113
Christian American, 241, 242
Christian Front, 241
Cigar Makers' International Union, 217
Civil Rights Act (1964), 338
Civil War, 5, 20; economic impact on the south, 7, 9; effect on unions, 42
Cleveland, Grover, 89
Cleveland Cloth Mills, 104
Clowes, Phil, 254
Cluett-Peabody, 179, 180
Coal miners' unions, 71-79, 137-53, 286-88; in Tennessee, 71-72; in Alabama, 72-75; in the southwest, 75; in Kentucky, West Virginia, 75-78
Coal River Collieries, 77-78
Coal Trimmers' Union, 68
Colored Alliance, 89
Colored Locomotive Firemen's Association, 59
Colored Longshoremen's Benevolent Association, 67
Commercial Secretaries Association, 37, 91
Commission on Industrial Relations, 54
Commissioner of Corporations, U. S., 91
Commonwealth Labor College, 161, 162
Communications Workers of America, 264
Communist Party, Communists, 105, 121, 130, 133, 137, 151, 215, 237, 264, 337; and National Textile Workers' Union, 106, 126; and Gastonia strike, 107-15 passim, 123; Workers' International Relief, 109; Young Communists, 110; International Labor Defense, 115, and Press Service, 109-10; efforts to organize Negroes, 154, 155-58, 182-83; and Sharecroppers' Union,

156-57; efforts to capture Southern Tenant Farmers' Union, 161-62; alleged in CIO, 247, 249, 259. *See also* National Miners' Union; National Textile Workers' Union; Sharecroppers' Union of Alabama
Confederacy, 3
Conference on Economic Conditions in the South, report quoted, 16-17
Congress of Industrial Organizations, 162, 203, 207, 241, 244, 341; forms organizing committee with United Textile Workers, 169-71; 1940 campaign for Textile Workers' Union, 173-75; iron and steel unions, 182-88; growth during New Deal, 182-201; Steel Workers' Organizing Committee, 184-88; and rubber workers, 188-91; and United Auto Workers, 191-92; and American Newspaper Guild, 192-94; and oil workers, 194-201; Petroleum Workers' Organizing Committee, 196; and longshoremen, 206-11; merger with AFL, 220 (*see* American Federation of Labor–Congress of Industrial Organizations); influence on AFL, 220-21; and World War II, 226-27; and oil workers, 233; postwar organizing campaign, 254-69; and NLRB elections, 265-66; Southern Organizing Committee, 254-59; and Negroes, 310-11
Conner, Bishop James A., 123
Conroe Manufacturing Co., 226
Continental Can Co., 284
Copolymer Co., 226
Craig, George, 254
Crawford, W. H., quoted, 184
Cuney, Norris Wright, 66-67
Curran, Joseph, 247

Dabbs, James McBride, quoted, 7
Dacus, Sol, 99
Dalrymple, Sherman, 189
Dalrymple, William, 143
Dan River Mills, 234, 259, 260, 278; strike (1930-31), 124-31
Danhof, Clarence H., quoted, 17
Daniel, Franz, 170
Daniel Construction Co., 279, 280
Daniels, Josephus, quoted, 88
Danville, Va., strike (1930-31), 124-31
Darlington Manufacturing Co., 277
Davis, Chester, 160
Davis, David, 21
Dawson, Francis W., 12

De Bardeleben, Charles F., Sr., 144-45, 147, 148
De Bardeleben, Henry, 144
De Bardeleben Coal Co., 74, 140, 144, 286
Debs, Eugene V., 92
Deering, Milliken & Co., 234, 236; Textile Workers' charges against, 276-78
Delta Cooperative Farm, 164
Delta Shipyards, 226
Democratic Party, 21, 74, 89
Department of Agriculture, U. S., 160, 291, 292
Department of Justice, U. S., 147, 290
Department of Labor, U. S., 107, 145, 168, 176
Divisional Coal Labor Board, 145
Dodge, Witherspoon, 170
Dorsey, Willie, 209-10
Douglass, Frederick, 49
Douty, H. M., quoted, 131
Drolet, Father Jerome A., 209-10
Du Pont Co., 226
Dubinsky, David, 236, 250
Duke, James P., 14
Dunlop, John T., quoted, 3, 309, 311
Dwight Manufacturing Co., 189

East, Clay, 158, 159, 160, 164
Eddy, Sherwood, 164
Elizabethton, Tenn., strikes (1929-30), 105-07, 121, 122
Emergency Committee for Strikers' Relief, 121, 127, 128
Emerson, Arthur Lee, 94
Emspak, Julius, 247
Esso Corp., 233
Evans, E. Lewis, 214, 215, 216
Evans, Mercer G., 56; quoted, 44, 55

Fair Employment Practices Committee, 228, 263
Farm-Labor Union of America, 93
Farm Laborers' and Cotton Field Workers' Union, 157
Farm Security Administration, 165
Farmers' Alliance, 88-90
Farmers' Educational and Cooperative Union of America, 90-92
Farmers' Union, 36, 37, 159
Farmers' Union of Alabama, 157
Faubus, Orval E., 161; sources of support for, 340
Federal Labor Union, 53

Federal Mediation and Conciliation Service, 113, 259
Federal Trade Commission, 168
Federation of Organized Trades and Labor Unions, 24
Fenton, Frank, 250
Fight for Free Enterprise, 244-45
Finklestein & Sons, 176, 178, 180
Firestone Co., 190
Fitzgerald, H. R., 131; quoted, 125
Flaxer, Abram, 247
Florida: slave percentage (1840), 6; "right-to-work" law, 320; licensing law, 329-30
Florida State Federation of Labor, 47
Food, Tobacco, Agricultural, and Allied Workers' Union of America, 237, 240-41
Ford Motor Co., 190
Fox, C. M., 172
Frank, Jerome, 160, 161
Friedman-Harry Marks, 176, 177-78
Fruit and Vegetable Producers' Union, 290
Fulton Bag and Cotton Mill, 81, 83

Gadsden, Ala.: strikes and antiunion violence, 188-90; union progress in, 227, 229, 256
Gaffney Manufacturing Co., 234
Galenson, Walter, quoted, 185
Galloway Lumber Co., 97
Galveston, Tex., and longshoremen's unions, 65-67
Galveston Daily News, quoted, 66, 67
Galveston Screwman's Benevolent Association, 65-66
Galveston Trades Assembly, 67
Gastonia, N.C., strike (1929), 106, 107-15, 123
Gastonia Gazette, 110; quoted, 111, 113, 115
Gaylord Corp., 213, 214
General Motors Corp., 191, 192
Georgia: slave percentage (1840), 6; bauxite, 18; unions in 1920's, 44, 102; 1934 strike suppression, 167-68
Georgia Railroad, 58
Georgia State Federation of Labor, 102, 170, 220
German-Americans, 45, 65, 105
Girdler, Tom, 187
Gold, Ben, 247
Goldwater, Barry, 339
Gompers, Samuel, 25, 26, 83; quoted,

80-81, 82; attitude on racial policies, 34-36
Goodyear Rubber Co., 188, 189, 190, 229-30
Googe, George, 102, 119, 130, 172, 207, 219, 248, 251, 253, 312; quoted, 211, 226, 250, 252
Gorman, Francis J., 117, 125-26, 169; quoted, 129-30
Gould, Jay, 23
Grady, Henry W., 12
Graham, Frank, 123, 228
Graham, Lewis, 41
Grange, decline of, 88
Graves, John Temple, quoted, 189
Great Southern Lumber Co., 99, 213
Green, William, 104, 110, 121, 125, 126, 128, 163, 168, 204, 214, 220, 221, 241, 247, 250, 253; quoted, 105, 122, 123-24, 129, 220; role in Elizabethton strike, 106-07; reception in Atlanta (1940), 221-22
Greene, Prince W., 82
Grenada County Weekly, quoted, 262-63
Grenada *Daily Sentinel-Star,* quoted, 262, 263
Grenada Industries Co., 261-63
Grundy Coal Co., 287
Guffey-Snyder Act, 150
Gulf Coast Metal Trades Council, 195
Gulf Oil Co., 196, 232
Gulf States Paper Corp., 283
Gulf States Steel, 189
Gulick, Charles A., quoted, 115

Hall, Covington, 97, 98
Hammond, William J., 41
Hampton Institute, 74
Harding, Warren G., 76
Hardman, J. B. S., quoted, 115
Harlan County, Ky., unionizing in, 137-39, 146-47
Harlan County Coal Operators' Association, 140, 146, 147
Harriet-Henderson Mills, 234; strike (1958-61), 274-76
Harrison, George, 273; quoted, 272
Hat, Cap, and Millinery Workers' Union, 220
Haymarket riots, 51
Hays, Arthur Garfield, 114, 115
Haywood, Allan, 255
Haywood, Bill, quoted, 96-97
Henderson, Donald, 161, 162, 238
Henderson, N.C., strike (1958), 274-76

Hickey, Thomas, 92; quoted, 93
Hickory Clothiers, Inc., 322
Hicks, Clarence J., 199
Higgens Co., 226
High Point, N.C., strike (1932), 131-32
Hill v. *State of Florida,* 244
Hillman, Sidney, 169, 170, 180, 190, 247
Hiss, Alger, 160, 161
Hod Carriers and Common Laborers' Union, 164
Hoey, Clyde, 113
Hoffman, Alfred, 102, 115, 116, 121; kidnapped, 106
Houston Maritime Commission, 205
Houston Milling Co., 239
Howe, Frederic, 160
Humble Oil and Refining Co., 199, 229, 231, 232, 329

I. N. Vaughn Co., 215
Ickes, Harold, 141; quoted, 142
Illinois Central Railroad, 52; 1911 strike, 53-54
Imperial Sugar Co., 238
Independent Colored Longshoremen's Association, 203
Independent Industrial Workers Association, 200-01
Independent Miners' Union, 141
Independent White Longshoremen's Association, 203
Industrial Lumber Co., 284
Industrial Workers of the World, 26, 69, 131-32, 138; and lumber workers, 93-94, 98
Ingalls Shipbuilding Co., 188, 226
Inland Steel Corp., 186
International Brotherhood of Boilermakers and Iron Shipbuilders, 52
International Brotherhood of Electrical Workers, 45, 46, 251, 264, 304
International Brotherhood of Paper Makers, 211, 212, 283, 284
International Brotherhood of Pulp, Sulphite and Paper Mill Workers, 211-13, 237; membership, 1961, 283; Calcasieu campaigns, 284-85
International Brotherhood of Railway Signalmen, 51
International Brotherhood of Teamsters, 289
International Harvester Co., 337
International Labor Defense, 156
International Ladies' Garment Workers Union, 164, 166, 168, 169, 175, 181,

220, 281-82, 316, 331, 341; and World War II, 236
International Longshoremen and Warehousemen's Union, 161, 238, 240; contest with ILA for Gulf ports, 206-09; activities in New Orleans, 209-11
International Longshoremen's Association, 65, 68, 69, 238, 239, 303; during New Deal era, 202-11; vs. ILWU, 206-11
International Paper Co., 212
International Pressmen and Assistants, 43
International Timber Workers' Union, 99
International Typographical Union, 41, 43-44
Interstate Order of Colored Locomotive Firemen, Engine Helpers, Yard and Train Service Employees and Railway Mechanics, 60
Interstate Virginia-Carolinas Typographical Association, 102
Irish-Americans, 60, 65, 66
Iron and steel workers' unions, 182-88
Irwin and Cone chains, 278
Irwin Mills, 173

J. P. Stevens Mills, 236, 271, 316
Jackson, Gardner, 160
Jenkins, L. L., 117
Johnson, Forney, 149
Johnson, Hugh, 147
Joint Labor Legislative Board of Texas, 36-37
Jones, Jerome, quoted, 38
Jones, Walter, 151, 152
Jones-Costigan Act, 291
Journeymen Stonecutters' Association of America, 46

Kennedy, John F., 305
Kennedy, Thomas, 169
Kent, Rockwell, 161
Kentucky: slave percentage (1840), 6; coal miners' unionization, 75-78, 137-39, 146-47; union membership in 1960's, 304
Kentucky Federation of Labor, 216
Kilby Car Manufacturing Co., 186
King, MacKenzie, 199
King Mills, 82
Kirby, John H., 95
Kirby Lumber Co., 97
Knight, O. A., 199; quoted, 231, 232-33
Knights of Labor, 10, 51, 63, 68, 71, 73,

75; history, 21-24; and Farmers' Alliance, 88, 89; and lumber workers, 94
Kohler strike, 343
Korean War, 265
Kroll, Jack, 254
Ku Klux Klan, 55, 126, 128, 150, 171, 183, 187

La Follette Committee, 144, 146
Labor's Protective Benevolent Mutual Aid Association, 61
Laffoon, Ruby, 139
Lahne, Herbert J., 171
Landrum-Griffin Act, 325
Lane Cotton Mills, 173
Lehman, Herbert H., 107
Leitch System of Industrial Democracy, 125, 127
Lester, Richard, 228
Lewis, John L., 77, 153, 162, 185, 186, 210, 241; quoted, 79, 149
Liggett and Myers, 215, 216, 217
Lilienthal, David E., quoted, 219
Little Cahaba Coal Co., 143
Lockwood, Green and Co., 101
Long, Huey P., 158
Longshoreman's Protective Union Association, 67
Longshoremen Protective Union Benevolent Association, 206
Longshoremen's unions, 60-70; race problems, 60-68; union destruction in Gulf ports, 68-70; during New Deal era, 202-11
Loray Mill, 107, 108, 109
Lorwin, Louis, quoted, 130
Louisiana: slave percentage (1840), 6; sulpher, 18; Communists in, 156; union membership in 1960's, 304
Louisiana Citizens' Committee, 251-52
Louisiana Cooperative Act, 290
Louisiana Farm Bureau, 294
Louisiana Federation, 46-47
Louisiana Longshoremen's Association, 204
Louisville Textile Co., 169
Lumber workers' unions, 93-100

McComb, Miss., strike violence (1911), 54
McCullogh, Spencer, 164
McDonald, David, 254, 255, 257, 272-73
McGrady, Edward F., 104, 129, 214; kidnapped, 106
Machinists' Union, 34, 52

McIntyre, Sherwood C., 307
McMahon, T. A., 83, 84, 116, 122, 126, 128, 169
Magnolia Petroleum Corp., 233
Mallory Steamship Co., 67
Manford Act, 243
Manhattan Shirt Co., 180
Manville-Jenkes Co., 107, 113
Marion, N.C., strike (1929), 115-18, 121, 122
Marion Manufacturing Co., 116
Marshall Canning Co., 238
Marshall Field Co., 173, 259
Mason, Lucy Randolph, 170, 190, 254, 341; quoted, 342
Masonite Corp., 249, 261, 264, 269
Meany, George, 247, 250, 253, 260, 271, 272, 292, 294
Meitzen, E. O., 92
Men's clothing workers' unions, during New Deal, 175-81
Merrill, Lewis, 247
Mexican-Americans, 239-40, 339
Meyers, Frederic, 307; quoted, 326, 327
Mid-Continent Petroleum Corp., strike against (1938-40), 197-99, 333
Militant Truth, 343
Miller, Carrol George, quoted, 64
Milliken, Roger, 277
Millner, George, quoted, 68
Mills, Clyde, 180
Mine, Mill and Smelter Workers' Union, 157, 182, 183-84
Miners' unions. *See* Coal miners' unions
Mississippi: slave percentage (1840), 6; CIO postwar campaign in, 261-63; "right-to-work" law, 320
Missouri and North Arkansas Railroad, strike (1922), 55-56
Mitch, William, 143, 151, 152, 185, 186
Mitchell, Broadus, 9, 12, 101, 115; quoted, 4, 13, 86
Mitchell, George S., 12, 104, 115; quoted, 184
Mitchell, H. L., 158, 159, 162, 164; quoted, 157
Mobile Maritime Committee, 205
Mobile Typographical Society, 43
Monroe Shock Absorber Co., 282
Monroe *World and News-Star*, 193-94
Montgomery Typographical Society, 43-44
Morgan (Southern Pacific) Lines, 203, 206
Murray, Philip, 79, 185, 201, 208, 241, 254, 255, 263; quoted, 258-59

Muste, A. J., 122
Myrdal, Gunner, 155

Nance, Steve, 170, 220
Nashua Manufacturing Co., 173
National Adjustment Commission, 69
National Agricultural Workers Union, 289, 290-94
National Association for the Advancement of Colored People, 156, 210, 338
National Association of Letter Carriers, 304, 336
National Bituminous Coal Wage Agreement, 287
National Farm Labor Union, 165, 251
National Industrial Recovery Act, 140, 141, 150, 166, 168, 175, 195
National Industrial Union of Forest and Lumber Workers, 96
National Labor Relations Act, 244, 277, 279, 310
National Labor Relations Board, 170, 171, 174, 176, 178-79, 186, 188, 191, 194, 196, 197, 198, 207, 208, 231, 233, 234, 237, 251, 258, 261, 264, 265-66, 277, 282, 285, 286, 287, 321, 323, 337, 338; "Kennedy NLRB," 324, 325-26; and "right-to-work" laws, 328-29
National Labor Union, 20-21
National Maritime Union, 195, 210
National Metal Trades Association, 27
National Miners' Union, 137, 138, 139, 141, 155
National Negro Labor Congress, 21, 239
National Open Shop Association, 27
National Progressive Union, 71
National Recovery Administration, 142, 166, 175, 176, 183, 189, 192, 195, 197, 215, 236; and regional wage differential, 147-50
National Right to Work Committee, 320
National Textile Workers' Union, 126, 155; role in Gastonia strike, 107-15
National Typographical Union, 41, 42, 155
National Union of Textile Workers, 82
National War Labor Board, 26, 196, 199, 225, 227-30, 232, 233, 234-35, 237, 239, 240, 245, 276, 279, 324
National Youth Administration, 162
Neal, John R., 113-14
Negroes, 46, 109, 124, 127, 180, 200; and slavery, 5-11; and National

Labor Union, 21; and AFL, 25, 29-36, 248-49, 269; and Knights of Labor, 22-23; northern migration, 26; and printers' unions, 42-43; and building trades unions, 48-49; as strikebreakers, 54, 58-59, 97, 112; and railroad unions, 57-60; and longshoremen's unions, 60-68, 202-03, 205, 207, 209-11; and coal miners' unions, 73, 74, 150-52; and textile unions, 81; and industrialization, 87, 88; and Populist movement, 90; as lumber workers, 94, 95, 96, 97, 99, 100; and racial issue in Gastonia strike, 111-12; in United Mine Workers, 150-52; Communists try to organize, 154, 155-57; in iron and steel unions, 182-84, 188; and ILWU, 207, 209-11; in tobacco workers' unions, 215, 216, 217; and canners' union, 239-40; and CIO, 258-59, 269; and pulp and paper workers' unions, 284; in agricultural workers' unions, 291; influence on present-day union organizing, 310-11; race issue as factor in southern union growth, 336-40; political alliances with labor, 339-40, 350

New Deal, 103, 135-222, 311

New Orleans, La.: as early union center, 20, 41; and longshoremen's racial problems, 60-64, 202-11, passim; general strike (1892), 62-63; street railway strike (1929), 103

New Orleans Daily News, 98

New Orleans Dock and Cotton Council, 63, 64, 69, 70

New Orleans and Great Northern Railroad, 99

New Orleans Screwmen's Benevolent Association, 60, 63, 65

New Orleans Steamship Association, 70, 203

New Orleans and Texas Pacific Railroad, 59

New Orleans Typographical Society, 41

New York Joint Dress Board, 281

New York World-Telegram, 192

Nicholls, William H., 12, 18

Norfolk Central Labor Union, 176

Norris-La Guardia Act, 205

North American Aviation Co., 226

North American Coal Co., 141

North American Rayon Corp., 172

North Carolina: slave percentage (1840), 6; union renewal in 1920's,

102; strikes (1932), 131-32; union membership in 1960's, 304-05

O'Daniel, W. Lee, 242, 243

Odum, Howard, quoted, 16

Oil, Chemical, and Atomic Workers, 304

Oil Field, Gas Well, and Refinery Workers' Union, 194

Oil Workers' International Union, 194-99, 227, 228; and Mid-Continent strike, 197-99, 231, 232; and World War II, 230-33

Oil workers' union, 194-201; and Mid-Continent strike, 197-99; dealings with Standard of New Jersey, 199-201

Oklahoma: "right-to-work" law, 319-20, 327; Negro-labor political alliances, 339-40

Open-shop movement, 26-27

Order of Railroad Conductors, 50, 91

Order of Railway Telegraphers, 51, 91

O'Sullivan Rubber Corp., 325

P. Lorillard Co., 215

Parade, 170

Patterson, Sherman, 343

Payton, Boyd, 276

Peel, John A., 116, 170

Pepperell Mills, 271

Petry, O. E., quoted, 220

Philip Morris Co., 215

Phillips Brothers Coal Co., 287, 288

Piedmont Organizing Council, 102

Pinchback, P. B. S., 61

Pioneer Mining Manufacturing Co., 15

Pollard, John W., 172; quoted, 172-73

Pollock, William, quoted, 272

Pope, Liston, 341-42

Populists, 10, 24, 89, 90

Powderly, Terence V., 23, 88, 89

Potofsky, Jacob, 176, 257, 272, 273

Pratt Coal and Coke, 15

Pratt Mines, 72

President's Committee on Farm Tenancy, 164

President's Committee on the Economic Conditions of the South, report quoted, 155

Pressman, Lee, 160, 247

Printers' unions, 41-45; and Civil War, 42; race problems, 42-43; antibellum growth, 43-45

Profile Mills, 173

Progressive Miners of America, 137, 140-41

Protective Order of Railway Trainmen, 59
Pulp and paper workers' unions, 211-14, 237, 283-85
Pure Oil Co., 196

Quill, Michael, 247

R. J. Reynolds Co., 104, 214, 217, 238, 272
Race issues. *See* Mexican-Americans; Negroes
Railroad Labor Board, 55
Railroad unions, 47, 50-60; machinists, blacksmiths, boilermakers, 51-52; and Illinois Central strike (1911), 53-54; strength in 1920's, 54-57; and race problems, 57-60
Railway Audit and Inspection Co., 204
Railway Labor Act, 310
Ramsey, John, 254
Ratchford, B. U., 107; quoted, 108
Reade Shirt Co., 177
Rebel, The, 92
Reconstruction, 4, 5, 88; effect on south, 9-11; and industrialization, 86-87
Reed Rubber Co., 191
Religion, and union growth, 341-43
Renner, George T., quoted, 4
Renters' Union, 92
Renters' Union of Oklahoma, 159
Republic Iron and Steel, 15
Republic Steel, 140, 185, 186, 187
Republican Party, 21, 74, 340, 350
Retail, Wholesale, and Department Store Union, 209, 210, 304
Reuther, Walter, 256, 263, 271, 273
Revere Copper and Brass Co., 321
Rhone, Ed, quoted, 207
Rieve, Emil, 169, 259, 260, 263, 264, 266
Riffe, John V., 259, 263
"Right-to-work" laws, 241, 242, 340; as attraction to industry, 319-21; effect on industrialization, 321; effect on union growth, 326-29; and NLRB elections, 328-29
Riverside Cotton Mills, 234; strike (1930-31), 124-31
Roosevelt, Franklin D., 149, 150, 168, 205; quoted, 155
Rostow, W. W., quoted, 4
Rubber workers' unions, 188-91
Rural Electrification Administration, 165
Ryan, Joseph, 203, 205

S and K Kneepants Co., 179
Saint Louis Lumberman, quoted, 96
St. Louis *Post Dispatch*, 164
St. Regis Paper Co., 212
Sampson, Flem D., 138
San Antonio, Tex., open-shop movement, 27
Santa Fe Railroad, 98
Scottdale Mills, 174
Scottsboro case, 156
Screwmen's Benevolent Association Number 2, 61
Seabrook Farms, 165
Selly, Joseph, 247
Sharecroppers' Union of Alabama, 156-57
Shell Oil, 233
Sherman Act, 287, 288, 290
Sherman and Sons, 175, 176
Sidele Fashions, Inc., 323
Simmons, Luther, quoted, 213
Sinclair, Harry F., 195
Sinclair, Upton, 159
Sinclair Oil Co., 195
Slavery: population (1840), 5-6; impact on south, 5-6; economic effects of, 7-9
Sloss Furnace Co., 15
Sloss-Sheffield Co., 186, 187
Smith, Edwin, 231, 232
Smith, Paul J., quoted, 124
Smith, Robert, quoted, 131
Social-Democratic Party, 92
Socialist League for Industrial Democracy, 159
Socialist Party, Socialists, 87, 92-93, 157, 158-65
Soil Conservation Service, 165
Sons of Vulcan, 182
South, the: region defined, 3; economic, demographic aspects, 4-7; impact of slavery, war, Reconstruction, 7-11; and industrialization, 11-19, 101; economic conditions, 1929-41, 154-55; effect of World War II on economy, 225; industry and the law, 319-31; industrial development, 319-23; legislation, 323-31; "right-to-work" laws, 326-27; NLRB elections, 328-29
South Carolina: slave percentage (1840), 6; union revival in 1920's, 102; strikes (1929), 118-20
South Carolina State Federation of Labor, 120
Southeastern Carriers' Agreement, 59
Southern Baptist Convention, 341

Southern Bell Telephone Co., 264
Southern Conference for Human Welfare, 239
Southern Conference of Teamsters, 251
Southern Cotton Oil Co., 241
Southern Cotton Textile Federation, 172, 235
Southern Federation of Telephone Workers, 264
Southern Industrial Council, 148
Southern Industrial-Fraternal Review, quoted, 74
Southern Labor Conferences, 246 (1940), 247 (1946)
Southern Labor Congress, 37-38
Southern Labor School, 312
Southern Labor Union, 287
Southern Lumber Operators' Association, 94, 95
Southern Lumberman, 97; quoted, 98, 99
Southern Negro Youth Conference, 239
Southern Negro Youth Congress, 215
Southern Organizing Committee, 129
Southern Pacific Lines, 69. See also Morgan Lines
Southern Railroad, 59
Southern States Industrial Council, 242
Southern Tenant Farmers' Union, 93, 157, 158-65; origins, 158-60; and New Deal, 160-61; Communists' attempt to take over, 161-63; strikes, 163-64; relations with AFL, 164-65
Southern Textile Bulletin, 84
Southern Textile Commission, 228
Southern Worker, 182
Southern Workman, quoted, 74
Southport Petroleum Corp., 228
Southwest Open Shop Association, 27
Spengler, Joseph J., 18
Stanberry, V. B., quoted, 4
Standard Fruit and Steamship Co., 203, 206, 208
Standard Oil of Louisiana, 200
Standard Oil of New Jersey, 232, 233; and independent unions, 199-201
Stalin, Josef, quoted, 155-56
Starling, Tom, 254; quoted, 191-92, 266
Starnes, R. W., quoted, 261
Steel, H. Ellsworth, 307
Steel Workers' Organizing Committee, 184-88
Steel workers' unions, 182-88, 304
Stith, Gerald, 41
Stocking, George, 16
Strasser, Arnold, 305

Supreme Court, U. S., 11, 146, 178, 189, 244, 277, 278, 288, 293, 329, 331; desegregation decision (1954), 310
Sylvis, William, 21
Syndicalists, 87

Taft-Hartley Act, 242, 251, 252, 285, 287; effect on union growth, 324-25
Talbot, Tom, 51
Talmadge, Eugene, 167
Tampa Shipbuilding Corp., 242
Taylor, Myron C., 185, 186
Taylor, W. B., 232, 233
Tennessee: slave percentage (1840), 6; iron industry, 14-15; bauxite, 18; coal miners' unions, 71-72; union membership in 1960's, 305
Tennessee Coal, Iron, and Railroad Co., 15, 72, 73, 74, 140, 184, 185, 186, 187, 229
Tennessee Federation of Labor, 127
Tennessee Valley Authority, 165, 218-20, 280, 287
Tennessee Valley Trades and Labor Council, 218-20
Texas: sulphur, 18; antiunion campaign (1920's), 27; Joint Labor Legislative Board, 91; Socialists in, 92-93; antiunion legislation, 242-43; union membership in 1960's, 304; Union Regulation Act (1943), 329; "right-to-work" law, 320, 326-27
Texas Co., 196, 231
Texas Independent Union Council, 238
Texas Rangers, 233
Texas Socialist Party, 92
Texas State Federation of Labor, 36, 91
Texas State Manufacturers' Association, 228
Texas Typographical Society, 42
Textile Workers' Organizing Committee, 169-71, 174, 175
Textile Workers' Union of America, 229, 259, 260, 261, 263, 266, 271, 272; formed, 171; and World War II, 233-36; and Henderson strike, 274-76; and race issue, 337
Textile workers' unions, 80-85; and upsurge in unionism (1929-30), 101-05; Elizabethton strike, 105-07; Gastonia strike, 107-15; Marion strike, 115-18; South Carolina strikes, 118-20; 1934-41 growth, 166-75; and World War II, 245
Thomas, Norman, 159; quoted, 121
Thomas, R. J., 243-44, 329

Thompson, Kenneth, 306, 307
Tidewater Labor Conference, 102-03
Tippett, Tom, 118; quoted, 110-11, 114
Tobacco Workers International Union, 214-18, 272
Tobin, Dan, 250
Trade Union Unity League, 156
Transport Workers Union, 210
Transportation Workers' Association of Virginia, 68
Tredegar Steel Co., 20
Trevellick, Richard, 21
Troy, Leo, 254
Trumpet, 343

Union Carbide, 252
Union Labor Party, 89
Union Manufacturing Co., 174
Union News, quoted, 152
Unions, southern: institutional setting, general development, 3-38; National Labor Union, 20-21; history (pre-1928), 20-38; Knights of Labor, 21-24; AFL, 1881-1928, 24-36; and political action, 36-37; pre-1932 development, by industry, 41-133; printers, 41-45; building trades, 45-49; railroad, 50-60; longshoremen, 60-70; coal miners, 71-79; textile workers, 80-85; agricultural organizations, 86-93; lumber workers, 93-100; revival (1929-30), 101-05; textile workers' strikes, 105-20; coal mining, 137-53; growth of United Mine Workers, 137-53; during Depression and New Deal, 137-222; and southern economic conditions, 1929-41, 154-55; and Communists, 155-58; textile and clothing, during New Deal, 166-81; CIO growth during New Deal, 182-201; AFL growth during New Deal, 202-22; war and postwar development, 225-94; and World War II, 225-45; postwar organizing campaigns, 246-69; AFL-CIO in 1950's, 1960's, 270-82; and postwar growth of paper industry, 283-85; coal miners', in postwar period, 286-88; agricultural, in Louisiana, 288-94; membership, quantitative aspects of, 297-308; growth—status, causes, prospects, 297-352; collective bargaining coverage, by industry, 305-07; factors influencing growth, 309-18; unity and diversity of growth, 311-18; industrial structure and location, 314-18; and

antiunion legislation, 319-31; effect on industrial development, 321-23; modern growth, 332-43; future of, 344-52
United Automobile Workers, 191-92, 227, 282, 292, 304, 329, 336; and race issue, 337
United Brotherhood of Carpenters and Joiners of America, 47, 99, 102, 302
United Canning, Agricultural, Packinghouse and Allied Workers of America, 161, 157, 217; and World War II, 237-41
United Fruit Co., 69, 203, 206, 208
United Garment Workers, 179, 181
United Machinists and Mechanical Engineers of America, 51
United Milk Producers of America, 289
United Mine Workers, 34, 137-53, 168, 169, 174, 183, 184, 185, 238, 240, 286-88, 322, 333; formed, 71; in Alabama, 73-75, 143-46; in southwest, 75; in West Virginia and Kentucky, 75-78, 137-39; and New Deal, 139-40; and rival unions, 140-41; and employers' attitudes, 141-43; unionizes Harlan County, 146-47; and wage developments, 147-50; racial practices, 150-52; and autonomy question, 152-53; quits AFL, 253-54
United Mine Workers Journal, 153
United Packinghouse Workers, and race issue, 336, 337
United Papermakers and Paperworkers' Union, 212, 213, 284; membership, 1961, 283
United Rubber Workers' Union, 227, 325; Gadsden campaign, 188-90; Memphis campaign, 190-91
United States Pipe and Foundry, 15
United States Steel Corp., 15, 16, 140, 185, 186
United States Shipping Board, 68, 70, 202, 203
United Textile Workers of America, 83-84, 85, 102, 104-05, 108, 119, 122, 124, 169, 253, 260, 266, 271; and Elizabethton strike, 106; and Marion strike, 115-18; and Danville strike, 124-31; in early New Deal period, 166-69; general strike, 1934, 167; and 1937 organizing campaign, 169-71; reorganization, 171-73; and 1940 CIO campaign, 173-75; and World War II, 235-36

United Transport Service Employees, 217

University of Tennessee, 159

Virginia: slave percentage (1840), 6; union revival in 1920's, 102

Vance, Rupert B., 7

Vance Knitting Mills, 174

Veteran's Industrial Association, 252

W. F. Aldrich Co., 252

Wages, and southern union growth, 334-36

Wagner Act, 146, 147, 174, 176, 178, 188, 189, 197, 200, 215, 238, 241, 330; effect on union growth, 323-24

Wallace, Henry, 160, 161

Walsh-Healey Act, 173, 287

War Labor Board. *See* National War Labor Board

Warmoth, Henry Clay, 61

Washington, Booker T., quoted, 34

Washington Manufacturing Co., 178

Watson, J. Tom, 242

Watterson, Henry, 12

Weisbord, Albert, 111; quoted, 108, 109, 110, 112

Weller, D. R., quoted, 200

West Virginia, coal miners' unions, 75-78, 141

West Virginia Miners' Union, 141

West Virginia Paper Co., 214, 284

Western Kentucky Coal Co., 140

Wharton, Vernon L., 11

White Legion, 183

Whittier Mills, 174

Williams, Lum, 99, 100

Wilson, Charles, quoted, 52

Winn, Will, 34-35

Wolchok, Samuel, 210

Wolman, Leo, quoted, 270

Women workers, and union growth, 340-41

Women's Trade Union League, 128

Wood, Charles G., quoted, 113

Woodbury, O. E., quoted, 128-29

Woodward, C. Vann, 10; quoted, 12-13

Woodward Iron Corp., 186, 187

Woolen and Worsted Federation, 235

Works Progress Administration, 155

World War I, 18, 55, 60, 67, 68, 79; effect on U. S. unionism, 25-26, 27; effect on textile industry, 83

World War II, 45, 163; effect on southern unions, 225-45; and War Labor Board, 227-30; and individual unions, 230-41; and antilabor activities, 241-45

Wyler, Edward, 216

Youngstown Sheet and Tube Corp., 186

Zimmerman, Charles, 169

WERTHEIM PUBLICATIONS IN INDUSTRIAL RELATIONS

Published by Harvard University Press

J. D. Houser, *What the Employer Thinks*, 1927

Wertheim Lectures on Industrial Relations, 1929

William Haber, *Industrial Relations in the Building Industry*, 1930

Johnson O'Connor, *Psychometrics*, 1934

Paul H. Norgren, *The Swedish Collective Bargaining System*, 1941

Leo C. Brown, S. J., *Union Policies in the Leather Industry*, 1947

Walter Galenson, *Labor in Norway*, 1949

Dorothea de Schweinitz, *Labor and Management in a Common Enterprise*, 1949

Ralph Altman, *Availability for Work: A Study in Unemployment Compensation*, 1950

John T. Dunlop and Arthur D. Hill, *The Wage Adjustment Board: Wartime Stabilization in the Building and Construction Industry*, 1950

Walter Galenson, *The Danish System of Labor Relations: A Study in Industrial Peace*, 1952

Lloyd H. Fisher, *The Harvest Labor Market in California*, 1953

Donald J. White, *The New England Fishing Industry*, 1954

Val R. Lorwin, *The French Labor Movement*, 1954

Philip Taft, *The Structure and Government of Labor Unions*, 1954

George B. Baldwin, *Beyond Nationalization: The Labor Problems of British Coal*, 1955

Kenneth F. Walker, *Industrial Relations in Australia*, 1956

Charles A. Myers, *Labor Problems in the Industrialization of India*, 1958

Herbert J. Spiro, *The Politics of German Codetermination*, 1958

Mark W. Leiserson, *Wages and Economic Control in Norway, 1945-1957*, 1959

J. Pen, *The Wage Rate Under Collective Bargaining*, 1959

Jack Stieber, *The Steel Industry Wage Structure*, 1959

Theodore V. Purcell, S. J., *Blue Collar Man: Patterns of Dual Allegiance, in Industry*, 1960

Carl Erik Knoellinger, *Labor in Finland*, 1960

Sumner H. Slichter, *Potentials of the American Economy: Selected Essays* edited by John T. Dunlop, 1961

C. L. Christenson, *Economic Redevelopment in Bituminous Coal: The Special Case of Technological Advance in United States Coal Mines, 1930-1960*, 1962

Daniel L. Horowitz, *The Italian Labor Movement*, 1963

Adolf Sturmthal, *Workers Councils: A Study of Workplace Organization on Both Sides of the Iron Curtain*, 1964

Vernon H. Jensen, *Hiring of Dock Workers and Employment Practices in the Ports of New York, Liverpool, London, Rotterdam, and Marseilles,* 1964

John L. Blackman, Jr., *Presidential Seizures in Labor Disputes,* 1967

Studies in Labor-Management History

Lloyd Ulman, *The Rise of the National Trade Union: The Development and Significance of its Structure, Governing Institutions, and Economic Policies,* 1955

Joseph P. Goldberg, *The Maritime Story: A Study in Labor-Management Relations, 1957,* 1958

Walter Galenson, *The CIO Challenge to the AFL: A History of the American Labor Movement, 1935-1941,* 1960

Morris A. Horowitz, *The New York Hotel Industry: A Labor Relations Study,* 1960

Mark Perlman, *The Machinists: A New Study in Trade Unionism,* 1961

Fred C. Munson, *Labor Relations in the Lithographic Industry,* 1963

Garth L. Mangum, *The Operating Engineers: The Economic History of a Trade Union,* 1964

David Brody, *The Butcher Workmen: A Study of Unionization,* 1964

F. Ray Marshall, *Labor in the South,* 1967

Published by McGraw-Hill Book Co., Inc.

Robert J. Alexander, *Labor Relations in Argentina, Brazil, and Chile,* 1961

Carl M. Stevens, *Strategy and Collective Bargaining Negotiations,* 1963

John T. Dunlop and Vasilii P. Diatchenko, *Labor Productivity,* 1964